AIDA Europe Research Series on Insurance Law and Regulation

Volume 8

The AIDA Europe Research Series on Insurance Law and Regulation is the first book series of its kind and area of specialization. It comprises volumes on topics researched and written with an international, comparative or European perspective.

The regulatory response to the financial crisis in 2008 has pushed towards the adoption of transnational principles and rules also in the field of insurance by encouraging the convergence of national regulations to common regulatory framework. The need for a common legal language emerges to fully understand the process of transnational convergence in place and its impact on national legislation. On the other hand, persisting national peculiarities must be examined in the light of the transnational convergence of rules and concepts. Moreover, new risks, business practices and customers' issues are emerging worldwide, so requiring increasingly global responses.

The scope of the series is to bring together academics, practitioners and policy makers in order to exchange views and approaches to the topics concerned, which are based on the new transnational dimension of insurance law, business and regulation. All contributions are peer reviewed.

Margarida Lima Rego • Simon Grima
Editors

Cross-Disciplinary Impacts on Insurance Law

ESG Concerns, Financial and Technological Innovation

Springer

Editors
Margarida Lima Rego
School of Law and CEDIS (Research Centre on Law and Society)
NOVA University Lisbon
Lisboa, Portugal

Simon Grima
Department of Insurance and Risk Management, Faculty of Economics, Management and Accountancy
University of Malta
Msida, Malta

ISSN 2662-1770 ISSN 2662-1789 (electronic)
AIDA Europe Research Series on Insurance Law and Regulation
ISBN 978-3-031-38525-4 ISBN 978-3-031-38526-1 (eBook)
https://doi.org/10.1007/978-3-031-38526-1

This Springer imprint is published by the registered company Springer Nature Switzerland AG
The registered company address is: Gewerbestrasse 11, 6330 Cham, Switzerland

Preface

Cross-Disciplinary Impacts on Insurance Law

ESG Concerns, Financial and Technological Innovation

What do you get when you mix insurance academics and professionals from different countries and cultures and add to this disruption such as new environmental, social and governance concerns, financial and technological innovation? When you combine insurance academics and professionals from diverse countries and cultures, infuse this blend with disruptive forces such as emerging environmental, social, and governance concerns, and the dynamism of financial and technological innovation, what emerges is a collective effort to identify and characterized the new, acceptable norm in twenty-first-century insurance.

Unlike their predecessors, the twenty-first-century insurers have a growing impact on cross-sector service provision by making available to their clients a wealth of expert knowledge and experience in Big Data analytics. Although the series has a predominant legal focus, in this volume, we wanted to explore the wider-angle viewpoint, strongly encouraging submissions of multi- or inter-disciplinary research, as reflected by the different scientific backgrounds of the two co-editors. We also wanted to extend our reach to diversify the volume of authors' profiles, inviting academics in various career stages, including students and sector practitioners, to submit their manuscript proposals.

When considering the wider-angle viewpoint beyond insurance, it is important to look at how insurance fits into the broader financial services industry and how it intersects with other areas of the economy. For example, the insurance industry is closely tied to the healthcare industry, as health insurance is one of the most important and widely purchased insurance products. Additionally, the insurance industry is also connected to the investment industry, as insurance companies often invest the premiums they collect in order to generate returns.

It is also important to consider the social and political dimensions of insurance, such as access to insurance coverage and the role of insurance in addressing environmental, social and governance concerns. Insurance plays a crucial role in protecting individuals and communities from financial loss, but access to insurance and the quality of coverage can vary greatly depending on factors such as income, race and location. It is essential to look at the interconnections between insurance, other industries and society as a whole to understand its impact and importance.

Insurance and insurance regulation are not isolated in a vacuum and are not independent entities, but influence and impact, in an outward perspective, and are influenced and impacted, in an inward perspective, (by) fields outside of their industry. Insurance regulations and policies can be affected by various factors, such as changes in the economy, advancements in technology, and shifts in consumer preferences, to name a few. Additionally, the insurance industry can have a significant bearing on the wider economy, making it important for the industry to operate within the framework of comprehensive regulations.

Insurance and its regulations are becoming more complex as the industry evolves and new products and services are introduced. Increasing technology use, changing regulations, and a more diverse customer base are some of the factors driving this complexity. This requires insurance providers to constantly update their knowledge and skills to deliver the best solutions to their clients. Additionally, customers are becoming more aware of their insurance needs and are demanding more personalised and flexible products, contributing to the industry's complexity.

Insurance regulations are necessary since not many angels roam the world, but one needs to understand and balance and rebalance the environment, social needs and economic requirements of populations when enforcing directives, laws and soft laws. That is in proportion to the size, complexity and nature of the firm and the economy. However, how can we ensure this? How can we ensure that we are not over-regulating or under-regulating? Regulating takes time and is usually reactive. How, then, can it answer the arising problems, especially if rebalancing the three pillars of sustainability, i.e. economic needs, social needs and the environment, are disrupted continuously with digitalisation, natural disasters, etc., and are surrounded by noise such as politics and corruption?

The interconnections between insurance, regulations, other industries, and society are complex and multifaceted. One must consider the following:

(a) Regulations: Insurance is heavily regulated at the local, state, and federal levels, with regulations aimed at protecting consumers, ensuring the stability of insurance companies and promoting competition in the industry. Regulations can significantly impact the insurance industry and affect how insurance products are designed, priced and marketed.
(b) Other industries: The insurance industry has strong connections to many other industries, including health care, investment and real estate. For example, the healthcare industry is closely tied to the insurance industry through health

insurance, and investment decisions made by insurance companies can significantly impact the overall financial market.
(c) Society: Insurance plays a crucial role in society by helping to protect individuals and communities from financial loss. However, access to insurance and the quality of coverage can vary greatly based on factors such as income, race and location, leading to disparities in financial protection and stability.

The interconnections between insurance, regulations, other industries and society are complex and far-reaching. Understanding these connections and how they impact the insurance industry and wider society is essential for making informed decisions and shaping a more equitable and stable future.

The idea of this book was to move away from the series' norm and delve beyond insurance, taking a wider-angle viewpoint. To delve into the transition of insurers from suppliers of products consisting of risk coverage and/or investment opportunities to the provision of a variety of different services and ultimately to the provisions of solutions by partnering with their clients to prevent failure, optimise their clients' operations and help them excel in their various economic sectors.

The chapters delved into theoretical, empirical and policy-oriented papers on topics exploring particular aspects of new trends and wider analyses leading to a more systematic understanding of the industry's socioeconomic role—insights on a broad spectrum of themes from a national, transnational, international or comparative perspective.

In the first part, the book focuses on the insurance industry's outward influence and impact by looking into its potential role in addressing environmental, social and governance concerns. Chapters delve into the insurance sector's contribution to Sustainable Development Goals, insurance as an accelerator of economic and social change and the role of insurance in dealing with disasters.

In the second and third parts, the book looks mostly into the inward influence and impact on financial and technological innovation insurance, respectively. In the second part, chapters go into the historical, definitional and implementational issues of financial services regulation in a small jurisdiction, government self-insurance risk pools, a comparison of efficiency levels of insurance companies and the impact of capital structure on the financial performance of insurance companies. In the third part, chapters address automatic vehicles and legal/insurance risks, the suitability of the protected cell company structure for shipping business, goods and services tax implications on the insurance sector and the effectiveness of recent policyholder-friendly laws at addressing complaints.

The book has a global outreach, including chapters of a more global nature and chapters looking into particular jurisdictions in different continents, including Europe, Asia and North America.

Lisboa, Portugal — Margarida Lima Rego
Msida, Malta — Simon Grima

Contents

Part I
Insurance and ESG Impact

The Insurance Sector's Contribution to the Sustainable Development Goals: A Story Worth Telling?

Maria del Val Bolívar Oñoro and Margarida Lima Rego

Abstract To remain competitive in the increasingly demanding and diverse global marketplace of the twenty-first century, some insurers have chosen to move away from their traditional position as mere suppliers of insurance products designed to cover insurable risks and/or provide investment opportunities, refashioning themselves as service providers in neighbouring sectors such as healthcare, and, more recently, being pushed to become what could now be described as solution seekers, creating their own ecosystems by offering customers the prospect of a strong and lasting value-creating partnership. This completely transforms their customer relationship from distant and sporadic to close and permanent in an attempt to create value, gain trust and increase customer satisfaction. This value creation could also enhance the industry's already very significant potential to being key players in contemporary society's global efforts to meet the United Nations' sustainable development goals ('SDG').

The actual or potential contribution of the insurance industry to furthering the SDG is also potentially relevant to the industry's work towards gaining trust and increasing customer satisfaction. In this chapter, we look at the industry's perceptions of, and narratives on, their actual contribution to the SDG. Our main focus is on existing reports that reflect how the industry presents itself to the world in this context. We conclude that insurers seem to be falling short when it comes to narrating their own contribution to the SDG. This appears to be, at least in part, a consequence of the industry's widespread lack of awareness and common misperceptions about the various economic, social and governance aspects of sustainability, as well as of the industry's actual and potential role in contributing to the furthering of some SDG. Our chapter includes a case study of Portuguese-based insurance company Fidelidade.

M. del Val Bolívar Oñoro (✉)
University of Alcalá, Madrid, Spain

M. L. Rego
School of Law and CEDIS (Research Centre on Law and Society), NOVA University Lisbon, Lisboa, Portugal
e-mail: margarida.limarego@novalaw.unl.pt

M. Lima Rego, S. Grima (eds.), *Cross-Disciplinary Impacts on Insurance Law*,
AIDA Europe Research Series on Insurance Law and Regulation 8,
https://doi.org/10.1007/978-3-031-38526-1_1

Keywords Insurance ecosystems · Sustainable development goals · ESG · Insurance reputation · Corporate narratives · P2P

1 Introduction

In the twentieth century, as before, insurers competed with each other for a share of the insurance market. Nowadays, however, the stakes have become much higher for insurers, as for many other businesses, since they are no longer competing only with their own kind: increasingly, "any firm that customers trust with their finances" is a potential competitor. This includes "shopping sites, payments players or ride-hailing apps".[1] Consequently, in addition to providing new opportunities for the most audacious to take advantage of this entire new world, the new globalized marketplace raises significant concerns for the insurance industry.

Customer satisfaction is now, more than ever, a key prerequisite for success.[2] Nonetheless, the relationship between insurance companies and their customers was characteristically sporadic: a contract was agreed, premiums were paid, and there was not much contact in between, until the occasional insured event occurred. Accordingly, insurers did not characteristically form a strong psychological bond with their customers. The sector has never enjoyed a good reputation: the insurance industry was never a favourite. "The overriding perception of insurance companies is that they're needed, but not liked, relied on, but not trusted".[3]

This does not place insurers in a favourable competitive position when compared with the major strongholds of the new sharing economy. As Eccles and Vollbracht affirm, "since insurance is all about trust, the media image of the insurance industry is critical to its visibility".[4] In the current digital era, customers have learnt to engage remotely and they expect a 24/7 service and easy interactions in everything they do.[5] Thus, if insurers maintain their traditional business model and fail to embrace this

[1] Payne and Whyte (2021).

[2] Schanz (2006), p. 377, refers to "the increasing relevance of reputation as one the insurance industry's key assets, offering attractive returns when properly cultivated but also threatening considerable damage if eroded or lost". "Considering the role of reputation in insurance, it is astonishing to note the relative shortage of (academic) attempts to thoroughly analyze this phenomenon and its specific ramifications for one of the world economy's most significant industries, which constitutes more than 8 per cent of global GDP. This state of affairs could arguably be viewed as a result of the industry's long tradition of operating in relative obscurity and isolation, in a heavily regulated environment characterized by limited competition and, accordingly, stakeholder interest and scrutiny" (p. 378). See also Eccles and Vollbracht (2006), pp. 395–408. Finally, see Swiss Re's "Reputation risk in the insurance industry" (2013). Available at http://www.oxfordmetrica.com/public/CMS/Files/1570/OM-report-for-Swiss-Re_2013c.pdf (Accessed: 20 December 2022).

[3] Eardley (2021).

[4] Eccles and Vollbracht (2006), p. 397.

[5] PwC, "Top insurance industry issues in 2021" p. 16. Available at: https://www.pwc.com/us/en/industries/insurance/assets/pwc-top-insurance-industry-issues-2021-compilation.pdf (Accessed: 20 December 2022).

new trend, they face increased exposure to disintermediation, disaggregation, commoditization and invisibility.[6] What is more, as PwC has pointed out, "insurers' legacy limitations (siloed processes, lack of single customer view across units, limited external connectivity, etc.) now look increasingly out of step with post-Covid-19 buying behaviour and distribution patterns".[7]

To remain competitive in the increasingly demanding and diverse global marketplace of the twenty-first century, some insurers have chosen to follow a development path which has led them away from the traditional position where they presented themselves to the world as mere suppliers of products—insurance products designed to cover insurable risks and/or, more recently, to provide investment opportunities; causing them to refashion themselves as service providers in neighbouring sectors such as that of healthcare; and, even more recently, pushing them from the position of mere service providers to becoming what could now be described as solution seekers, creating their own ecosystems by offering customers the prospect of a strong and lasting partnership.

Accordingly, insurers put their knowledge of, and experience in, Big Data analytics to good use with a view to optimizing their customers' own businesses or activities. They focus on non-insurance specific value creation by helping corporate customers thrive in their various economic sectors by becoming more efficient and preventing failure, as well as helping individual make better or more informed life choices.[8]

This completely transforms their customer relationship from distant and sporadic to close and permanent in an attempt to create value, gain trust and ultimately increase customer satisfaction. Much of this is achieved through the creation of ecosystems which, according to the definition provided by EY, "are networks of companies that choose to collaborate and can collectively produce a higher level of business value than any individual collaborator can produce on its own".[9]

These ecosystems are typically composed of a single leading company, the orchestrator, which provides a platform of core capabilities, and the participants,

[6]Catlin et al. (2018), p. 3.

[7]EY, "COVID-19: How insurers can meet the evolving needs of their customers". Available at: https://www.ey.com/en_gl/financial-services-emeia/covid-19-how-insurers-can-meet-the-evolving-needs-of-their-customers (Accessed: 20 December 2022).

[8]Singh (2021), "Insurers should leverage the ecosystem model to secure their future": "ecosystems will account for 30% of global revenues by 2025. Insurers agree too: 84% of insurance executives consider ecosystems an important strategy and 54% are actively seeking ecosystem capabilities". Available at: https://www.thoughtworks.com/insights/blog/platforms/insurers-should-leverage-the-ecosystem-model-to-secure-their-fut#:~:text=Insurers%20should%20leverage%20the%20ecosystem%20model%20to%20secure%20their%20future,-Blogs&text=Insurers%20need%20new%20and%20disruptive,an%20underwhelming%20global%20financial%20market (Accessed: 20 December 2022). Accenture, "The Ultimate Guide to Insurance Ecosystems" (2022). Available at: https://insuranceblog.accenture.com/the-ultimate-guide-to-insurance-ecosystems (Accessed: 20 December 2022).

[9]Messineo (2020), p. 2.

who offer complementary services, features or functionalities.[10] Once these are functional, customers engage with the ecosystem, paying for various products and services, but also benefiting from the added value of the whole.[11]

There is limited research on ecosystems and insurance aside from the contributions written by large consulting firms such as McKinsey & Company,[12] Ernst & Young,[13] PwC,[14] and Accenture.[15] These contributions are not generally aimed at or even refer in passing to the industry's role in furthering sustainable development goals.

As private businesses, insurance companies are called upon to contribute to achieving the United Nations' Sustainable Development Goals ('SDG').[16] This was clearly stated in the Resolution adopted by the UN General Assembly on 25 September 2015, entitled "Transforming our world: the 2030 Agenda for Sustainable Development": Section 67 of this resolution states that "we call upon all businesses to apply their creativity and innovation to solving sustainable development challenges".

Although the issue of how insurers are creating or merging into different ecosystems as a survival strategy in the digital collaborative global economy has already been explored to some extent, no light has been shed thus far on the synergy between these ecosystems and the industry's actual or potential contribution to the SDG. In our view, such ecosystems, as well as the use of insurers' pre-existing and ever-increasing expertise in the unlocking of very large amounts of data, enhance their potential to become very significant actors in contemporary society's global efforts to meet the United Nations' sustainable development goals ('SDG'). It is also our belief that the industry's potential as SDG contributors, if adequately showcased, might also have a very positive impact on its overall reputation.

In this chapter, we look at the insurance industry's perceptions of, and narratives on, the sector's actual contribution to the SDG. Our main focus is on existing reports which reflect how the industry presents itself to the world in this context. We aim to

---

[10] Ibidem.

[11] Ibidem.

[12] McKinsey & Company, "Ecosystems in insurance: The next frontier for enhancing productivity". Available at: https://www.mckinsey.com/industries/financial-services/our-insights/insurance-blog/ecosystems-in-insurance-the-next-frontier-for-enhancing-productivity (Accessed: 20 December 2022); McKinsey & Company, "Ecosystems and Platforms: How insurers can turn vision into reality". Available at: https://www.mckinsey.com/industries/financial-services/our-insights/ecosystems-and-platforms-how-insurers-can-turn-vision-into-reality (Accessed: 20 December 2022).

[13] Payne and Whyte (2021).

[14] PwC, "Top insurance industry issues in 2021" p. 16. Available at: https://www.pwc.com/us/en/industries/insurance/assets/pwc-top-insurance-industry-issues-2021-compilation.pdf (Accessed: 20 December 2022).

[15] Accenture, "The Ultimate Guide to Insurance Ecosystems" (2022). Available at: https://insuranceblog.accenture.com/the-ultimate-guide-to-insurance-ecosystems (Accessed: 20 December 2022).

[16] Pérez Pérez et al. (2021), p. 3.

verify the extent to which this contribution is adequately presented and, therefore, whether, in this context, it also plays a role in the industry's effort to gain trust and increase customer satisfaction. This study includes a case study of Portuguese-based insurance company Fidelidade.

2 Insurance and the Sustainable Development Goals

2.1 The Inclusion of Insurance Companies in the UN Sustainable Development Agenda

Particular attention should be paid, in this context, to the United Nations Global Compact,[17] which was launched by the former UN Secretary-General Kofi Annan in 2000 with a view to bringing businesses and the United Nations together to work towards advancing societal goals.[18] The UN Global Compact purports to be the world's largest corporate sustainability initiative. It is "[a] call to companies to align strategies and operations with universal principles on human rights, labour, environment and anti-corruption, and take actions that advance societal goals".[19] In short: to "help us transform the world through business".[20]

According to the UN Global Compact, "[s]ustainability begins with a principled-based approach to doing business".[21] It encourages businesses to incorporate its Ten Principles:

> Human Rights: Principle 1: Businesses should support and respect the protection of internationally proclaimed human rights; and Principle 2: make sure that they are not complicit in human rights abuses. Labour: Principle 3: Businesses should uphold the freedom of association and the effective recognition of the right to collective bargaining; Principle 4: the elimination of all forms of forced and compulsory labour; Principle 5: the effective abolition of child labour; and Principle 6: the elimination of discrimination in respect of employment and occupation. Environment: Principle 7: Businesses should support a precautionary approach to environmental challenges; Principle 8: undertake initiatives to promote greater environmental responsibility; and Principle 9: encourage the development and diffusion of environmentally friendly technologies. Anti-Corruption: Principle 10: Businesses should work against corruption in all its forms, including extortion and bribery.[22]

---

[17] UN Global Compact. Available at: https://www.unglobalcompact.org/ (Accessed: 20 December 2022).

[18] Ibidem.

[19] Ibidem.

[20] Ibidem.

[21] UN Global Compact Mission and Principles. Available at: https://www.unglobalcompact.org/what-is-gc/mission/principles (Accessed: 20 December 2022).

[22] The Ten Principles are derived from: the Universal Declaration of Human Rights, the International Labour Organization's Declaration on Fundamental Principles and Rights at Work, the Rio Declaration on Environment and Development, and the United Nations Convention Against Corruption.

In addition to the UN Global Compact, at the 2012 UN Conference on Sustainable Development, the UN Environment Programme Finance Initiative (UNEP FI)'s Principles for Sustainable Insurance (PSI) were launched as a global framework for the insurance industry to address environmental, social and governance (ESG) risks and opportunities.[23]

In the wake of these initiatives, the Sustainable Development Goals (SDG) were adopted by the United Nations in 2015 in the UN General Assembly resolution of September 2015: "Transforming our world: the 2030 Agenda for Sustainable Development".[24] This Agenda is "a plan of action for people, planet and prosperity". It recognizes the eradication of poverty in all its forms and dimensions as "the greatest global challenge and an indispensable requirement for sustainable development". It establishes 17 Sustainable Development Goals (SDGs) and 169 targets,[25] and its mission is therefore the worthiest of all missions.

> The SDGs are based on the concept that our social and economic development objectives must be rooted in the principles of environmental, social and economic sustainability. It is therefore important that we develop multi-disciplinary approaches with community participation for developing an effective implementation strategy.[26]

This includes the entire global community and thus the insurance sector. The latter is explicitly mentioned in target 8.10, which aims to "strengthen the capacity of domestic financial institutions to encourage and to expand access to banking, insurance and financial services for all". However, our focus in this chapter is not on this particular target as the underlying assumption is that insurance companies already are—or in some cases have the potential to become—key actors in the achievement of a number of SDGs.

---

[23] UNEP FI Principles for Sustainable Insurance (PSI). Available at: https://www.unepfi.org/psi/ (Accessed: 20 December 2022).

[24] United Nations, "Transforming our world: the 2030 Agenda for Sustainable Development". Available at https://dgs.un.org/2030agenda (Accessed: 20 December 2022).

[25] (1) No Poverty, (2) Zero Hunger, (3) Good Health and Well-being, (4) Quality Education, (5) Gender Equality, (6) Clean Water and Sanitation, (7) Affordable and Clean Energy, (8) Decent Work and Economic Growth, (9) Industry, Innovation and Infrastructure, (10) Reduced Inequality, (11) Sustainable Cities and Communities, (12) Responsible Consumption and Production, (13) Climate Action, (14) Life Below Water, (15) Life On Land, (16) Peace, Justice, and Strong Institutions, (17) Partnerships for the Goals.

[26] Swaminathan and Kesavan (2016), p. 127.

2.2 Reported Contribution of Insurance Companies Towards the SDGs

The UN Global Compact's multi-year strategy "is to drive business awareness and action in support of achieving the Sustainable Development Goals by 2030".[27] Therefore, the following question is being asked within the reporting procedure: "Which of the following Sustainable Development Goals (SDGs) do the activities described in your COP address?". This raises questions as regards the main SDGs in which insurance companies can make their biggest contributions and the real involvement of the sector in global efforts to achieve these goals.

Some publications have tried to draw the lines between those SDGs where insurance companies can make a substantial contribution and those where their role is ancillary at best. There appears to be some disagreement as to which SDGs insurance companies can make their biggest contributions.[28] However, there is consensus on the crucial contribution of the industry to SDG (13) Climate Action, and SDG (3) Good Health and Well-being.[29]

This chapter's main focus is on how the insurance industry views itself in the context of SDG contributions. As mentioned above, there is a section on the UN Global Compact's website that allows us to check which sectors are reporting activities to advance the SDG. Unfortunately, we have found no information on the data collection date, or the procedures followed. Some inconsistencies are difficult to understand or explain. We collected all the answers to the question above from the Communications of Progress of the registered (life and non-life) insurance companies, a total of 164.[30] The results can be seen in Fig. 1.

---

[27] UN Global Compact. Available at: https://www.unglobalcompact.org/ (Accessed: 20 December 2022).

[28] The German Agency for International Cooperation (GIZ) published a report called "Inclusive Insurance and the Sustainable Development Goals: How insurance contributes to the 2030 Agenda for Sustainable Development". In this document, they maintain that insurance is a primary level contributor in six SDG: (1) No Poverty, (2) Zero Hunger, (3) Good Health and Well-being, (5) Gender Equality, (8) Decent Work and Economic Growth, (13) Climate Action; and a secondary level contributor in five more SDGs; (4) Quality Education, (9) Industry, Innovation and Infrastructure, (10) Reduced Inequality, (11) Sustainable Cities and Communities, (17) Partnerships for the Goals. The World Bank Group has also developed a publication on the matter. For them, the SDG on which Insurance has a Significant Impact are: (13) Climate Action, (11) Sustainable Cities and Communities, (3) Good Health and Well-being and (10) Reduced Inequality, whereas the SDG on which Insurance has a Strong Impact are (1) No Poverty, (8) Decent Work and Economic Growth and (2) Zero Hunger. Moreover, in the PSI framework, an inquiry working paper on this issue was released in June 2015. The paper is called "Insurance 2030: Harnessing Insurance for Sustainable Development" and it highlights the possible contribution of insurance to all SDG.

[29] Ibidem.

[30] As insurance companies join and leave the UN Global Compact, it should be clarified that this analysis was conducted in March 2022, and the number of companies was rechecked on March 29th. Only 126 of the 164 were considered as the remainder are new incorporations and their CoPs had not been released yet.

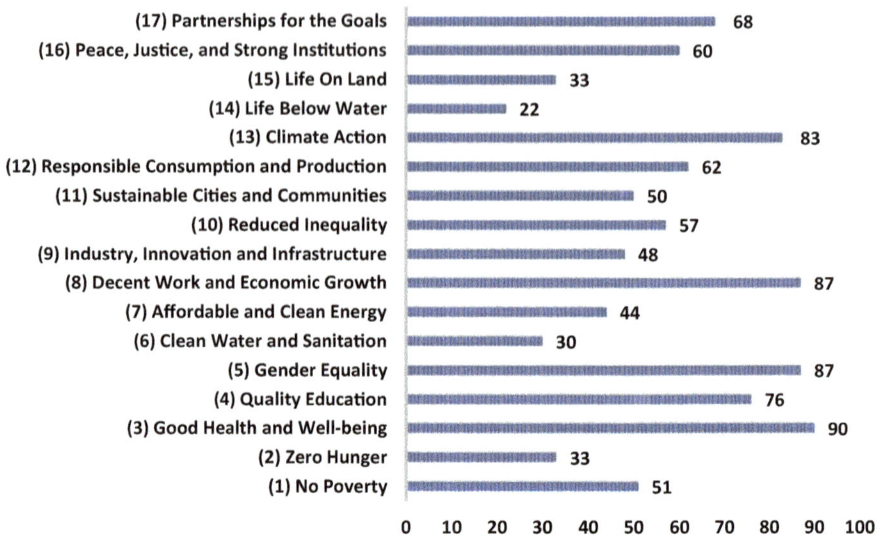

Fig. 1 Reported contributions to SDG

This graph shows that insurance companies report that they are effectively contributing or making efforts to contribute to those targets in respect of which there is consensus as to the industry's key role, (13) Climate Action, and (3) Good Health and Well-being.

The number of companies that report contributing towards the achievement of targets (5) Gender Equality and (8) Decent Work and Economic Growth is similarly high. However, while the analyses we mentioned above suggested that insurance companies could have a strong impact in (1) No Poverty and (2) Zero Hunger, only 51 and 33 companies respectively believe that they are making contributions in these areas.

Moreover, it is interesting to see that none of the reports addressed the contribution of insurance companies to target numbers (12) Responsible Consumption and Production, and (16) Peace, Justice, and Strong Institutions, and almost half of the reporting companies believe that they are still working towards the achievement of those targets.

It also appears incoherent that many insurance companies believe that they are contributing to target (13) Climate Action but fail to mention the other closely related SDG, specifically, (6) Clean Water and Sanitation, (7) Affordable and Clean Energy, (11) Sustainable Cities and Communities, (14) Life Below Water and (15) Life on Land.

If an insurer is indeed contributing to target (13) Climate Action, it is surely also contributing to (14) Life Below Water and/or (15) Life on Land. Life below water and life on land appear to be dichotomous, in the sense of being collectively exhaustive of all forms of life on the planet, albeit not mutually exclusive. In fact, none of the SDG are mutually exclusive, although some answers seem to assume that they would be. Assuming that climate action is aimed at improving the planet's liveability, then if one is contributing to climate action, by definition, one is also improving life below water and/or life on land. However, the number of times SDG (13) is mentioned is far greater than the sum total of (14) and (15) mentions. And we should bear in mind that, their not being mutually exclusive, the same insurers could refer to (13), (14) and (15). So either not all SDG received the same degree of attention in the data collection which preceded the elaboration of these reports, or at least some respondents thought that (14) and (15) should only be directly identified when their contribution was directly aimed at furthering such SDG, rather than SDG (13).

We have also concluded that the answers provided by insurance companies to the UN Global Compact on the extent of their contribution to achieving the realization of the SDG do not always fully capture the essence of the Communication on Progress and the extended documentation provided. For instance, in the documents provided to comply with their requirements under the UN Global Compact, some companies touch upon certain matters regarding the environment or gender equality, but no contributions to these targets are recorded on the webpage.[31] This comment is also true the other way around, that is to say, some companies appear to be contributing to all SDGs but, in their extended documentation, they confine their work to just a few targets.[32]

Our findings confirm the general claim by Eccles and Vollbracht according to which "substantial evidence exists that companies are indeed not reporting sufficiently about value drivers that shareholders and other stakeholders – and the companies themselves – consider important in building the value of an insurance company".[33]

While their claim is of a general nature, being unrelated to sustainability, the information gaps identified by these authors make it difficult for companies and any interested stakeholders to measure their contribution to furthering SDG. If they are not properly measured and displayed, this underplays the advantages that might otherwise be drawn from this contribution, to the company itself, society or the planet.[34]

The reports that we have analysed typically do not provide information on actual authorship, it being unclear which department or person is responsible, in each company, for the work of compiling and processing the data relating to the company's contributions and drafting the reports. These information gaps might

[31] Examples of this would be the companies Odessa Agente De Seguros S.A de C.V. and Peña Verde SAB with regard to (13) Climate Action, or Axis Specialty U.S Services INC with regard to (5) Gender Equality.

[32] BPI Vida e Pensões provides a good example of this statement. The company appears to be making contributions to all the SDG but in the extended documentation confines its work to eight targets (1,7,8,9,12,13,16,17). UN Global Compact Communication in Progress. Available at: https://www.unglobalcompact.org/participation/report/cop (Accessed: 20 December 2022).

[33] Eccles and Vollbracht (2006), p. 405.

[34] Ibidem.

be the result of the act of reporting being seen as someone's task, rather than everyone's task, and that someone not holding all the data nor the power to retrieve it without the good will of their colleagues, who may not have the incentives they would need to prioritize the identification and reporting of contributions to SDGs.

2.3 Barriers to Such Contributions Faced by Insurance Companies

The UN Environment Programme Finance Initiative (UNEP FI) aims "to raise awareness of the contribution that the insurance industry is already making to sustainability and to identify major challenges and opportunities that lie ahead".[35] It has identified the following structural barriers to sustainable insurance:

(i) the pervasiveness of misperceptions about the relevance of economic, social and governance issues to the insurance business and/or about the apparent irreconcilability of sustainability concerns with a mind-set predominantly oriented towards the pursuit of profit;
(ii) the institutional rigidity of this heavily regulated sector, regulatory frameworks providing external barriers and the organizational structures of the insurance companies themselves providing internal barriers to these contributions, since neither has been specifically designed to encourage them;
(iii) the insurance sector's lack of capacity of in mostly developing countries where contributing would be most critical.[36]

Given our focus on the industry's perceptions, the first of these barriers—that of misperceptions—becomes especially apparent and is therefore also worthy of special note.

We believe that, to a great extent, the incongruities we have spotted in the insurance companies' reports on their contributions to the SDGs can perhaps be at least partly explained by the very different levels of awareness about the SDGs of those who prepare such reports. What we mean is the following: generally speaking, there is a much greater level of awareness that the environment and the climate crisis are a core sustainability concern than the level of awareness that sustainability concerns also include other general societal core values, such as the fight against

[35] UNEP Finance Initiative. The inaugural report of the Insurance Working Group of the United Nations Environment Programme Finance Initiative. "Insuring for Sustainability: Why and how the leaders are doing it" (2007), p. 10. Available at: https://www.unepfi.org/fileadmin/documents/insuring_for_sustainability.pdf (Accessed: 20 December 2022).

[36] UNEP Finance Initiative. The inaugural report of the Insurance Working Group of the United Nations Environment Programme Finance Initiative. "Insuring for Sustainability: Why and how the leaders are doing it" (2007), p. 11. See also pp. 50–52. Available at: https://www.unepfi.org/fileadmin/documents/insuring_for_sustainability.pdf (Accessed: 20 December 2022).

poverty and hunger, the protection of basic human rights, justice, peace and effective institutions.

As Pfeifer and Langen highlight, "so far climate change aspects have been the dominant aspect in managing sustainability risks and opportunities (in insurance)".[37] Thus, when asked about their role in furthering the SDGs, the link between insurance and the environment is the first thing that comes to the mind of those in charge of preparing the reports sent to the UN Global Compact.

The second of these structural barriers to sustainable insurance seems to be directly linked to the information gaps identified in the previous section, at least when it comes to internal organizational barriers within insurance companies. We should look at existing law and legislative initiatives in order to understand the types of external barriers stemming from existing regulatory frameworks and whether efforts can be identified that could help to overcome such barriers. Here, our focus is on EU law, given the high degree of harmonization of insurance regulation in the European Union. Even though soft law lacks the coercive force of hard law, there is a wide range of examples that show that the former is often presented as a first step towards the achievement of a common goal that could lead to the latter on a specific matter.

The existing EU legal framework is not yet in tune with sustainability concerns. Currently, the major piece on this matter is Commission Delegated Regulation (EU) 2021/1256 of 21 April 2021 amending Delegated Regulation (EU) 2015/35 as regards the integration of sustainability risks in the governance of insurance and reinsurance undertakings.[38] In addition, the European Commission has put forward some proposals relating to insurance and sustainability in the Solvency II Directive,[39] i.e., a Proposal for a Directive of the European Parliament and of the Council amending Directive 2009/138/EC as regards proportionality, quality of supervision, reporting, long-term guarantee measures, macro-prudential tools, sustainability risks, group and cross-border supervision,[40] and a Proposal for a Directive of the European Parliament and of the Council establishing a framework for the recovery and resolution of insurance and reinsurance undertakings and amending Directives 2002/47/EC, 2004/25/EC, 2009/138/EC, (EU) 2017/1132 and Regulations (EU) No 1094/2010 and (EU) No 648/2012.[41]

This comprehensive 'review package' was created bearing in mind that insurance "is a prerequisite for many activities regularly carried out by businesses, financial

[37] Pfeifer and Langen (2021).

[38] https://eur-lex.europa.eu/legal-content/EN/TXT/?uri=celex%3A32021R1256 (Accessed: 20 December 2022).

[39] EIOPA, "EIOPA welcomes Solvency II proposals from the European Commission on sustainability" (2021). Available at: https://www.eiopa.europa.eu/media/news/eiopa-welcomes-solvency-ii-proposals-european-commission-sustainability_en (Accessed: 20 December 2022).

[40] https://eur-lex.europa.eu/legal-content/EN/TXT/?uri=CELEX:52021PC0581 (Accessed: 20 December 2022).

[41] https://eur-lex.europa.eu/legal-content/EN/TXT/?uri=CELEX:52021PC0582 (Accessed: 20 December 2022).

market participants and in individual households" and that the sector "offers solutions for retirement income and helps channel savings into financial markets and the real economy". Thus, the aim of the previous legislative instruments is to "ensure that insurers and reinsurers in the EU keep investing, and support the political priorities of the EU", such as post-Covid recovery and channelling funds to implement the European green deal.[42]

Aside from the insurance-specific legislation, the EU has two main Directives that should be mentioned: Council Directive 2004/113/EC of 13 December 2004 implementing the principle of equal treatment between men and women in the access to and supply of goods and services[43] and Council Directive 2000/43/EC of 29 June 2000 implementing the principle of equal treatment between persons irrespective of racial or ethnic origin. In addition, there is a Proposal for a Council Directive on implementing the principle of equal treatment between persons irrespective of religion or belief, disability, age or sexual orientation. All these laws may have a direct impact on the SDG as they seek to guarantee the right to equality and non-discrimination. Although the last proposal might seem old (2008), it is still very much alive, there having been multiple efforts of reaching an agreement to approve it, some of which recent.[44]

The Proposal for a Directive of the European Parliament and of the Council on Corporate Sustainability Due Diligence and amending Directive (EU) 2019/1937,[45] according to the explanatory text, aims to fulfil the European Union objective of delivering on the SDG by implementing "comprehensive mitigation processes for adverse human rights and environmental impacts in their value chains, integrating sustainability into corporate governance and management systems, and framing business decisions in terms of human rights, climate and environmental impact, as well as in terms of the company's resilience in the longer term".

EIOPA is also pursuing some activities on sustainable finance with the aim of reflecting "the need for global action to enable decisive progress on the transition to a more sustainable economy".[46] Moreover, "sustainable finance is a strategic priority area in EIOPA's work programme 2022–2024, and the Commission's Strategy for

[42] European Commission, "Insurance rules' review: encouraging solid and reliable insurers to invest in Europe's recovery". Available at: https://ec.europa.eu/info/publications/210922-solvency-2-communication_en (Accessed: 20 December 2022).

[43] https://eur-lex.europa.eu/legal-content/EN/TXT/?uri=celex%3A32004L0113 (Accessed: 20 December 2022).

[44] Consejo, 'Outcome of the 3625th Council meeting Employment, Social Policy, Health and Consumer Affairs Employment, Social Policy and Health issues Luxembourg, 21 and 22 June 2018'. https://www.consilium.europa.eu/media/35974/st10202-en18.pdf (Accessed: 20 December 2022).

[45] https://eur-lex.europa.eu/legal-content/EN/TXT/?uri=CELEX%3A52022PC0071 (Accessed: 20 December 2022).

[46] EIOPA, Sustainable finance. Available at: https://www.eiopa.europa.eu/browse/sustainable-finance_en?field_term_topic_type_tid%5B%5D=218 (Accessed: 20 December 2022).

financing the transition to a sustainable economy encapsulates work by EIOPA in delivering on the Green Deal".[47]

EIOPA's seven key areas of activity on sustainable finance for 2022–2024 are the following:[48] integrating ESG risks in the prudential framework of insurers and pension funds, consolidating the macro/microprudential risk assessment of ESG risks, promoting sustainability disclosures and a sustainable conduct of business framework, supporting supervision of ESG risks and supervisory convergence in the EU, addressing protection gaps, promoting the use of open source modelling and data for climate change risks and contributing to international convergence for the assessment and management of sustainability risks.

These topics have great potential indeed to contribute to the SDGs, but there is no mention of these goals in the report on sustainable finance activities for the period 2022–2024.[49] We do not mean to imply that EIOPA's choice not to use the UN classification of 17 SDGs should necessarily be directly categorised as a problem. However, it might suggest a different approach towards established priorities in the field of sustainability. Given the relevance of misperception as a barrier to furthering the SDGs, having different standards might generate further confusion among insurers and other stakeholders and that would consequently lead to underperformance in the sector's contribution to the achievement of the SDGs.

In conclusion, while the European Commission's reflection paper entitled "Towards a Sustainable Europe by 2030"[50] states that "[t]he EU is leading a comprehensive shift of the financial system to a sustainable path", it is quite clear from the brief overview above that much remains to be done. This includes enacting the above-mentioned legislative proposals, some of which have been pending for a long time, clarifying priorities, and generally improving awareness of all aspects of the SDGs.

2.4 Reputation: A Great Incentive to Overcome the Barriers to Contributing to the SDGs

In addition to the more obvious benefits of doing good by making things better for the people and for the planet, assuming that a company's contribution to that collective effort is viewed positively by society, what follows if this contribution

[47] Ibidem.

[48] Ibidem.

[49] EIOPA, Sustainable Finance Activities 2022–2024. Available at: https://www.eiopa.europa.eu/sites/default/files/publications/other_documents/eiopa-sustainable-finance-activities-2022-2024.pdf (Accessed: 20 December 2022).

[50] European Commission, Directorate-General for Communication, Towards a sustainable Europe by 2030: reflection paper, Publications Office, 2019, https://data.europa.eu/doi/10.2775/676251.

is adequately made known to the public is an improvement in the company's reputation.

It is undisputed among scholars that a good digital reputation positively impacts a company's financial and non-financial performance.[51] Moreover, Barta, Balanche, Flavian and Terre contend that "implementing the SDGs (stimulus) increases users' intentions to remain loyal to the organization (response) (. . .)". In fact, some authors argue that "in terms of strategies to improve the firm's financial and nonfinancial performance, the variety of SDG-related themes covered (breadth) and the distribution of non-financial disclosure among the SDGs (concentration) appear to be determining factors for improving the effectiveness of digital reputation for the performance of the company".[52] There is evidence that "social influencer CEOs are extensively posting on SDGs; which is subsequently leading in leveraging their corporate reputation and organizational identity within the society".[53]

Assuming that individual insurance companies and the industry as a whole would benefit from adequately displaying the sector's contribution to society's efforts to meet the SDG, then it is in their best interest to showcase all their individual and collective achievements. The absence of an integrated perception of such achievements and their inadequate or incomplete reporting, perhaps due to the insufficient awareness of each company and their staff of some SDG and, consequently, of their actual contribution to meeting these goals, appear to be hindering the industry in its efforts to showcase this contribution. In other words, insurers are currently not taking full advantage of their actual contribution to the SDGs.

Some studies have shown that a failure to align one's interests and values with those of one's customer base may lead to loss of market share: insurance customers may jump ship in search of providers that are perceived to be better at understanding their needs[54] or at furthering their shared values, which is one of the strongest points of many companies created under the umbrella of the collaborative platform economy, where data shows a growing appetite for business models that exploit the shared-interests-and-values psyche.[55]

[51] Schena et al. (2022), pp. 315–325. Available at: https://www.sciencedirect.com/science/article/abs/pii/S0148296322006294 (Accessed: 20 December 2022). Ramos and Casado-Molina (2021), pp. 121–130.

[52] Online corporate. . .Ibidem.

[53] Grover et al. (2019), pp. 39–52. Available at: https://www.sciencedirect.com/science/article/abs/pii/S0268401218312428 (Accessed: 20 December 2022).

[54] Kawohl et al. (2020), "Successfully shaping insurance ecosystems": "Insurers need to better understand the needs of their customers. Thus, they need to create intelligent ecosystem offerings. Besides, they must be perceived as preferred partners in relevant ecosystems to complement them with their offerings. In other words, insurers need to become "ecosystem-capable"." Available at: https://www.ecosystemizer.com/blog/successfully-shaping-insurance-ecosystems (Accessed: 20 December 2022).

[55] Rego and Carvalho (2020).

There is a growing emergence of technology-based peer-to-peer (P2P) insurance models.[56] These can pose a risk to traditional business for consumer (B2C) insurance companies like Fidelidade, because insured persons can "pool their risk and capital, self-organize and self-administer so as to minimize their losses and maximize their gains" with these new models.[57] The issue is that at least part of the reason insurance customers use these models is because of their sense of community. This part is sometimes so important that it even overrides the financial reasons for choosing one product over another. For instance, customers can choose a model that donates excess funds to an NGO pursuing a cause that is deemed fair by all the members within a given risk pool but, other than by donating to someone who does contribute to the cause, in this example, platform economy is not contributing in any particularly significant way to furthering the SDG.

Morell, Espelt and Senabre Hidalgo have argued that the "limited digital perspective of the SDGs in its own definition (. . .) and the current stage of the platform economy, still expanding, do not cover all the challenges defined in the SDGs".[58] Conversely, some insurance companies are not only contributing to the SDGs, but their potential to work between traditional and digital methods is indeed an advantage to their potential contribution to the achievement of a set of goals aimed at all, even those without access to digital technologies.

Insurance companies are expected to excel when using blockchain technology, due to their innate capacity to manage large amounts of data.[59] Some examples for health and life insurance companies are: the development of interoperable and comprehensive health records, supporting administrative and strategic imperatives with smart contracts, detecting fraud more effectively, improving provider directory accuracy, simplifying the application process by making it more client-centric and facilitating a dynamic insurer/client relationship.[60] Such recent developments offer many opportunities to furthering the sector's contribution to the SDGs, as some authors have highlighted.[61] One clear example is provided by the development of interoperable and comprehensive health records, which is set to have a direct, substantial impact on SDG (3) Good Health and Well Being. The expectation is that such records will allow earlier detection and treatment of diseases. From a public health perspective, in addition to improving individual healthcare, the applicability of these techniques on developing countries may also allow for very significant advances in the tracking of diseases, thereby providing a much better basis for achieving global solutions to global health threats.

---

[56] Ibidem; Zornoza (2016).

[57] Ibidem, p. 30.

[58] Fuster Morell et al. (2021), p. 10.

[59] Amponsah et al. (2021).

[60] Deloitte, Blockchain in health and life insurance Turning a buzzword into a breakthrough. https://www2.deloitte.com/us/en/pages/life-sciences-and-health-care/articles/blockchain-in-insurance.html (Accessed: 20 December 2022).

[61] Parmentola et al. (2022), pp. 194–217.

This brings us to a paradox: while insurance companies might be better positioned than some of their current competitors to develop significant contributions to the achievement of the SDGs, they might be losing ground to those competitors precisely due to their perceived weaker performance in this area because they are not adequately communicating their contributions, which is key to their success, in clear terms even to the UN Global Compact.[62]

Some palpable improvement in the current state of affairs could be achieved if, every time an insurance company believes that it is contributing to achieving a single SDG, it were to further analyse the repercussion of that contribution on other SDGs. This idea includes reflecting on the people in charge of those reports and the role that SDGs have in the company's corporative values. By doing so, it will be conveying a more integrated vision of its contribution to achieving the SDGs. For instance, when a company reports on a contribution to target (13) Climate Action, further analysis should be carried out to determine whether it is contributing to more than one environmental target. This would naturally require specific training for those in charge of drafting SDG-related reports, but the message would then be clear and transparent.[63]

3 Fidelidade as a Case Study

The earliest origins of Fidelidade date back to 1808, when insurer Bonança was founded.[64] The company operated like every other traditional insurance company for a long period of time: there was an initial contact with the potential customer, but no further communications or exchanges took place after the policy was finalised, other than those revolving around the payment of the premium, until an insured event happened and a claim was made. Fidelidade no longer purports to be a mere supplier of products or even a multiservice provider, but positions itself as a solution seeker, playing the role of orchestrator in different ecosystems that bring together multiple actors in order to generate added value for their customers. These ecosystems are now reputed to be key to its success.

[62] Barta et al. (2022), pp. 209–211.

[63] Eccles and Vollbracht (2006), pp. 395–408.

[64] The company's official denomination is Fidelidade - Companhia de Seguros, S.A. Although Bonança, its predecessor, was founded in 1808, the name Fidelidade only appeared on the market in 1835. After a succession of mergers and acquisitions, Fidelidade is currently the result of a merger in 2012 of insurers Fidelidade Mundial and Império Bonança. At that time, the company was owned by the State-owned Caixa Geral de Depósitos Group. Today, it is no longer a State-owned insurer, having been acquired by the Fosun International Limited Group in 2014.

3.1 *Fidelidade's Deep-Dive into Ecosystems*

According to Fidelidade, the shift towards ecosystems is interlinked with the digitalization of its business, a process in which it created a substantial portfolio of digital assets and best practices along the insurance value chain.[65] An accelerator mode was activated to drive the change, aimed at increasing efficiency and enhancing the overall customer experience through the creation of a transformational environment.[66] An innovation hub was created to improve and enhance the group's capacity to implement transformational projects. Bearing this in mind and following its own value chain, Fidelidade deep dived into five ecosystems: mobility, home, health, aging and lifestyle.[67]

A clearer picture of what is at stake comes from looking at some of the digital products launched to achieve this goal, according to the literal descriptions provided by Fidelidade: the company launched an app aimed at helping users to improve some aspects of their driving while earning points which can then be exchanged for vouchers with partners that are suppliers of products or services in sectors that are unrelated to insurance, such as food and drinks, energy, entertainment; another app was launched combining travel insurance with some travel preparation assistance using devices such as an intelligent travel shareable checklist; a healthcare app was launched to allow remote consultation with a team of specialist doctors, including videocalls with the doctors, as well as the possibility of attaching or sharing exams or images with them; another app was launched which suggests challenges that help users to adopt a healthy lifestyle, awarding prizes when users overcome the challenges; yet another app was launched to link users with all sorts of home service providers, including, among others, cleaning and maintenance workers, plumbers and electricians; another app was launched to cater to the needs of the elderly, linking them with caregivers and home help services; another app was launched to assist pet owners; and yet another "integrates an individual life insurance product with savings solutions that allow customers to define and achieve their life goals in a simple and fun way".[68]

3.2 *Reported Integration of the SDG into Fidelidade's Ecosystems*

According to Fidelidade, its contribution to the SDG is focused on the following goals: (3) Good Health and Well-being, (8) Decent Work and Economic Growth,

---

[65] Center for Transformation: Fidelidade, "Innovation: Imagining the Future" p. 16.

[66] Ibidem, p. 17.

[67] Ibidem, p. 18.

[68] All the products have been described as stated in: Ibidem, pp. 28–35.

(10) Reduced Inequality, (11) Sustainable Cities and Communities, (13) Climate Action and (17) Partnerships for the Goals.[69] While some of the measures taken in this regard are not industry-specific, such as creating an award to support the good work carried out by the third sector, many of them bear clear links to insurance.

Fidelidade's contribution to SDG (3), as per its own account, has been built around investment in new applied technology innovations as well as in innovative products and services.[70] It is based on the two pillars of longevity and prevention. The company aims to accompany the scientific and technological research on longevity, strengthen the social protection of its customers, and contribute to mitigating the vulnerability and social exclusion linked to the aging process. Fidelidade also aims to be a key player in the field of prevention by designing new products and services and fostering healthy behaviour. The actions taken involved providing remote access to primary health care, ensuring national coverage and the high quality of the providers, reducing the grace period for preventive medicine coverage, promoting healthy living through such initiatives as the healthy habits test, nutritional guidance and the get-fit programme, and launching a health protection programme for people aged 60+.

With respect to SDG (8), Fidelidade's reported actions on the area of decent work and economic growth foster balance between working time-personal life and quality of life, reflection on the development of an integration policy for people with disabilities, and the creation of a feedback culture and investment in rejuvenating the teams. Its intention is to build trust among all the people that make up the ecosystem.

SDG (10) is focused on reducing inequalities and the company reports that it contributes to this goal with the Fidelidade Community Award. This prize aims to strengthen the social sector, contributing to the mitigation of inequalities in the area of health and ageing for people with disabilities or permanent impairments. Fidelidade also highlights the importance of aligning its investment policy with the Principles of Sustainable Insurance.

According to the Group, it contributes to SDG (11) through its "work in product and service innovation, digitalization and promoting the improvement of service quality" because this "keeps pace with the trends in the development of technology

---

[69]This section reflects the information provided by Fidelidade in the following documents. Translations are by the authors': Fidelidade Insurance Group, "2020 sustainability report". Available at: https://www.fidelidade.pt/PT/a-fidelidade/QuemSomos/QuemSomos/Documents/Sustainability%20Report%202020.pdf (Accessed: 20 December 2022); Fidelidade, "2021 Annual Report". Available at: https://www.fidelidade.pt/EN/fidelidade/investor-relations/financial-information/Documents/200_Fidelidade_Annual_Report_EN_2021_v2.pdf (Accessed: 20 December 2022); Fidelidade, "Estrategia". Available at: https://www.fidelidadecomunidade.pt/estrategia/ (Accessed: 20 December 2022).

[70]In addition, in 2014 the Group acquired one of the largest healthcare providers in Portugal: Espísito Santo Saúde, owner of the brand Luz Saúde, who runs a chain of private hospitals and clinics in Portugal.

and capitalizes on its potential for the positive transformation of some of the main societal challenges".

As regards SDG (13), Fidelidade also states that it has "been working on the problem of climate change, both in the careful assessment of customers' risk, in order to be able to propose more adequate coverage, and in the management of processes related to climate events in Portugal, as in 2018 during storm Leslie. Products and services that contribute to minimizing environmental impacts are also being developed and predictive models are being developed to improve risk management".[71]

Regarding the partnerships for SDG (17), Fidelidade explains that the "internationalization is a strategic priority for diversification and the creation of synergies and transfer of innovation between companies and, above all, between markets. But it is also a commitment to the development of the markets where the Group decides to operate, whether in the development of people, the creation of infrastructures or the provision of services and solutions to the population".[72]

These are the company's contributions as reported by Fidelidade. Some data can be easily verified, such as the creation of the Fidelidade Community Award, but some other information, for instance, its contributions in the SDG (13), are more difficult to track. Factchecking these reports is beyond the scope of this chapter. We should, however, point out that such reports would have much to gain if companies were to enrich them by providing references to external, verifiable sources corroborating their contributions.

3.3 *Towards a Greater Integration of SDG into Ecosystems*

Fidelidade's annual report 2020 reads as follows:

> The Group's human resources are evenly distributed between the genders. The recruitment and selection process fully respects the equal opportunities principle, and selection is according to the curriculum and skills profile of each candidate. Thus, when recruiting the Group does not discriminate based on gender/ethnicity/nationality or any other factors.[73]

The group clarifies that even in areas where most managerial positions are held by men, there has been an increase in the number of women in these posts.[74] This is an

[71] Fidelidade, "Estrategia". Available at: https://www.fidelidadecomunidade.pt/estrategia/ (Accessed: 20 December 2022).

[72] Ibidem.

[73] Fidelidade. "Annual Report 2020": In 2020, 38.0% of "Senior Management" and "Line Management" positions were held by women (69 employees), compared to 36.3% in the previous year, which is equivalent to 3 more women occupying positions of greater responsibility. Available at: https://www.fidelidade.pt/PT/a-fidelidade/informacoes_legais/informlegais/Documents/RC_Fidelidade_2020_EN.pdf (Accessed: 20 December 2022).

[74] Fidelidade. "Annual Report 2020": In 2020, 38.0% of "Senior Management" and "Line Management" positions were held by women (69 employees), compared to 36.3% in the previous year,

effort that aligns with SDG (5), but the company does not mention any work done on this matter in its report to the UN Global Compact. This might mislead customers and lead them to opt for a company that more openly defends gender equality.

In another example, launching health insurance for people aged 60+ is indeed an action that works towards SDG (3), but its major contribution is to target 8.10, which, as the only one of the 169 targets explicitly mentioning insurance, refers to the expansion of access to insurance for all. Nevertheless, this is not mentioned in Fidelidade's materiality matrix and related documentation.

Target 8.10 can be the cornerstone for a more thorough integration of the SDGs into insurance ecosystems, if one considers the remote villages in developing countries whose risks might be largely uninsurable due to the lack of publicly available data. The Fidelidade Group operates not only in Portugal but also in Peru, Bolivia, France, Angola, Macao, Chile, Spain, Cabo Verde, Paraguay and Mozambique. If we follow the UN data,[75] Angola, Cabo Verde and Mozambique are among the least developed countries in the world. According to the UN Conference on Trade and Development, "at least eighteen of the 169 Sustainable Development Goal targets refer explicitly to the least developed countries, and dozens more are of central importance to their development success (. . .) This is why UNCTAD argues that the LDCs is the battleground where the Sustainable Development Goals will be won or lost".[76]

Bearing in mind that poor data affects the possibility of offering insurance and that the lack of insurance makes it impossible to develop businesses that could help to feed the population in some of the places where famine is most widespread, it is not difficult to identify windows of opportunity for Fidelidade to carry on groundbreaking work to further some key SDGs. It is not the aim of this chapter to comment on whether or to what extent such work has already been carried out. Our point is simply that, for the most part, this is absent from the company's sustainability reports. Thus, one may safely conclude that Fidelidade has yet to acknowledge and showcase its full potential as a key player in furthering SDGs.

In this example alone, working towards better access to insurance for all could trigger a contribution to the following goals: (1) No Poverty, (2) Zero Hunger, (3) Good Health and Well-being, (4) Quality Education, (6) Clean Water and Sanitation, (7) Affordable and Clean Energy, (8) Decent Work and Economic Growth, (9) Industry, Innovation and Infrastructure, (10) Reduced Inequality,

which is equivalent to 3 more women occupying positions of greater responsibility. Available at: https://www.fidelidade.pt/PT/a-fidelidade/informacoes_legais/informlegais/Documents/RC_Fidelidade_2020_EN.pdf (Accessed: 20 December 2022).

[75] UN Department of Economic and Social Affairs Economic Analysis, "LDCs at a Glance". Available at: https://www.un.org/development/desa/dpad/least-developed-country-category/ldcs-at-a-glance.html (Accessed: 20 December 2022).

[76] Achieving the Sustainable Development Goals in the Least Developed Countries. Available at: https://unctad.org/publication/achieving-sustainable-development-goals-least-developed-countries (Accessed: 20 December 2022).

(11) Sustainable Cities and Communities, (12) Responsible Consumption and Production, (13) Climate Action, (15) Life On Land, and (17) Partnerships for the Goals.

In another example, the COVID-19 outbreak of forced more than 70% of Fidelidade's workforce in Cabo Verde to switch to teleworking. As some people did not have the equipment and infrastructure to be remotely connected, Fidelidade decided to make a significant investment in improving these connections. This is a direct contribution to SDG (9) Industry, Innovation and Infrastructure, but, if correctly articulated, can also have a broad impact in the community. For instance, if the new internet connection can be used for children to get a better education, there is an impact on SDG (4) Quality Education; if it allows others to set up their own new small businesses, it can have an impact on SDG (8) Decent Work and Economic Growth. Fidelidade can also look at these infrastructures as a potential touching point to open new markets in Cabo Verde and make further contributions to the development of the country, as in the example provided above.

Fidelidade has the knowledge and the financial capacity to trigger changes that positively affect the sustainable development of the world. These actions will trigger a constructive financial impact for those countries and the company itself. However, the most important consideration is that, as we live in a globalized world where each country is in constant contact with the others, it will be building the global trust that is needed to stay relevant in today's insurance market—if its actions are adequately integrated into the company's corporate narrative when reporting on its contributions to achieving the SDGs.

3.4 *Lessons That Arose from Fidelidade as a Case Study*

Following on from the previous section, we can conclude that insurance companies could tap into their own, as well as the sector's, contributions to furthering the SDGs as a means to survive in the midst of the new business models, just as much as the SDGs need the sector's contribution to be successfully achieved. If insurance companies wish to compete against new business models in this new global arena, they first need to structure their vision and correctly articulate all the work that they already carry out and optimize their potential in planning more work that they can also undertake to achieve the SDGs. They then need to align the narrative so that all this work is more visible to the world. This also happens to be the key to a successful ecosystem, because a process cannot work properly if any of its parts are missing. Understanding this is crucial, but communicating how insurers can and do use their expertise to build a better world is no less important.

Adequate communication of the sector's key contribution to achieving the SDGs will enhance the reputation of insurance companies, thereby increasing society's trust in the sector. Insurers who are successful at this will be better equipped to compete with the new business models for a market share and make the world a better place at the same time.

4 Conclusions

The survival of traditional insurance companies has been threatened by the advent of digitalization,[77] the emergence of P2P business models and the sharing economy, and the ever-increasing competition from non-insurance specific global players. To remain competitive in the increasingly demanding and diverse global marketplace of the twenty-first century, some insurers have reacted by creating and merging into ecosystems.

Within these ecosystems, communication with insurance customers is constant and both parties reap benefits from their close interaction. For instance, accidents are less likely to happen when rewards for good drivers are provided through an app, thus insurers will receive fewer claims and will be able to assess the risk more accurately, while customers will reduce the possibility of suffering injuries and will get vouchers for things they like.

The non-insurance specific value creation enabled by the new insurance-based ecosystems also enhances the industry's already very significant potential to being key players in contemporary society's global efforts to meet the United Nations' sustainable development goals. In its turn, the actual or potential contribution of the insurance industry to furthering the SDGs is also potentially relevant to the industry's work towards creating value, gaining trust and increasing customer satisfaction. This is not only good in itself, as insurers who choose to do this will be working towards a better world, but it might also be of strategic importance, as it could help to improve the individual reputation of each insurer and the collective reputation of the industry in the current, digital era and to combat the loss of customers tempted by more recent business models with better communication skills.

We do not dispute that the insurance industry can and already does contribute significantly to the achievement of SDGs, but we have found that this contribution is not yet adequately displayed in sustainability reports. Discrepancies, inconsistencies and information gaps were found to be the norm in such reports. This appears to be, at least in part, a consequence of the industry's widespread lack of awareness and misperception about the various economic, social and governance aspects of sustainability, as well as of the industry's actual and potential role in contributing to some SDGs.

Fidelidade has proven to be a very fertile source of information for our case study by providing a good illustration of what we perceive to be a more general trend among some of the most dynamic, innovative insurance companies which already contribute in different ways to furthering the SDGs and yet do not have a complete, coherent, clear and accessible narrative that adequately showcases all the different aspects of their current work in furthering the SDGs.

[77] Struve (2009).

References

Books, Book Chapters and Articles

Amponsah AA, Adekoya AF, Weyori BA (2021) Blockchain in insurance: exploratory analysis of prospects and threats. (IJACSA) Int J Adv Comput Sci Appl 12(1)

Barta S, Belanche D, Flavian M, Terré MC (2022) How the implementation of sustainable development goals affects customers' perceptions and loyalty towards organisations. In: 26th Corporate and Marketing Communications Conference: Conference Proceedings. https://www.unic.ac.cy/cmc2022/wp-content/uploads/sites/33/2022/05/Book-of-Proceedings-CMC2022.pdf. Accessed 20 Dec 2022

Catlin T, Lorenz JT, Nandan J, Sharma S, Waschto A (2018) Insurance beyond digital: the rise of ecosystems and platforms. https://www.mckinsey.com/industries/financial-services/our-insights/insurance-beyond-digital-the-rise-of-ecosystems-and-platforms. Accessed 20 Dec 2022

Eccles RG, Vollbracht M (2006) Media reputation of the insurance industry: an urgent call for strategic communication management. Geneva Pap Risk Insur Issues Pract 31:397

Fuster Morell M, Espelt R, Senabre Hidalgo E (2021) Data for sustainable platform economy: connections between platform models and sustainable development goals. Data 6–7:10

Grover P, KumarKar A, Vigneswara Ilavarasan P (2019) Impact of corporate social responsibility on reputation—insights from tweets on sustainable development goals by CEOs. Int J Inf Manag 48:39–52

Parmentola A, Petrillo A, Tutore I, De Felice F (2022) Is blockchain able to enhance environmental sustainability? A systematic review and research agenda from the perspective of Sustainable Development Goals (SDGs). Bus Strategy Environ 31:194–217

Pérez Pérez C, Benito Osorio D, García Moreno SM, Martínez Fernandez A (2021) Is sharing a better alternative for the planet? The contribution of sharing economy to Sustainable Development Goals. Sustainability 13

Pfeifer D, Langen V (2021) Insurance business and sustainable development. In: Sarfraz M, Ivascu L (eds) Risk management. Institut für Mathematik

Ramos C, Casado-Molina AM (2021) Online corporate reputation: a panel data approach and a reputation index proposal applied to the banking sector. J Bus Res 122:121–130

Rego ML, Carvalho JC (2020) Insurance in today's sharing economy: new challenges ahead or a return to the origins of insurance? In: Marano P, Noussia K (eds) InsurTech: a legal and regulatory view, AIDA Europe Research Series on Insurance Law and Regulation 1. Springer Nature Switzerland AG 2020

Schanz KU (2006) Reputation and reputational risk management. Geneva Pap Risk Insur Issues Pract. 31:377–381. https://doi.org/10.1057/palgrave.gpp.25

Schena R, Secundo G, De Fano D, Del Vecchio P, Russo AA (2022) Digital reputation and firm performance: the moderating role of firm orientation towards sustainable development goals (SDGs). J Bus Res 152:315–325

Swaminathan MS, Kesavan PC (2016) Achieving the sustainable development goals. Curr Sci 110: 127–128

Zornoza A (2016) Peer-to-peer insurance. Primera Aproximación a los Seguros entre Pares, R.E.D.S. núm. 9, July–December

Other Online Resources

Accenture (2022) The ultimate guide to insurance ecosystems. https://insuranceblog.accenture.com/the-ultimate-guide-to-insurance-ecosystems. Accessed 20 Dec 2022

Deloitte (2022) Blockchain in health and life insurance. Turning a buzzword into a breakthrough. https://www2.deloitte.com/us/en/pages/life-sciences-and-health-care/articles/blockchain-in-insurance.html. Accessed 20 Dec 2022

Eardley J (2021) Bad reputation: changing the perception of insurance. https://www.the-future-of-commerce.com/2021/01/28/perception-of-insurance/. Accessed 20 Dec 2022

EIOPA (2021) EIOPA welcomes Solvency II proposals from the European Commission on sustainability. https://www.eiopa.europa.eu/media/news/eiopa-welcomes-solvency-ii-proposals-european-commission-sustainability_en. Accessed 20 Dec 2022

EIOPA (2022a) Sustainable Finance Activities 2022-2024. https://www.eiopa.europa.eu/sites/default/files/publications/other_documents/eiopa-sustainable-finance-activities-2022-2024.pdf. Accessed 20 Dec 2022

EIOPA (2022b) Sustainable finance. https://www.eiopa.europa.eu/browse/sustainable-finance_en?field_term_topic_type_tid%5B%5D=218. Accessed 20 Dec 2022

European Commission (2019) Insurance rules' review: encouraging solid and reliable insurers to invest in Europe's recovery. https://ec.europa.eu/info/publications/210922-solvency-2-communication_en. Accessed 20 Dec 2022

European Commission - Directorate-General for Communication (2019) Towards a sustainable Europe by 2030: reflection paper. https://data.europa.eu/doi/10.2775/676251. Accessed 20 Dec 2022

EY (2020) COVID-19: how insurers can meet the evolving needs of their customers. https://www.ey.com/en_gl/financial-services-emeia/covid-19-how-insurers-can-meet-the-evolving-needs-of-their-customers. Accessed 20 Dec 2022

Fidelidade (2021) Annual Report 2020. https://www.fidelidade.pt/PT/a-fidelidade/informacoes_legais/informlegais/Documents/RC_Fidelidade_2020_EN.pdf. Accessed 20 Dec 2022

Fidelidade Insurance Group (2021) 2020 sustainability report. https://www.fidelidade.pt/PT/a-fidelidade/QuemSomos/QuemSomos/Documents/Sustainability%20Report%202020.pdf. Accessed 20 Dec 2022

Fidelidade Insurance Group (2022) 2021 Annual Report. https://www.fidelidade.pt/EN/fidelidade/investor-relations/financial-information/Documents/200_Fidelidade_Annual_Report_EN_2021_v2.pdf. Accessed 20 Dec 2022

Fidelidade Insurance Group, "Estrategia". https://www.fidelidadecomunidade.pt/estrategia/. Accessed 20 Dec 2022

German Agency for International Cooperation (GIZ) (2017) Inclusive Insurance and the Sustainable Development Goals: how insurance contributes to the 2030 Agenda for Sustainable Development. https://us.milliman.com/-/media/milliman/pdfs/2021-articles/5-11-21-inclusive-insurance-and-the-sustainable-development-goals.ashx. Accessed 20 Dec 2022

Kawohl J, Lange J, Rosenbaum M, Nguyen H (2020) Successfully shaping insurance ecosystems. https://www.ecosystemizer.com/blog/successfully-shaping-insurance-ecosystems. Accessed 20 Dec 2022

McKinsey & Company (2020a) Ecosystems and platforms: how insurers can turn vision into reality. https://www.mckinsey.com/industries/financial-services/our-insights/ecosystems-and-platforms-how-insurers-can-turn-vision-into-reality. Accessed 20 Dec 2022

McKinsey & Company (2020b) Ecosystems in insurance: the next frontier for enhancing productivity. https://www.mckinsey.com/industries/financial-services/our-insights/insurance-blog/ecosystems-in-insurance-the-next-frontier-for-enhancing-productivity. Accessed 20 Dec 2022

Messineo G (2020) Ecosystem in insurance: three steps to a winning strategy. https://www.ey.com/en_us/insurance/ecosystems-in-insurance-three-steps-to-a-winning-strategy. Accessed 20 Dec 2022

Payne C, Whyte J (2021) Ecosystems: why they matter to insurers and the imperative for action. https://www.ey.com/en_pt/financial-services-emeia/ecosystems-why-they-matter-to-insurers-and-the-imperative-for-action. Accessed 20 Dec 2022
PSI framework (2015) Insurance 2030: harnessing insurance for sustainable development. https://www.unep.org/resources/report/insurance-2030-harnessing-insurance-sustainable-development. Accessed 20 Dec 2022
PwC (2021) Top insurance industry issues in 2021. https://www.pwc.com/us/en/industries/insurance/assets/pwc-top-insurance-industry-issues-2021-compilation.pdf. Accessed 20 Dec 2022
Singh D (2021) Insurers should leverage the ecosystem model to secure their future. https://www.thoughtworks.com/insights/blog/platforms/insurers-should-leverage-the-ecosystem-model-to-secure-their-fut#:~:text=Insurers%20should%20leverage%20the%20ecosystem%20model%20to%20secure%20their%20future,-Blogs&text=Insurers%20need%20new%20and%20disruptive,an%20underwhelming%20global%20financial%20market. Accessed 20 Dec 2022
Struve J (2009) Harnessing network effects: a Web 2.0 primer for the insurance industry. https://www.perrknight.com/2009/10/01/harnessing-network-effects-web-2-0-primer-insurance-industry/. Accessed 20 Dec 2022
Swiss Re (2013) Reputation risk in the insurance industry. http://www.oxfordmetrica.com/public/CMS/Files/1570/OM-report-for-Swiss-Re_2013c.pdf. Accessed 20 Dec 2022
UN Department of Economic and Social Affairs Economic Analysis (2021) LDCs at a Glance. https://www.un.org/development/desa/dpad/least-developed-country-category/ldcs-at-a-glance.html. Accessed 20 Dec 2022
UNEP Finance Initiative (2007) The inaugural report of the Insurance Working Group of the United Nations Environment Programme Finance Initiative: Insuring for Sustainability: why and how the leaders are doing it. https://www.unepfi.org/fileadmin/documents/insuring_for_sustainability.pdf. Accessed 20 Dec 2022

Maria del Val Bolívar Oñoro obtained her Dual Ph.D. in the University of Alcala (Spain) and Maynooth University (Ireland) in 2021, after defending her dissertation: *"The Right of People Living with HIV to Private Health Insurance in Spain"*. Currently, she is a Posdoctoral Fellow at the University of Alcalá ("Programa Propio UAH"), Madrid, Spain. She was a Margarita Salas Postdoctoral Fellow (funded by the Spanish Government, *NextGenerationEU*, *Plan de Recuperación Transforamación y Resilencia* and the University of Alcala) at NOVA School of Law in 2022. Her research is focused on the intersection between the Right to Health, Equality and Non-discrimination and the Freedom to Conduct a Business of Insurance Companies.

Margarida Lima Rego is full professor and dean of NOVA School of Law. As an academic, she has taught different courses and published in a wide range of topics within Private Law, with a special focus on Contract Law and Insurance Contract Law. She is an active researcher at CEDIS, the School's R&D Unit, where she founded and coordinates the NOVA Knowledge Centre for Data-Driven Law. She is the holder of the Jean Monnet Module in EU Insurance Law: Challenges in the SDG Era. Margarida has been a member of the Board of Appeal of the European Supervisory Authorities since December 2021. Previously, she was Of Counsel to Morais Leitão, where she headed the insurance, reinsurance and pension funds cross-practice team, having left the firm in July 2019 to pursue her academic career on a full time basis. She is still an active legal consultant who is regularly sought on varied subject matters of Portuguese and Lusophone Law, having contributed to dispute resolutions before the courts of several jurisdictions in Europe, Africa and North and South America. Current positions include: President of AIDA Portugal; member of the Executive Committee and Scientific Committee of AIDA Europe; of the Scientific Committee of CILA; of the Presidential Council of AIDA World.

Insurance Is Accelerating Economic and Social Change in the United States: A Legal and Sociological Perspective

Kathleen M. Defever

Abstract Insurance does not receive the full, rigorous interdisciplinary analysis to which it is due. The availability of insurance in a society is a critical factor in determining the potential economic success and social health of that society. The confluence of insurance principles, law, and sociology in the United States has only been addressed a few times over the past century, but for the most part, multidisciplinary analysis of the insurance concept has not been comprehensively performed.

Currently, insurance is accelerating economic and social change in the United States. This chapter analyzes insurance from a legal and sociological perspective, and highlights how, and why, the American insurance regime has reinforced the ever-widening wealth gap in the United States, led to large migrations of people within the country, and even contributed to the staggering increases of corporate power which now threaten the fabric of American democracy.

Keywords Insurance · Law · Insurance law · Sociology · Economics · Political science · Democracy · United States · Deregulation · Enforcement · Risk society

Insurance does not receive the full credit due for the concept's role in the wealth and development of our world societies. Insurance, when kept true to its original conceptual purposes,[1] is a tool for communities to provide more security, and therefore increase sustainable equality and overall stability of resources. When

[1] "The general principles of insurance... are always the same; insurance is a generic conception covering the methods of obtaining security, of which the modern devices are but specific, highly elaborated, and scientifically tested examples." Sumner and Keller (1927), p. 749.

K. M. Defever (✉)
DePaul University College of Law, Chicago, IL, USA

University of Connecticut School of Law, Hartford, CT, USA

Ghent University Faculty of Law, Ghent, Belgium
e-mail: Kathleen.Defever@ugent.be

M. Lima Rego, S. Grima (eds.), *Cross-Disciplinary Impacts on Insurance Law*,
AIDA Europe Research Series on Insurance Law and Regulation 8,
https://doi.org/10.1007/978-3-031-38526-1_2

members of a society are protected from significant suffering due to hardship,[2] an overall increase in wealth and happiness naturally follows. Insurance also promotes innovation by reducing the negative impacts of failure when a new venture is attempted.[3] The availability of insurance in a society is a critical factor in determining the potential economic success of that society.

A study of the evolution of insurance in the United States reveals recent trends which have reinforced the ever-widening wealth gap, led to large migrations of people within the country, and even contributed to the staggering increases of corporate power which now threaten the fabric of American democracy. This chapter explores current societal change in the United States, as well as the impacts the modern state of insurance products and regulation have on the economy, and on the insurance consumer. I will highlight some trends developing in economic markets and insurance regulation which can be linked directly to the societal changes evolving in the United States today.

1 Insurance and Society

Insurance is notably overlooked in the field of social science. As American insurance law scholar Tom Baker wrote, "Although there is significant research literature on insurance and risk, it remains relatively small compared to the importance of insurance to society. Given the enormous size of insurance institutions relative to contemporary Western economies, it is surprising that most social scientists and historians have paid so little attention to insurance."[4] But there are a few social scientists who have studied insurance over the decades, and legal experts who artfully combined the field of sociology with the study of insurance law. I will mention several of these individuals and their studies throughout this chapter, and provide citations to the works of others.

As early as the 1920's, Yale University sociologists Sumner and Keller collaborated on a four-volume treatise titled "The Science of Society," discussing political science and sociology, and referring to the concept of insurance multiple times throughout the text.[5] In the introductory section, they immediately establish the importance of insurance, explaining that when societies first developed insurance as a concept, it was necessary to assist them against the uncertainties of life, particularly when cooperation in small social groups was essential, because otherwise a person could starve to death, or be attacked by outsiders competing for the same resources. At the time, these social groups did not "realize [insurance's] full nature and

[2] Sumner and Keller (1927), pp. 326–328, 331.

[3] Ewald (2002), pp. 298–299; Wasow and Hill (1986), p. 63. All risks are potentially insurable. See Baker and Logue (2013), p. 2. See Pearson (2017), pp. 5–9.

[4] Baker and Simon (2002), p. 12; See also Ericson et al. (2003), p. 3.

[5] See Sumner and Keller (1927).

function."[6] Sumner and Keller were so certain of the importance of insurance in a society that they equated life in a society to a "species of insurance."[7]

In 1960, law professor Spencer L. Kimball published a thorough and thoughtful book titled, "Insurance and Public Policy." Like Tom Baker, he noted the tendency for insurance to be overlooked, observing, "Unlike the banks or the railroads or the automobile manufacturers, insurance never occupied the center of the stage in the drama of American political life. Nevertheless, no broad discussion of insurance in American society should neglect the place of the insurance business in the distribution of power."[8]

In 2003, three Canadian scholars authored the book "Insurance as Governance," stressing that insurance is a key, powerful component of political sociology, and should be included in every sociological investigation. They noted that the role of insurance in risk distribution impacts how all institutions and individuals function within a society.[9] Scholars who have studied insurance, whether from the viewpoint of sociology, political science, or law, agree that insurance is a powerful economic and social force which impacts each and every member of society.

1.1 Brief History of Relevant Insurance Evolution

While insurance is a concept that has probably been in existence for as long as humans have lived in social groups,[10] the modern form of large-scale, consumer-oriented insurance wasn't born until just before the industrial revolution.[11] As people left their agrarian lifestyles and moved to cities for employment in factories, they began living in dense housing, and found their risks increasingly intertwined. For example, if a fire occurs in a city, it is highly likely to impact at least several homes or businesses. In fact, during the nineteenth century there were dozens of fires that

[6] Sumner and Keller (1927), p. 20.

[7] *Id.*

[8] Kimball (1960), p. 308.

[9] Ericson et al. (2003), pp. 4, 43.

[10] Research tentatively suggests that insurance, in a mutual form, existed during the times of Confucius (551 B.C. to 479 B.C.) and Mencius (372 B.C. to 289 B.C.). Kang (1997), p. 103; Ancient Phoenician merchants reduced their shipping risks by dividing cargoes and placing them on different ships, and the fourth Century B.C. Greeks loaned money tied to ships and their cargoes, only to be paid back when the ships arrived safely at their destinations—if the ship was lost, the debt was forgiven. Abraham (2005), p. 1; The first known commercial insurance contract was written in 1343 in Genoa, Italy, to insure sea cargo. Fondazione Mansutti (2015), p. 13. *See* Defever (2018).

[11] Excluding merchant-oriented policies, i.e. commercial coverages. For example, the first private fire insurance institutions were developed in Great Britain just before the Industrial Revolution, partly due to the unfolding, increasing ability of the common man (non-noble) to own property, and partly due to the increase of the wealth of the new industrial businessmen (circa mid-1600's), and then subsequently in response to the frequency and severity of fires occurring in areas with dense populations. Pearson (2017), pp. 3–4.

burned not only entire neighborhoods of major cities, but sometimes burned cities almost to the ground.[12] The industrial revolution also brought about increased specialization of labor. As people ceased to grow their own food or make their own clothing, and took jobs in factories or the service industry, they became more reliant on others for their basic needs. Dependency on other people (here, people who have never met one another) brings added uncertainty, and therefore, added risk.[13]

As the twentieth century began, further increases in the specialization of labor and the rapid adoption of additional modern technologies made the concept of insurance for risk-spreading more viable and important than ever. In the United States, the insurance industry was growing at a rapid pace. Americans sought security for their new-found wealth, and protection from the vulnerabilities which their new dependencies brought about. In fact, Americans in the mid-twentieth century were so security-conscious that the time period became known as "the insurance age".[14]

Insurers were marketing their products accordingly. What was previously a mostly unregulated economy in which individuals bore the brunt of not only their own risks, but also widespread negative impacts—whether from risks undertaken by others, or due to uncontrollable natural disasters—transformed into a society in which people purchased insurance coverage and took responsibility for their own social costs,[15] with the intention that this responsibility would also benefit the larger group. There was a "sense of responsibility for the welfare of those less fortunately situated."[16]

At the same time, there was a push for more social insurance, and the social security system was established, as well as health insurance for the elderly (Medicare) and the economically-disadvantaged (Medicaid). These programs would generally be as far as the United States would take the concept of government-provided social insurance, but in other places around the world, such as Western Europe and Japan, the social insurance programs became much more extensive.

Interestingly, because during the twentieth century American insurance companies were so successful with their marketing to convince the public of the virtues of the insurance product, the public reacted by advocating for more government-managed social insurance, therefore undercutting the free enterprise, private insurance economy.[17] However, at the end of the twentieth century there was a strong

---

[12] For example, the fires of Chicago in 1871 and Boston in 1872, Baranoff (2003), p. 119. In 1666, the Great Fire of London gutted the city.

[13] "In variety of vocations, there is less chance to sense group-advantage and risk, and the powerful take his insurance on himself." Sumner and Keller (1927), pp. 330–331.

[14] Kimball (1960), p. 30.

[15] i.e. personal property loss, disability, lack of income/poverty due to death or hardship, etc.

[16] Kimball (1960), pp. 303–304.

[17] Kimball (1960), p. 311.

drift in the United States toward individual insurance provided by insurance corporations, and less reliance on social programs.[18]

In the twenty-first century, the demand for individualizing risk is certainly more prevalent. Overall, Americans embrace individual risk as an honorable concept.[19] People who take economic risks are considered admirable entrepreneurs, boldly following the American dream. It became virtuous to take individual risk and provide for one's own insurance protection, rather than receive government assistance in any form.[20] This mentality is not limited to the United States. In fact, world societies as a whole have become so "risk-centric" since the Industrial Revolution that well-known sociologist Ulrich Beck contends that our modern societies are best labeled as "risk societies".[21]

Ulrich Beck believes that while the "modern" industrial era was preoccupied with the distribution of wealth, the "post-modern" era is focused on the "prevention, minimization, and channeling of risk."[22] Although sociological theorists disagree about whether society has changed so much that new analytical approaches are needed, Beck's theory does seem to correlate with the decrease of the more socially-minded insurance organizations such as mutual associations, and the concurrent increase in the corporate shareholder-driven insurance model, during the second half of the twentieth century.[23]

2 The Broader Socio-Economic Context: Rapid Changes in American Society

In the United States there has been a clear and demonstrable trend toward the elimination of economic regulation, starting in the 1980s. Corporate interests promoted a "free" or "self-regulating" market, and the privatization of services which had previously been maintained by the government.[24] Although there have been many pushes for the privatization of social security, to date these have not been successful. While there is much discussion about how the insurance industry is highly regulated in some aspects, and in fact subject to more regulation than most industries, this dialogue distracts from the more important analysis of how much regulation is needed, and whether or not the current level of regulation is sufficient, or effective.

---

[18] Ericson et al. (2003), p. 6.

[19] Taking personal responsibility is an ethical pillar of insurance. Long (1971), p. 38.

[20] Baker and Simon (2002), pp. 3–4; McCluskey (2002), p. 148.

[21] Ritzer (2011), p. 72.

[22] Ritzer (2011), p. 72; See Beck (1986).

[23] See my discussion of the history and decline of mutual insurance companies in Defever (2018), pp. 10–11. Also see Bainbridge (1952), p. 21.

[24] McMichael (2012), p. xiii.

While upon a cursory view the United States insurance regulatory landscape does appear powerful and exhaustive, in reality, critical aspects are weak and often ineffective. Although individual state Insurance Commissioners do monitor solvency and premium rates, and investigate fraudulent claims, there is a complete lack of uniformity of the insurance codes. In addition, the existing insurance regulations intended to protect the consumer during market transactions (sales) and claims processing are either minimal in scope or not enforced (or both). Not every state has a dedicated insurance code for consumer protection,[25] and those that do exist are not enforced with any noticeable vigor.

Because the availability and quality of insurance has such a profound impact on the economy and society as a whole, thoughtful governmental regulation of the insurance market is critical. Nobel-prize winning economist Joseph E. Stiglitz writes, "... social returns are not well aligned when competition is imperfect," for example, "where risk markets... are absent (one can't for instance, buy insurance against many of the most important risks that one faces)."[26] Without regulation, a balanced, robust economy and a healthy society cannot be achieved.[27]

Notably, the decades-long trend of U.S. market deregulation has also led to multiple economic crises, of which the Great Recession of 2008-09 was the worst.[28] The United Nations Department of Economic and Social Affairs noted that the Great Recession "exposed the flaws of market deregulation, requir [ed] government intervention, [and] dealt a blow to... conventional wisdom..."[29] One "flaw" which has become quite glaring is the rapidly increasing wealth gap.

[25] Many states/territories classify their insurance regulations under the broader umbrella of "financial regulation," and do not have an exhaustive, separately dedicated insurance code. Many states/territories do not have a dedicated Department of Insurance and/or an Insurance Commissioner, including Arizona, District of Columbia, Indiana, Michigan, Minnesota, Missouri, Montana, New Jersey, New York, Oregon, Rhode Island, Tennessee, Vermont, Virginia, and the U.S. territories of Guam, Northern Mariana Islands, and Virgin Islands. National Association of Insurance Commissioners (NAIC). Of the states which do have substantial insurance regulation, many of them either have not adopted the National Association of Insurance Commissioners (NAIC) model insurance consumer protection laws (most relevantly the Unfair Trade Practices Act and the Unfair Claim Settlement Practices Act), or have adopted their own simpler code with far fewer protections (see Alabama, for example). Others have failed to adopt any consumer protections at all. For example, the state of Mississippi has not adopted the Unfair Claim Settlement Practices Act, and a Mississippi state court took the extra step to hold that the act would not apply to insurance claims adjusting in the state. See Defever (2018), pp. 18–20.

[26] Stiglitz (2013), p. 42.

[27] Heimer (2002), p. 118.

[28] Stiglitz (2013), p. 43; See Reinhart and Rogoff (2009).

[29] McMichael (2012), p. 302, quoting UNDESA.

2.1 Increasing Wealth Gap

During the last thirty years, economic inequality in the United States has increased swiftly. Put simply by Joseph E. Stiglitz, "the rich are getting richer, the richest of the rich are getting still richer, the poor are becoming poorer and more numerous, and the middle class is being hollowed out."[30] All statistics aside, it has been a common point of discussion in the United States that the vast majority of the wealth is held by the "top 1 percent" of earners, with the remaining 99 percent holding only a small fraction of wealth in comparison. For example, from 1990 to 2010, the bottom 90 percent of earners only saw a 15 percent increase in their wages, while the top 1 percent saw an additional 150 percent increase, and the top 0.1 percent had a 300 percent increase. After the Great Recession, the wealthiest 1 percent held 225 times the wealth of the typical American.[31] Stiglitz explains:

> This trend is far greater in America than in most of Europe and comes out of the distinctively American policies, ranging from tax systems that are less progressive, safety nets and social protections systems that are weaker...[etc.], especially after ... [the] deregulatory fervor [of the 1980s].[32]

International economists agree that the inequality in the United States had reached the level where it is inefficient and bad for economic growth.[33] Insurance, which is by definition a safety net used to provide increased security, is most certainly at the core of the dynamics which cause wealth inequality.

For example, as income increases, so does the amount of wealth at risk, and therefore, more insurance is demanded. If and when more insurance is issued, economic actors are both able to protect against bearing the full weight of unanticipated losses and participate in investments which bear some risk.[34] Because the risk of loss is then spread amongst society through the insurance risk pool, society receives a net gain in wealth when significant losses are compensated with insurance coverage. Insurance supports the creation of additional wealth, and wealth increases the demand for insurance.[35] Insurance and prosperity have a mutually complementary relationship. When insurance is not uniformly or substantially available, safety nets are weakened, consumers are forced to take on increased risk and bear the full impact of their economic losses, and the societal wealth gap increases. For wealthy Americans and corporate entities, insurance is an available and effective tool for the prevention of large economic losses. However, as we will discuss further, for the average American consumer, needed insurance is not always available, and even

[30] Stiglitz (2013), p. 9.

[31] Stiglitz (2013), pp. 9–10.

[32] Stiglitz (2013), p. xxxii.

[33] Stiglitz (2013), p. xv, citing The Economist; McMichael (2012), pp. 287–288.

[34] Such as investing in property which may be damaged or destroyed, a business which may experience income loss, or, in the case of institutional investors, perhaps issuing loans to cover a mortgage taken on a new home.

[35] Wasow and Hill (1986), pp. 122, 134.

when it is, it does not always appropriately compensate for the losses which are incurred.

2.2 Increasing Corporate Profits

The deregulation of American industry has led to an increased ability for corporations to make more profits, and to retain more of this profit. Since the beginning of deregulation in the 1980s, American industries have worked to achieve monopoly power (often in violation of antitrust laws) and circumvent government regulations, including finding creative ways to favorably interpret the U.S. tax code. Large corporations have, for the most part, been able to avoid significant taxation. Despite a posted corporate tax rate of approximately 21%, corporations often are able to avoid most, if not all, of their taxes through tax planning strategies.[36] Corporate profits are at an all-time high.

Also as a result of this fervor for deregulation, when consumers entrust their funds to large business entities such as banks and insurance companies, they find that more of their funds are being "kept" by these corporations, whether through predatory lending and abusive credit card practices;[37] increased fees and penalties imposed by banks, merchants, service providers (including insurers), and creditors; or the failure to disburse funds under contractual agreements. The U.S. Consumer Protection Bureau reports that more money is being retained by financial institutions through consumer financial transactions than ever before—in 2019 banking consumers paid $15.47 billion in overdraft and insufficient fund fees, alone.[38] With the American government refusing to increase regulation on behalf of the consumer, corporations have increased fees, penalties, and even fraudulent activity, with little to no oversight.[39] In January 2022 the Bureau launched an initiative to curb billions of dollars in exploitative "junk" fees, which have been levied on bank accounts, credit cards, and other financial products for years—often illegally.[40]

American consumers can easily surmise where the additional corporate profits are allocated. Corporate executive salaries are at an all-time high,[41] and major shareholders have become rapidly wealthier over the past several decades. These shareholders comprise the afore-mentioned one percent which holds more than 225 times the wealth of the average American. The wealth gap in the United States is now

---

[36] Scott (2021).

[37] Stiglitz (2013), p. 47.

[38] Consumer Financial Protection Bureau (2021).

[39] A representative example can be found in the 2016 Wells Fargo & Company fake (bank) account scandal.

[40] Consumer Financial Protection Bureau (2022).

[41] Harvard Law School Forum on Corporate Governance (2022).

equal to, or larger, than it was during the "roaring" 1920's,[42] and the American middle class has shrunk almost to the point of disappearance, while a small percentage becomes incredibly wealthy and the rest fall into mid- to low-income or poverty classifications.

2.3 Unregulated Corporate Power Influencing American Policy-Making

The ability of American corporations to avoid government regulation (and, as we will discuss, the majority of costly lawsuits) has increased their economic power significantly. However, other recent changes in the American laws have granted corporate actors another type of power—heavy political influence and the ability to, in essence and sometimes also in fact, author their own regulations with little to no interference.[43]

Of course, the U.S. government has never been completely free of influence from private economic actors, particularly those which are very well-funded. Over the recent decades, private lobbyists have regularly been hired to ensure the "voices" of corporations and organizations are heard.[44] However, a major upheaval occurred in the United States in the year 2010, when the U.S. Supreme Court decided the *Citizens United* case.[45] In *Citizens United,* the highest court in the United States held that the free speech clause of the First Amendment of the United States Constitution[46] prohibits the government from restricting independent expenditures for political campaigns by corporations, including nonprofit corporations, labor unions, and other associations.[47]

Since then, American corporations are able to create and promote their own advertisements in support of (or in opposition to) political candidates. Hundreds of millions of dollars are spent on these advertisements every year. Politicians, while technically not the direct recipients of the funds, are very sensitive to the campaigns which are promoted by large corporations and organizations. The influence of these "big money interests" (also called Super PACs[48]) has ballooned to the point that the average American voter is now, just over ten years later, beginning to notice that

---

[42] Colombo (2019), citing Saez and Zucman (2020); Stiglitz (2013), pp. 5–6.

[43] Stiglitz (2013), pp. 59–60.

[44] Stiglitz (2013), p. 407 citing OpenSecrets.org.

[45] Citizens United vs. FEC, 558 U.S. 310 (2010).

[46] "Congress shall make no law respecting an establishment of religion, or prohibiting the free exercise thereof; *or abridging the freedom of speech*, or of the press; or the right of the people peaceably to assemble, and to petition the Government for a redress of grievances." Constitution of the United States, First Amendment (emphasis added).

[47] Wikipedia, Citizens United vs. FEC.

[48] "PAC" stands for political action committee.

their vote has been effectively "diluted," because politicians are paying more attention to the messages of lobbyists and corporate donors than they are to the results of actual elections.[49]

Unfortunately, corruption of the American democracy is now a recognized reality amongst the majority of citizens.[50] Scholars across the fields of law and economics agree that the *Citizens United* case needs to be overturned, or federal law needs to be created that reinstills campaign contribution limits. The weighty influence of corporate money needs to be curtailed from corrupting and controlling the American democratic system of public representation.

3 The Insurance Consumer Experience in Twenty-First Century American Society

The confluence of economic deregulation, increasing corporate wealth and power, the erosion of democratic principles through essentially a weakening of the power of the vote, and the rapidly expanding wealth gap, has changed American society substantially. Naturally, the view of the concept of insurance through the lens of American society has also undergone a shift, as well as the resultant nature and design of the insurance product. The most commonly understood purpose of today's insurance is the offsetting of personal or commercial risks through the purchase of a bilateral contract, or insurance policy.[51] As we have discussed, the incredible risk-spreading ability of insurance also opens doors to increased wealth for a society. This means not only are new, uncertain economic endeavors possible, but consumers are also protected from negative impacts of natural catastrophes, and other events causing economic failures. Without the availability of adequate insurance, a considerable amount of economic activity would never occur, and the average consumer,

---

[49] *See* current disconnect between 70% of Americans supporting Roe v. Wade abortion rights protections and the recent elimination of those long-established rights by the newly politically-minded Supreme Court justices. See Pew Research Center (2022). Hundreds of millions of private dollars have been spent by wealthy corporate owners, through their political organizations (super-PACs) on anti-abortion messaging in the United States, in the past decade. Open Secrets.org (2012–2022).

[50] Despite that the Supreme Court reassured Americans in the *Citizens United* opinion that "the appearance of influence or access" for big donors "will not cause the electorate to lose faith in our democracy." Polls show that approximately eighty percent of Americans disapprove of the weight of money in politics, and about the same number of voters would like the Citizens United decision to be reversed. *Citizens United vs. FEC*; Chayes (2020), p. 371; Vandewalker (2020).

[51] Baker and Simon (2002), p. 37; Technically, the modern insurance product is "a mechanism for contractually shifting burdens of a number of risks by pooling them," Rubin (2013), p. 254. However, consumers typically do not contemplate the actual pooling of risk with other insureds, so they often make the assumption that their premiums are paid into a special—perhaps individual—fund which they draw from at a later date.

employee, and business owner would not have the ability to recover from a misfortune.[52]

The current changes unfolding in American society are causing a weakening of the consumer's power as a market actor. The decrease in effective consumer protections results in an increase of corporate wealth and influence, which contributes to the widening wealth gap and ultimately, undermines democracy. Now that we have set the broad social, historical, and regulatory stage, we will take a closer look at the American insurance landscape, by narrowing specifically on the insurance consumer.

3.1 *The Lack of Insurance Regulation Results in the Unavailability of Justice*

As we discussed, the state of regulations protecting the American insurance consumer is less than ideal to support a healthy insurance market. Because the U.S. states widely fail to enforce the consumer insurance codes,[53] insurance consumers seeking relief from abusive practices are then forced to file a lawsuit alleging a violation of the common (court-created) law.[54] Therefore, the responsibility for enforcing promised protection is ultimately falling on the insured. This is fundamentally problematic, because lawsuits in the United States are prohibitively expensive and extremely time-consuming, taking anywhere from one to ten years, with no guarantee of a positive result.[55]

---

[52] Hacker (2019), p. 159; Wasow and Hill (1986), p. 63.

[53] See Defever (2018), pp. 15–21.

[54] And/or the state insurance code, although in many states this cause of action is unavailable.

[55] This author is a licensed consumer insurance plaintiff's attorney with well over a decade of experience. For a detailed investigation and explanation of the factors causing lawsuits in the United States to be an ineffective substitute for the enforcement of insurance consumer protection regulations, see Defever (2018), pp. 14–21. That article explains that although there are attorneys willing to take clients on "contingency" (meaning the client will not pay for the attorney's services unless that attorney is successful in securing a settlement or verdict—therefore ostensibly removing the cost barrier for a policyholder to bring suit)—insurance contingency lawyers are a very small sector of the American legal field, due to the inherent high risk of subsidizing expensive litigation with no guarantee the attorneys will be paid for their services. In fact, plaintiff's insurance lawyers working on contingency are in such high demand that they only accept a tiny fraction of the potential clients who seek their services—naturally, those few policyholders who have an excellent factual claim and extremely valuable insurance coverage. Additionally, in some states it is nearly impossible to locate a contingency lawyer because the state does not have developed insurance bad faith law and/or does not allow the attorney to recover extracontractual damages, punitive damages, or attorney's fees. The existence of contingency attorneys does not even begin to address the rampant failures of enforcement by state authorities.

The average cost of insurance litigation is between $10,000 and $35,000 per year.[56] The median household income in the United States in 2020 was $67,521.[57] Therefore, the average American family cannot afford to file a lawsuit, no matter how meritorious its claim may be. Even if consumers somehow manage to finance a suit, at an alarming cost of approximately 1/6th to 1/2 of their yearly income, they have no guarantee of a positive result. For nearly all Americans, this risk is far too high. Consequently, litigation—and therefore justice—is simply not an option.[58] This is obviously an inefficient, less-than-ideal method to achieve any level of consumer protection, much less the level necessary to support a healthy economy.

While we can see that deregulation and the failure to enforce existing regulations has an underappreciated impact on the American consumer of insurance, American sociologist Carol Heimer takes the analysis one step further, noting that the absence of regulatory checks on the self-interested behaviors of insurers raises questions about *whose* welfare is being optimized under the current regulatory structure. Heimer posits that perhaps rather than regulating to protect the consumer and the health of the economic markets, our American regulators are governing *for* insurance.[59] Keeping Heimer's suggestion in mind, we now turn to a deeper analysis of the consumer's experience in the insurance marketplace.

3.2 Victims of Large Losses Experience Significant Delays, Are Underpaid, or Are Never Paid

As we have established, insurance is purchased for security, and to aid in recovery from a negative event. When policyholders have paid premiums over an extended period of time, thus taking capital which could be allocated elsewhere in the economy and choosing to invest it in insurance coverage, those policyholders do so with the expectation that the insurance company will make them whole after a covered event.

Before the 1990s, insurance claims were often paid with little fanfare. However, in the early 1990s, insurance companies discovered that their claims departments could be transformed into profit centers. They searched for methods to reduce

---

[56] Assuming the case is not settled in less than one year, and assuming active attorney litigation for each year. Figure based on research by the University of Denver's Institute for the Advancement of the American Legal System and author's own observations. These figures have likely increased significantly since the study was conducted.; Gerety (2011), p. 16.

[57] Shrider et al. (2021).

[58] Defever (2018), p. 17; also note that some attorneys work on "contingency," meaning they will not be paid for their services until they reach a successful settlement or verdict. Claimants have a difficult time locating a willing contingency attorney due to the inherent nature of the risks involved in insurance suits; see also fn 55.

[59] Heimer (2002), p. 136.

payment to policyholders.[60] Thirty years later, it has become common for large loss claimants to fail to receive their benefits when they are needed, and fail to receive their full benefits owed.[61]

Delayed and unfairly denied coverage payments cause an unanticipated shift in capital in the economy. Instead of the capital flowing to the policyholders at the time they need to be made whole again, the capital stays in the insurance corporation. This causes a one-way flow of capital resources (the insurance premiums) to the insurance industry—thus enriching corporate executives and major shareholders, and reducing the wealth of the policyholders.

This redistribution of wealth occurs not only when claims are unfairly denied, but also when claims are underpaid, or unnecessarily delayed. Wealth is taken out of the market and placed into the corporate coffers. Over time, and across millions of insurance claims, this is causing changes in the economic and social fabric of the United States. When consumer protection laws are weak or unenforced, a redistribution of resources occurs, and value is either misappropriated or destroyed.[62] The growth of the unprecedented wealth gap in the United States is directly fueled by the unfair claims denials and underpayments which are now common in the insurance industry.

3.3 *Rebuilding After Natural Disasters Is Smaller, Cheaper, and Slower*

Recent evidence shows that communities impacted by property claim delays and denials are not recovering quickly, and in many cases, not recovering at all. For example, there are numerous areas devastated by wildfires which have taken many years to recover. Slow and substandard insured recoveries are no longer the exception in the United States, but the norm. For example, in Northern California's Sonoma County, the area impacted by the Tubbs Fire in 2017 was still seeing repairs and rebuilds in 2022—five years later. In 2017 approximately 1/3 of fire victims in

---

[60] In the 1990's the majority of the largest American insurance companies instituted a massive change within their claims departments, turning the claims department from simply claim processing centers to newly-created income sources. Feinman (2010), pp. 56–66.

[61] *See* research by United Policyholders, author's own observations, the numerous books and investigations addressing improper insurance claims handling since 1990, and, for example, the order by California's Insurance Commissioner John Garamendi to impose a fine and reopen all disability claims at insurance company UnumProvident in 2005, after the discovery of a pattern and practice of unfair claims management.; *See* Defever (2018), pp. 16–17; As a general rule, the larger the claim, the higher the probability that claim will be either denied entirely, denied in part, or significantly delayed. When insurers delay claims payments, the unpaid monies stay in an interest-bearing account, and profit continues to be made while the benefits continue to be held by the corporation.

[62] Long (1971), p. 35.

the North Bay of California reported that their claims were delayed by late claim payments and delays in communications with the insurance company. This increased to forty-four percent by 2020.[63] Policyholders also reported being significantly underinsured, and therefore unable to rebuild to their previous standards.[64] A large percentage of policyholders reported that they have chosen to not rebuild at all. This can be observed by visiting the Sonoma County area, where pre-existing driveways now lead to either empty lots or permanently-parked RVs, instead of homes.[65]

3.4 Property Values Decrease

When policyholders are unable to rebuild to the same or similar quality standards of their pre-disaster property, or simply cannot rebuild at all, their property value decreases. Of the surveyed victims of the 2017 North Bay Fires of Northern California, seventeen percent reported that they will not rebuild their homes. Sixty-four percent of victims reported they do not have enough insurance to cover the full cost of repairing or rebuilding.[66] Although it is unclear from the survey if there is overlap in these two categories, the most conservative calculation yields the conclusion that sixty-four percent of victims have suffered a decrease in their property values, either due to the inability to rebuild, or the construction of a new building of lesser value than their previous home. In the highly-valued California North Bay area, this easily totals tens of millions of dollars in lost property values. As noted above, much of this value was not merely destroyed by the forces of nature, but was shifted to a corporate insurance company when that company retained the property owner's insurance premiums instead of paying the benefits the policyholder had a legal right to recover. Another example of this occurred in Paradise, California, which led to even larger questions about the role insurance plays in American society.

In 2018, the town of Paradise, California burned to the ground.[67] Subsequently, insurance companies withdrew entirely from the area. Homeowners who wished to rebuild and then sell their properties found themselves unable to sell, because for a home to sell in the United States, mortgage lenders require buyers to secure property insurance coverage. Potential purchasers of property in Paradise either could not

---

[63] United Policyholders Survey Results (2022).

[64] See Klein (2018), pp. 34–111.

[65] While it is not clear without further investigation whether these are the result of underinsurance or other causes, the collected data does lead to the conclusion that a large percentage of them are likely due to the chronic underinsurance of properties.

[66] United Policyholders Survey Results (2022).

[67] Ninety-three percent of the town was destroyed by fire. Paradise had a population of approximately 30,000 people before the fire. Helsel and Johnson (2019).

secure the needed insurance coverage, or the coverage they located was up to ten times more expensive than before the wildfire.[68] As a result, property sales slowed and property values decreased.

3.4.1 The Problem with Paradise

The lack of availability of insurance causes additional impacts on society. When identifiable groups of people cannot obtain the needed insurance for financial transactions, social hierarchies are created and/or strengthened.[69] For example, in Paradise the pre-fire residents became worse off because their properties became more difficult to sell, due to the decreased availability and increased costs of insurance. Therefore, their properties became less marketable, and less valuable. The potential Paradise property buyers were also negatively impacted because they were either prevented from purchasing property, or they were forced to spend more money to make the purchase. The entire community, or social group, found itself worse off, financially. Widespread failures of insurance such as these also cause human migration, which in the aggregate, can lead to massive societal shifts, of which the impacts are not fully understood.

3.5 *Human Migration*

Due to the many extreme weather events in the United States—hurricanes, fires, earthquakes, etc, hundreds of thousands of people are displaced from their homes each year. A large number of these persons never return, many of them due to the fact that they were either uninsured or severely underinsured, and therefore unable to repair or rebuild. People become disconnected from their friends and family, forced to find new employment, and struggle to locate replacement housing due to housing shortages.[70] Entire social groups are displaced and forced to reintegrate elsewhere. The full economic and social impact of this is extremely difficult to quantify.[71]

---

[68] Friedman (2020).

[69] For a discussion on insurance availability and social hierarchies, see Baker and Simon (2002), p. 32 and pp. 116–140.

[70] Internal Displacement Monitoring Center (2019).

[71] Frankenberg et al. (2015).

3.6 Slow Recoveries Have a Detrimental Impact on Human/Social Capital

When insureds suffering a loss are forced to dedicate months or even years of their time and energy to the attempts to recover their insurance benefits, not only is the recovery of their full participation in the market delayed, but the delayed process leading to recovery is an ongoing loss to market productivity. Instead, if funds are promptly paid to the claimant, the claimant is able to reinvest them in a quicker recovery, therefore placing those funds actively back into the economy. The widespread, unlawful withholding of insurance benefits is an exponential drag on the American economy that is so massive it may be incalculable.

Even if the exact monetary amount of benefits withheld could be estimated; the value of the emotional, psychological, and physical damages would be inestimable. All of society is impacted by a large-scale loss of human capital, social capital, loss of work product, loss of enjoyment and health, increased stress, damaged interpersonal relations, increased burdens on the healthcare system, and shortened lifespans.

For example, in the American field of workers compensation insurance, benefits for injured workers have diminished to the point that a loss for a worker can cause an immediate financial crisis for the family. Many workers never recover financially. As a result, the injured employee contributes far less to the economy, over a longer period of time.[72] Both the employee's reduction in productivity and resources, as well as the decrease in their contribution to the economy, have a net detrimental impact on society. Oftentimes these injured workers are then forced to seek other government-provided benefits, like welfare or government-subsidized housing, which are paid for by taxpayers. This is not an ideal or efficient structure for recovery.

While I will make no attempt to determine whether the most economically and socially beneficial method for recovery lies in solely private insurance coverage, solely government coverage, or a combination of the two—what we can safely conclude from the activity before us is that the current insurance scheme is failing American citizens on multiple levels.

3.7 Private Insurance vs. Insurance Provided by the Government

The power of private insurers to set rates and make determinations about the availability of coverage renders them the gatekeepers to the potential for increased

[72]McCluskey (2002), p. 154.

wealth.[73] Of course local state regulators[74] have a great deal of influence on this process, regulating rates and sometimes also insurance availability.[75] But the availability of insurance can have a profound impact on not only individual economic actors, but the entire society. This is evident in the Paradise problem, where potential home buyers and sellers were unable to make real estate transactions. In another example, when consumers do not have the resources to purchase an auto insurance policy, they can be prevented from driving an automobile. The inability of an individual or a family to satisfy basic needs has a ripple effect on their community, even more particularly when that party is forced to seek government assistance, which is taxpayer-funded.

Under some circumstances, governmental institutions offer critical insurance coverage, such as coverages for risks that are higher or more costly than what the private insurance industry is willing to insure, i.e. flood coverage for properties in areas of high flood or hurricane risk, earthquake coverage for properties in earthquake-prone areas, or high risk auto coverages for drivers with poor driving records. However, these government-offered policies are limited in scope, coverage, and quality, and the premiums are often unaffordable for those who need the coverage the most.

Further, according to many insurance industry analysts and scholars, the industry's decision-making process can be exceptionally inefficient and unjust, and actually creates and increases societal risks.[76] The private insurance sector, through its own underwriting and determinations of available rates and coverages, has an enormous impact on society, its institutional actors, and the economy. One example of private insurance's widespread impact can be found in the recent blanket denials of all business income loss claims in the United States, in the aftermath of the Covid-19 pandemic.

---

[73] Arguably, this ability also renders insurance companies as regulators of economic and social activity. See Heimer (2002), p. 119; Baker and Logue (2013), p. 10.

[74] In the United States, insurance is regulated almost entirely at the state level, with only a few exceptions. 15 U.S.C. Sect. 1012(b); See Defever (2018), p. 15.

[75] Insurance Commissioners primarily monitor insurance companies for solvency, regulate premium rates, and investigate and prosecute fraudulent insurance claims. Thomas (2012), p. 390; Wasow and Hill (1986), p. 135; Defever (2018), p. 16. One example of the regulation of availability—the State of California's Department of Insurance has mandated that insurers of properties at high risk for wildfires could not cancel policies within certain periods of time after a wildfire had occurred in the area.

[76] Ericson et al. (2003), pp. 12–13; See the conclusions based on research performed by United Policyholders; etc.

3.8 *Business Income Loss Insurance*[77] *and Covid-19*

When the Covid-19 pandemic forced the closure of nearly all businesses while most of the United States went into quarantine, business owners assumed that their insurance coverage would reimburse them for their losses. The vast majority of them were incorrect. By contrast, in Europe, many of these coverages were granted. In some countries, state governments mounted special tribunals to promptly decide whether private insurance coverage should be granted or not.[78] In the United States, that has not happened. Lawsuits will continue for many years into the future.

American insurance companies denied all claims for business income loss coverages, typically citing a "virus exclusion" in the policy, but also commonly citing that the covid-19 virus was not physically found on the insured premises. Businessowners were forced to file lawsuits in order to seek coverage.[79] The vast majority of businessowners hired lawyers with no special expertise in insurance law, largely due to the afore-mentioned lack of attorneys with experience in consumer insurance law, but also due to the commonly-held underappreciation of the complexity of the field.[80]

Although there is a colorable argument that because the commercial coverages were written as all-risk policies, which automatically cover all risks to the commercial activities of the insured unless that risk is explicitly excluded,[81] this argument was not presented. Instead, insureds often pointed to the vague language of the common "virus and bacteria" exclusions, claiming that these exclusions did not apply. Insureds also argued that the virus was present on their business premises (ostensibly satisfying the requirement of a direct, physical loss), or, that they were covered for their losses under the "civil authority" clause, because businessowners were precluded from conducting business due to the quarantine orders of a civil authority.

In response, insurance companies claimed that the virus exclusions *did* apply, arguing that the industry anticipated pandemic claims and intended to exclude damages which resulted from business closures.[82] They challenged claimants to prove that the virus was present on their business premises and caused a direct,

---

[77] Also known as Business Interruption insurance, and typically an element found in a commercial policy.

[78] See the United Kingdom, for example.

[79] For a nation-wide record of lawsuits filed for business interruption coverage, See the University of Pennsylvania Carey Law School's "Covid Coverage Litigation Tracker," (2022), showing nearly 2500 cases filed as of May 13, 2022.

[80] Author's observations.

[81] Which, in the United States, places the burden on the insurers to prove that pandemic closures are *not* covered.

[82] Interestingly, most of the virus exclusions never directly addressed human-carried viruses, but instead referenced "viruses and mold" being present on a property. There were some recent virus exclusions which specifically mentioned pandemics and human-carried viruses, but these clauses were far less common.

physical loss. They construed the civil authority clause as inapplicable. Broadly speaking, despite some good evidence to the contrary, and despite the common law doctrine that ambiguity in an insurance contract is to be construed against the insurance company (contra proferentum), the insurers' defense has been overwhelmingly successful in courts across the nation.[83]

Whatever the proper legal interpretation, the result is that American businesses were not able to receive insurance coverage to compensate for their income loss during the pandemic closures. In this case, the insurance company strategy to turn their claims departments into profit centers seems to have been overwhelmingly successful. In order to prevent a large-scale collapse of the American economy, the U.S. government was forced to intervene. A federal loan and grant program was offered to assist millions of businesses to recover.[84] However, the program was not available to all businesses, so hundreds of thousands of businesses entered bankruptcy. In effect, because businesses were unable to receive the disputed insurance coverage for their losses, the American taxpayer then funded—through their taxes paid to the U.S. government—the loans and grants which were needed to offset these losses. When private insurance failed to mitigate a devastating risk, American taxpayers became *ex post facto* insurers.[85]

3.8.1 Taxpayers as Unwilling *Ex Post Facto* Insurers and Self-Insureds

The afore-mentioned examples of claim underpayment, lack of coverage availability, and unfair claims denials all frequently result in more burden on the American government and the U.S. taxpayer. In another example, the American government and taxpayer bore the cost of the loss-mitigation efforts during the Great Recession. Although the market crash of 2008-09 was not due to the direct actions of insurers, or any failure to provide insurance, it is nonetheless another prominent example of post-loss burden-shifting. Banks and other financial institutions took on bad risks which ultimately resulted in the U.S. government needing to provide "bail out" funding to avoid what would have been an even worse market crash. Because the government is funded by tax revenue, the U.S. taxpayers became the *ex post facto* insurers for the risks taken by large financial corporations.

Due to the combination of a multitude of factors, including increasingly narrow and unavailable insurance coverages, the underpayment and delayed payment of

[83] For more on Covid-19 cases and their results, please see the University of Pennsylvania "Covid Litigation Tracker".

[84] See U.S. Small Business Administration programs (2022); The American Rescue Plan Act of 2021 (2021); and U.S. Department of the Treasury (2022).

[85] Whether insurance can, by definition, be offered *ex post facto* is beyond the scope of our discussion here. Our observations are for the sake of performing a sociological comparative analysis, weighing the different methods which have been used to aid in economic recoveries, and making a critical analysis of the role (and potential role) that insurance in its many forms may or may not have played.

claims, the lack of availability of experienced insurance consumer counsel, the unaffordability of justice through litigation, the aggressive claim-denial techniques of insurance companies, and the unwillingness of American government representatives (such as Insurance Commissioners) to proactively enforce insurance codes or create new consumer protections—a large number of today's American insurance consumers are resigned to accepting their claim denial, or walking away with far less than what they need (and legally deserve) to fully recover.

The consumer has also been forced to accept risks they are unable to obtain coverage for (therefore, in effect, self-insuring), and to insure *ex post facto* the increasingly large risks undertaken by powerful corporations.[86] These trends are deeply troubling for the United States, because research shows that risk regimes which subscribe to more "free market" and deregulated economic principles, which in turn support weaker and less protective state insurance and security systems, are clearly more productive of poverty.[87] Perhaps sociologist Carol Heimer's suggestion is correct, and the U.S. government is, in fact, governing *for* insurance. The lack of regulation of the American insurance industry has lead to record corporate profits, which has in turn lead to a wider wealth gap and more corporate power in the American political landscape, which leads to even worse results for the American insurance consumer. This *lack* of regulation is just as damaging as a body of regulations which *actively* aids unfair behaviors of insurers—much in the way that a lie by omission is still considered a lie.

4 Redefining Insurance in American Society

According to sociologist Ulrich Beck, a person's rank in a class structure creates a social risk position. In other words, some people are more impacted by the increase of risks than others. Typically, the lower-class, economically-disadvantaged are forced to take on more risk in their daily lives, and therefore bear the consequences of negative events more often.[88] Additionally, people who have to pay more for insurance will have less disposable income to spend on other things.[89] The classes with fewer economic resources are impacted more readily by the lack of affordable insurance than the upper classes.

[86]Even as more and more risks are immeasurable, insurers gamble anyway. Ericson et al. (2003), p. 9.

[87]Ericson et al. (2003), p. 41, citing Goodin et al. (1999), and Atkinson (1999, 2000).

[88]Beck (1986), p. 23.

[89]Baker and Logue (2013), p. 14.

4.1 *All Social Classes Are Impacted*

However, in what Beck coins "the boomerang effect," even those who produce or profit from risks will also be struck by them, and this effect breaks up the normal patterns of class. An excellent example is when the wealthy classes have benefited from energy production which causes environmental pollution, but that same pollution causes unavoidable negative impacts to all of society, including those higher-class individuals who initially profited.[90] Law professor Martha McCluskey summarizes the concept well, "[P]olicies that *embrace* risk always also *redistribute* risk. The problem--for society as a whole and for insurance in particular—is not *how much* risk versus security is good policy, but *whose* risk and *whose* security is good policy."[91] Arguably for a healthy society, risk should be spread with intention, and with some degree of equality.

4.2 *What Is "Risk" in American Society?*

Beck takes the concept one step further and prompts us to ask ourselves the ethical question, "How do we wish to live?". What kind of risks are considered acceptable in our societies, and what is not wanted? When, as societies, we make determinations about what kind of risks we are willing to accept, who is able to obtain insurance for those risks and who is not, how much the insurance costs and who pays for it—we are making ethical determinations which involve our own, unique societal philosophy, culture, and politics. Beck believes that "Risk determinations are an unrecognized, still undeveloped symbiosis of the natural and the human sciences, of everyday and expert rationality, of interest and fact." These risk determinations require cooperation across all disciplines.[92]

5 Toward Positive Social Change and Improved Insurance Economies

We can see how American society's lack of appreciation for the concepts of risk and insurance, combined with the lack of industry regulation and ethically-driven, long-range risk management (by both private and government actors) is accelerating economic inequality, and exposing more Americans to increased hardship. Understandably, people are feeling increasingly disgruntled and dissatisfied, and are

[90] Beck (1986), pp. 23, 37–38.
[91] McCluskey (2002), p. 145.
[92] Beck (1986), pp. 28–29.

seeking social change. If the American consumer is able to successfully demand better insurance availability and more comprehensive coverages,[93] not only would consumers recover more quickly from unfortunate events, but the improvement in the insurance market will lead to better economic equality and stability and ultimately, increased wealth and happiness for all of society. Americans need to take a hard look at how they define risk, and what kind of insurance they would like to be available, and for whom. Truly, insurance, both as a social concept and as a product, has such a profound impact on our societies that "life in a society" can be aptly described as a "species of insurance."[94]

As insurance law professor Tom Baker wrote in 1996, "Insurance arrangements form a material constitution, one that operates through routine, mundane transactions that nevertheless define the contours of individual and social responsibility. For that reason, studying who is eligible to receive what insurance benefits, and who pays for them, is as good a guide to the social compact as any combination of [U.S.] Supreme Court opinions."[95] As we can see, a deep analysis of insurance, insurance law, the corresponding political landscape, and the surrounding social system, is critical if we are to bring about positive change.

References

15 U.S.C. Sect. 1012(b)
Abraham KS (2005) Insurance law and regulation: cases and materials, 4th edn
American Rescue Plan Act of 2021 (2021). https://www.whitehouse.gov/american-rescue-plan/, White House.gov. Last visited June 20, 2022
Atkinson A (1999) The economic consequences of rolling back the welfare state. MIT Press
Atkinson A (2000) Can welfare states compete in a global economy? In: Ericson R, Stehr N (eds) Governing modern societies. University of Toronto Press, pp 259–275
Bainbridge J (1952) Biography of an idea: the story of mutual fire and casualty insurance. Doubleday & Company, Inc.
Baker T (1996) On the genealogy of moral hazard. Tex Law Rev 75:237–292
Baker T, Logue K (2013) Insurance law and policy. Wolters Kluwer
Baker T, Simon J (2002) Embracing risk. The University of Chicago Press
Baranoff D (2003) A policy of cooperation: the cartelisation of American fire insurance, 1873-1906. Financial History Review, pp 119–136
Beck U (1986) Risk society: toward a new modernity. Sage Publications
Chayes S (2020) On corruption in America, and what is at stake. Penguin Random House LLC
Colombo J (2019) America's wealth inequality is at roaring 20's levels. Forbes. https://www.forbes.com/sites/jessecolombo/2019/02/28/americas-wealth-inequality-is-at-roaring-twenties-levels/?sh=1486b7ac2a9c. Last visited June 19, 2022
Consumer Financial Protection Bureau of the United States Government (2021) CFPB research shows banks' deep dependence on overdraft fees – overdraft and non-sufficient fund penalties

[93] "Insurance is a remarkably adaptable phenomenon," Long (1971), p. 23.

[94] "Life in a society is a species of insurance," Sumner and Keller (1927), p. 20.

[95] Baker is a University of Pennsylvania professor of insurance and the holder of degrees in both law and sociology. Baker (1996), pp. 236, 291; Ericson et al. (2003), p. 50.

made up two-third of reported fee revenue. https://www.consumerfinance.gov/about-us/newsroom/cfpb-research-shows-banks-deep-dependence-on-overdraft-fees/. Last visited June 19, 2022
Consumer Financial Protection Bureau of the United States Government (2022) Consumer financial protection bureau launches initiative to save Americans billions in junk fees – agency seeks public input on fees on bank accounts, credit cards, and other financial products. https://www.consumerfinance.gov/about-us/newsroom/consumer-financial-protection-bureau-launches-initiative-to-save-americans-billions-in-junk-fees/. Last visited June 19, 2022
Defever KM (2018) Comparative analysis of European Union and United States insurance law systems – with emphasis on consumer protection law. Eur J Commer Contract Law (Paris Legal Publishers) 2(3):9–27
Ericson R, Doyle A, Barry D (2003) Insurance as governance. University of Toronto Press
Ewald F (2002) The return of Descartes's malicious demon. In: Baker T, Simon J (eds) . Embracing risk, The University of Chicago Press, pp 298–299
Feinman JM (2010) Delay deny defend: why insurance companies don't pay claims and what you can do about it. Delden Press
Fondazione Mansutti (2015) The fascinating history of insurance: posters, books, fire marks and policies / L'Affascinante storia dell'assicuraione: Manifesti, libri, targhe, polizze
Frankenberg E, Laurito M, Thomas D (2015) The demography of disasters. International Encyclopedia of the Social & Behavioral Sciences: Second Edition, pp 101–108
Friedman N (2020) High cost of wildfire insurance hurts California home sales, Realtor.com Real Estate News and The Wall Street Journal. https://www.realtor.com/news/real-estate-news/high-cost-of-wildfire-insurance-hurts-california-home-sales/. Last visited June 19, 2022
Gerety C (2011) Excess and access: consensus on the American civil justice landscape. University of Denver Institute for the Advancement of the American Legal System
Goodin R, Heady B, Muffels R, Driven HJ (1999) The real worlds of welfare capitalism. Cambridge University Press
Hacker J (2019) The great risk shift. Oxford University Press
Harvard Law School Forum on Corporate Governance (2022) CEO compensation increase trends. The President and Fellow of Harvard College. https://corpgov.law.harvard.edu/2022/02/15/ceo-compensation-increase-trends/. Last visited June 19, 2022
Heimer CA (2002) Insuring more, ensuring less: the costs and benefits of private regulation through insurance. In: Baker T, Simon J (eds) Embracing risk. The University of Chicago Press, pp 116–145
Helsel P, Johnson A (2019) Paradise regained. NBC News. https://www.nbcnews.com/news/us-news/paradise-regained-year-after-camp-fire-resilient-town-rebuilds-n1077991. Last visited June 19, 2022
Internal Displacement Monitoring Center (2019) Global report on internal displacement: United States, California wildfires, urban expansion and the risk of displacement. https://www.internal-displacement.org/sites/default/files/publications/documents/2019-IDMC-GRID-spotlight-united-states.pdf. Last visited June 20, 2020
Kang Z (1997) Assurances modern en Chine: Une continuité interrompue (1801-1949). Risques 31: 103–120
Kimball S (1960) Insurance and public policy. The University of Wisconsin Press
Klein KS (2018) Minding the protection gap: resolving unintended, pervasive, profound homeowner underinsurance. Conn Insur Law J 25:34–111
Long JD (1971) Ethics, morality, and insurance: a long-range outlook. The Indiana University Sesquicentennial Series on Insurance, Bureau of Business Research, Indiana University
McCluskey M (2002) Rhetoric of risk and the redistribution of social insurance. In: Baker T, Simon J (eds) Embracing risk. The University of Chicago Press, pp 146–170
McMichael P (2012) Development and social change: a global perspective. SAGE Publications
National Association of Insurance Commissioners (NAIC)., https://content.naic.org/state-insurance-departments. Last visited January 7, 2023

Open Secrets.org (2012–2022) Abortion policy/anti-abortion PACs contributions to candidates. https://www.opensecrets.org/political-action-committees-pacs/industry-detail/Q14/2020. Last visited June 19, 2022

Pearson R (2017) Insuring the industrial revolution: fire insurance in Great Britain 1700-1850. Routledge

Pew Research Center (2022) About six-in-ten Americans say abortion should be legal in all or most cases. https://www.pewresearch.org/fact-tank/2022/06/13/about-six-in-ten-americans-say-abortion-should-be-legal-in-all-or-most-cases-2/. Last visited June 19, 2022

Reinhart C, Rogoff K (2009) This time is different: eight centuries of financial folly. Princeton University Press

Ritzer G (2011) Classical sociological theory. McGraw Hill

Rubin HW (2013) Dictionary of insurance terms. Barron's Business Guides

Saez E, Zucman G (2020) Trends in U.S. income and wealth inequality: revising after the revisionists. National Bureau of Economic Research

Scott M (2021) "What's Wrong With the American Tax System," Investopedia. https://www.investopedia.com/articles/personal-finance/082415/whats-wrong-american-tax-system.asp. Last visited June 19, 2022

Shrider EA, Kollar M, Chen F, Semega J (2021) U.S. Census Bureau, Current Population Reports, Income and Poverty in the United States: 2020. U.S. Government Publishing Office, Washington, DC, pp 60–273

Stiglitz JE (2013) The price of inequality: how today's divided society endangers our future. W.W. Norton & Company

Sumner W, Keller A (1927) Science of society. Yale University Press

Thomas J (2012) In: Heiss H (ed) Insurance contract law between business law and consumer protection. Dike Zurich, USA

United Policyholders Survey Results (2022) 2017 north bay fires survey results. https://uphelp.org/media/surveys/. Last visited June 19, 2022

United States Department of the Treasury (2022) Assistance for small businesses. https://home.treasury.gov/policy-issues/coronavirus/assistance-for-small-businesses. Last visited June 20, 2022

United States Small Business Administration (2022) Loan programs. https://www.sba.gov/funding-programs/loans/covid-19-relief-options. Last visited June 20, 2020

University of Pennsylvania Carey Law School (2022) COVID coverage litigation tracker. https://cclt.law.upenn.edu/. Last visited May 13, 2022

Vandewalker I (2020) "Since Citizens United, A Decade of Super PACs," The Brennan Center for Justice. https://www.brennancenter.org/our-work/analysis-opinion/citizens-united-decade-super-pacs. Last visited June 19, 2022

Wasow B, Hill R (1986) The insurance industry in economic development. New York University Press

Kathleen M. Defever holds a Juris Doctorate (J.D.) with a specialization in International Law from DePaul University College of Law in Chicago, Illinois, USA; a Master of Insurance Law (LLM) from the University of Connecticut School of Law, Hartford, Connecticut, USA; and is currently a doctoral fellow on the subject of Microinsurance at Ghent University Faculty of Law and Criminology, Ghent, Belgium. Ms. Defever is a practicing consumer insurance attorney in San Francisco, California, as well as a licensed public insurance adjuster. E-mail: Kathleen.Defever@ugent.be.

The Role of Insurance in Dealing with Disasters: The Case of Agricultural Insurance

Sara Landini and Kyriaki Noussia

Abstract One of the big challenges in the last years is the coverage of costs arising from catastrophic events. Due to climate change disasters are becoming more frequent and the classic tools of risk management and risk transfer are not enough. The increase in natural disasters, also due to climate change, requires a consideration on the means of transferring systemic risks characterized by low frequency and high harmfulness. In this case funding and prevention are two keywords. Until now the instrument, in addition to public compensation schemes, was the insurance contract together with reinsurance. In addition, thanks to new technologies, instruments beyond the classic insurance contract are offered on the market. This chapter will consider the catastrophic risk within the agricultural sector and discuss the management—also in terms of prevention—of catastrophe risk, its insurance coverage, index-based insurance, the use of cat-bonds. The chapter analyzes the state of the art in agricultural risk insurance according to the CAP Common Agricultural Policy in the European Union; it considers the possible causes of the insufficient diffusion of insurance coverage as a tool for the resilience of agricultural enterprises and proposes tools to reduce costs, simplify management and shift the attention of farmers to insurance.

Keywords Agricultural insurance · Insurance · Natural disasters · Catastrophe risk · Climate change · Cat-bonds · Calamities

---

S. Landini (✉)
University of Florence, Florence, Italy
e-mail: sara.landini@unifi.it

K. Noussia
University of Reading, Reading, England, UK
e-mail: k.p.noussia@reading.ac.uk

M. Lima Rego, S. Grima (eds.), *Cross-Disciplinary Impacts on Insurance Law*,
AIDA Europe Research Series on Insurance Law and Regulation 8,
https://doi.org/10.1007/978-3-031-38526-1_3

1 Premise

Climate change poses new challenges for businesses. One of the most affected sectors is the agricultural one with heavy repercussions in terms of health and social protection, food security and food safety.

One of the tools that could allow the resilience of agricultural enterprises hit by catastrophic events is the insurance contract, which however in postmodern reality is undergoing important changes in its structure and which has to compete with alternative instruments having a hedging function.

The second part of the chapter deals with the issue of agricultural risk and its evolution within the European continent and the centrality of the insurance instrument in the translation of the costs of adverse events. The third part of the chapter analyzes the different insurance layers: reinsurance, mutual funds, premium insurance coverage with particular attention to subsidized coverage with public funds. We therefore note the reduced number of insurance coverage due in particular to the costs and the difficulty for insurers to cope with adverse events that are increasingly the size of a catastrophic event since even frequent events are becoming more and more catastrophic. Precisely for this reason parametric policies can simplify and reduce the costs of contract execution. The fourth part of the chapter is dedicated to these. The fifth part of the chapter reflects on possible levers that move the interest of agricultural enterprises to insurance such as access to credit. Finally, the sixth part of the chapter is dedicated to alternative instruments to insurance coverage such as cat bonds and to parametric policies where the pay out is connected exclusively to a trigger and which end up losing a hedging function and having only a gambling function.

2 Catastrophic Risk in Agriculture

Catastrophic events in agriculture are one of the major causes of over-indebtedness of agricultural entrepreneurs as emerged from the report "Risk Management and Agricultural Insurance Schemes in Europe" (2009) of Joint research center of EU Commission.[1]

The current increase in catastrophic events linked to climate change and the reduction of public resources to deal with the major damages, leads to reflections on the possibility of finding private sources of funding and systems to prevent or reduce damage, in particular damage to production.

Funding and prevention are the two primary needs in case of environmental catastrophic events. An efficient answer to such instances could be found in insurance contracts. The insurers will indemnify the insured party in case of losses. At the same time, in order to avoid moral hazard and in order to reduce the risk, the insurer

[1]Tangermann (2011), p. 13.

will impose by contract to the insured party rules of conduct ordered to reduce or avoid losses. In this term the insurance contracts play a relevant role both in funding and in prevention. However, a drop of insurance demands emerges in the agricultural sector.

The insurance coverages are inadequate with respect to the farmers' needs, and unsustainable in term of cost of coverages.[2] The causes of high premiums are basically: adverse selection problems—only those who are more exposed to risks are interested in concluding an insurance contract—and high cost for losses assessment. Even in case of state subsidies for the payment of premium the bureaucracy represents strong constraints to the development of insurance coverages. Insurance should aim to implement the contractual coverages of damage in case of environmental catastrophes by identifying contractual templates that represent an answer to the above-mentioned problems. The second European climate change program launched in October 2005 (ECCP II) [3] focused on options also for the adaptation to the effects of climate change. Moreover, the risk management aspects are perfectly in line with the Sendai Framework for Disaster Risk Reduction 2015–2030,[4] which is the successor to the Hyogo Framework for Action (HFA) 2005–2015. [5] The Sendai framework presents innovations over previous works, with particular emphasis on disaster risk management compared to disaster management. This change is perfectly in line with the innovative perspective proposed. The Priority 1 of Sendai Framework for Disaster Risk Reduction 2015–2030 "Understand the risk of disaster", includes policies and practices for disaster risk management, including the aim to promote the incorporation of knowledge on disaster risks, including disaster prevention, mitigation. Moreover, the action plan on the Sendai Framework for Disaster Risk Reduction 2015–2030[6] is also addressed so as to promote the use of mechanisms for disaster risk financing, risk transfer and insurance, risk-sharing, and retention. The intention is to propose possible strategies that allow sustainable and adequate funding and prevention actions against catastrophic environmental events. An efficient answer to such instances can be found in insurance contracts: the insurer agrees to indemnify the insured person trying to avoid moral hazard and encouraging

[2]Glauber (2004), pp. 1179–1195; Musser and Patrick (2002); The CAP towards 2020: Meeting the food, natural resources and territorial challenges of the future. EC Communication (COM (2010) 672); Commissione Europea (2011).

[3]European Commission, Climate change: start of the second European Climate Change Programme, https://ec.europa.eu/commission/presscorner/detail/en/IP_05_1330 (last visited Jan 30, 2020).

[4]UNDRR, Sendai Framework for Disaster Risk Reduction 2015-2030, https://www.undrr.org/publication/sendai-framework-disaster-risk-reduction-2015-2030 (last visited Jan 30, 2020).

[5]UNDRR, Hyogo Framework for Action 2005-2015, https://www.undrr.org/publication/hyogo-framework-action-2005-2015-building-resilience-nations-and-communities-1 (last visited Jan 30, 2020).

[6]*See* Key Area 3 - Promoting EU risk informed investments; UNDRR, Sendai Framework for Disaster Risk Reduction 2015-2030, https://www.undrr.org/publication/sendai-framework-disaster-risk-reduction-2015-2030 (last visited Jan 30, 2020).

conduct that can counteract the effects of a harmful event. In addition to insurance contracts, amongst the risk transfer mechanisms, it is necessary to consider the mechanism of the creation of dedicated funds financed by the subjects exposed to risk and sometimes by public interventions. These funds often operate as last resort insurance. The importance of private sector in risk disasters management is taken into account, particularly in the work of UNISDR—United Nations Office for Disaster Risk Reduction—"Disaster Risk Reduction PPP (Private Sector Partnership) Post 2015 Framework - Private Sector Blueprint Five Private Sector Visions for a Resilient Future". In 2017 the European Commission adopted the EU Adaptation Strategy[7] which aims to make Europe more climate resilient. This has also been amended in 2021. The European Commission adopted its new EU strategy on adaptation to climate change on 24 February 2021. The new strategy sets out how the European Union can adapt to the unavoidable impacts of climate change and become climate resilient by 2050. The Strategy has four principle objectives: to make adaptation smarter, swifter and more systemic, and to step up international action on adaptation to climate change.[8] The Commission encourages all Member States to adopt comprehensive adaptation strategies and provides funding to help them build up their adaptation capacities and act. Moreover, the European Commission has developed a Green Infrastructure Strategy aiming to ensure the protection, restoration, creation and enhancement of green infrastructure.[9] The Commission in recent communication on the Multiannual Financial Framework (MFF) mentioned a more common agricultural policy (CAP) will have to support the transition to a fully sustainable agricultural sector development of dynamic rural areas, ensuring healthy, safe and high quality food for over 500 million consumers.[10] On 1 June 2018, the European Commission presented the legislative proposals on the future of the CAP for the period after 2020.[11]

The cost of coverages against environmental catastrophic events represents the main constraint to their diffusion. The causes of high premiums are: i) adverse selection problems (only the most vulnerable subjects are interested to be insured), the diversity of catastrophic events and the difficulty of identifying homogeneous

[7]European Commission, EU Adaptation Strategy, 2017, https://ec.europa.eu/clima/eu-action/adaptation-climate-change/eu-adaptation-strategy_en (last visited 26 July 2022).

[8]https://ec.europa.eu/clima/eu-action/adaptation-climate-change/eu-adaptation-strategy_en (last visited Jan 30, 2020).

[9]European Commission, EU strategy on Green Infrastructure, https://ec.europa.eu/environment/nature/ecosystems/strategy/index_en.htm (last visited Jan 30, 2020).

[10]COM (2018) 322 final – Regulation QFP.

[11]Proposal for a Regulation of the European Parliament and of the Council establishing rules on support for strategic plans to be drawn up by Member States under the Common agricultural policy (CAP Strategic Plans) and financed by the European Agricultural Guarantee Fund (EAGF) and by the European Agricultural Fund for Rural Development (EAFRD) and repealing Regulation (EU) No 1305/2013 of the European Parliament and of the Council and Regulation (EU) No 1307/2013 of the European Parliament and of the Council (COM/2018/392 final - 2018/0216 (COD).

classes of insured persons sharing the same insured risks; ii) the cost of coverages for catastrophic event is linked not only to the nature of the covered risk, but also to the costs of the operation. The assessment of losses in case of natural catastrophic events is extremely expensive in term of settlement costs, so the premiums for their coverage are necessarily high. With reference to settlement costs, it is possible to consider in particular:

(I) cost for the technical assessment of the declared damage (existence and consistency of the damage):

- equipment costs;
- survey costs (staff expenses, personal expenses);
- consultancy costs.

(II) for assessing the possible adoption of prevention techniques
(III) for assessing the existence of possible causes of exclusions (e.g. verification whether an intervention has taken place prior to the technical assessment, such as harvesting the product or replacing the crop prior to the technical assessment), of any possible co-causes (causes in addition to the catastrophic events like technical causes due to the negligence of the insured).
(IV) for assessing long-term damage.

In addition to the costs for damage assessment, also the costs for the adoption of prevention measure are important. In the case of agricultural insurance, the costs of prevention include regular field visits to check the production trend and any agronomic advice to be given to the insured. In any case such costs are significantly counterbalanced by the risk reduction.

3 The Different Layers of Risk Coverage

With regards to the agricultural sector presently we have different levels of insurance coverage with pyramid structure:

A first layers is represented by public reinsurers.

An example could be represented by Flood Re, which offers reinsurance coverage for flood risk respect both to homeowners and to production.[12]

In order to pay for the claims that will arise from policies passed to Flood Re there is a central fund which will comprise of two elements:

[12] https://www.floodre.co.uk (last visited 26 July 2022).

- Premiums on flood risks passed to Flood Re by insurers.[13]
- Levy: the annual levy is paid by all insurers authorized to operate in the sector of home insurance in the UK.[14]

A second level is formed by private reinsurers.

In Italian agricultural sector special reinsurance Plans adopted by the Ministry of Food and Forestry Policies provide for reinsurance intervention arrangements "to support the competitiveness of agricultural enterprises by reducing the consequences of atmospheric adversities through the facilitated agricultural reinsurance business contracted by insurance companies".[15]

The main feature introduced since the Agricultural Plan of 2013 includes:

- the expansion of reinsurance policy types, including all experimental and innovative policies compatible with Community law, avoiding constraints on pre-defined contractual types. All the reinsurance techniques available on international markets can be used, widening the supply and competition of insurance products, resulting in lower reinsurance costs.
- Provision of the possibility of non-proportional "stop loss" reinsurance, in order to increase the reinsurance leverage.

A third level is formed by private insurance contracts.

With regards to the present situation in Italian Agricultural Sector, that level represents a strategic point of view. However, it needs to be said that Italy was one of the first countries in Europe dealing systematically with the management of the risks in agriculture with the establishment of the National Solidarity Fund (hereinafter FSN) according to Act. N.364 of May 25, 1970, an instrument that institutionalized the principle of solidarity for businesses that suffer damage caused by variables outside their control.

Public spending on FSN interventions over the first thirty years has been absorbed by more than 70% by compensatory interventions and active defense plans.[16] Since the nineties, there has been a trend reversal: expenditures for the aforementioned interventions have been reduced, except for a few isolated exceptions; the insurance volumes and their public facilities have recorded a steady but gradual growth, to the profound reform of the FSN enshrined by Legislative Decree (D. lgs.) 102/2004, adopted in implementation of Act no. 38 of 7 March 2003, entitled "Financial interventions in support of agricultural enterprises".[17] In addition to systematically ordering the previous legislation, this legislation has updated the national discipline of agricultural risk management, especially, in order to adapt it to the new

[13] https://www.floodre.co.uk (last visited 26 July 2022).

[14] https://www.floodre.co.uk (last visited 26 July 2022).

[15] Ministero Delle Politiche Agricole e Forestali. Decreto 7 Febbraio 2003.

[16] https://bio-protocol.org/exchange/minidetail?type=30&id=9182077 (last visited July 26, 2022).

[17] Ministero Delle Politiche Agricole e Forestali. Decreto 7 Febbraio 2003.

Community guidelines and to modernize the risk management tools available to agricultural enterprises.[18]

The common European Agricultural policy needs to be modernized according to the new challenges posed by climate change and by the fluctuation in agricultural products pricing.[19] Moreover, it must be simplified for do it with a minimum level of administrative burden and must be made more compatible with the other EU policies to maximize their contribution to the ten priorities of the Commission and Sustainable Development Goals (SDGs).

In the work program for 2017, the Commission has carried out a broad consultation on the simplification and modernization of the CAP. For the year 2021–2022 a transition regulation is in force. The regulation 2020/21 includes a strong contribution to European Green Deal. The new CAP was formally adopted on 2 December 2021. After extensive negotiations between the European Parliament, the Council of the EU and the European Commission, agreement was reached on CAP reform and. The new CAP is due to be implemented from 1 January 2023.[20]

Nevertheless, the subsidized agricultural insurance market manifested in Italy in the last three years, evident signs of suffering. ISMEA (Institute of Services for the Agricultural Food Market) in its 2018 report, underlined that in 2017, the insured

---

[18] Ministero Delle Politiche Agricole e Forestali. Decreto 7 Febbraio 2003; In particular, we have to consider Regulation (EU) No. 1306/2013 of the European Parliament and of the Council on the financing, management and monitoring of the common agricultural policy and repealing Council Regulations (EEC) No. 352/78, (EC) No. 165/94, (EC) No. 2799/98, (EC) No. 814/2000, (EC) No. 1290/2005 and (EC) No. 485/2008.This Regulation lays down the rules on the financing of expenditure under the Common Agricultural Policy (CAP), including expenditure on rural development. Furthermore, it sets forth provisions on the (i) farm advisory system, (ii) the management and control systems to be put in place by the Member States, (iii) the cross-compliance system and (iv) clearance of accounts. This system may also cover the promotion of conversions of farms and the diversification of their economic activity, risk management and the introduction of appropriate preventive actions to address natural disasters, catastrophic events and animal and plant diseases, as well as the information related to climate change mitigation and adaptation, biodiversity and protection of water, as set out in Annex I to this Regulation. Another fundamental EU regulation is Regulation (EU) No. 1308/2013 of the European Parliament and of the Council establishing a common organization of the markets in agricultural products and repealing Council Regulations (EEC) No. 922/72, (EEC) No. 234/79, (EC) No. 1037/2001 and (EC) No. 1234/2007. This Regulation establishes a common organization of the markets for agricultural products, namely all the products listed in Annex I to the Treaties with the exception of the fishery and aquaculture products as defined in European Union legislative acts on the common organization of the markets in fishery and aquaculture products. Agricultural products covered by these provisions include cereals, rice, sugar, seed, olive oils and table olives, fruits and vegetables, wine, tobacco, and milk. According to this Regulation preventive instruments such as harvest insurance, mutual funds and green harvesting should be eligible for support under the wine support programs so as to encourage a responsible approach to crisis situations.

[19] https://agriculture.ec.europa.eu/common-agricultural-policy/cap-overview/cap-glance_en (last visited July 26, 2022).

[20] https://agriculture.ec.europa.eu/common-agricultural-policy/cap-overview/cap-glance_en (last visited July 26, 2022).

values relating to crops stood at 4981 million euros, the lowest figure since 2010.[21] Compared to 2016, a decrease of 5.8% is observed, after the decline of 5.4% recorded in 2016.[22] The entire amount of premiums was slightly less than 337 million euros, with a 4.5% decrease on an annual basis, while the average level of tariffs was 6.8%.[23]

The ISMEA 2021 report[24] shows that the number of insured companies is still too low, around 76,000 units against almost 705,000 agricultural holdings benefiting from CAP payments. The persistent territorial concentration and limitation of the insured base, in conjunction with the unfavorable trend in claims rates for agricultural sector, finds the inevitable reflection in the progressive increase in the rates applied by insurance companies, with national average rates that in the 2020 campaign they reached the record value of 9.06%.

The same conclusions can be reached regarding other EU countries.[25]

In UK firms provide farm or crop insurance. Agricultural insurance is purchased by agricultural producers to protect against either the loss of their crops due to natural disasters, such as hail, drought and floods, or the loss of revenue due to farm-specific risks. According to the Report of CRED (Center on Epidemiology of Disasters), the total reported economic losses in the United Kingdom caused by weather- and climate-related calamities during 2020 amounted about to US$33.5 billion (£23.7 billion), as a result average economic losses caused by weather- and climate-related extremes in the United Kingdom per annum were US$1.6 billion (£1.1 billion) between 2000 and 2020 inclusive. The CRED also reported that there were 3750 fatalities caused by weather- and climate-related extremes in the United Kingdom between 2000 and 2020 inclusive. The most common weather- and climate-related extremes that affect the United Kingdom are storms, flooding, extreme temperatures, droughts, and to a far lesser extent, earthquakes, wildfires, and land movement. Insurance industry revenue in this sector is forecast to grow. New product development through technological innovation and better financial returns from insurers' investments are expected. However, as demonstrated in the past five-year period, revenue is subject to sudden changes in financial markets. The

[21] Report on risk management in agriculture, Rome, 2018. https://www.ismeamercati.it/flex/cm/pages/ServeAttachment.php/L/IT/D/6%252Ff%252Fa%252FD.e19e6e1c4492e2a7d686/P/BLOB%3AID%3D9191/E/pdf?mode=inline, pp. 47, 81 (last visited July 26, 2022).

[22] Report on risk management in agriculture, Rome, 2018. https://www.ismeamercati.it/flex/cm/pages/ServeAttachment.php/L/IT/D/6%252Ff%252Fa%252FD.e19e6e1c4492e2a7d686/P/BLOB%3AID%3D9191/E/pdf?mode=inline, pp. 47, 81 (last visited July 26, 2022).

[23] Cafiero et al. (2007); Glauber (2004), pp. 1179–1195; Musser and Patrick (2002); D'auria et al. (2011), p. 27; Capitanio and Cioffi (2011). The CAP towards 2020: Meeting the food, natural resources and territorial challenges of the future. EC Communication (COM (2010) 672); Commissione Europea (2011).

[24] ISMEA Report on risk management in agriculture, Rome, 2021.

[25] *See* Brunette (2019) (last visited Jan 30, 2020).

level of public subsidies that the agricultural sector receives over the next five-year period will significantly affect industry demand.[26]

In EU, the CAP, as in the Report of the EU Commission COM (2018) 322 final,[27] must be modernized to respond to these challenges, it must be simplified for do it with a minimum level of administrative burden and must be made more compatible with the other EU policies to maximize their contribution to the ten priorities of the Commission and, the last level is risk retention for the amount of the deductible. Insurance contracts usually provide for a deduction leaving a part of the risk to the insured person who will arrange it. The provision of deductible amount is a means to avoid moral hazard of the insured party and to improve the use of precautionary measures by the insured party. In fact, the part of risk deducted from the coverage will be retained by the insured party who needs to manage it. There may be two types of deductibles. It is possible that the insurer covers the full amount of claims of an entity greater than a certain amount and the insured maintains the risk of harmful events within that limit. It is possible that the policyholder is committed to always supporting part of the risk within the limits indicated.

It is also important to consider the importance of Catastrophe (CAT) bonds in this field. A (CAT) bond is a high-yield debt instrument that meant to raise money in case of a catastrophe such as a hurricane or earthquake. It is usually insurance-linked. In fact, it has a special condition that states if the issuer, such as the insurance or reinsurance company, suffers a loss from a particular predefined catastrophe, then its obligation to pay interest and/or repay the principal is either deferred or completely forgiven.[28]

4 Index-Based Insurance: Are They Insurance Contracts?

With regards to the contractual coverages of disasters different solutions have been proposed in agricultural sector. Index-based insurance is a type of insurance where the amount of compensation is predetermined on the basis of the achievement of certain target indexes like climate or weather indexes.[29] The advantages of this mechanism are well known: reduction of settlement costs; greater chance of predetermining losses and therefore better reinsurance capabilities; correction of adverse selection problems; all insured are subject to the same terms, conditions, and winnings, which virtually eliminates the problem of adverse selection for insurers. These contracts require qualifying actions to determine whether they are insurance contracts or derivative contracts for the purposes of the applicable law.[30]

---

[26] Agricultural Insurance in the UK - Market Research Report, 2020.

[27] COM/2018/322 final - 2018/0132.

[28] *See* par. 5.

[29] Skees and Collier (2010).

[30] Stout (1996), pp. 38, 39; Stout (1995), p. 53; Stripple (1998).

From a legal point of view, there are also issues of qualification of the contract for the authorization of the national public insurance market in relation to EU directives in this field and, most recently, considering the Directive 138/2009/EC as Solvency II.[31] The limit of this tool is that it does not allow any damages prevention measures to be evaluated. It is said that these policies reduce the moral hazard as the "pay-out" is based on an independent basis and on an exogenous weather parameter, independent of the insured's behavior. This aspect does not detract from the "winning" certainty that can represent a disincentive from the adoption of damage prevention measures.[32] Secondly, based on losses directly related to the calamitous event which are more easily verifiable and quantifiable. It is important to take into account the loss of profit (income in case of natural persons) or loss of revenue. Both need to be structured through careful legal drafting techniques so that the contract also contains conditions for the prevention and containment of damage[33] and it covers the risk of a catastrophic event, not of a risk of patrimonial losses independent from a catastrophic event. This distinction is important for both public authorizations, where cover is provided by an insurance company, and for access to public subsidies—like in the case of agricultural risk coverage. The limits to this solution are that it does not eliminate adverse selection phenomenon as the covered event will be a certain type of catastrophic event. Thus, only subjects most exposed to that risk will be interested in that kind of insurance coverage. It is evident that both solutions, i.e., index-based insurance and insurance for loss of profit, fail to reach the objective of adequate, in term of responds to farmers' needs, and sustainable coverage, in terms of costs. Particular blockchain applications may occur in the claims settlement phase in the case of indexed policies that allow you to correlate the amount of the indemnity to certain indices. The basic concept of parametric solutions is that, instead of indemnifying for the actual loss incurred, parametric insurance covers the probability of a predefined event happening, and pays out according to a predefined scheme. In the agricultural sector, index-based insurance is spreading and is generally parameterized to meteorological indices. It is doubtful whether these contracts can be considered insurance contracts, as the indemnification is based on index. They could be considered derivatives because they don't respect the indemnification principle, that is a defining characteristic of insurance. It is our opinion that these contracts are insurance contracts because they are based on the compensation of a loss where the determination of the loss is calculated thanks to the use of algorithms that can help in reducing human errors and also frauds in the process of losses assessment.

[31] Doff (2007); Eling et al. (2007), sf.69.

[32] Landini (2013), pp. 228 ff.

[33] *See* conditions for compensation arising from the adoption of prudential conduct by the claiming party.

5 Levers to Insurance

Moreover, it is important to find levers to pull farmers toward the conclusion of agricultural insurance. Both solutions essentially aim to cover losses but do not consider the need for business continuity and support in managing the over-indebtedness crisis than the catastrophic event. This issue is very sensitive in European Commission policy. The EU adopted in June 2019 the Restructuring and Second Chance Directive 2019/1023[34] that would allow viable business in distress to be rescued and honest but bankrupt individuals to be given a second chance. According to the goals of the proposal of the directive it is the need for more targeted rules which are necessary to make restructuring frameworks more efficient; it is also the rules on company managers' duty of care when nearing insolvency which also play an important role in developing a culture of business rescue instead of liquidation, as they encourage early restructuring, prevent misconduct and avoidable losses for creditors. Equally important are rules on early warning tools. One of the problems in case of indebtedness, is that the enterprise, especially SMEs, have not resources to pay professionals able to manage the crises in advance. It is important, in addition to coverages for losses caused by calamities, to have insurance contracts providing for legal and commercial assistance in managing the crisis when certain levels of debts are reached and to manage the crisis in advance providing for monitoring of the patrimonial situation of the insured enterprise. This kind of insurance service could be distributed together with agricultural coverages in case of calamities to enhance the interest of farmers toward insurance coverages and considering the usual correlation between losses in case of calamities and indebtedness. Agricultural insurance could also represent an instrument to facilitate access to credit. Thus, another lever could be the provision of better conditions in loan contracts in the case of insurance coverage against natural catastrophe having an impact on the agricultural production. The borrower may enjoy better economic conditions if his business is protected against natural disasters. The presence of such insurance coverage would help to reduce credit risk and help access to credit. With regard to this solution, attention should be paid to the risk of possible agreements between banks and insurance companies that could impose insurance contracts that are neither adequate nor sustainable. It should be said that the problem is solved in the guidelines adopted by EIOPA (European Insurance Authority) and by national authorities.[35]

---

[34] Rasekh and Rosha (2021).

[35] Mortgage life and other credit protection insurance, when adequately developed and targeted, can be beneficial for consumers, offering policyholders and their estates protection in the event that they become unable to pay a loan. Despite the benefits, national competent authorities have reported issues and risks related to these types of insurance products that may lead to consumer detriment, as reported in EIOPA's 2019 Consumer Trends Report. These risks include unmitigated conflicts of interests, aggressive sales techniques, and high commissions. In UK payment protection insurance is of particular interest regarding bankruptcy of the debtor. Payment Protection Insurance (PPI) is an insurance contract generally taken out at the time of a loan or credit card. The law states that this

6 Cat Bonds and Disasters: The Case for Agricultural Insurance

International experiences using alternative catastrophe risk management arrangements have shown that in both the public sector sponsored schemes (e.g., for hurricanes) or the private sector initiatives (e.g., investment bank sales of catastrophe insurance), innovations have allowed better risk control for the insureds and for small insurers who usually direct risks to the market. Catastrophe risk poses a unique challenge to the insurance industry. Catastrophic risks in primary markets tend to be spread temporally more than spatially. The pricing of catastrophe reinsurance is based on the notion of spreading risk over time. The securitization of catastrophe risk, happens via catastrophe bonds which pay investors high yields, but are subject to default on all or part of principal and interest if a catastrophic event occurs during the life of the bond; contingent surplus notes which essentially install and instigate rights which allow the insured party to issue debt to pre-specified buyers in the event of a catastrophic event; exchange traded catastrophe options, catastrophe equity puts, catastrophe swaps and weather derivatives.[36] The emergence of catastrophe (CAT) bonds as a new method of catastrophic risk management, unites the disaster law's approach to compensation and risk-spreading with other branches of finance and portfolio management.[37]

CAT Bonds were first developed in the U.S. market after two major catastrophic events: starting from hurricane Andrew in 1992 and the Northridge earthquake in 1994, and following with the events of 1992 and 1994, insurance providers became increasingly averse to insurance policies covering certain events in specific areas and additionally the premiums rose quickly. [38] CAT bonds were therefore devised to transfer insurance risk borne by insurance and reinsurance companies to the financial markets. CAT bonds are essentially securities used, also by insurance companies, to transfer the risks borne as a result of issuing insurance policies to the financial markets.[39] Insurers see the CAT Bonds as a way to diversify their reinsurance capabilities and strengthen the access to capital markets; CAT Bonds are used in

---

contract is an asset in the bankruptcy, as is the right to complain if it was mis-sold. Where a PPI contract signed before the date of the bankruptcy, the right to claim compensation belongs to the bankruptcy trustee. For more information, see https://www.gov.uk/guidance/ppi-after-bankruptcy.

[36] Pollner (2001). Available at: https://papers.ssrn.com/sol3/papers.cfm?abstract_id=632627.

[37] Chen (2012). Available at https://doi.org/10.2139/ssrn.2141591.

[38] Polacek, A., Catastrophe bonds: A primer and retrospective, https://doi.org/10.21033/cfl-2018-405.

[39] Polacek, A., Catastrophe bonds: A primer and retrospective, https://doi.org/10.21033/cfl-2018-405, What is a Catastrophe bond? - Artemis - resource library Artemis.bm - the Catastrophe bond, insurance linked securities & investment, reinsurance capital, alternative risk transfer and weather risk management site, https://www.artemis.bm/library/what-is-a-Catastrophe-bond/ (last visited Jan 30, 2020); Edesess, M., Catastrophe bonds: an important new financial instrument, https://risk.edhec.edu/publications/Catastrophe-bonds-important-new-financial-instrument (last visited Jan 30, 2020).

order to complement the reinsurance options available. There are substantial differences reinsurance products and CAT Bonds. Traditional reinsurance contracts offer reinstatement provisions, which reset coverage when the reinsurance limit is exceeded. No such provision is generally found in a CAT bond structure. Reinsurance also tended to be annual contracts, whereas CAT bond coverage typically covers events that may occur over a 3-to-4-year period. Furthermore, contracts of insurance and reinsurance are subjected to the principle of utmost good faith. The doctrine of utmost good faith and *uberrima fides* existing in English law is somehow attenuated in other European countries, like Italy,[40] but execution of the contract in good faith is still a fundamental principle of the Italian legal system, which establishes the standard of conduct that a reinsured must satisfy, in order to reap the benefits of its reinsurance agreement, either in the placement/underwriting of business, or in the subsequent stage of the submission of claims to the reinsurer. On the contrary, CAT Bonds market is purely transactional: no good faith issue may be conceivable, and this is a relevant factor in increasing certainty. It may be critical in fact for an insurer selling this risk to be able to claim full credit on its financial statements for all risk transfers, including CAT Bonds. Since CAT Bonds are fully collateralized with the bond proceeds protected by a reinsurance trust for the benefit of the ceding insurer, provided that the documentation is properly and accurately drafted, the ceding insurer should rely on a relatively smooth and quick collection of reinsurance.

6.1 Agricultural, Cat Bond and Parametric Insurance

Agriculture is a risky business and farmers face risks making their incomes volatile as confronted with losses due to bad weather or crop diseases or with the risk of catastrophic losses, all of which pose serious financial problems. Given the above, and the long experience living with risk, farmers have developed several well-honed strategies such as spreading their bets by growing a mix of crops and crop varieties. Also, communities provide another layer of protection against risk via community funds, credit groups, and kin-support networks. However, with the uncertainty entailed, farmers are withheld from specializing in their most profitable alternatives, essentially trading off higher income to reduce risk exposure. Agriculture insurance is provided by the private for-profit sector, governments (public), and other, mostly non-profits (mutual groups, NGOs, etc.). Private agricultural insurance is focused on insuring farm business losses. Index-based insurance serves the need to overcome the problems of traditional forms of crop insurance. And even if it also provides cover against specific perils, yet contracts are written against events defined and recorded at regional levels rather than at individual farm levels. Index-based

[40] For instance, the consequences of misrepresentation and non-disclosure of material facts set out under articles 1892 and 1893 c.c. are somewhat less severe than those existing in English law.

products broaden the scope for insuring against named perils, widening the number of assured farmers who can be served by the same index contract. Public agricultural insurance has tried to fill the gap left by the private sector, especially for meeting the insurance needs of the many smallholders who cannot afford to pay the full costs of insurance.[41] Parametric (at times 'index') risk insurance is insurance that pays out benefits on the basis of a predetermined index (e.g., rainfall level, wind speed, Richter scale) for loss resulting from weather and catastrophic events, using a model to calculate the payout of the insurance policy and to closely mirror the actual damage on the ground; thus enabling a much more rapid payment as no loss adjusters are required after the event to assess the actual damage.[42] Index-based insurance include resilience bonds/parametric resilience insurance, i.e., financial instruments whose cash flows depend on the occurrence of contractually settled catastrophic events and part of the economic value of the investment is devoted to finance resilience actions.[43] Fully parametric agriculture insurance is an efficient and scalable solution for agriculture risks that cannot often be accommodated via traditional insurance schemes.

In June 2021, Generali issued the first ever "Green cat bond" whereby the investment of the collateral in assets with a positive environmental impact and the allocation of the solvency capital was released towards eligible "green assets" and inherently green forms of insurance business. The transaction targets both asset side (green investments) and liability side (insurance policies) making it the very first capital management and reinsurance product. It also provides a new and innovative capital management tool for a sector that will face an escalating frequency and severity due to climate change. The bonds were welcomed and over-subscribed so far.

6.2 *The Need for Parametric Block-Chain Climate Risk Insurance*

Insurers, usually, would calculate premiums via the assessment of past risk as this has been evaluated and has been quantified of claims made in the past. This is a form of ex-post retrospective underwriting works well for well tested through time insurance products which allow resort to records of claims and payments, but not for new products whereby no such records to provide similar data exist, and in such cases usually *in situ* measurements of the risk posed are used as a method for underwriting. This method is costly and, therefore, instead remote sensing was initially thought as a way of alternative risk assessment. However, such data mining is not straightforward. Another method is that of the geographical underwriting of

[41] Hess and Hazell (2018).

[42] Navarro-Martin (2017).

[43] Pagano et al. (2019), pp. 305–332.

risk, as risk of exposure to hazards often varies geographically, which, in turn, means the spatial variation in exposure leaves room for varied insurance rates geographically. However, index-based insurance was considered mostly appropriate for agricultural insurance combined with remote sensing via satellites which allows for cost-effective, reliable, and impartial information and data on agriculture and a continuous flow of information to develop long-term datasets with stable characteristics over time. In the case of agricultural/crop insurance, the application of remote sensing stems from the concern of government to control fraud in agricultural insurances. To date the adoption of the technology in claim-based insurance is not pervasive. However, index-based insurance has a greater potential for uptake by the insurance industry as combined with the method of remote-sensing applied in it, it allows the redesign of insurance business via the development of insurance products in new areas and with new customers; thus, allowing the industry to develop new markets, non-reachable without remote sensing and have agricultural insurances with lower costs.[44] This, together with the adoption and combination of parametric insurance, via the use of blockchain technology, seems to be a solution to lead the way forward towards precise risk calculation and affordable premium for agricultural insurance.

Innovative technologies are rarely implemented, increasing vulnerability. Communities often manage risks via solidarity, cooperation, and trust among rural communities or via diversification. However, this can result in lower income. The creation of a parametric—yet via blockchain—climate risk agriculture insurance can increase agricultural resilience to climate change through offering a more accessible index insurance product via bespoke tailor—made standardized and customized insurance products, along with significant innovations to automate pay-outs and reduce the transaction costs via the use of the technology of blockchain.

The Global Innovation Lab for Climate Change, a lab which identifies, develops, and launches sustainable finance instruments that can drive billions to a low-carbon economy issued such a product for Blockchain Climate Risk Crop Insurance which serves as a standardized, digital index crop insurance platform for smallholder farmers that addresses the impacts of climate change on crop production by making insurance more transparent, efficient, and scalable.[45] The Blockchain Climate Risk Crop Insurance addresses supply and demand barriers by improving insurance with reduced claim cycles and transaction costs, and increased transparency and trust via smart contracts on a blockchain. Instead of lengthy processing of claims, weather data automatically triggers pay-outs, giving farmers the means to react promptly to the weather event. Also, the use of index insurance reduces costs since the system relies on easily verifiable data, thus resulting in a much lower cost of processing claims and probably lower fraud potential. By creating templates for

---

[44] De Leeuw et al. (2014), pp. 10889–10894.

[45] The Lab, Blockchain Climate Risk Crop Insurance, https://www.climatepolicyinitiative.org/wp-content/uploads/2020/08/Blockchain-Climate-Risk-Crop-Insurance_instrument-analysis.pdf (last visited 30 January, 2022).

blockchain-based insurance products, it allows farmers and end-consumers to use the tools provided to create their own customized insurance product, at a lower cost.

Challenges to the instrument may be: a) persisting low demand due to farmers being unaware of the product's value, or because despite the transaction costs reductions, insurance premiums remain higher than what farmers are willing to pay; b) a basis risk as a result of poor designed products, the distance between the index measurement location and the actual production field, the extension of the area covered and its variability; or c) the perception that the use of blockchain protocols may automatically lead to significant environmental co-impacts at scale.

However, it is innovative as it is addressing the lack of trust in insurance products farmers and it is at the same time enabling higher standardization of insurance products and it is commercially viable under all scenarios from a business perspective, as it has been tested so far, and it is catalytic and actionable. Overall, the instrument offers the possibility to create standardized and customized insurance products, and as it will be available via mobile phones it will allow farmers to react promptly to weather events, increasing resilience of vulnerable crops in remote locations. [46]

7 Conclusions

Climate change requires rethinking the insurance contract in order to bring it closer to the new needs of agricultural businesses and to make coverage sustainable for insurance companies. We need to rethink to make damage compensation and risk mitigation tools complementary. New technologies can help by providing indexed systems for determining damage and monitoring tools for agricultural enterprises that allow a better risk assessment, the identification of tailor-made mitigation systems, continuous monitoring of their implementation, alert systems where implementation is necessary. mitigation tools, a speeding up of liquidation procedures to favor the more rapid recovery of the affected companies.

The meteo-climatic analyzes, based on data from the World Meteorological Organization (WMO), show that in the year 2020 we have had an average temperature anomaly of plus 1.2 Celsius degrees compared to the pre-industrial period. The year 2020 can be placed among the three hottest years of the historical series considered (data from 1981 to 2010), despite the observation of the phenomenon of "La Nina", with its effect of contrasting the increase in temperatures. The areas in which particularly high temperatures were observed, compared to the historical average, include the Arctic belt and Siberia, where anomalies above +5 Celsius degrees were recorded. It is also known that the rise in global temperatures is also

[46] The Lab, Blockchain Climate Risk Crop Insurance, https://www.climatepolicyinitiative.org/wp-content/uploads/2020/08/Blockchain-Climate-Risk-Crop-Insurance_instrument-analysis.pdf (last visited 30 January, 2022).

related to an increase in the frequency of extreme phenomena. The year 2020, in particular, was characterized by a high number of fires, which mostly hit Australia and the USA, as well as flood phenomena and floods, which affected various areas of Asia and Africa. A severe drought hit South America, particularly in the areas between Brazil, Paraguay, and Argentina. Numerous tropical storms were detected 30 of which 13 categorized as hurricanes.

Climate change requires rethinking synergies between the different tools to strengthen the resilience of agricultural businesses: insurance contracts, reinsurance, mutual funds financed by farmers, derivatives. It is also a question of finding new levers that push farmers to take out insurance by finding links between insurance and credit facilities (thanks to the reduction of the risk of insolvency due to catastrophic events), including consultancy services. Therefore, it is necessary to simplify the bureaucracy in subsidized coverage also through the automation of the contract conclusion processes. Block chain and smart contracts technology can also help in creating better tailor-made insurance services and it can rend the assessment of losses faster and cheaper.

Finally, it is a question of rethinking the complementarity between indemnity protection in the event of a disaster provided by insurers and risk prevention and mitigation tools.

References

Agricultural Insurance in the UK - Market Research Report, 2020., www.ibisworld.com

Artemis - resource library artemis.bm - the Catastrophe bond, insurance linked securities & investment, reinsurance capital, alternative risk transfer and weather risk management site. https://www.artemis.bm/library/what-is-a-Catastrophe-bond/

Brunette M (2019) Chocs climatiques pourquoi les agriculteurs francais sont ils si mal assures, July 24, 2019. https://theconversation.com

Cafiero C, Capitanio F, Cioffi A, Coppola A (2007) La gestione del rischio nelle imprese agricole tra strumenti privati e intervento pubblico. Agriregionieuropa 8:1

Capitanio F, Cioffi A (2011) Gestione del rischio in agricoltura ed intervento pubblico. Evoluzione, sostenibilità e prospettive del sistema italiano, in Rivista Economia e Diritto Agroalimentare; Commissione Europea, (2010)

Chen JM, Postmodern Disaster Theory (September 5, 2012). MSU Legal Studies Research Paper No. 11-17. https://doi.org/10.2139/ssrn.2141591

D'Auria R, Capitanio F, Adinolfi F, Di Domenico M, Guido M (2011) La gestione del rischio in agricoltura nella futura politica di sviluppo rurale dell'UE. Agriregionieuropa 27

De Leeuw J, Vrieling A, Shee A, Atzberger C, Hadgu KM, Biradar CM, Keah H, Turvey C (2014) The potential and uptake of remote sensing in insurance: a review. Remote Sens 6:10888–10912. https://doi.org/10.3390/rs61110888

Doff R (2007) Risk management for insurers: risk control, economic capital and solvency II. Risk Books, London

Edesess M. Catastrophe bonds: an important new financial instrument. https://risk.edhec.edu/publications/Catastrophe-bonds-important-new-financial-instrument

Eling M, Schmeiser H, Schmit JT (2007) The solvency II process: overwiew and critical analysis. Risk Manag Insur Rev 10(1):sf.69

European Commission (2010) The CAP towards 2020: Meeting the food, natural resources and territorial challenges of the future, EC Communication (COM (2010) 672
European Commission (2011) Legal proposal for the CAP after 2013
European Commission, Climate change: start of the second European Climate Change Programme. https://ec.europa.eu/commission/presscorner/detail/en/IP_05_1330
European Commission, EU strategy on Green Infrastructure. https://ec.europa.eu/environment/nature/ecosystems/strategy/index_en.htm
European Commission, EU Adaptation Strategy, 2017. https://ec.europa.eu/clima/eu-action/adaptation-climate-change/eu-adaptation-strategy_en
Glauber J (2004) Why subsidized insurance has not eliminated disaster payments? Am J Agric Econ 86(5):1179–1195
Hess U, Hazell P (2018) Innovations and emerging trends in agricultural insurance. GIZ
Landini S (2013) From environmental insurance to environmental derivatives? Eur Energy Environ Law Rev:228 ff
Musser WN, Patrick GF (2002) How much does risk really matters to farmers? In: Just RE, Pope RD (eds) A comprehensive assessment of the role of risk in U.S. agriculture. Kluwer Academic Publishers, Boston/Dordrecht/London
Navarro-Martin M (2017) Parametric insurance, applications in agriculture, climate and disaster risk and pandemics. World Bank
Pagano AJ, Romagnoli F, Vannucci E (2019) Flood risk: financing for resilience using insurance adaptive schemes. Agrochimica:305–332
Polacek A. Catastrophe bonds: a primer and retrospective. https://doi.org/10.21033/cfl-2018-405
Pollner J. Catastrophe risk management: using alternative risk financing and insurance pooling mechanisms (February 2001)
Rasekh A, Rosha A (2021) Restructuring and insolvency in Europe: policy options in the implementation of the EU Directive. International monetary fund, May 2021
Skees JR, Collier B (2010) New approaches for index insurance: ENSO insurance in Peru. In: Kloeppinger-Todd R, Sharma M (eds) 2020 vision for food, agriculture, and the environment, focus 18 innovations in rural and agriculture finance. International Food Policy Research Institute, Washington, DC
Stout I (1995) Betting the bank: how derivatives trading under conditions of uncertainty can increase risks and erode returns in financial markets. J Corp Law 21:53
Stout I (1996) Insurance or gambling? Derivatives trading in a world of risk and uncertainty. Brookings Rev 14:38, 39
Stripple J (1998) Securiting the risk of climate change, in IIASA, IR- 98 098 December, Austria
Tangermann S (2011) Risk management in agriculture, and the future of the EU's common agricultural policy. ICTSD 34:13
The Lab, Blockchain Climate Risk Crop Insurance. https://www.climatepolicyinitiative.org/wp-content/uploads/2020/08/Blockchain-Climate-Risk-Crop-Insurance_instrument-analysis.pdf
UNDRR, Sendai Framework for Disaster Risk Reduction 2015-2030. https://www.undrr.org/publication/sendai-framework-disaster-risk-reduction-2015-2030
UNDRR, Hyogo Framework for Action 2005-2015. https://www.undrr.org/publication/hyogo-framework-action-2005-2015-building-resilience-nations-and-communities-1

Sara Landini Full professor of economic law at the University of Florence; teacher of Insurance law at the actuarial school—CISA (Interacademic Center for Actuarial Sciences). Her research interests span from insurance and reinsurance to AI, digital technologies, data protection, ethics, environmental law. She has written extensively and advises regularly in these fields. She is also a qualified barrister (Florence Bar Association). She studied at Florence University Law School, She got the PhD with a thesis in Insurance law. PI of International projects. Director of Scientific Journals. She has been a visiting professor in Europe (Germany, Spain, Norway, Hungary), Asia (Japan), Australia (Sydney).

Kyriaki Noussia is an Associate Professor in Law at the School of Law, University of Reading UK. Her research interests span from insurance and reinsurance to AI, digital technologies, shipping, arbitration and environmental law. She has written extensively and advises regularly in these fields. She is also a qualified barrister (Athens Bar Association) and an accredited arbitrator and mediator. She studied at the Athens University Law School (LLB), University of Essex (LLM) and University of Southampton (PH.D.). She has been a visiting professor in Europe (Germany, France, Italy, Turkey, Greece), Asia (China), Australia (Sydney, Melbourne, Queensland) and the USA (Columbia NY USA).

Part II
Financial Innovation in Insurance Regulation

Historical, Definitional, and Implementational Issues of Financial Services Regulation in a Small Jurisdiction

John A. Consiglio

Abstract This paper provides a discussion about certain definitional and historical context issues revolving around the generic term of "regulation," and particularly financial services (FS) regulation. The importance of familiarity with salient happenings in the chronicles of financial services regulation, and the great difficulty in arriving at clear pictures of how, and which, attributes can be appended to desired regulatory formats, are discussed and reflected in the results of a study of facets of these issues as carried out in 2021 in a small FS jurisdiction.

Keywords Small jurisdiction · Financial services · Historical background · Implementation issues · Insurance · Securities · Banking

1 A Brief Historical Background

The banking, insurance, and securities businesses of the Medicis (first bank in 1397 and now making a comeback in New York); the Sforzas (who are reputed to have built their banking business on the remnants of the Viscontis (1277–1447) in Milan, Italy; the Rothschilds (who shrewdly planted a banker son in every feuding early European main city); similar other banking "greats" from pre-nineteenth century Europe; those even further back of the financial world in the times of the Qing and Song (960–1279), and Ming (1440s) dynasties in China; and elsewhere in Asia and the Americas; these fascinating banking stories all survived and thrived in social, cultural, and political contexts which by no stretch of the imagination can be considered as analogous to today's in terms of "regulation". Indeed the term as such never really appears in the legal, or even the political, chronicles of those times.

Therefore, it is fair to consider these and others as being contexts where the activities were such where, if regulation was "felt" at all, it was more a case of implicit direction of something exclusively conducted within the term of the nation

J. A. Consiglio (✉)
Department of Banking and Finance, Faculty of Economics, Management and Accountancy, University of Malta, Msida, Malta

M. Lima Rego, S. Grima (eds.), *Cross-Disciplinary Impacts on Insurance Law*, AIDA Europe Research Series on Insurance Law and Regulation 8,
https://doi.org/10.1007/978-3-031-38526-1_4

state. Even as explorers and traders figure prominently in the histories of so many colonizing nations, and these often being described as "pioneers" of much of the trading or services activity taking place, any ideas of "regulating" activity was perceived as actually being something that hampers trade and the activities of markets. If "regulation" was there at all it was only more akin to custom and habit, and indeed working practices, that few would really think or worry about at all, even as it indeed would be carried out, and potentially also "exported", as such. Of course in essence many nations were closed national economies, where in fact more concern was given to the notions of durability and legitimacy of national decision making.

Today's world is one where regulation is factually on the rise across the whole universe. One interpretation of this could be that it became an inevitability when the state stepped back from public ownership of economic activities, for example through the process of privatization.[1] But the style and the way that political delegation has been passed on to regulatory authorities has not followed anywhere near a uniform pattern. Administrative traditions, different attributes of institutional endowment, market structures and business cultures, legal and soft law structures (more on the latter below), these and other factors have all influenced the creation of regulatory authorities and implementation styles.

Much seems to suggest that the overriding view of regulation in long past history must, so far, remain one where the activity would be predominantly perceived as tantamount to "interference", carried out in any form on the activity subjected to it. The activity would be essentially seen as being governed, altered, controlled, indeed even possibly guided and steered, in some way or other. It remained however deliberate "interference" in a chosen activity. And it is against such discussion of the background from past history and chronicles that any consideration of actually defining regulation must be contextually placed. One will find it hard to answer simple questions such as "When was regulation born? When did it first come in? When did governments wake up to this as being a necessary activity which they would at some point start feeling that they should control or influence?"

No dates will ever provide a full answer to all of these questions. IMF records show that between 1980 and 2003 approximately 75% of the organisation's member-states had some form of institutional or national crisis in their banking services sectors.[2] That time span precedes 2008 and the US subprime-lendings crisis, and, a year later, the crisis in Greece which from here into future years, *inter alia,* morphed specific EU-funded institutional bailouts into obligatory international bail-in requirements, and specific institution recovery and resolution processes as conceptually evolving via the EU's efforts towards a banking union.

But these may probably only be considered as developments happening in our own times. And they do not in reality provide anywhere near a complete historical

---

[1] For fuller analysis of the issues of financial services privatization *vide* Consiglio (2006b).

[2] *Vide "Bank Soundness and Macroeconomic Policy in the EU CCs – 1980 to 1996"* – J.A. Consiglio (Malta European Studies Association, EDRC University of Malta, Malta). For a longer-spanning, some 300 years, view of financial crises, see also Quinn and Turner (2020).

picture of how, for example, interdependence and international cooperation (or even the lack of it[3]) were instrumental in evolving today's theories and practices in the world of financial services regulation. The 1970s were times when slowdown in productivity rates were being recorded in many economies, particularly in Europe. But ruling policies in many countries up to the late 20th century were of a strongly interventionist character. And then, even before the turn into the 21st century, during for example the 1980s, economic policies in many developed countries moved towards more reliance of the forces of the market and of competition It can be a matter for debate whether this was essentially a knee-jerk reaction to how Japan, and the newly industrializing countries (NICs), were asserting themselves on the world stage.

Such changes in the thrust of central government policies are not of course anywhere near being novel in the history of regulation. If these were times which then led to widespread feelings that regulation played a part in hampering the workings of markets, and instrumental, at least partly, in worsening of economic conditions, one can then understand and appreciate why we have eventually evolved into today's endless saga of regulation-deregulation-and-constant-reregulation. Indeed much of deregulation can be validly considered as an expression of regulation not having worked properly, and in fact imposing on practitioners various forms of operational costs that far exceeded any presumed benefits.

The context of today's regulatory environment is of course very different to that of the past. All purpose and process of financial services regulation today exists in a context of this being an activity which is no longer exclusively conducted within only the closed frontiers of the domestic nation state. There is much in today's international relations reality that is based on the factor of *interdependence*.[4] But that does not mean that among states and geographical regions, the factors of trade, monetary flows, technology, communications, the activities of multinational enterprises and other non-state actors, that all of these as such are resulting in any forms of totally harmonized regulatory activity. Continued blips and issues as the EU works its way towards a harmonized Capital Markets Union these are possibly a good example of this. An all encompassing history of regulation is, seen in such contexts, still both unwritten and, inevitably so, still evolving.

[3]The BCCI (Bank of Credit and Commerce International) crisis (1972 *et seq*) is often cited as a classic example of the big voids In inter-country regulatory liaison and cooperation which facilitated criminality at a then unprecedented level.

[4]*Vide e.g.* Lieber (2008).

2 Definitional Issues

With this consideration of some history elements as a generally wide background—and there can indeed potentially lie much more history that can be related to it—the definitional issues of regulation can be equally wide. Most uses of the term assume that the activity regulated is of a general economic nature, and the concept becomes practically equal to governmental intervention. This view was considered in Moran's (1986) seminal study[5] as both expansive and unsatisfactory because it both "fails to distinguish regulation from the general exercise of public power, of which it is only a part", and also because it "fails to [sufficiently] recognize that much regulation is carried out by private institutions". Clearly the latter part of this position has over time come to be much questioned and modified, specifically of course in the sense that in the modern world of financial services most regulation would appear to be mostly influenced, created, and implemented, by some form or other of state- created and controlled bodies.

Also to be considered here is the fact that in daily practice two vital elements deserve consideration. Again one carries with it a tinge of times-past, but the other still remains much of our own times. And, too, a fine historic inspiring thread between the two is not incorrect to conceive. The first is the reminiscence of much *self-regulation* failure in the past. 1973–1975 were years of dramatic crashes of several small, but also important, ('secondary' they were perhaps euphemistically described as!) banks in Britain, and over following years the UK experience was one where, up to Professor Jim Gowers' important study in 1982 reviewing the failure within the country of investor protection, the country had actually laboured under a structure where several self- regulatory organizations (SROs), had been failing.[6] The experiment, or experience, of self-regulation had been an ongoing one of over half a decade, but it had failed to deliver what was really needed for the citizens of the land.

The other element of practice can however be said to still be a very much alive and practically daily reality. It is that of *soft law*. This is now perhaps best described as that concept of rule-based relationships, evolving over time, or through practice, or even as a result of specific agreements, where under the non-following of agreed rules and/or practices, and/or agreements of the structure or system, entails the offending individual or organization being subjected to certain agreed sanctions. In soft law very often such sanctions are structured in a manner that benefits the other complying member individuals or institutions in the system—e.g. fines, not being retained as member or subscriber to the system—and naturally this often has dire

[5]Moran (1986), pp. 185–201.

[6]Various chronicles (*vide e.g. The Journal of the Institute of Bankers*) show that during the Sixties in the City of London there existed something like six associations of both a lobbying and self-regulatory nature. These were concerned with sectorial business activity, e.g. mortgage, agricultural, merchant, and commercial banking, and by the 1980s the more influential of these had become FIMBRA (Financial Intermediaries Managers and Brokers *Regulatory* Association), and LAUTRO (Life Assurance and Unit Trust *Regulatory* Association).

economic consequences for those hit. Over time the history and experience of regulation has come to see and accept soft law as often becoming the basis of subsequently drafted laws which give a formal law character to generally accepted practices or conventions.[7] It is perhaps the best illustration of a regulating process that works bottom-upwards.

It is not incorrect to consider whether in our times it is only academics who concern themselves with issues such as that of what is, or can be, an all-encompassing definition of regulation, let alone financial services regulation. In the day-to-day world out there it is much more likely that the bigger number of practitioners will be tagging on to the term their own private or public view of what, and how, regulation should be or should be done. In the wake of the post-2008 economic crisis the then new EU financial sector chief, Michel Barnier, sought to reassure London's bankers that "new regulation introduced would be both "*smart*" and "*proportionate*". "To ensure confidence we *need* regulation. And much better supervision. But smart, *effective,* and proportionate regulation", he added. His view was that for all of this the three main priorities were: well-*supervised* institutions, well *capitalised* institutions, and *responsible* institutions.[8]

The descriptive adjectives which over time have been tagged on to "regulation" have been endless, and would easily (and proudly?) make it to Roget's Thesaurus. Good, bad, complicated, simple, effective or ineffective, efficient or inefficient, technical, smart, coherent, exaggerated, well-drafted, competent, powerful, holistic, neutral, non-political, non-lobbyist, cheap, costly, "sufficient",[9] otherwise, and so on and so forth. The descriptions can indeed be endless. For those facing the workings of any drafters of law, or regulation, but not only for them, also for the implementers, these descriptions and undoubtedly others are always attributes and characteristics to be considered, sought, or avoided, according to the objectives being aimed at.

There was much debate in such sense in the United Kingdom around 2000 when what must perhaps be considered as that country's major contemporary piece of financial services law in our times—the Financial Services and Markets Act 2000—was about to be enacted. Would that monumental piece of legislation, and the institutions it envisaged, over time come to be such as to include all that is right, and eschew all that is wrong, with regulating? Eventually two attributes made it to the top in that law, viz:

Prudential regulation, *which* is that corpus of regulation, which deals with the *financial soundness* of regulated institutions and, through them, the financial markets, and *Business Conduct* regulation which is regulation which is mainly concerned with the way in which the products of financial services institutions are constructed, marketed, and sold.[10]

---

[7] **Author's University of Malta "Banking Regulation" Course Notes, 2004.**

[8] **Barnier** (2010).

[9] **For a discussion on too much legalization, herein also applicable to Regulation, *vide* Said** (2021).

[10] Blair et al. (2001).

Prudence, and correct business conduct (what are often also referred to by many as 'good governance rules') actually became the elements that underlined the creation and setting up of structures for the implementation and administration of regulation. When the UK opted for removing its former single regulator, the Financial Services Authority (2001–April 2013), and created two authorities instead, i.e. the Prudential Regulation Authority and the Financial Conduct Authority (in 2013), this development actually set loose a big debate about that methodology of "doing" regulation. That twin peaks setup was not in fact a universally adopted one for regulatory governance. After its summer 2015 stock market crash China seriously mulled over having a single 'super-regulator' for bringing together its banking, insurance, and securities regulators into a single super-commission. Poor inter-agency coordination was also mentioned as one of the reasons for the contemplated change.[11] Fabri (2006) points out that the debate over single 'super regulator' setups, and on whether a single regulatory system is more efficient than a multi-agency structure, must remain such as requiring analysis which is wider than mere abstract consideration of attempts at *ad hoc*istic solutions to rising situations. He correctly points at the fact that "neither the EU Commission, nor the various EU financial services Directives, stipulate how a member state's regulatory structures should be designed." But he also clearly points out that "recent EU Directives explicitly require member states to set up *effective* supervisory *agencies* with sufficient competence and power to implement the relevant rules."[12]

Twin, or multiple (see e.g. the US), or single, or other possible formal national structures of regulation, do not of course in essence modify the omnipresent reality of every regulation process, everywhere, viz that it is a two-level process[13] involving regulators and regulated (sometimes also referred to as 'regulatees'). The character of the process is in essence a top-down process. But one should not be exaggeratedly dogmatic about this. The realities of market capture can conceptually also be considered as that part of the regulatory process which at some points is reflected by the bottom-to-top "contribution" towards new regulation evolution. In normal circumstances, and more often than not over time, it would necessarily have to be *acceptance* by all concerned of the regulatory process which would result in the fulfilling of what is laid down in said regulations by way of a pattern which is correct, ordinary, usual and formal. When considering this *sine qua non* reality Braithwaite[14] interprets regulatory policy as complex, and also paradoxical, in ways that require us to attend to both the *substance* and the *politics* of specific regulatory regimes.[15] Risk and regulation are currently in a constant process of reconceptualisation, and there is much to suggest that a main cause of this process

[11] Tham and Lim (2015).

[12] Fabri (2006).

[13] Kagan (1982).

[14] Braithwaite (2002), and Course notes.

[15] This is also an important element faced by teachers of regulation: to what extent must their courses hold back from morphing into law courses poure and simple?

continues to be with us as some form of extending aftermath of the realities of institutional and national economic crises.

Dynamic market economies, as they blend with responsiveness to political and normative demands for fairer financial services, health, safety, environmental protection, and fairness generally, cannot do without the central process of contemporary governance. As Kagan (1982) had showed, a solid process of understanding regulation's ambient, its varieties, vulnerabilities, virtues, and processes, is one way of making regulation more acceptable.

3 Opinion Indicators

How do financial services practitioners, operating either as regulators, or as firms licensed to sell products/services in markets, feel and react to such historical and definitional issues? This is a different question to that of how does a country's financial services industry look at its own regulators. This latter issue was specifically and empirically tackled by Scicluna, Seychell et al. in 2018/2019 in an exercise that used a five-factor model (incorporating conscientiousness, agreeableness, neuroticism, experiential openness, and extroversion) to fully interpret such perception in one specific small jurisdiction, i.e. the small island Republic of Malta in the Mediterranean.[16] On the other hand, what we have here researched are reactions to the former of these questions, in again the same jurisdiction, which indeed, in the relatively short history of its banking environment,[17] actually has a very good experience and history of regulation in both financial services, and other, sectors.

In this jurisdiction the originally chosen sample base for our enquiries was 2500 persons from the industry being invited to respond, with 1687 (67.5%) validly accepting to do so. Eventual margin of error worked out at 4 to 5%, and the gender composition resulted in 61% being male, 38% being female, and 1% refusing to answer that question. The responding cohort must be related to a financial services sector which, over a period of almost two decades (2000–2019), saw total national employment grow from 7388 to 12,229, at an annual growth rate of 10.5%. This can be considered as very much indicative of a sector of workers who are eager to come forward with stances, beliefs, and suggestions for an important facet—i.e. regulation itself—of their calling: in fact some 13.8% of the total number of workers in the country employed in this sector responded to our invitation. The country's overall total employment level grew by 4.6% over the same period, and in 2020 the financial services sector was in fact contributing 8.7% of National Gross Value Added.[18] The

[16] Scicluna et al. (2019), pp. 16–56.

[17] *Vide e.g.* Consiglio (2006a).

[18] The National Employment Policy Document 2021-2030 (Ministry for Finance & Employment, Malta).

different age cohorts of our respondents worked out as follows: 0–15 years: 0%; 16–25: 3.8%; 26–40: 30.2%; 41–65: 57.1%; 65+: 8.9%.

The views of workers everywhere naturally go through morphing processes as one proceeds through life, and when we asked about the number of years that respondents had been working in this sector this provided the following figures: 1 to 10 years: 8.9%; 11–30: 26.8%; 31.50: 64.0%; 50 years+: 0.3%. Such working years would clearly have been spent either in pure regulatory functions, i.e. as regulators (6.2%), or in the wider licensed organizations (the regulatees/ed) operating in the markets (93.8%). Those whose work was strictly in employment with/in Malta's regulators[19] indicated the extent of their experience as regulators (in age groupings) as follows: 1 to 5 years: 0.2%; 6–15: 15.8%; 16–30: 36.3%; 31–50: 45.6; 50+: 2.1%. The suggestion here is that Malta's regulator cohort is one which is almost equally subdivided between young and older workers. But this element must also be considered in the light that over recent years practically all of Malta's FS regulatory bodies (excepting possibly the Malta Stock Exchange) increased the levels of their employment in the wake of much stronger focus and pressure (both internal and foreign) on doubtful goings-on in the country's sector, such insistence coming from, inter alia, bodies like the local Financial Intelligence Analysis Unit (FIAU), the International Financial Action Task Force (FATF), the EU's Venice Commission, and other international oversight organizations. It was a situation which, potentially, had been building up over a number of years: indeed in 2017 the jurisdiction of Malta had placed 85th in a ranking of 92 financial centres surveyed by the Zyen Global Financial Services Index.[20]

Our approach to these respondents with regards to the first area of this study, i.e. the relevance of historical evolution of regulation, was aimed at finding out whether they in fact felt that this is a matter which practitioners in this economic sector should be feeling as necessary at all for their jobs. The reactions here were more or less closely balanced. It may somehow seem related to a generally felt stance, in most callings in life it seems, that collectively, in the group of financial services workers here, theoretically seen as a conceptually homogeneous grouping, those who said that such awareness of history was "Very important", i.e. only 24.9% of respondents, was in fact the lowest. Perhaps the popular old American slang dictum "History is bunk" is what inspires the attitudes of those who think and feel in such fashion. But there was also the sector of those who feel that an awareness of the historical evolution of FS regulation "Is necessary" for their job: this summed up to 36.3% of respondents; whilst those with the view that such awareness is "Not relevant" were 38.8% of the total responding cohort.

---

[19]Whilst the Malta Financial Services Authority (MFSA) is the country's main financial services regulator, it is also correct to consider the Financial Intelligence Audit Unit (FIAU), the Central Bank of Malta (CBM), and the Malta Stock Exchange (MSE) as having their own strictly defined financial regulatory intervention functions.

[20]Times of Malta (2017) – *"Malta slips to 85 of 92 in global financial services"* – (December 12).

This part of the study became more specific in the composition of such awareness level groupings when it sought to find out what market practitioners considered as having been the main regulatory history events which have most impacted their work. Respondents were asked to grade 1,2,3, etc upwards, with 1 going to the development or event which they considered as having been most important for the sector in their professional consideration. Certainly the list of events provided can never be considered as including all that has happened in regulation in our contemporary times, but it may still be potentially considered as a generally broad and encompassing picture. We show hereunder the main events posited for consideration and ranking, and how respondents' reactions mapped out in terms of individuals' final rankings of importance of these developments:

Respondents' Rankings

- The Lehman crisis in 2008 and its aftermaths. *1*
- The Greek crisis from 2009 and its aftermaths. *2*
- The Basle process from 1974 onwards 3
- Malta becoming an EU member-state in 2004 *4*
- The birth of the UK's PRA and FCA in 2013 *5*
- The UK's Financial Services & Markets Act 2000 *6*
- Pre-20th century governmental interventionist policies in Europe *7*
- The EU's SEA (Single European Act) for unifying markets of 1986 *8*
- The UK's "secondary banking crisis" in 1973–75 *9*
- Any other event of your choice (please specify) *10*

Perhaps to be expected was the outcome that the two important crises occurring close to each other, i.e. the US-sub-prime and Greece's,[21] would be considered as the major contemporary impacts in today's regulatory environment. The thinking is strong that the all-pervading aura of sector cross-border contagion was the root of the birth of the European Banking Union (EBU) in 2012, and its ensuing banking (the EBA), securities markets (ESMA), and insurance and occupational pensions (EIOPA) authorities. These today, are sometimes described as practically, inch by inch, leaving little room for any much form of individual domestic regulatory creativity. That the earlier Basle process,[22] from the initial Basle Accord in 1988, to then its Basle 1A development in 2007, then 2 in 2008, and then 3 in 2010, that this process and continuing pattern ranks third in most practitioners' view as the historically most relevant regulatory event, this too has been viewed as also very significant. Gauci's (1999) view that "the majority of members forming the Basle

[21]Certainly US regulators cannot be considered as not having reacted. For example, in 2009 in California, Maryland, and Minnesota regulators pushed up to 84 the number of bank deemed as failures amid the soured economy and rising defaults on loans. The Federal Deposit Insurance Corporation (FDIC) took over the Affinity Bank based in Ventura California, the Bradford Bank in Baltimore Maryland, and the Mainstreet Bank in First Lake, Minnesota. (The Sunday Times, August 30, 2009).

[22]The Basle Committee of Bank Supervisors was formed within the Bank for International Settlements in 1974.

Supervisors Committee of the Bank of International Settlement are also members of the EU", and thus totally influence European Union financial sector regulation, this too can be considered as very relevant in this context.[23]

Scicluna et al.'s (2019) work in this area[24] can be interpreted as having summed up to an overall view that both regulatees and regulators in Malta generally deserve to be viewed positively. Three years from that study we have attempted a possibly more specific and direct search for views of the overall regulatory situation in Malta's financial services sector, and the percentage of those who felt that they were "Very satisfied" was, at 23.8%, the lowest when compared to those who said that they were "Moderately satisfied (38.7%), and those who expressed themselves as being "Not satisfied at all" (37.5%). Clearly, and perhaps inevitably, some practitioners in the sector 'want it all'. To a specific question as to which of a randomly chosen list of regulatory attributes they would give their support, the outcome in terms of "Preferred Regulatory Attribute ranking", resulted as follows:

Desired regulatory attribute	*Ranking*	*% respondents*
Relevant	1	19.9
Efficient	2	16.7
Holistic	3	14.8
Effective	4	12.8
Good	5	12.6
Non-political	6	10.5
Cheap	7	7.2
Least intrusive	8	5.5

Certainly, as suggested in the first part of this study, to each of the above desired attributes individuals will always add their own purely subjective nuancing description. "Good" regulation, for example, can always be considered in some contexts of "beauty is in the eye of the beholder" or "one man's wine is another's poison" adages, and such positions apply in the case of every other attribute included above, or even not included at all. But it is indicative of a certain disposition towards perhaps a fatalistic acceptance of the potential all-pervasiveness of regulation in certain situations, that having regulation which is "least" intrusive ranked lowest in respondents' rankings.

So, beyond merely describing an overall character for desired types of regulation, this enquiry moved into seeking a more direct expression of feelings about the actual present state of regulation of financial services in Malta. Respondents were presented with a range of 'rough, ready, and general' descriptions of what actually regulation can be described as, and were asked to specifically say whether they agreed or disagreed with such description. Clearly this range here leaves out several of the

[23] Gauci (1999).

[24] *Op cit.*

characteristic descriptions of regulation to which reference has been made in the first part of this study.

Do you feel that in Malta the FS sector is:	*Yes: %*	*No:*
Badly regulated?	32.4	67.6
Over regulated?	78.9	21.1
Inefficiently regulated?	19.2	80.8
Effectively regulated?	57.7	42.3
Needs more regulation?	20.1	79.9
Needs less regulation?	62.7	77.3
Conforms to international requirements?	83.2	16.8
Too costly?	70.4	29.6
Moderately costly?	21.8	78.2
Relatively cheap?	13.3	86.7

But, here again, nuances can be felt to exist in every one of the above descriptions of regulation in this industry in this jurisdiction. To take for example the always debatable element of the price of regulation. Discussion about the extent to which regulators can operate in a totally autonomous matter will always include this element as an important component. Obviously not all participants are of the same size and have identical depths to their pockets. It is inevitable that individual respondent reaction will vary to general enquiry about its overall satisfaction with the two key issues of the present structure of regulation in the country—inter alia here the issue of single or multi-peak regulator structures—and also, very important, feelings about the country's main regulator i.e. the Malta Financial Services Authority (MFSA). In these two areas our respondents reacted as follows:

Structure

Satisfaction with a single-peak structure	Yes: 68.2%	No: 31.8%
Preference for a more specialised multi-peaked structure:	Yes: 41.4%	No: 58.6%

Is the MFSA:

Competently managed?	Yes: 44.1%	No: 48.2%	Have no answer: 7.7%
Staffed by competent personnel?	Yes: 60.3%	No: 30.7%	Have no answer: 9.
Fully independent of government control?	Yes: 30.4%	No: 62.3%	Have no answer: 7.3%
Adequately financed?	Yes: 44.3%	No: 25.1%	Have no answer: 30.6%

With financial services generally accepted in Malta as being one of the main pillars of the country's economy, that a substantial number of respondents were not in a position to express a view as to whether the nation's main financial services authority is adequately financed for its current level of operations, this must be considered as a matter for concern. In 2019 the Malta Financial Services Authority Act was amended in substantial parts, and one of the main changes provided for the hiving off into an independent agency the country's Companies Registry which in fact had previously formed part of the MFSA, and had indeed been an important source of the Authority's income. That situation changed importantly into one where the Authority is now highly dependent on annual government budget subventions, given also that its authority or otherwise for raising fines from licensed firms who transgress regulation is the subject of a big legal debate as we write. This situation does not seem to be a totally homogeneous one with regards to other local regulators or administrative tribunals.[25]

4 Conclusions

This analysis has presented a multifaceted picture of FS regulation in a small jurisdiction, initially within historical and definitional contexts, and then relating these elements to several issues which can certainly be considered as applicable to the general view of regulation practically everywhere. It is not a matter for debate that in essence regulation remains some form of *imposed control* by a superior authority. For many the view is only of a process of "*Interference* in how I conduct my business", but certain more pragmatic views also see it as a *necessary activity* everywhere. But *lesser regulation* does *not* always bring *better functioning* of financial services markets. Some operators may try to be neutral and live and operate as if in realty "regulation" were *not existing at all*, and all that really exists is, according to the old Edward Kane position, "*constant reregulation*". Others will insist that either regulators are *always controlled by governments* or, in any hypothetical absence of that, *control by lobbyists*. And others, furthermore and even more highly debatable, that regulation's "*failure*" is in fact evidenced by the processes of deregulation and/or reregulation.

It is a matter for consideration that inherent in much of modern regulation is the insistence on *good* governance, to the hues of which reference has already been made above. One view is that good governance, in seeking to be pro-people, and in our context very much pro-licensed FS firms, will effectively end up as "good" regulation.[26] This of course is applicable to all sectors, e.g. the public sector,

[25] *Vide e.g.* local bank BOV being fined €2.6m by the Financial Intelligence Analysis Unit (FIAU), for failing to identify the full beneficial ownership in some of its customers' accounts. (Times of Malta, Dec 18, 2021).

[26] *Vide e.g.* O'Dea (2020). See also Zammit (2020).

provision of utilities, civil society structures, and of course financial services. Very often this issue, within the general context of in fact precisely its relationship with regulation, comes to a point of doubt as to whether regulators (even rating agencies have been similarly drawn into such questioning) do in fact need to be themselves regulated. Some regulatory bodies have given thought to the issue, and possibly tried to solve it by introducing serious in-house rules for themselves.[27] Others have acted differently, in that careful watch is kept on "trending" in regulation, and on acting in a manner that they come over as being essentially seen providing only the key deliverables of public protection, and helping in some way in national sustainable economic growth.[28] The "language" and "actions" of the every regulatory body often take priority in such an approach.[29]

Despite that the Basle process and system have reached the highly developed stage where inter-regulator availability of information can be considered as standing at a high level, no modern system of financial regulation relies entirely on disclosure and its related devices. As much, if not more, importance is given to techniques used for authorization (or licensing). Some of these techniques have reached standard techniques, and the obvious objective here is the creation of a perimeter (certainly differently effective in different jurisdictions) from which unauthorized persons are excluded, and within which the regulator can exert a level of control over unauthorized persons. In essence the nub always remains to which extent the regulator is both able and willing to punish non-compliance with, in an ultimate stage, also final exclusion from the regulated activity.

Willingness to regulate, correctly, properly, effectively, will possibly always remain an essentially political issue. That willingness lies alongside, shoulder to shoulder, with the big area of whether regulation, constantly or otherwise, *imposes unaffordable costs* on both regulators and regulates, and governments to boot. This is a field which still offers much room for further research. What is also, even at this stage, certain is the fact that too many factors still militate against the possibility of totally harmonized regulatory practices internationally. This perhaps is the case that, similar to what inspired the birth of the European Union as from its early conception, the conflict and contrast between the two forces of (a) "unity" and (b) "in diversity" (for which read also "different cultures", will remain an immovable reality of regulation for ever into the future.

---

[27] In October 2019 the Malta Financial Services Authority (MFSA) formally approved its manual on *Corporate Governance Framework Of the Malta Financial Services Authority.*

[28] Notice, for example, how Annual Reports often make constant reference to increases (or otherwise) in the number of new licences, and classifications thereof, as issued in every year of operating.

[29] Muscat Azzopardi (2019).

References

Barnier M (2010) Barnier reassures City bankers. . . . Malta Today, March 3
Blair M et al (2001) Blackstone's Financial Services & Markets Act 2000. Blackstone Press Ltd, London
Braithwaite J (2002) Restorative justice and responsive regulation. Oxford University Press, NYK
Consiglio JA (2006a) History of banking in Malta. Progress Press, Malta
Consiglio JA (2006b) Privatisation of financial services in the EU CEECs – relating the analysis to the case of a small island nation. Ph.D thesis, University of Malta
Fabri D (2006) A single unified supervisory authority for financial services in Malta and beyond – some legal and regulatory issues. Id-Dritt, University of Malta, Law Students Society, vol XIX
Gauci S (1999) Regulation of international banking. Ph.D thesis, University of Bristol
Kagan RA (1982) with Bardach E. – Going by the book: the problem of regulatory unreasonableness. Temple University Press, NYK & London
Lieber RJ (2008) Foreign policy. Routledge
Moran M (1986) Theories of regulation and changes in regulation; the case of financial markets. Polit Stud XXXIV:185–201
Muscat Azzopardi N (2019) The reputation of regulation. Times of Malta, June 28
O'Dea J (2020) Governance has to be good. Times of Malta, Nov 6
Quinn W, Turner JD (2020) Boom and bust. Cambridge University Press
Said M (2021) Too many legal rules. Times of Malta, Dec 22
Scicluna L, Seychell S, Spiteri J, Grima S (2019) The Maltese financial services industry's perception on the regulators: an empirical analysis. Eur Res Stud J XXII(1):16–56
Tham E, Lim BK (2015) After market crash, China mulls single super-regulator. Times of Malta, Nov 18
Zammit L (2020) Governance for the public sector. Times of Malta, Nov 6, 2020

John A. Consiglio Ph.D., was a professional banker for over 42 years with Barclays, MidMed, and HSBC banks in Malta. He studied at the Universities of Rome, Manchester Business School, Wales, New York, and Malta. After retiring he became an academic at the University of Malta, and was also a Governor on the Board of the Malta Financial Services Authority. He was also for ten years Chairman of the National Fiscal Board of Special Commissioners. He presently chairs the Revenue Remissions Supervisory Board and is a member of the MFSA's Resolutions Committee which implements the EU's BRRD. He is author of several books and published studies on banking history, financial regulation, and economic issues. He is a Fellow of the London Chartered Institute of Banking and Finance and was its President in Malta for several years.

Public/Private Risk Financing Innovation: The Case of Government Self-Insurance Risk Pools in the United States

Peter C. Young

Abstract Innovative practices are not often associated with local authorities, and certainly not very small public bodies (villages, schools, towns), but in the USA the success of local government self-insurance pools flies in the face of that notion. Over 75,000 (out of a total of 84,000) local bodies have come to participate in pools and—indeed—they were collectively/collaboratively responsible for their creation. Starting in 1974, these pools have provided risk financing across most traditional lines of insurance—property, liability, life, and a range of specialty lines. In fact, reinsurance pools have also emerged; pools of pools it might be said. Perhaps most significantly, many of these pools have extended their activities well beyond risk financing and have become what might be called risk management pools. As such, the real innovation may not just be seen in providing a myriad of risk coverages to small public bodies but to providing relatively advanced risk management programs to thousands of these bodies; bodies that otherwise simply would not have the capacity to take on these activities themselves. In achieving this range of sophistication, the case is easily made that pooling is the most important example of public sector innovation in USA local governments.

Keywords Group self-insurance pools · Public sector innovation · Public risk management · Adaptive practices · Public risk financing

1 Introduction

The public sector has long presented challenges for the insurance industry. While the oft-cited argument continues to resonate that the public sector presents obstacles through insurance procurement processes, and other management and controls requirements, other more fundamental factors seem more influential. Among other key features of the public sector is its role as the 'risk manager of last resort' for

P. C. Young (✉)
University of St. Thomas--Opus College of Business, Minneapolis, MN, USA
e-mail: pcyoung@stthomas.edu

M. Lima Rego, S. Grima (eds.), *Cross-Disciplinary Impacts on Insurance Law*, AIDA Europe Research Series on Insurance Law and Regulation 8,
https://doi.org/10.1007/978-3-031-38526-1_5

society. This suggests a wide and varying exposure to threats (and opportunities), with emergent challenges resting just over the horizon. Add to this the fact that many of society's most pressing threats—pandemics, military adventurism, climate change—are complex and do not align with political borders. This suggests that very often only collaborative action can lead to effective responses.

The need for innovation is evident, and—to be clear—technological advances such as AI and Big Data are making major adaptive/innovative contributions to assessing and addressing risks across all boundaries. Here, however, the chapter examines a fifty-year experiment in what ultimately might be called public/private collaborative risk management. More commonly referred to as risk pools or group self-insurance pools, their longevity is suggestive of a successful innovation in response to crises in risk financing. However they are also illustrative of what might be called an innovation platform, that is, a space where the commercial insurance industry was able to produce innovations of its own. The story of pooling is an underexamined topic in its own right, but here it is presented as a case study for innovation within the public sector that ultimately yielded a range of opportunities for innovation/adaptation within the commercial insurance sector.

Two initial points deserve mention. First is the popular view that governments are unable to be innovative due to a number of constraints—legal and philosophical factors, the nature of the work and responsibilities, the structure of public bodies and the connectivity between those bodies and the public they serve. This chapter offers a considered look at this issue, arriving at a view that while there are institutional, legal, and political constraints, risk management is a centralized role for public organizations. Government is risk management.

Second, the emergence of pools reveals a line of thinking that connects directly with research on leadership for organizational adaptability and on complex adaptive systems. While an examination of complexity and adaptability serves as something of a subtext in this chapter, it is worth highlighting here that the concept of "independent agents operating/innovating/adapting within networks" features prominently in the story of pooling, suggesting that whatever conclusions are drawn in this chapter must recognize the organic foundations of pooling as a phenomenon. Command-and-control leadership and practice does not play much of a role in the emergence and evolution of pooling.

So, pooling is an innovation. But the ultimate matter of concern here is pooling's role as an innovation platform for both the public sector and the commercial insurance sector.

2 Setting the Scene

2.1 Two Adjacent Developments

In order to understand present thinking on pools this chapter begins with brief consideration of two related developments—developments, each of which could warrant an entire book, but which cannot be ignored as they provide contextual insight for understanding the need for and influencing factors in innovation.

2.1.1 The Evolving Nature of Risk Management

Over the past twenty years it has been possible to argue that the nature of risk management has undergone a 'swerve.'[1] That is, by virtue of the evolutionary track it has followed, risk management has—rather unexpectedly—become something different. Michael Power[2] provided an early insight into this unanticipated change, arguing that—to paraphrase—the risk management of everything might easily become the risk management of nothing; but others have offered similar critiques.[3] It is useful to understand this change as it reconstitutes the playing field for both pools and the commercial insurance world.

Risk management is a field of study and practice that emerged in the late 1940s (narrower antecedent functions had existed prior to that time). Snider offered an early attempt to conceptualize risk management as a practice by framing private sector risk management around insurance-buying.[4] What is significant about this initial orientation was (1) its establishment of *risk* (measurable uncertainty) as the central concern, (2) that this—in turn—focused on assessing and addressing *threats* (largely ignoring upside risks, that is, opportunities), and finally (3) that the obvious focus was *insurable risks*—a subset of all measurable uncertainties that present sufficient data to support insurance pricing. This view has altered somewhat, but its imprint is seen in the continuing view of risk management as a finance oriented, systems and controls measure keyed to dealing with threats to an organization.[5]

2.1.2 Expansion and Integration

Over time an increasing sophistication among practitioners introduced alternative risk financing possibilities[6] and an expanding range of proactive risk controls.[7] This included loss prevention initiatives like workplace health and safety programs, business continuity management, supply chain management, disaster preparedness and crisis management. [8] Developments in adjacent fields, including operations management, introduced methods such as total quality management (TQM) that

[1] Andersen and Young (2022).
[2] Power (2009), pp. 849–855.
[3] Miller (2009), pp. 157–180.
[4] Snider (1956), pp. 30–35.
[5] Williams et al. (1998).
[6] Punter (1999); Weiss (2007), pp. 31–45.
[7] Schmit and Roth (1990), pp. 455–470.
[8] Crockford (1982), pp. 169–179; Haimes (1992), pp. 314–321; Dickinson (2001), pp. 360–366.

were adapted for risk management.[9] While these innovations and adaptations were important advances for risk management, they retained a primary focus on measurable exposures that present the possibility of losses. In the initial phases of this expansion, it was common for these various technical functions to not communicate with one another. But the idea of integration slowly emerged, first promoted by finance theorizing and practices.

Financial risk management emerged in the 1970s as a major development of the field to include consideration of more complex credit, foreign exchange, interest rate, commodity price, and investment exposures.[10] New tools, generally identified as *derivatives*, enabled diversification of economic exposures and fostered levered investments in highly complex positions.[11] In addition to these benefits, however, the complexity of such derivative portfolios has often made it difficult for top managers to understand the risk exposure these tools introduced—e.g. the1994 bankruptcy of Orange County in California.[12]

Nonetheless, the diversification perspectives inspired a view that risk management requires an integrated enterprise-wide orientation to effectively determine aggregated corporate exposures.[13] This unitary risk management rationale was shown to improve the ability to consistently assess the riskiness of corporate investments where risk-adjusted returns of internal capital allocations form a basis to optimize shareholder value.[14] It also fully introduced the idea that risk management involved the pursuit of *opportunities* as well as the mitigation of *threats*.

Actual practices were evolving in a similar direction. By the 1990s risk management practices could be described as involving a range of technical functions including insurance-buying, financial risk management, risk monitoring, IT security, and quality controls. This growing collection of risk management activities prompted consideration of how to better integrate specialized functions to avoid overlaps and gain operating efficiencies.[15] This move toward integration ultimately led to the emergence of Enterprise Risk Management (ERM) frameworks.[16] It might be argued that the advancement of ERM benefited from a convergence of theory and practice, in that practitioner adaptations were reinforced by a more theoretically-based rationale for integrated and holistic risk management. Critical to this chapter, however, is the fact that no comparable rationale has emerged in the public management sphere—nor in reality anywhere outside the world of publicly-traded firms.[17]

---

[9] Hall (1992).

[10] Christoffersen (2011).

[11] Pernell et al. (2017), pp. 511–541.

[12] Nocco and Stulz (2006), pp. 8–20; Halstead et al. (2004), pp. 293–315.

[13] Doherty (1985).

[14] Nocco and Stulz (2006), pp. 8–20.

[15] Haimes (1992), pp. 314–321.

[16] Beasley et al. (2005), pp. 521–531.

[17] Hinna et al. (2018), pp. 110–128.

2.1.3 Enterprise Risk Management

The ERM frameworks formalized integrative risk management practices through various guidelines or standards, adding—at least indirectly—enforceable requirements to existing theoretical and practical motives. Two particular frameworks have become predominant and influential.[18] The Committee of Sponsoring Organizations of the Treadway Commission (COSO) defined ERM as *"a process, effected by an entity's board of directors, management and other personnel, applied in strategy-setting and across the enterprise, designed to identify potential events that may affect the entity, and manage risks to be within its risk appetite, to provide reasonable assurance regarding the achievement of entity objectives."*[19] The International Organization for Standardization (ISO) describes ERM in a similar manner, although it is viewed as a more 'principles based' approach, which arguably makes the framework more generally applicable across sectors.[20]

In the US, COSO became associated with the Sarbanes-Oxley Act of 2002 (SOX) as it was interpreted as providing authoritative guidance for compliance with SOX.[21] SOX legislation[22] was a reaction to major corporate scandals at the time—e.g., Enron, Tyco International and WorldCom. COSO itself emerged from the professional accounting and auditing communities, so it is not a particular surprise that its ERM framework is centred on internal control processes where adherence to the ERM practices often became conceived as an internal audit responsibility.[23] Excepting COSO, many frameworks around the world subsequently folded into ISO 31000.[24] Both COSO and ISO 31000 have been updated.[25]

---

[18]COSO (2004); ISO (2009) *Risk Management – Principles and Guidelines* [ISO 31000]. International Organization for Standardization. Accessed November 1, 2019. https://www.iso.org/iso-31000-risk-management.html.

[19]Moeller (2007).

[20]ISO (2009) *Risk Management – Principles and Guidelines* [ISO 31000]. International Organization for Standardization. Accessed November 1, 2019. https://www.iso.org/iso-31000-risk-management.html; ISO (2018) *Risk Management - ISO 31000 Update*. International Organization for Standardization. Accessed November 1, 2019. https://www.iso.org/iso-31000-risk-management.html.

[21]Tsay (2010), pp. 52–57.

[22]United States Congress. 2002. H.R.3763 - *Sarbanes-Oxley Act of 2002*. Accessed August 10, 2019. https://www.congress.gov/bill/107th-congress/house-bill/3763.

[23]Williamson (2007), pp. 1089–1119.

[24]IRM. 2002. *A Risk Management Standard* – published jointly by the Institute of Risk Management (IRM), the Association of Insurance and Risk Managers (AIRMIC) and the Public Risk Management Association (Alarm). https://www.theirm.org/media/6827/arms_2002_irm.pdf; AS/NZS 4360:2004:: Standards New Zealand https://www.standards.govt.nz/shop/asnzs-43602004; ISO. 2009. *Risk Management – Principles and Guidelines* [ISO 31000]. International Organization for Standardization. Accessed November 1, 2019. https://www.iso.org/iso-31000-risk-management.html.

[25]COSO. 2017. *Enterprise Risk Management – Integrating with Strategy and Performance* (Executive Summary). Committee of Sponsoring Organizations of the Treadway Commission. Accessed

The emergence of COSO and ISO 31000 have been hugely impactful in shaping both thinking and practice regarding ERM. However, as Power[26] and others have observed, there are difficulties in achieving the vision. [27] One central barrier appears to be the holistic aspirations of ERM where it declares an interest in a vast and expanding range of non-quantitative and non-financial uncertainties—uncertainties, unknowns, complexities—that prove impervious to the application of conventional financial management, control, and decision-making techniques.[28] This arguably provides the conditions for a 'swerve' in risk management, as ERM seeks to maintain the view that it is both a continuation and an extension of traditional approaches—oriented around financial and accounting concerns—while nevertheless also asserting that risk management serves a more wide-ranging purpose not really captured in conventional theorizing and practice.[29]

2.1.4 The Emergence of Risk Leadership

The emerging concept of risk leadership might be seen as a technical advancement on ERM, but it is very early days. A few comments are warranted, however, because several parts of the pooling story feature the role of leadership.

One adjustment to the early ERM templates specified the integrative function of a central coordinating risk management office, which also introduced the formal role of a Chief Risk Officer (CRO) as leading the expected risk governance processes.[30] The CRO title was first observed in the mid-1990s[31] but the need for a CRO position only received serious attention after the major corporate scandals in the early 2000s.[32] The global financial crisis 2007–2009, and—not least—the collapse of Lehman Brothers, served as a motivation for further reviews of the risk governance processes in financial institutions.[33] Pronouncements by the Basel Committee on Banking Supervision and Organization for Economic Co-operation and Development[34] further solidified the importance of the CRO.

May 1, 2021. https://www.coso.org/; ISO. 2018. *Risk Management - ISO 31000 Update*. International Organization for Standardization. Accessed November 1, 2019. https://www.iso.org/iso-31000-risk-management.html.

[26] Power (2009), pp. 849–855.

[27] Gordon et al. (2009), pp. 301–327; Dickinson (2001), pp. 360–366; Lim et al. (2017), pp. 75–90; Lundqvist (2014), pp. 393–429; McShane et al. (2011), pp. 641–658.

[28] Slywotzky and Drzik (2005), pp. 78–91.

[29] Paape and Speklé (2012), pp. 533–564.

[30] Liebenberg and Hoyt (2003), pp. 37–52.

[31] Lam (2003).

[32] Grant and Visconti (2006), pp. 361–383; Kallio (2007), pp. 165–175.

[33] McDonald and Robinson (2009).

[34] BIS. 2010. *Principles for Enhancing Corporate Governance*. Basel Committee on BankingSupervision, Bank for International Settlements. Basel, Switzerland; BIS. 2020. History of the Basel Committee, Bank for International Settlements. Bank for International Settlements.

Interestingly, consideration of what a CRO actually is managing has produced pressure to better understand (1) what it means to lead in response to complexity, risk, and uncertainty, and (2) where the CRO 'vantage point' resides in the organization and how s/he influences the seemingly diverse and widely distributed practices? It is these considerations that have triggered the view that a CRO is just one particular type of leader. Rather, leaders operate at all levels of an organization, community, or society and they may also assume risk management roles, which has led to the introduction of *risk leaders* and *risk leadership* to serve as a more generalizable terminology.[35] A provisional description of risk leadership might be:

> Risk leadership, consistent with all leadership, anticipates a moral relationship between leaders, followers, and other stakeholders that recognizes and accounts for the presence of contextual factors. Key characteristics of that relationship are that it is trust-based, attuned to rights and responsibilities, and includes a recognition of the emotional dimension and a commitment to the common good. It differs from other leadership concepts in the technical focus, which is to thoughtfully engage the challenges driven by the presence of complexity, risk, uncertainty and the unknown.[36]

2.1.5 Focus on Public Sector Risk Management

The first thing to establish regarding public risk management in the US is the profound presence of *collaborative risk management*, in the form of risk pooling, which will become the central subject of interest for the balance of the chapter. Upwards of 80% of all governmental entities participate in pools, which offer risk financing solutions of course, but also varying levels of risk management services.[37] This would logically, and correctly, lead to the conclusion that non-collaborative risk management is largely the provenance of federal government agencies, state governments, and large localities (roughly speaking, communities with over 100,000–150,000 residents).

Public practices outside pooling. Early efforts to implement risk management in public organizations focused on threats to physical assets—fire, theft, and motor vehicle accidents—due largely to broad exemptions from legal liability.[38] Gradual erosion of legal immunities, alongside transfer of responsibilities to local governments has been judged as a key influence in the adoption of risk management practices.[39]In the 1970s growing liability exposure led to dramatic increases in

Accessed January 20, 2020 on https://www.bis.org/bcbs/history.htm; OECD. 2010, 2015. Principles of Corporate Goverance. Organization for Economic Cooperation and Development. Accessed September 10, 2019 on https://www.oecd.org/corporate/principles-corporate-governance/.

[35] Holberton (2019).

[36] Andersen and Young (2020).

[37] Association of Governmental Risk Pools—AGRIP. 2021. Accessed August 15, 2021. https://www.agrip.org.

[38] Olson (1979), pp. 485–504.

[39] Todd (1969), pp. 285–295; Posner (1998); Szymendera (2016).

insurance premiums, and—in many instances—insurance was simply unavailable. This crisis led to a major public risk management innovation, risk pooling. [40]

Developments in Europe have been somewhat comparable—excepting the pooling phenomenon—resulting in broadly similar public sector risk management conditions today.[41] Many European countries have mutual insurance companies specifically focused on government entities, which has made access to insurance coverage in the market less problematic. And note that the European mutuals also began in response to difficulties obtaining commercial insurance.[42] Despite a less restrictive legal environment and other differences with the US, changing societal expectations,[43] partially influenced by the European Union,[44] have been motives. Alongside those factors particular concerns about environmental threats and emergency responses have driven a focus towards more formal and structured risk management approaches.[45]

Risk management efforts in government institutions mostly adopt control-based approaches—in accordance with a traditional risk management cycle of identification, assessment, handling, and monitoring of exposures. This is partly a consequence of budgeting and auditing standards imposed in the US by the Government Accountability Office, and in the EU by the Internal Audit Service. This, in turn, has led governmental bodies to adopt risk management practices that conform to private sector risk management standards—including most recently the established Enterprise Risk Management, or ERM, frameworks.[46] The few surveying studies of public sector risk management are mainly undertaken by professional associations and consultancies that monitor members or clients. These limited windows on public practices reveal mainly adoption of traditional risk management approaches—primarily, but not exclusively, focused on pre-ERM technical practices.[47]

In sum, public risk management practices (even when including the particularities of pooling risk management efforts) tend to rely on the transference of private sector practices despite the fact that the public sector operates in a distinctly different environment—different risk exposures and responses, goals and purposes that rest

---

[40] Young (1989), pp. 40–54; Young and Reed (1995), pp. 96–112.

[41] OECD 2021. Public Integrity Handbook: Risk Management. Accessed January 10, 2021. https://www.oecd-ilibrary.org/sites/ebbed075-en/index.html?itemId=/content/component/ebbed075-en.

[42] Blanchard (1916), p. 430.

[43] Beck (1989), pp. 86–103.

[44] Jeynes (2012).

[45] Federation of European Risk Management Associations (FERMA) 2021. www.ferma.eu; Young et al. (2022).

[46] Bracci et al. (2021), pp. 205–223; Braig et al. (2011); Bullock et al. (2019), pp. 75–87; Association of Federal Enterprise Risk Management (AFERM). www.AFERM.org.

[47] Public Risk Management Association. 2021. Resources. Accessed March 24, 2021. https://www.primacentral.org.; Association of Local Authority Risk Management (2021). ALARM (alarmrisk.co.uk); Public Risk Management Organization (PRIMO-Europe) 2021. https://primo-europe.eu; Association of Federal Enterprise Risk Management (AFERM). www.AFERM.org; Federation of European Risk Management Associations (FERMA) 2021. www.ferma.eu.

on an underlying requirement to balance political and economic objectives.[48] Fundamentally it seems important to observe that the public sector not only does risk management; it is risk management. There are two primary reasons for this.

2.1.6 Government Is a Risk Manager of Last Resort

Public risk management often is described as presenting three basic facets.[49] The *managerial* facet relates to the administrative aspects of risk management efforts. The second and third roles, *regulatory* and *stewardship* add distinct features to public risk management.

Moss[50] refers to government as, fundamentally, a risk regulator. This is seen in financial sector oversight, criminal law, taxation policy, social security, building codes, and obviously much more. Stewardship refers to values-based practices applied where private, non-governmental, public-sector institutions, and governmental bodies attempt to exert beneficial influences on communities, societies—and indeed—the planet.[51]

Underlying this view, Pesch[52] concludes that "*public administration involves two incompatible and even contradictory meanings ... the practice of public administration can be seen as an attempt to find a workable equilibrium between the two.*" He characterizes these incompatibilities as government's political and economic roles. The political role entails responsibility to structure society and maintain order to advance welfare and societal interests. The economic role rests on beliefs that a liberal society obliges government to act with restraint being mindful of individual citizen interests.[53]

2.1.7 Public Risks Are Categorically Different

From this line of reasoning certain risks may be deemed *public*; namely risks that:

- cannot be broadly distributed or transferred in consideration of social equity towards responsible parties able to bear the risk.
- produce externalities (or imbued with externalities and spillover effects) that cannot be captured in market-based pricing.
- are caused by political processes (from extreme events like social unrest to erosion of common values and public trust).

---

[48] Hinna et al. (2018), pp. 110–128; Smith and Fischbacher (2009), pp. 1–12.

[49] United Kingdom Strategy Unit (2002). Risk: Improving Government's Capability to Handle Risk and Uncertainty. London: Strategy Unit Report.

[50] Moss (2002).

[51] Holzmann and Kozel (2007), pp. 1–6; IRGC (2005).

[52] Pesch (2008), pp. 170–193.

[53] Moss (2002); Bozeman (2007).

- have catastrophic outcomes with wide-spread scope and impact—displaying high levels of uncertainty, e.g. climate change.
- threaten public order, exercise prevailing public values, or erode commonly accepted social and political processes.
- affect the value of public assets and the ability to perform public administrative functions while balancing political and economic concerns.[54]

Public risks provide a different context for risk management—so much so they appear categorically different from private sector exposures. The nature of risks, the legal, political, and moral dimensions as well as the scope and scale of outcomes suggest that direct appropriation of private sector risk management practices—while offering useful technical contributions—leaves serious shortcomings. The nature of public risks also go some way in explaining the difficulties commercial insurers face when interacting with public entities.

3 Risk Pools: An Innovation in Public Sector Risk Financing

Although a 1949 California law is sometimes cited as the opening chapter of the pooling story in the US, no risk pools were formed over the ensuing 25 years. Thus the more widely-accepted inception period for pooling is the years 1972–1974 when the Texas state legislature debated and then enabled counties, school districts, and municipalities to form three separate pools; pools which—more or less—simultaneously began operations in 1974.[55]

Since the 1970s risk pools have grown in size and number arriving at a point where they have become the dominant facilitator of risk financing for local governments.[56] Further, they have had a major impact on the practice of risk management in—particularly—small public bodies. Pools do also exist in Canada and Australia, with preexisting public sector mutual insurance companies in Europe standing as both precursors and analogs to pooling.

3.1 Antecedents: European Public Risk Mutuals

Reference to European mutuals provides a wider context for understanding pools. Long-serving mutual insurance companies specializing in public bodies can be

[54] Young (2016).

[55] Mendoza (2014), p. 53.

[56] Association of Governmental Risk Pools—AGRIP. 2021. Accessed August 15, 2021. https://www.agrip.org.

found in several European countries. The historical motives for their creation vary, but in most cases a failure of commercial insurance markets to meet the needs of public entities was a catalyzing feature. The UK offers one particular example, where Municipal Mutual Insurance was formed in 1903 in response to exactly that issue.[57] Due to the failure of an ambitious expansion agenda, Municipal Mutual collapsed in the early 1990s and a partial, somewhat artificially constructed commercial insurance market emerged from the wreckage.[58]

Elsewhere, the fortunes of mutuals have been brighter. KommuneForsikring in Denmark (now part of Gjensidige), along with mutuals in Norway and Ireland, and the unusual public captive insurance approach adopted in Sweden illustrate a longer-term commitment to collaborative risk financing.[59]

European mutuals are highly related to pools, for though they are considered legally incorporated insurance carriers they share many conceptual and functional features. For example, mutuals and pools both:

- Are owned by the policyholders (the public entities that buy coverage serve as the owners and directors of the organization, though the Danish mutual now has a different ownership structure).
- Specialize in addressing the risks of public entities.[60]
- Focus on sharing the organization's profitability with its owners (in the form of lower premiums, dividends, or both).
- Are subjected to different treatment from conventional insurers by regulators and the courts (though this is less the case in Europe).
- Tend to view their role as including risk management services in addition to risk financing.[61]

3.2 US Public Entity Risk Pooling

Since 1970, local governments in the US have experienced two major insurance crises, the first occurring in the mid-1970s and the second in the mid-1980s. These crises were the result of wider cyclical commercial insurance market factors, the states of the economy preceding each episode, insurance industry management practices, episodic large-loss experiences, and inherent insurance pricing

[57] Hood and Young (2005), parts 6 and 7.

[58] Fone and Young (2000).

[59] Kommunal Landspensjonskasse—KLP 2021. Accessed August 11, 2021. http://www.klp.no; KommuneForsikring—KF. Accessed August 12, 2021). https://www.cobx.org; Irish Public Bodies 2021. Accessed August 10, 2021. https://ipb.ie/; Swedish Public Captives. Accessed August 12, 2021. https://www.captiveinsurancetimes.com.

[60] Hood and Young (2005), parts 6 and 7.

[61] European Institute for Risk Management—EIRM. 2009. "*Public Risk Financing in Europe*." Accessed July 20, 2021. www.eirm.net.

problems.[62] The riskiness (at a minimum, the perceived riskiness) of local governments—owing to significant changes in tort liability laws—undoubtedly was a factor as well.[63]

The rhythms of the insurance underwriting cycle are well studied,[64] but the particularities of public entities' experiences were especially severe, resulting in a 20-year period in which local governments had been able to afford commercial insurance (especially liability insurance) only at significant cost—if insurance was available at all.[65]

In response, local governments, governmental associations, and even state governments sought and obtained legal authorization to create alternative risk financing mechanisms to provide coverage for local governments. These mechanisms, then commonly referred to as *group self-insurance pools*—to legally distinguish them from commercial insurers—enabled local governments within a given state to pool together risks and resources to finance the costs of fortuitous losses. Initially, the pools provided mainly general liability and workers' compensation coverage for members. However, pooling today provides a range of coverages, from property coverage to employee benefits and most things between.[66] Indeed, even reinsurance pools operate today.[67]

A 1988 study of pools found that approximately 200 public risk financing pools operated in the United States.[68] Those pools, with an estimated aggregate membership of between 15,000 and 20,000 entities, were present in almost all regions of the country (although more than half of the pools were located in California). Nearly all pools were homogeneous as to membership; that is, school districts pooled with school districts, counties with counties. The pools were homogeneous as to member population/size as well. Almost all pool participants were associated with small communities. The pools themselves, however, varied widely in terms of size; the smallest pools reported three to five participating governments and the largest reported 1100 to 1300 members.In 1994 a follow-up study was conducted to understand the degree to which the pooling environment had changed.[69] The findings indicated there were at least 400 pool funds in operation, and that these pools had an aggregate membership of 30,000 to 35,000 local entities. Pools still remained the preserve of small public bodies.By 1994, pooling had more evenly spread throughout the United States. More than half of the pools were sponsored by associations (leagues of cities, counties, school board associations, etc.) and the

[62] Abraham (2001), pp. 85–109.

[63] Olson (1979), pp. 485–504.

[64] Cummings et al. (1987), pp. 246–262; Weiss (2007), pp. 31–45.

[65] Young and Reed (1995), pp. 96–112.

[66] Association of Governmental Risk Pools—AGRIP. 2021. Accessed August 15, 2021. https://www.agrip.org.

[67] National League of Cities. Accesses July 24, 2021. https://www.nlcmutual.com/.

[68] Young (1989), pp. 40–54.

[69] Young and Reed (1995), pp. 96–112.

estimated aggregate member contributions were thought to be about $5.5 billion. Although no further sector-wide studies have been undertaken, by 2021 an estimated 450–500 pool funds operated in the United States and evidence suggests that approximately 75,000 local governments purchase one or more coverages through pools. The net contributions were estimated to be $25 billion in 2020.[70]

Here it is helpful to pause to consider a question that becomes central to the purpose of this chapter. Given the seeming success of pools, why did commercial insurers have such difficulty insuring public organizations? At one level it could be argued that pools, owned by their local government members, somehow better understood the public sector and, when properly incentivized, better exerted controls over loss experience.[71] Alongside this, the option for members to leave their pool to avoid loss costs was simply not a serious option—at least in the sense that any problems or outstanding claims would directly revert to the departing members. So the interests, motives, and stakes were different, and—perhaps—this may offer an adequate answer.

3.3 Governance, Operations, Performance

Authorization and Formation. Risk financing pools would have been difficult, if not impossible, to form until state legislatures permitted an exemption from prohibitions on the commingling of public funds.[72] The State of California established a *joint powers authority* statutory provision in 1949, which, though it did not lead to the immediate formation of pools in that state, eventually served as a template—note that over half of all pools in the mid-1980s were based in California.[73] Owing to the early influence of California law and pool formations, a majority of pools throughout the US are organized under joint powers agreements.

Related to the matter of legal status is the question of sponsorship or pool ownership. About half of all pools were formed by a sponsoring association such as a state municipal league or association of counties. Of the non-association pools, the majority were established by cooperative agreements between local entities, though there also are instances of specific individuals or organizations (e.g., a local insurance agent) serving as a catalyst for pool formation.[74] If any current trend can be detected, it has been in non-association pool formations, though this

---

[70] Association of Governmental Risk Pools—AGRIP. 2021. Accessed August 15, 2021. https://www.agrip.org.

[71] Pumford (1986).

[72] Mendoza (2014), p. 53.

[73] Pumford (1986).

[74] Young (1989), pp. 40–54.

just may be due to the fact that most all state-wide associations have already formed pools.[75]

Pools versus Pool Funds. Initially most pools focused on single issues—legal liability or workers' compensation/employers' liability. However, over time many pools expanded into a wider range of coverages--property, boiler & machinery, employee benefits, and more. In the early years, the terms 'monoline' (single coverage), multi-line (multiple related coverages), and 'fleet' (a wide range of coverages) pools served as a typology. Those terms still are employed, but it is more useful to understand the distinction between pools and pool funds.Most joint powers legislation took care to place limitations on the commingling of financial resources—that is, commingling between and among pool members.[76] Consequently, while it was permissible for, say, ten municipalities to create a fund for workers' compensation coverage, the commingling across types of coverage (e.g. workers' compensation and property) was either prohibited or limited to special circumstances. The concern with this possibility was that members might not want all coverages on offer but would still be required to share in the pool of all risks.

There is a particular technical point to emphasize about commingling. Regardless of other considerations, risk pooling (commingling) relies on implicit or explicit actuarial principles. While pools were legally defined as something distinct from commercial insurance, in fact the only practical way to develop a workable financing structure in the early days was through the adoption of principles of insurance pricing and commercial data. Partly this was due to the influence of consulting actuaries and brokers advising on pool formation, but it is difficult to imagine risk pools operating otherwise.

The existence of pool member homogeneity is an indirect way commingling is influenced by both legal and actuarial considerations. While aggregated pool participation reveals virtually all types of local entities, individual pools tend to be specific to types of members. A review has found pools focused on municipalities, counties, townships, school districts, as well as special districts such as county appraisal districts, housing authorities, municipal utility districts, regional special education consortia, port authorities, hospitals, special services cooperatives, water districts, drainage districts, zoological societies, nutrition councils, and river authorities. However, recent evidence of some relaxation in requirements for pool homogeneity has been noted and deserves further investigation.[77]

The preceding describes *pools,* but what about *pool funds*? An early solution to the problem of commingling across coverage types was the creation of separate pool funds for each coverage offered. And thus a pool might control several funds. The term *pool fund* does lead to a counting problem in describing the pooling world,

---

[75] Association of Governmental Risk Pools—AGRIP. 2021. Accessed August 15, 2021. https://www.agrip.org.

[76] Cypher and Grinnell (2007).

[77] Association of Governmental Risk Pools—AGRIP. 2021. Accessed August 15, 2021. https://www.agrip.org.

however. In measuring participation in the pooling sector an answer scanning legal filings for pool formation would produce one estimate. According to AGRIP, that method would yield approximately 250 pools.[78] However, as noted, within any one pool multiple funds might exist. Using pool funds as the measure, it is likely there may be up to 500 pool funds. Add to this the fact that a local government might participate in one or more of those funds (is this then counted as one participant in total or as one participant for each pool fund?). Further complicating matters, one local government might participate in more than one entirely separate pool.

Although it may seem surprising, obtaining a full and accurate count of pool participation thus remains somewhat elusive. The oft-repeated statements that 'nearly 80%' or 'over 75,000 local governments' participate in pools, should be accepted with some caution. It is easy to suspect that there is double-counting and some other inaccuracies in play. Nevertheless, this does not detract from the profound transformation of risk financing in the US public sector. It seems safe to assume the vast majority of the 84,000 public entities are involved in pooling.[79]

Pool Governance. Almost all pools have a governance structure organized around a board of directors/chief executive. The board typically consists of representatives of pool membership and are elected in about half the cases and appointed in about a quarter of the cases. Some pool boards are partially elected and partially appointed. The relationship of the board to the pool varies in a number of key ways, but the distinction between sponsored (by associations) and non-sponsored pools offers one illustration in which board/pool relationships may differ. Non-sponsored pool boards derive from the membership and are therefore presumed to be directly responsive to members. Sponsored pool boards derive from pool membership as well but may also be selected from the wider sponsoring organization. Frequently, for instance, the chairperson of a pool board is the executive director of the sponsoring organization.The issue of conflict of interests/purposes may arise (and has arisen) in sponsored pool settings. Association interests and member interests (even pool management interests) do not always coincide. As one example of this point, risk financing pools ordinarily rely on the principle of rate and risk relationships—that is, within some structured approach to pricing, higher risks pay more for coverage than do lower risks. This rate "discrimination" is a convention of risk pooling but occasionally associations may view pools as a *benefit* of association membership, suggesting that members should not be discriminated against. It is unclear how such issues are resolved, and pool governance is a subject requiring additional investigation.

Pool Management. There is a wide degree of variation and size in pool staffs. Research suggests that on average pools have a staff of six. However, the largest

---

[78] Association of Governmental Risk Pools—AGRIP. 2021. Accessed August 15, 2021. https://www.agrip.org.

[79] Association of Governmental Risk Pools—AGRIP. 2021. Accessed August 15, 2021. https://www.agrip.org.

pools might have a staff of 100, while the smallest may have only a single part-time administrator.[80]

The specific in-house/outsourcing dynamic has been subject to circumstantial influences. For example, over time there has been a rather general movement away from early reliance on third party administrators providing a wide range of management services (e.g. claims management, actuarial and financial management, legal counsel, IT management, and so on), and toward greater use of in-house services. This is most likely to occur in larger pools, where the motives for doing so are argued to be better controls and coordination, as well as growing managerial confidence.

However, alongside this phenomenon the commercial insurance sector has responded. The 'unbundling' of insurance and risk services has allowed a range of managerial services to become available in ways that heretofore were not possible. Further 'gaining confidence' has been a two-way street. Pool managers have become more knowledgeable and confident in their capabilities, but likewise, pools have organized the public sector market, and so many of the uncertainties that influenced commercial insurers' prior understanding of public sector risks have moderated. For example, some commercial insurers now sell their coverages to pools; workers' compensation coverage serving as a rather ironic illustration of this change.[81] To be clear about this point, some pools have become group insurance buyers, and in fact some pools are completely managed by commercial third party providers.

It should be noted that there are several interesting questions about decisions to partner or outsource. Further comment will appear here, but two features are prominent with respect to in-house v. outsourcing. First, pools are themselves a product of outsourcing, as they exist in a quasi-public/nonprofit world and thus have something of a vendor status *vis á vis* the membership. Second, the processes of (and risks to) the outsourcing services is understood in only general terms—adherence to procurement rules, for example—but the particular issues are not well-studied.

Pool Financial Performance. Perhaps the key (or a key) question would be directed to evidence of financial performance. A simple answer might be that their long-term existence seems to demonstrate financial viability, and this observation cannot be dismissed out of hand. Nevertheless, very little study has been undertaken to provide a detailed assessment of financial performance for the pooling movement as a whole. Here, what currently may be said to describe the financial state of the pooling scene would include:

- It has been estimated that member contributions to pools totaled more than $25 billion in 2020.[82] Thus one observation is that pooling involves significant levels of public funds, which reflects thousands of individual governmental decisions to commit resources to pools.

---

80 Young and Reed (1995), pp. 96–112.

81 Safety National Mutual. Accessed August 15, 2021. https://www.sfmic.com/.

82 Association of Governmental Risk Pools—AGRIP. 2021. Accessed August 15, 2021. https://www.agrip.org.

- While commingling in a *fund* seems self-evident, there are different ways pools operate in terms of the actuarial management of those funds. Most commingle, but there are pools that do not commingle at some levels—or at all; *protected cell pools* segregate members into separate accounts, providing only some risk transference to the pool itself. Somewhat ironically these approaches track with one of the oldest forms of insurance in the US—the farm mutual.[83]
- Historically, pool rates were derived from insurance industry data—the Insurance Services Office, a rating bureau, in particular.[84] This was a natural decision since—at the outset—pools had no past data on which to estimate future claims, but also because the consulting actuaries who assisted pools in rate development had knowledge of and access to relevant information. Over time, however, pools have demonstrated some movement away from insurance industry-based pricing, and now rely to a larger degree on their own loss experience, as well as accumulated data from the pooling sector as a whole. As previously noted, the presence of consulting actuarial services provides both a technical understanding of financial performance, as well as a transference of a better understanding of financial management to pool managers.
- A member's contribution (known as the *premium* in commercial insurance—a term not customarily used, often not even allowed, in pooling) consists not just of the expected losses that will be paid, but also of the expenses and overhead charges for pool administration. Pool charges for expenses (*expense loading*) are similar to insurance methods but reveal some distinct differences. The principal differences are that (1) most pools do not have to pay federal or state income taxes, (2) most pools do not have to pay insurance premium taxes, (3) most pools do not have to make participation commitments to state guaranty funds, high-risk pools, or other arrangements mandated by a state insurance regulator, and (4) a number of pools do not have to make allowances for agent and broker commissions. These differences are not trivial and could—everything else being equal—account for a 10 to 20 percent difference between a pool's contribution rate and a comparable commercial insurer's premium.[85]
- In the most common commercial insurance transactions the premium paid is the sum total of what an insured owes the insurer under the contract. However, some cooperative (or mutual) types of insurers utilize an assessment feature to their pricing scheme, which means that the insurer could require additional contributions if losses exceed some predetermined level. That assessibility may be limited or unlimited. Most pools are assessable pools (more than 8 out of 10), and of those assessable pools, nearly 70 percent have unlimited assessment features. Refunding, rebating, and dividend distributions are other means by which contributions may be adjusted. A majority of pools use one or more of these tools to

---

[83] Wright et al. (1994), pp. 1–5.

[84] Public Risk Management Association—Pooling Section 1986. Interview with Harold Pumford, Head of the Pooling Section. Annual Conference, Boston MA. May 14–16.

[85] Young and Reed (1995), pp. 96–112.

offset the contribution costs if loss experience is favorable. Another widely used measure is discounting, whereby the pool discounts that initial contribution based on the supposition that the pool will be able to prevent losses from rising to a level that would warrant the undiscounted contribution.

- In 1992, the Governmental Accounting Standards Board (GASB) released Statement 10, which serves as a broad directive on pool accounting practices.[86] GASB 10 is almost universally adopted as the basis for issuing financial reports, which has gone a long way toward standardizing pool reporting and allowing for more transparency of pooling performance (at least for direct stakeholders). GASB 10 has not only promoted standardization but has had a significant effect on how pools reserve for losses, on how they report losses, and on matters related to investment returns, discounting, maintenance of surplus/contingency funds, and other financial issues.
- Since most pools are not taxable entities, financial analysis of pooling performance is not influenced by state or federal income tax considerations. This advantage over commercial insurance companies is offset by the restrictions that exist for investment of funds. Although insurance companies are subject to regulatory restrictions with respect to the riskiness of investments, public entity restrictions are even more stringent, and the standards that govern public-sector investment practices apply almost universally to pools.[87]
- Finally, it is worth remembering the return of commercial insurers to the public sector risk financing marketplace. Reinsurance and excess-loss insurers have played a role in insuring pools nearly from the beginning, but primary insurers have returned as well—to the extent that some pools are not really risk pools per se, but group purchasing pools. This suggests two things: first, commercial insurers see value in participating, and second, the reappearance of insurers implies something about the market as a whole. Pools appear to have made insuring public entities somehow more attractive.

It might be tempting to conclude that the financial performance of pooling is positive based on the preceding evidence. External actuarial assessments, along with independent audits and other indicators speak to that conclusion—at least as those assessments pertain to individual pools. However, with respect to the pooling community as a whole, there has been virtually no effort to expand analysis beyond individual pool experience. Further, there is some evidence of pool failures and there is further evidence that some pools have experienced crises, though details of their recovery stories are not well understood.

Therefore, while there is indirect evidence of positive financial performance, an overall assessment of pools has not been undertaken. Numerous assumptions cannot be tested—for example, comparisons of pooling financial performance across pools are difficult to construct, which then yields problems in

---

[86] Governmental Accounting Standards Board (2021). Accessed August 20, 2021. https://www.gasb.org/st/summary/gstsm10.html.

[87] Young and Reed (1995), pp. 96–112.

benchmarking and more formalized standards of practice? And it is likely that opacity prevents some questions from even being identified let alone asked. A good example would be the question of decision-making processes around assessments among pools. In sum, it seems possible to conclude that—in particular—pools could be judged to be performing successfully, but—in general—it is difficult to draw conclusions for the pooling sector as a whole.

3.3.1 Pooling as Risk Management

In the very early years of pooling considerable resistance arose—mainly from the insurance industry. The essence of that opposition was concern that public bodies were being permitted to compete unfairly and inappropriately in a private market. This argument contained an element of irony as the industry had largely abandoned the public sector on two occasions, but there is a philosophical argument regarding the appropriateness of governments competing—while possessing built in advantages—with commercial insurers.[88] Although this argument occasionally reappears a counterargument asserts local governments have a responsibility for *risk management* and that creating risk pools merely illustrated local governments' efforts to respond to a particular risk management problem.

This counterargument might be summarized as follows:

> The idea of pooling is simple in one sense, and technically complex in another. In the simpler sense pooling is a means of protection; if a group of individuals pool their time and effort, they can provide for a common response that is more effective than could be provided through individual initiative. This is an example of resource pooling, which commonly has the goal of extending capabilities. In the more complex sense, the pooling of risks, while offering some of the capacity-expanding features that resource pooling provides, focuses more on the matter of risk or uncertainty reduction. Pooling can improve predictability, stabilize budgeting and forecasting, and reduce fear and worry.[89]

The distinctions between *risk* and *resource pooling* are not always visible to the casual observer and, in fact, they do overlap. However, it seems important to recognize the two distinct outcomes possible through pooling: (1) The pool participants are able to achieve more than they can as individuals, and (2) uncertainty and risk can be reduced.

Employing actuarial principles, risk financing pools can structure financing arrangements to provide a stable flow of funds into the pool, funds that are adequate to cover the sporadic outflows that occur due to losses. However, even in the early days, pools were also expressly providing resource pooling. Initially this included a relatively narrow range of activities (pools advising on risk control measures and providing loss-recovery assistance), but over time the resource pooling activities extended into affiliated risk control measures. The expansion of the resource pooling

[88] Young (1989), pp. 40–54.

[89] Young (1989), pp. 40–54.

idea was further influenced by the examples of many unrelated public sector efforts at enhancing local public body capacities—mutual aid agreements, group purchase programs (for schoolbooks, auditing services, equipment), circuit-riding managers, regional cooperatives—all represented activities that seek to provide benefits by enhancing capacities, not necessarily from reducing uncertainty.[90]

Owing to the resource/risk pool line of reasoning, the justification emerged that the essential purpose of pools was providing *risk management* (*collaborative risk management*) to members. That is, the decision to provide risk financing was a specific risk management decision based on a response to circumstances that affected member communities' overall abilities to manage their risks. Pointedly, it was argued in the early days of pooling, if the commercial industry reentered the public sector market and offered attractive terms and conditions, the pools would buy commercial insurance instead of pooling their risks—but they would remain the risk managers of their members.

A number of pools now expressly follow this line of reasoning and thus it is important to acknowledge the emergence of what might be seen as a distinct (or at least idealized) pooling form—the *risk management pool*. In that capacity, the pool not only provides risk financing arrangements but also provides risk assessment, control, training, and management services. The evidence that the risk management pool idea has taken hold is visible today. Pools do engage commercial insurers to purchase insurance if the terms are attractive, do engage reinsurers and insurance brokers to acquire a range of technical services, and do employ third party administrators (actuarial consultancies, claims management providers for example) that specialize in serving pools.

However, it is here where a reminder of the earlier discussion of public sector risk management practices needs to directly connect with the risk management pool idea. As a conduit for risk management among thousands of local governments, pooling has an enormous impact. However, the practices that are followed within pools does appear to follow the more traditional insurable risk orientation first espoused by Snider in 1956, meaning that pools too are transferring private sector practices into the services they provide.

3.3.2 A Summary Assessment of Pooling

It is critical to re-state here that pools exist almost completely outside the boundaries of insurance regulation. As such, for insurance regulators pooling holds up a mirror to current insurance regulatory assumptions and practices. From a political standpoint, for example, a central question emerges: does the nature of public risk exposure introduce an argument for different legal and regulatory considerations, expectations, and conclusions? This, in turn, raises another question. Does different treatment—essentially one might say, granting permission for less transparency—

[90] Hazenberg et al. (2013).

directly contradict broader public sector transparency expectations and requirements: public access to records, open meetings, public reporting, sunshine/sunset laws?[91]

A review of the various enabling laws does find that transparency/reporting requirements were not prominently featured in early authorization and enabling legislation. This might to be due to the pressurized context of the insurance crises. Relatedly, recall that pools were defined as 'group self-insurance' arrangements—partly as a legislative work-around—and as a result were exempted from regulatory requirements normally imposed on risk financing (that is, insurance) organizations.[92] A few states, such as Wisconsin, New York, and Washington, however, do have some narrow regulatory requirements in place.[93]

Over time improvements in reporting were introduced—the aforementioned Governmental Accounting Standards Board (GASB) Statement 10 serves as an example.[94] Nevertheless, it must be conceded that pools exist in a regulatory 'gray space' which means that assessing overall pooling sector financial performance is not easily undertaken. It is possible this state of existence is not entirely unacceptable to pools. There have been occasional examples of sharp dealing in the pooling world so a lack of oversight or transparency could aid and abet such practices. Far more commonly, however, comfort in this gray area may be due to the prospects of increased managerial flexibilities, and obviously, the absence of compliance costs associated with regulation (and taxes). Early estimates suggested that the lack of formal regulation may have given pools up to a 15–20% pricing advantage when compared with commercial insurance.[95]

But is the right question being asked here? Pool-wide data may be painstakingly difficult to gather—albeit possible—but a point worth considering is whether conventional insurance metrics would be a relevant benchmark for analysis. It does seem that risk pooling can only be structured around conventional actuarial principles, but even there—in generally descriptive terms—pools only really align with mutual insurance companies—and in fact, only with the historic farm and factory mutuals.[96] This is to say that they function more as *spreading* 'timing risk', rather than providing loss *sharing* mechanisms. The distinction is a fine one, but as with farm mutuals a pool makes a good faith estimate of future claims, but often allows for additional—often unlimited—assessments to cover unexpected losses. The renewed involvement of commercial reinsurers and excess loss underwriters may have muted the need for such draconian assessments, but pool members are expected to be available to add additional funds when necessary. It is worth considering

[91] Kopits and Craig (1998); Palermo (2014), pp. 322–341.

[92] Young (1989), pp. 40–54.

[93] Randall (2021).

[94] Governmental Accounting Standards Board (2021). Accessed August 20, 2021. https://www.gasb.org/st/summary/gstsm10.html.

[95] Young (1989), pp. 40–54.

[96] Wright et al. (1994), pp. 1–5.

whether this implies that the member's *capacity to tax* (or to access public funds through intergovernmental appropriations and transfers) then serves as the ultimate source of excess loss financing, and indeed whether this possibly contributes to making pools categorically different from commercial insurance?[97]

Therefore, speculatively, pools should not be judged solely on actuarial principles. Pools are intended to provide continuity, a long-term orientation, and stability—some also might say "budget smoothing." In this sense, it may be better to consider pools to be a form of *social insurance*, where—yes—actuarial considerations are embedded, but where practical social/political considerations also are central objectives.[98] However, as pools also provide collaborative risk management, this role moves pools somewhat beyond the realm of social insurance into what may be called *social risk management*. Social Risk Management is a term in circulation within the academic and practitioner literature but has not generally been applied to pools.[99]

4 Discussion

4.1 Pools as Innovation

Pools represent a *prima facie* innovation for the simple reason that they did not exist before 1974, they proliferated, and continue to exist fifty years after their inception. The scale and scope of the pooling movement further indicates that this was not a unique or one-off innovative opportunity. All true, but a more clinical description of pools as an innovation is required.

A useful way to begin is to consider a wider interpretation of innovation and then to ask how it is seen to occur. Innovation and adaptation have been variously defined, but a reasonably acceptable summary would be that adaptation is a response to conditions that involves—largely—the reimagining, and/or restructuring and redeployment of existing means to address those conditions, while an innovation is—perhaps—a type of adaptation that involves the creation of heretofore non-existent means to address a condition.[100] The boundary line is not clear, so pools might—from varying vantage points—be described either as an adaptation or an innovation. Here this lack of precision does not disrupt consideration of pooling, so perhaps a provisional resolution of the terminology is to say that pools are an innovation that nevertheless also involve adaptations of existing resources.

How is innovation initiated? Previously, the initiating step of pooling innovation was described as the work (and inventiveness) of policy entrepreneurs, public sector

[97] Young (1989), pp. 40–54.
[98] Atkinson (1991), pp. 113–131.
[99] Holzmann and Kozel (2007), pp. 1–6; IRGC (2005).
[100] Grobman (2005), pp. 350–382.

associations, and state government leaders and legislators. Significantly, the presence of so-called insurance crises was a catalyzing agent, which resonates with the ERM adoption literature where ‘response to crisis’ has been cited as the most frequent motive for adoption.[101]

Response to crisis is a motive, but how was the response initiated? In accordance with relevant academic literature on crisis management, leadership plays an essential role. It is true that self-organizing responses sometimes exist in place of explicit leadership. (Kellerman 2008) In non-crisis situations, both leader-influenced and self-organizing adaptations can exist—often side-by-side. In both crisis and in general conditions, leadership on innovation, or Leadership for Organizational Adaptation (LOA) research offers some insights into innovation initiation.[102]

LOA envisions three interlocking leadership components —Entrepreneurial Leadership, Enabling Leadership, and Operational Leadership— which considers both leadership roles in innovation as well as the nature of those innovation processes, often referenced as *dynamic capabilities*. Enabling Leadership presupposes a ‘space’ where entrepreneurial innovations and adaptions engage operational considerations to translate ideas into action

Entrepreneurial Leadership emphasizes the generation and development of new ideas—including adaptive and innovative responses to threats or opportunities (in both a reactive and proactive sense) are observable in or outside the system/organization. Enabling Leadership focuses on the conversion of ideas into functional adaptations and innovations. Operational Leadership illuminates an effort to transpose the organization into an adaptive mode.

In an ecosystem, basic laws of nature provide system structure and coherence. Organizations and communities, as social systems, are different. They are constructed systems susceptible to human interference, constrained only by morality, social policing, and the enforceable rules that may pertain. So, Operational Leadership, also serves a ‘regulatory’ function—maintaining overall organization structure, integrity, and functionality in compliance with laws and social norms. In both LOA and wider ranging study of Complex Adaptive Systems (CAS), the ‘regulatory’ term is schema (more informally we might say ‘rules of the road’). That is, all agents with a system understand that there are rules and values that are commonly held.[103] However it is not widely understood how these develop and are enforced. Regarding pools, we might say that regulation could be a source and enforcer of schema. Other rules and laws do already serve as schema (investment rules, and general laws pertaining to governmental bodies). But the formation of pooling schema and their enforcement and monitoring is not well understood. It is for this reason that the limited presence of insurance-oriented regulation in pooling

[101] May and Koski (2013), pp. 139–159; McShane et al. (2011), pp. 641–658; Andersen and Young (2021).

[102] Uhl-Bien and Arena (2017), pp. 9–20; Uhl-Bien and Arena (2018), pp. 89–104.

[103] Ospina (2016), pp. 275–287.

deserves greater attention. That greater attention might not result in any change, but there are gaps and inconsistencies in the logic of the present approach to oversight.

Second, the functioning of a complex system does seem to require some artificial structures that are not necessary in, say, an ecosystem. For example, if all 'agents' within a pool are empowered to identify a risk and respond to it, that could mean that all agents might independently decide that insurance is needed and then would individually seek out a broker. The degree of inefficiency and the failure to attend to economies of scale in such an approach is mind-boggling. Relatedly, agents might independently decide that varying elements of a new policy on IT security is needed, but it is unclear how those insights self-organize and find their way to organization-wide decision makers. Clearly some degree of conscious 'connective tissue' is needed. In conversational terms, these issues suggest a role for risk leaders and leadership, which—in complex systems—has been described as:

> (Facilitating)...(b)oundary spanning, organizing and implementing aligned actions, promoting cross-functional training, joint planning and decision-making, deploying resources across units to foster interconnectivity.[104]

Thus, with respect the question of who initiates, there is a leadership dimension that seems to involve different skills, knowledge, abilities than more conventional views of leadership. When overlaid on the actual emergence of pooling, it may be reasonably argued that the earliest leaders (policy leaders, associations, legislatures) followed the general outline of CAS/LOA thinking.

So the ignition point for pooling was two crises of insurance unavailability and unaffordability. Independently, various agents, initially operating as agents within public sector systems and networks, recognized the need for a solution. Existing networks were then exploited (as just one example, the Public Risk Management Association—PRIMA—which formed the Pooling Section as a forum for information exchange) to share ideas and ultimately develop the idea of an alternative risk financing solution. The rest of the story has been previously outlined.

It seems the case that the pooling movement might be framed as a demonstration of a Complex Adaptive System, and that the story of the entrepreneurs, influencers, and other leaders illustrates how emergent leadership (rather than assigned leadership) was the basis for initiating the innovation and then providing sufficient substance to facilitate enactment. And, in fact, since many of these leaders evolved into the leaders of the pools themselves, they became responsible for actualizing and maintaining that innovation. And, using the language of LOA, the pooling movement served as an Enabling space.

But is it proper then to view individual pools as fractal CAS within the larger pooling movement? The evidence yields a provisional 'yes' as an answer. Broadly, the varying nature of the pools suggests that much of the development of pools was unique to each situation (even when adhering to the guidance provided by joint powers authorizing legislation). Partly these differences were due to whether policy

---

[104] Uhl-Bien and Arena (2018), pp. 89–104.

entrepreneurs or associations provided the leadership, partly it was due to the memberships (e.g. school districts vs. county governments), partly to exogenous factors such as geographic setting, population, and logistical factors. And, significantly, it is evidenced in the fact that pooling was new, and it was new to all the original pools at the same time, so there was not a great deal of past history and received wisdom to rely on.

Finally it should be noted the expansion of pool services are indicative of organizational learning, adaptation, and innovation. For example, the evolution of pools from providing a single line of insurance to members, to the frequently observed risk management pool framework reveals an innovating/adapting dynamic.

4.2 Pools as an Innovation Platform

Pooling might be defined as an innovation platform in two senses. The building block that resides within the platform is public/private collaboration—arguably an innovation itself, but then the manifestation of that collaboration yielded further innovations—the novel or adapted uses of tools, techniques, expertise, and support. Innovation created the pools, then innovation led to collaborative risk management, which in turn produced innovative or adaptive solutions.

What were the factors that allowed the platform to be built?

As suggested previously pooling illustrates intra- and inter-sector collaboration. From the standpoint of collaboration within the public sector pools, there were/are three relationship vectors. The first is local entity-to-local entity; the second is local entity-to-association the third is local entity/association-to-regional entity. Each was and is critical to the formation of the pooling movement.

To be clear, collaboration was fraught with issues, particularly around resource- and risk-sharing. Practically speaking commingling of resources and risk was not permitted or only permitted in limited ways prior to pooling—e.g. there were legal/regulatory barriers. A political barrier is observable in the debate over (1) whether and (2) on what terms governmental entities could enter the 'risk financing business.' That debate, while obviously interesting, need not be detailed here. Rather, it is through the evidence of the restrictions that ultimately emerged (or were imposed) that an outline of the legal/political tensions can be discerned. For example:

- Pools were restricted to a very limited number of risks (commonly workers' compensation, or general liability).
- Cross-subsidization of coverages was not permitted; and members participated in all coverage pool funds.
- Members were confined to a single state.
- Pools were not subject to insurance regulation (they were 'group self-insurance' arrangements). However, they were required to file annual reports with the state risk manager.

- As much by necessity as by fiat, pool members held form of entity in common (towns with towns, school districts with school districts).
- Certain state requirements for handling, investment, and management of public funds were applicable. Bidding requirements were enforced as well.

4.2.1 Platform Emergence

Given the detail provided previously, it is sufficient here to say that pools identified necessary functional and operational elements, and not surprisingly the mutual insurance model served as a generic template. In the earliest stages, typically, risk management consulting firms served as facilitators of mapping organizational structure, building job descriptions, establishing operational frameworks and, obviously more.[105]

Logically, nearly the earliest step was to explore pricing methods, that is, the means by which pools determined the contributions. Almost invariably this required actuarial consultancy involvement. Among other things, aggregated past loss data were typically not available for members of a specific pool, nor was actuarial expertise much on hand in public entities. Thus, engagement with the actuarial community—particularly actuarial consulting firms—was an obvious and common-sensical response. Interestingly, while the capabilities of actuaries were rarely an issue of concern, questions regarding data quality were present. Simply expressed, if commercial insurers (presumably relying on their public sector clients' claims data) determined that public entities were uninsurable, or only insurable at prohibitive rates, how would pricing pool contributions—based on that same commercial insurer data—produce a more affordable price?

What appears to have emerged in response is a flexible approach to underwriting where the initial determination of rates (based on existing data) were adjusted by discounts, favorable or flexible terms were granted for timing and payment of contributions, and most significantly where most pools instituted unlimited assessments provisions—meaning additional contributions could be collected if claims exceeded available funds. Although this may have been the only structure possible, it does suggest a hedging accommodation whereby the wider financial resources of each member were pledged to deal with any/all covered losses. It has been argued by pool leaders, however, that this hedge also was the psychological glue that held together pools, providing a concrete motive for greater emphasis on risk management ('if we cannot afford to pay for losses, we must prevent them'). Peer pressure has also been cited as a factor; individual pool members did not want to be seen as the weak link.[106]

Following those earliest collaborative efforts, the question of sourcing necessary expertise led to the identification of—primarily—third party service providers

[105] Pumford (1995).

[106] Pumford (1995).

(TPAs), who already had begun to emerge in response to the more widespread movement toward alternative risk financing. The fact that unbundling was already well underway must be seen as the windfall it was for pooling. Absent that development, accessing technical expertise would have proven to be much more difficult.

Interactions between pool boards and executives (and staff in some cases) and TPAs produced interactive effects that led to extensions of the original scope of activity—notably a wider range of coverages and support services. It is at this point that the idea of *risk management pools* takes shape—arguably in the late 1980s-early 1990s.[107]

A matter of political philosophy remains, in a very real sense, unresolved as often is the case with public policy issues. There persists a view—though no longer widely shared—that public entities (via pooling) should stay out of private markets, especially when they enjoy numerous regulatory exemptions and advantages. However, from a practical standpoint the fact that commercial providers have significantly re-entered the market has diminished the most forceful opposition. This is why it has been observed that pools have organized the public sector insurance market.[108]

But how did pools organize the market? Broadly this was accomplished by:

- facilitating the aggregation of public sector loss data.
- raising attention among governmental leaders of the importance of loss prevention, reduction, and control.
- aiding local officials in better understanding the structure and dynamics of the insurance market.
- introducing, at least, a perception of orderliness to public sector risks.
- more vividly revealing insurer's role in the risk management value chain.
- introducing a sharper picture of local government's risk concerns, which ranged far from conventional insurable risks, leading to an awareness of the distinction between traditional take-it-or-leave-it transactions and the need for different thinking about how local governments actually perceived their challenges.
- pooling exposures (resource pooling) offsetting some inherent problems in traditional approaches to risk financing.[109]

Harkening back to the chapter's opening comments on complex systems, it is possible to recast the preceding discussion as an example of an adaptive system in action. The process of the adaptation or innovation is set out in the discussion above, but the innovation *itself* was the stabilization of the risk financing and services market, primarily through the reduction of uncertainty. Thus—and perhaps without being fully conscious of the eventual outcomes—pooling established a platform that was a legally sturdy but otherwise open system where adaptations could occur.[110]

[107] Young and Reed (1995), pp. 96–112.

[108] deSpelder (2021).

[109] Pumford (1995).

[110] Young (2016).

4.2.2 Returning to the Regulation Question

Perhaps the issue to which most readers will be drawn is the matter of regulation—or its absence. At least three questions are raised in the earlier discussions. (1) What does the limited regulatory environment for public risk pooling say about regulation in general, and especially insurance regulation, (2) Is there something about the public setting that alters the argument for regulation of pools as financial institutions, and (3) More clinically, is the absence of regulation a spur to innovation, and if so, at what cost?

The constraints of insurance regulation are often cited as general barriers to innovation. The benefits of, and rationale for, insurance regulation have long been debated and this is not the place to revisit the philosophical underpinnings. However, perhaps useful to this chapter the following list of oft-cited motives for insurance regulation serve as a reminder:

- Elimination of the marginal firm under a competitive environment is contrary to the basic purpose of an insurance institution.
- Consumers are unable to evaluate the insurer's promises of future performance.
- Complete freedom of entry of new insurance firms is not desirable due to fiduciary considerations and the significant opportunities for fraud.
- Intensive unregulated competition in marketing insurance may produce unfair loss-adjusting practices, misleading policy language and monopolization.
- It is broadly (though not without controversy) in the public interest for consumers to have access to insurance coverage.[111]

It is clear from an examination of the pooling story that subjecting pools to conventional insurance regulation was viewed as a barrier to pool formation and function. So given longevity of the pooling phenomenon, the question might be asked, did allowing insurance-like organizations to operate significantly outside conventional insurance regulation prove much of a risk? Yes, questions regarding transparency remain an issue worthy of further exploration—especially in a public environment—but perhaps publicness may make pooling categorically distinct from commercial insurance. Or other public sector-specific rules and regulations proved sufficient to keep pools out of difficulties. Or pools may have just been lucky. How otherwise to explain the continuing 50 year-long existence of pooling?

In any event a case can be proposed that the absence of regulation has been—seemingly—not a particularly negative or restrictive factor. Still, the lack of regulation does raise the broader question of why member entities should desire that commercial insurers (from which the might purchase one coverage) be regulated while they do not have that expectation—or concern—about coverage acquired through an unregulated pool.

[111] Williams et al. (1998).

It is clear that the question of regulation requires further consideration. What exactly is the active agent that allows pools to exist unregulated—reasonably safely and successfully—at least relative to the conventional ways insurance is regulated? And, as an innovation platform, does this feature open a door for a wider field of innovation for commercial insurers—or is it just an invitation for mischief.

4.2.3 What Might the Future Hold?

It is very early days in considering an answer to this question, though AGRIP has taken on the task of long-range forecasting.[112] However, returning to Complex Systems thinking provides one way forward.

Recent research has introduced the idea that work in Complex Adaptive Systems (CAS) poses possibilities for further innovation in public (even society-wide) settings.[113] Pools already exist as innovation platforms, and thus have, let it be called, 'standing' in serving as risk management innovators and platforms—that is, enabling space. It must be emphasized, certainly, that most pools today would not particularly define themselves as such. Indeed, most would blanch at the thought of describing themselves as aggressively seeking additional responsibilities. So, here, consider existing pools as possessing the potential to serve as innovation platforms—whether or not they actively seek to do so.

There is a wide-ranging literature on adaptive organizations and though it would be informative to review, a thorough-going discussion would dramatically expand this chapter. However, consider a few observations on possible linkage between pooling and the LOA/CAS frameworks.

- The notion of networks and interactions between independent agents presents an opportunity to test how pools can distribute risk responsibilities throughout the organization and the pool membership.
- Risk management pools facilitate the use of basic tools, such as, risk registers, reflecting the idea of creating a comprehensive list of critical organizational/community risks and uncertainties to develop a useful view of the pool's overall risk profile. The basic methods of identification, analysis, and assessment are helpful, but also have limitations as they assume an ability to foresee major events, as well as free and unimpeded flows of information. A better understanding of interactive agent networks may help diagnose how ongoing agent interactions might serve to identify emergent risks and unexpected events.
- The tensions that catalyze innovation and adaptive responses seem to require further analysis perhaps utilizing new analytical methodologies. How leaders

[112] Association of Governmental Risk Pools—AGRIP. 2021. Accessed August 15, 2021. https://www.agrip.org.

[113] Andersen and Young (2021).

might actively seek or promote tensions, or stressors, could shine a new light on emergent risk assessment and consciousness about uncertain conditions.
- The idea that engaging networks of independent individuals around the organization, pool, or communities may be, in some way, a "better" approach to sensing emergent changes in order to make needed innovative and adaptive decisions.
- There is a particular tension between exploring new opportunities and exploiting existing activities. In business settings control-based management approaches seek to optimize the economies of the existing activity and to eliminate 'wasteful digressions'. In the public sector the dynamics are similar but obviously the context is quite different. Achieving the right balance between exploiting the present and exploring for the future is a key strategic concern that also seems to fit squarely within the public risk management agenda. Thinking about how to mediate this agenda offers echoes the risk management issue of prioritizing and aligning the past, the present, and the future as evolving states of being.
- Alongside these implied leadership capabilities in the face of complexity, there are more distinctly risk-related competencies, skills, abilities, and attributes. They would probably include an understanding of complexity and networks, an understanding of entrepreneurial contexts, awareness of innovation and adaptive processes, and a more nuanced view on how strategies actually come about and take form in real organizations and pools.

Demonstrably the seed of change within pools resides in a more conscious embedding of the idea that pools are or could be innovation platforms, and that it would entail some reconsideration of the roles and mindsets of leaders, managers, and employees—and even TPAs. It is, in this sense, not a matter of giving everyone extra duties, but more a matter of doing differently what they already do.

The key would seem to be extending the risk management pool concept to align more fully with the present and future direction of risk management. This does assume somewhat different ways of thinking as well as an expansion of horizons. Leadership approaches are likely to require reevaluation. AGRIP, the US association of pools is investing in better understanding long-range forecasting in complicated times, so there is evidence that emergent thinking is moving in a direction similar to new thinking on risk management.[114]

But here, of course, the chapter finally arrives at the question of pools as an innovation platform for the insurance sector.

To begin, it must be conceded that within progressive insurance sector organizations business strategizing, product and service development and innovation, are pursuing better efforts to imagine the future through the lens of complexity. But the essential difference between corporate efforts and pooling innovation platforms is the governing principle of inter-sector collaboration. Is there a collaborative role for

[114] Association of Governmental Risk Pools—AGRIP. 2021. Accessed August 15, 2021. https://www.agrip.org.

insurance in solving the widest ranging risk management challenges for local governments, their communities, their regions, and indeed the planet.

The act of engagement with pools is, it must be conceded, fraught with challenges. Notably, public-private collaborations come freighted with legal, political, and social questions that feature concerns such as favoritism, back door deals with vendors, failure to recognize issues related to the public interest and the common good—and more. These are not insignificant issues, but they exist in all contexts and—public-private partnerships abound. The threats are—if not always adequately addressed—at least reasonably well understood.

So what are possible innovations in this setting? Allowing for the commonly held view that we cannot ever really know what the 'next big thing' will be (such is the nature of complexity), five illustrative considerations for insurance sector engagement might be:

1. *Building resilient governments, communities, societies.* This already is a huge subject with many initiatives underway. However, the knowledge and capacities of the insurance sector might be more directly brought to bear here.[115]
2. *Community risk management.* A largely unexplored area within modern public sector risk management is how the ERM idea might better integrate the risk management of, say, a city government with the risks of the community at large.[116]
3. *Ground level solutions for large scale threats (and opportunities).* Recent events have brought the subject of large-scale risks to the fore. Emergency management, disaster response, and emergent global risks are challenges that are being addressed, but the integration of the risk financing dimension here is not well understood.[117]
4. *Long-term forecasting.* Certainly forecasting is a well-established provenance in the insurance sector, and it can be said that social insurance programs require extensions into extremely long-term forecasting. Relying on new technologies and insurance expertise, can this orientation to forecasting be applied elsewhere.[118]
5. *Improved interconnectivity.* Understanding the interconnective dimensions of the global risk environment is a subject of interest and study. How might risk financing better inform addressing risk interconnectivity.[119]

This discussion ends here with one very practical matter regarding collaborative risk management via pooling. The direct buyer-seller relationship between an organization and its insurer is—almost invariably—between a risk manager (the risk manager may be a pool) and an underwriter. Intermediaries play a functional role in many

---

[115] Bovaird and Quirk (2013).

[116] Bhattamishra and Barrett (2010), pp. 923–932.

[117] Boughton (1998), pp. 2–5.

[118] Healy and Malhotra (2009), pp. 388–406.

[119] Rana et al. (2019), pp. 37–45; Ospina (2016), pp. 275–287.

transactions and there are situations where other specialists may be involved. Nevertheless, the current reframing of risk management give rise to three observations.

1. Risk managers (pools) and the organizations they represent have a broad and ecumenical view of the challenges that a complex world presents. And not only does this broad view extend far beyond classically insurable risks, it also is a highly integrated view—meaning that, for example, a city administration building is exposed to the risk of fire (it is "an exposure"), but within the organization it has many levels of existence. It is a productive asset, it may have multiple roles, it has strategic value, it is interconnected with other assets (and liabilities), and it may have specific relationships with a variety of stakeholders. Interconnectivity shapes the risk manager's view of an organization's risks, while this is much less the case for an insurer.
2. Preventing or reducing the impact of losses remains operationally critical, but consideration of the importance of unmeasurable phenomena and interconnectivity means that the language of *sustainable resilience* has become more fully the language of risk management. And, yes, pursuing opportunities is part of the risk management remit.
3. The holistic—perhaps even organic—approach to modern risk management presents the question of 'who' is the client/partner. Or to put it more practically, risk managers may be the historic and primary client to whom insurance is sold, but if "everyone is a risk manager within the scope of their responsibilities," who are the risk management decision-makers? Put even more practically, are there new possibilities for insurers to interact more directly with others within a client organization?

5 Concluding Observation

The specific subject of pools is very much US-centric, but the broad background discussion in this chapter is widely applicable, and so the chapter concludes with a very brief comment on a more relaxed interpretation of what has been discussed here.

Pools can be, and often are, innovation platforms. That is, they serve as forums for public sector risk management innovation; indeed their very presence constitutes an advantage—they exist, they have standing. It must be said that external consultants and other TPAs historically have engaged clients with creative problem solving and these existing form of—it might be said—collaboration are important and will continue to exist. Where the idea of pools as innovation platforms diverges from such commercial transactions is to—in a philosophical sense—separate commerce from problem solving. This does strike a rather idealistic tone, and it is true that the previous innovations often arose due to profit-seeking motives. However, public sector risk management concerns are society's concerns and there must be space for consideration of these risk management challenges that draws on available expertise and contains—at least in part—the chance for no-strings attached exploration of solutions.

But do such spaces exist in Europe or elsewhere? They could, conceivably, start with a blank sheet of paper, but one effort in Denmark serves as an example. In 2004 KommuneForskring (a mutual dedicated to public sector clients) established a center for the study of public sector risk management—the European Institute for Risk Management. During its ten-year existence it evaluated subjects of interest to public entities in Denmark, it established a (ultimately) pan-European association for risk management geared toward top executives in local authorities (PRIMO—it still exists) and created forums for a range of training and education programming. Certainly, Kommuneforsikring had a commercial motive—better control of expenses, as public sector risks are tricky even in Denmark--but that endeavor did have independence and became self-sustaining. Innovation platforms can arise from other circumstances. Where might they next appear?

References

Abraham KS (2001) The rise and fall of commercial liability insurance. Virginia Law Rev 87(1): 85–109

Andersen TJ, Young PC (2021) Strategic risk leadership: context and cases. Routledge, Abingdon, UK

Andersen TJ, Young PC (2022) Public risk leadership: reshaping public sector risk management. Unpublished manuscript. Copenhagen Business School

Andersen TJ, Young PC (2020) Strategic risk leadership: engaging a world of risk, uncertainty, and the unknown. Routledge, Abingdon, UK

Association of Federal Enterprise Risk Management (AFERM). www.AFERM.org

Association of Governmental Risk Pools—AGRIP (2021) Accessed August 15, 2021. https://www.agrip.org

Atkinson AB (1991) Social insurance. The Fifteenth Annual Lecture of the Geneva Association. Geneva Pap Risk Insur Theory 16(2):113–131

Beasley MS, Clune R, Hermanson D (2005) Enterprise risk management: an empirical analysis of factors associated with the extent of implementation. J Account Public Policy 24:521–531

Beck U (1989) On the way to the industrial risk-society? Outl Argum Thesis Eleven 23(1):86–103

Bhattamishra R, Barrett C (2010) Community-based risk management arrangements: a review. World Dev 38:923–932

BIS (2010) Principles for Enhancing Corporate Governance. Basel Committee on BankingSupervision, Bank for International Settlements. Basel, Switzerland

Blanchard RH (1916) Municipal fire insurance in Great Britain and the United States. Natl Municipal Rev 5:430

Boughton G (1998) The community: central to emergency risk management. Aust J Emerg Manage 13:2–5

Bovaird T, Quirk B (2013) Reducing public risk and improving public resilience: an agenda for risk enabled government strategies. In: Staite C (ed) Making sense of the future: do we need a new model of public services? Birmingham, UK: INLOGOV.

Bozeman B (2007) Public values and public interest: counterbalancing economic individualism. Georgetown University Press, Georgetown, Washington DC

Bracci E, Tallaki M, Gobbo G, Papi L (2021) Risk management in the public sector: a structured literature review. Int J Public Sector Manage 34:205–223

Braig S, Gebre B, Sellgren A (2011) Strengthening risk management in the US public sector. McKinsey & Company
Bullock JB, Greer RA, O'Toole LJ Jr (2019) Managing risks in public organizations: a conceptual foundation and research Agenda. Persp Public Manage Gov 2(1):75–87
Christoffersen P (2011) Elements of financial risk management, 2nd edn. Elsevier, Waltham, MA
COSO (2004) Enterprise Risk Management – Integrated Framework. Committee of Sponsoring Organizations of the Treadway Commission. Accessed May 1, 2021. https://www.coso.org/
COSO (2017) Enterprise Risk Management – Integrating with Strategy and Performance (Executive Summary). Committee of Sponsoring Organizations of the Treadway Commission. Accessed May 1, 2021. https://www.coso.org/
Crockford GN (1982) The bibliography and history of risk management: some preliminary observations. Geneva Pap Risk Insur 7:169–179
Cummings JD, Outreville JF (1987) An international analysis of underwriting cycles. J Risk Insur 54(2):246–262
Cypher T, Grinnell C (2007) California state legislature senate local government committee report: governments working together: a citizen's guide to joint powers agreements. Senate Publications, Sacramento, CA
deSpelder J (2021) Interview with AGRIP Board member and Administrator/CEO County Road Association Self-Insurance Fund (CRASIF), November 17th
Dickinson G (2001) Enterprise risk management: its origins and conceptual foundation. Geneva Pap Risk Insur 26:360–366
Doherty NA (1985) Corporate risk management. McGraw-Hill, New York, NY
European Institute for Risk Management—EIRM (2009) Public Risk Financing in Europe. Accessed July 20, 2021. www.eirm.net
Federation of European Risk Management Associations (FERMA) (2021). www.ferma.eu
Fone M, Young PC (2000) Public sector risk management. Butterworth-Heinemann Publishing, London, UK
Gordon LA, Loeb M, Tseng C-Y (2009) Enterprise risk management and firm performance: a contingency perspective. J Account Public Policy 28:301–327
Governmental Accounting Standards Board (2021) Accessed August 20, 2021. https://www.gasb.org/st/summary/gstsm10.html
Grant RM, Visconti M (2006) The strategic background to corporate accounting scandals. Long Range Plan 39(4):361–383
Grobman GM (2005) Complexity theory: a new way to look at organizational change. Public Adm Q 29:350–382
Haimes YY (1992) Toward a holistic approach to total risk management. Geneva Pap Risk Insur 17: 314–321
Hall P (1992) Living with TQM. Risk Management 39(3), Gale Academic OneFile. Accessed 20 May 2021
Halstead JM, Hegde S, Klein LS (2004) Orange county Bankruptcy: financial contagion in the municipal bond and bank equity markets. Financial Rev 39:293–315
Hazenberg R, Hall K, Ogden-Newton A (2013) Enterprise solutions: public service mutuals. RSA, London UK
Healy A, Malhotra N (2009) Myopic voters and natural disaster policy. Am Polit Sci Rev 103(3): 388–406
Hinna A, Scarozza D, Rotundi F (2018) Implementing risk management in the Italian public sector: hybridization between old and new practices. Int J Public Adm 41(2):110–128
HM Treasury. (2004). The orange book: Management of risk principles and concepts. Retrieved from http://www.hmtreasury@gov.uk/media /3/5/FE66035B-BCDC-D4B31057A7707D2521F.pdf
Holberton D (2019) What makes a successful risk leader? Risk Management. Accessed December 3, 2020. http://www.rmmagazine.com/2019/04/01/what-makes-a-successful-risk-leader/

Holzmann R, Kozel V (2007) The role of social risk management in development: a world bank view. IDS Bull 38:1–6
Hood J, Young P (2005) Risk financing in UK local authorities: is there a case for risk pooling? Int J Public Sector Manage 18:Parts 6 and 7
IRGC (2005) Risk governance: towards an integrative approach. International Risk Governance Center, Lausanne
Irish Public Bodies (2021) Accessed August 10, 2021. https://ipb.ie/
IRM (2002) A Risk Management Standard – published jointly by the Institute of Risk Management (IRM), the Association of Insurance and Risk Managers (AIRMIC) and the Public Risk Management Association (Alarm). https://www.theirm.org/media/6827/arms_2002_irm.pdf
ISO (2009) Risk Management – Principles and Guidelines [ISO 31000]. International Organization for Standardization. Accessed November 1, 2019. https://www.iso.org/iso-31000-risk-management.html
ISO (2018) Risk Management - ISO 31000 Update. International Organization for Standardization. Accessed 1 November 2019. https://www.iso.org/iso-31000-risk-management.html
Jeynes J (2012) Risk management: 10 principles. Routledge, London, UK
Jondle DT, Maines D, Burke MR, Young PC (2013) Modern risk management: managing risk through the ethical business culture model. Center for Ethical Business Cultures Papers and Reports, p 11
Kallio TJ (2007) Taboos in corporate social responsibility discourse. J Bus Ethics 74:165–175
Kellerman B (2008) Followership: how followers are creating change and changing leaders. Harvard Business School Press, Boston, MA
Kommunal Landspensjonskasse—KLP (2021) Accessed August 11, 2021. http://www.klp.no
KommuneForsikring—KF. Accessed August 12, 2021). https://www.cobx.org
Kopits G, Craig J (1998) Transparency in government operations. International Monetary Fund, Washington, DC
Lam J (2003) Enterprise risk management: from incentives to controls. Wiley, Hoboken, NJ
Liebenberg A, Hoyt RE (2003) The determinants of enterprise risk management: evidence from the appointment of chief risk officers. Risk Manage Insur Rev 6:37–52
Lim CY, Woods M, Humphrey C, Seow JL (2017) The paradoxes of risk management in the banking sector. Br Account Rev 49:75–90
Lundqvist SA (2014) An exploratory study of enterprise risk management: pillars of ERM. J Account Audit Finance 29:393–429
May PJ, Koski C (2013) Addressing public risks: extreme events and critical infrastructures. Rev Policy Res 30:139–159
McDonald LG, Robinson P (2009) A Colossal failure of common sense: the inside story of the collapse of Lehman brothers. Three Rivers Press, New York, NY
McShane M, Nair A, Rustambekov E (2011) Does enterprise risk management increase firm value? J Account Audit Finance 26:641–658
Mendoza MA (2014) Reinsurance as Governance: *Government* Risk Management Pools as a Case Study in the Governance Role Played by Reinsurance Institutions. Connect Insur Law J 21:53
Miller KD (2009) Organizational risk after modernism. Org Stud 30:157–180. https://doi.org/10.1177/0170840608101475
Moeller RR (2007) COSO enterprise risk management: understanding the new integrated ERM framework. Wiley, New York, NY
Moss D (2002) When all else fails: government as the ultimate risk manager. Harvard University Press, Cambridge MA
Municipal Mutual Insurance. Accessed July 25, 2021. https://www.mminsurance.co.uk
National League of Cities. Accesses July 24, 2021. https://www.nlcmutual.com/
Nocco B, Stulz R (2006) Enterprise risk management: theory and practice. J Appl Corp Finance 18: 8–20

OECD (2021) Public Integrity Handbook: Risk Management. Accessed January 10 2021. https://www.oecd-ilibrary.org/sites/ebbed075-en/index.html?itemId=/content/component/ebbed075-en
Olson WA (1979) Governmental immunity from tort liability - two decades of decline: 1959-1979. Baylor Law Rev 31(4):485–504
Ospina SM (2016) Collective leadership and context in public administration: bridging public leadership research and leadership studies. Public Adm Rev 77:275–287
Paape L, Speklé R (2012) The adoption and design of enterprise risk management practices. Eur Account Rev 21:533–564
Palermo T (2014) Accountability and expertise in public sector risk management: a case study. Financ Account Manage 30(3):322–341
Pernell K, Jung J, Dobbin F (2017) The hazards of expert control: chief risk officers and risky derivatives. Am Sociol Rev 82:511–541
Pesch U (2008) The publicness of public administration. Adm Soc 40:170–193
Posner PL (1998) The politics of unfunded mandates: whither federalism? Georgetown University Press, Georgetown, Washington DC
Power M (2009) The risk management of nothing. Account Org Soc 34(6-7):849–855
Public Risk Management Association—Pooling Section (1986) Interview with Harold Pumford, Head of the Pooling Section. Annual Conference, Boston MA. May 14-16
Pumford H (1986) Interview with Chairman of the PRIMA-Pooling Section. June 1986
Pumford H (1995) Interview with Executive Director of the Association of Governmental Risk Pools (AGRIP). January 1995
Punter A (1999) The spectrum of alternative risk financing opportunities the changing risk landscape: implications for insurance risk management. Aon White Paper Series, London, UK
Rana T, Wickramasinghe D, Bracci E (2019) Public sector reform implications for performance measurement and risk management practice: insights from Australia. Public Money Manage 39: 37–45
Randall D (2021) Interview with Vice-President of Public Entity Underwriting at Safety National Mutual, November 10th
Safety National Mutual. Accessed August 15, 2021. https://www.sfmic.com/
Schmit JT, Roth K (1990) Cost effectiveness of risk management practices. J Risk Insur 57:455–470
Slywotzky A, Drzik J (2005) Countering the biggest risk of all. Harv Bus Rev 83(3):78–91
Smith D, Fischbacher M (2009) The changing nature of risk and risk management: the challenge of borders, uncertainty and resilience. Risk Manag 11:1–12. https://doi.org/10.1057/rm.2009.1
Snider HW (1956) Reaching professional status: a program for risk management. Corp Risk Manage Curr Probl Persp 112:30–35
Swedish Public Captives. Accessed August 12, 2021. https://www.captiveinsurancetimes.com
Szymendera SD (2016) Workers' Compensation: Overview and Issues. Congressional Research Service. https://fas.org/sgp/crs/misc/R44580.pdf
Todd JD (1969) The risk management function in municipal government. J Risk Insur 36:285–295
Tsay B-Y (2010) Designing an internal control assessment program using COSO's guidance on monitoring. CPA J 80:52–57
Uhl-Bien M, Arena M (2017) Complexity leadership: enabling people and organizations for adaptability. Org Dyn 46(1):9–20
Uhl-Bien M, Arena M (2018) Leadership for organizational adaptability: a theoretical synthesis and integrative framework. Leadership Q 29:89–104
United Kingdom Strategy Unit (2002) Risk: Improving Government's Capability to Handle Risk and Uncertainty. Strategy Unit Report, London
United States Congress (2002) H.R.3763 - Sarbanes-Oxley Act of 2002. Accessed August 10, 2019. https://www.congress.gov/bill/107th-congress/house-bill/3763
Weiss M (2007) Underwriting cycles: a synthesis and further directions. J Insur Iss 30:31–45

Williams CA, Smith ML, Young PC (1998) Risk management and insurance, 8th edn. Irwin/MGraw-Hill, Boston, MA

Williamson D (2007) The COSO ERM framework: a critique from systems theory of management control. Int J Risk Assessment Manage 7:1089–1119

Wright J, Wadsley V, Artandi J (1994) The history of the national association of mutual insurance companies, a century of commitment, 1895-1995. NAMIC, Indianapolis, USA, hal (1994), pp 1–5

Young PC (1989) Local government risk financing and risk control pools: understanding the forms, functions, and purposes. Public Budget Finance 9:40–54

Young PC, Reed BJ (1995) Government risk-financing pools: an assessment of current practices. Public Budget Finance 15:96–112

Young PC, Grima S, Gonzi RD (2022) Public sector leadership in assessing and addressing risk. Emerald studies in finance, insurance, and risk management. Emerald Publishing, Abingdon, UK

Young PC (2016) State and local government series: risk management and leadership. Lexis-Nexis Sheshunoff Publishing, Albany, NY

Peter C. Young PhD holds the 3M Endowed Chair in International Business, and is a Professor of Risk Management at the University of St. Thomas' Opus College of Business. He holds a Ph.D. in Risk Management from the University of Minnesota and a Master's Degree in Public Administration from the University of Nebraska-Omaha.

Professor Young has been a visiting professor to City University in London and Aoyama Gakuin University in Tokyo, and Glasgow Caledonian University in Scotland. Most recently, he was awarded the Otto Mønsted Visiting Professorship at Copenhagen Business School for research excellence in risk management.

Comparison of Efficiency Levels of Turkish Insurance Companies with VZA Malmquist Total Factor Efficiency Analysis

Serap Vurur and Letife Özdemir

Abstract Any change in the efficiency of insurance companies has a direct impact on financial markets and economic development. In this study, the development of the efficiency of the companies in the insurance sector traded on Stock Exchange Market Istanbul in the period of 2016–2020 is examined. Efficiency values were calculated using the Data Envelopment Analysis (DEA) method. The change in efficiency values during the period was measured using the Malmquist Total Factor Productivity Index. As a result of the analysis, it was determined that three companies out of the six companies included in the study were operating effectively in all periods. To be effective, inefficient businesses need to reduce their inputs and outputs. When we examine the average efficiency values of the periods, 2019 was more efficient for the insurance industry than other years. According to the total factor productivity index, the insurance industry showed an average annual productivity increase of 5.6% in 2016–2020. This increase in productivity in the sector resulted from technological progress. The findings show that most insurance companies are growing steadily. This chapter will contribute to policymakers and insurance institutions taking appropriate steps to develop relevant policies to increase the efficiency of insurance institutions in Turkey.

Keywords Efficiency · Insurance industry · Data envelopment analysis (DEA) · Malmquist total factor productivity index

S. Vurur
Afyon Kocatepe University, Bolvadin Faculty of Applied Sciences, Department of Accounting and Finance Management, Afyonkarahisar, Turkey

L. Özdemir (✉)
Afyon Kocatepe University, Faculty of Economics and Administrative Sciences, Department of International Trade and Finance, Afyonkarahisar, Turkey

M. Lima Rego, S. Grima (eds.), *Cross-Disciplinary Impacts on Insurance Law*, AIDA Europe Research Series on Insurance Law and Regulation 8,
https://doi.org/10.1007/978-3-031-38526-1_6

1 Introduction

Insurance ensures financial security for both individuals and institutions. Insurance is a tool used to cover the damages that may arise from recognizing risks. Insurance contracts are essential elements of financial planning as they enable more precise future planning. The insurance sector is one of the most critical elements of the economy due to the number of premiums it collects and the socio-economic role of covering personal and commercial risks. Financial management of unexpected risks is a significant challenge for governments and institutions worldwide. Climate change, increasing dependence on digital technologies, socio-economic trends such as globalization and urbanization, the frequency of floods and hurricanes, cyber-attacks, and infectious disease outbreaks create high financial, economic, and social costs each year.

Insurance can make significant contributions to reducing financial fragility in the economy and the recovery of both the economy and companies. The increasing demand for life insurance and non-life insurance policies has fueled the development of the insurance industry worldwide. Gross premium increases in life and non-life branches in the insurance sector continue. The insurance industry experienced financial losses in the last quarter of 2018.

With the movement of the stock markets in 2019, insurance companies benefited from this activity and achieved positive investment returns. This has enabled pre-Covid 19 insurance companies to have a substantial profit and high equity structure.[1]

According to the OECD's 2021 report, the insurance industry has generated income from its activities despite declining premium volumes in some branches. However, losses in the financial markets in the first quarter of 2020 affected the insurance industry's profitability. The amount of damage payments made by insurance companies is unknown, mainly due to the debates over whether insurance companies are responsible for job losses due to workplace closures in 2020.

In 2020, accurate global premiums fell by 1.3%, accounting for about a third of the decline in GDP. Global insurance demand is projected to grow above a trend of 3.3% in 2021 and 3.9% in 2022, with a much faster recovery from the 2008–2009 global financial crisis. The economic recovery will increase premiums by 10% above pre-COVID-19 crisis levels in 2021, and the global insurance market is expected to reach US$7 trillion by the end of 2022.[2]

The insurance sector is one of the leading actors and banks in the financial system in developed countries. Funds managed by insurance companies in developed countries are one of the most significant sources of financial markets. When

[1] "OECD Insurance Statistics 2020" <https://www.oecd-ilibrary.org/finance-and-investment/oecd-insurance-statistics-2020_adfe5566-en> Accessed March 11, 2021.

[2] Swiss Re World insurance: The recovery gains pace. Sigma, 3 (Swiss re Institute 2021) <https://www.swissre.com/institute/research/sigma-research/sigma-2021-03.html> Accessed March 11, 2021, p. 12.

Table 1 Number of insurance companies

	2019	2020	2021
Non-life	38	38	42
Life	4	4	6
Life/Retirement	18	18	15
Reinsurance	2	3	3
Total	62	63	66

developing countries are evaluated in this respect, it is seen that the share of the insurance sector in the financial markets in these countries is limited. The banking sector in Turkey has a share of 89.9% in the finance sector, with an asset size of TL 6.1 trillion as of the end of 2020. The insurance and private pension sector, on the other hand, ranks second in the finance sector with a share of 4.5% and an asset size of 307.8 billion TL.[3] This situation shows the importance of the insurance sector for Turkey. This study is aimed at examining the performance of insurance companies traded on Stock Exchange Market Istanbul by reviewing the case of the insurance sector in Turkey.

2 Turkish Insurance Sector

As of 31.12.2021, there are 66 companies in the sector, 63 of which are insurance and pension companies, and 3 are reinsurance companies. Forty-two operate in non-life, six in life, and 15 in life and pension branches of the insurance companies (Table 1).

It was predicted that the COVID-19 epidemic would trigger the deepest recession since the 1930s, and the global gross domestic product (GDP) will contract by approximately 3.7% in 2020. This is expected to result in a decrease in insurance demand. Although a 1.5% increase is expected in the non-life premium volume in the sector, it is predicted that it will cause a 4.4% contraction in the life premium volume and a 1.3% contraction in the total premium production (Fig. 1).[4]

The Turkish insurance industry's total premium production in non-life and life branches increased by 19.3% to 82.6 billion in 2020. It provided guarantees amounting to TL 129 trillion to the real sector. In 2020, the ratio of premium production to GDP reached 2.78%. Considering that this ratio was 2.05% in 2015

[3]"Turkish Insurance Association Sector Report" (Turkish Insurance Association (TIA) 2020) , <https://tsb.org.tr/media/attachments/2020_YILI_SEKT%C3%96R_RAPORU.pdf> Accessed 05 October 2021, p. 12.

[4]TIA p. 2.

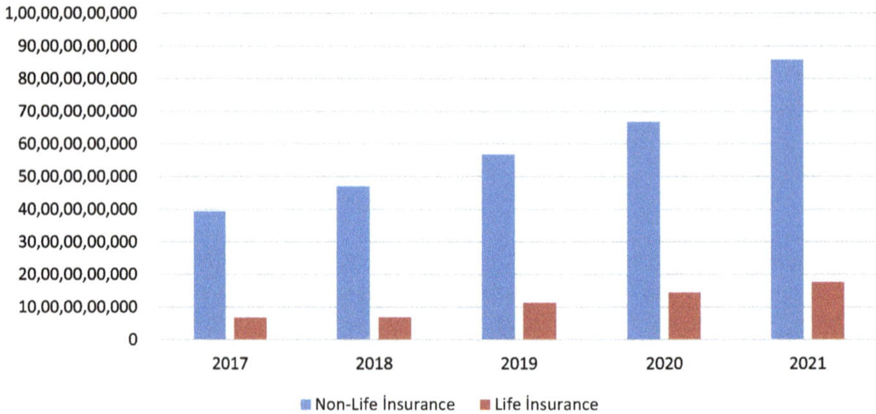

Fig. 1 Premium Production. Source: The author has edited from the data of the Turkish Insurance Association

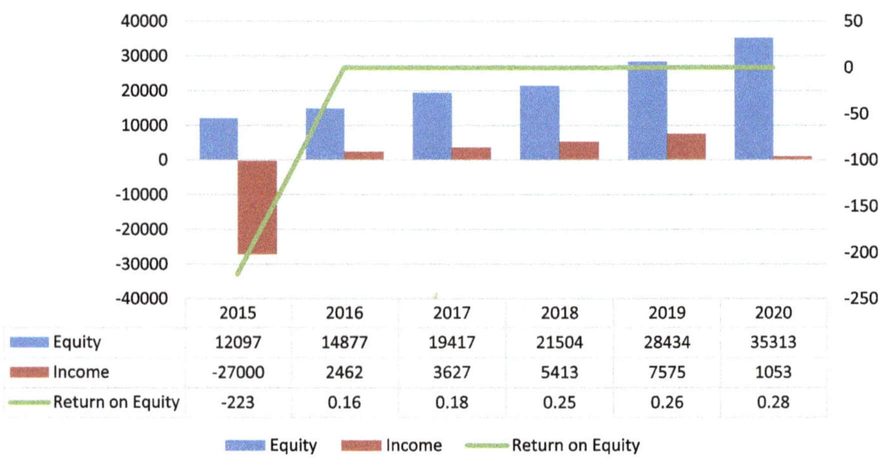

Fig. 2 Profitability Development of the Insurance Industry. Source: The author has edited from the data of the Turkish Insurance Association

and has gradually increased over the years, it is concluded that the Turkish insurance sector has demonstrated a stable growth performance (Fig. 1).[5]

As shown in Fig. 2, the total assets of insurance companies increased by 32.8% to 232 billion TL, their total equities increased by 32.2% to 28 billion TL, and their total profits were 7 billion TL. It is seen that the profitability of the insurance sector has shown a continuous increase since 2016.

[5] "Report on Insurance and Private Pension Activities in Turkey in 2019" (Insurance and Private Pension Regulation and Supervision Agency, 2020) <https://seddk.gov.tr/tr/raporlar/sigortacilik-ve-bes-faaliyetleri> accessed March 11, 2021, p. 7.

The Turkish Insurance Association has not yet published the 12-month data for 2021. For this reason, the data for 2021 will be evaluated over 11 months. According to the statistics announced by the Insurance Association of Turkey, the sector grew by 23.3% in the 11 months of 2021. However, due to the increase in inflation, the actual premium increase in the sector was only 1.6%. In the January-November period, the non-life branch grew by 24.4%, while total premium products in the life branch increased by 18.2%. When inflation is taken into account, real growth has been relatively low. The actual standard change in the sector is due to the contraction in traffic and life branches. The traffic branch contracted by 9.2% in real terms, while the life branch contracted by 2.6%. It is observed that the high inflation experienced hurt the insurance sector.

According to the data of the Turkish Insurance Association, the non-life sector made a technical profit of approximately five billion in the first nine months in 2021. Technical profitability decreased by 29% compared to the same period of 2020. The insurance industry predicts that 2022 will be a very challenging year. Increases in exchange rates and inflation may lead to a decline in the growth rate of the Turkish economy and may also lead to a contraction in the insurance sector.[6] Interest in insurance contracts has increased during the pandemic process. The increased interest in the insurance sector and the difficulty in replacing assets due to increases in asset prices due to inflation have made insurance necessary. This situation creates an advantage for the sector.

3 Literature Review

Banks and insurance companies are financial intermediaries used to channel savings and investments, especially in developed economies. Therefore, any change in the efficiency of insurance companies has a direct impact on financial markets and economic development. The effect of insurance companies on the financial market and economy has created extensive literature on the subject, especially in developing countries. Hwang and Tong-Liang,[7] Eling and Luhnen,[8] Barros et al.,[9] Mandal,[10] Al-Amri,[11] Nourani et al.,[12] Akhtar Muhammad,[13] Battal and Fahad,[14] Masud

[6]Özen and Grima (2020), p. 46.

[7]Hwang and Kao (2006), p. 699.

[8]Eling and Luhnen (2010), p. 1497.

[9]Barros et al. (2005), p. 244.

[10]Mandal (2014), p. 115.

[11]Al-Amri et al. (2012), p. 362.

[12]Nourani et al. (2016), p. 879.

[13]Akhtar (2018), p. 677.

[14]Battal et al. (2018), p. 20.

et al.,[15] Almulhim,[16] Nausad et al.,[17] Kaffash et al.[18] studies can be given as an example.

When some studies in the literature on developing countries are examined, it is seen that the effectiveness of insurance companies in these countries has increased over the years. Nausad et al. examined the efficiency of 30 companies, consisting of conventional and Tekaful insurance companies, in the Saudi stock market, using 2015–2018 with the DEA method.[19] The study concluded that most insurance companies operating on the Saudi stock exchange are efficient. Masud et al. investigated the efficiency of life insurance companies in Malaysia from 2012–2016 using the DEA method. The study's findings show that total factor productivity in the Malaysian insurance industry increased by 2.5% from 2012 to 2016. The results show that the overall progress in the industry is due to technological change.[20] Battal and Fahad investigated the efficiency of five insurance companies traded on the Iraqi stock exchange between 2005 and 2014 using the Malmquist index. The results show that Iraqi insurance companies showed negative growth under review. According to the Malmquist total productivity index, negative growth reached 15%.[21]

Some studies deal with the insurance industry from different perspectives in different periods in Turkey. It has been observed that different analysis techniques are preferred in studies on the insurance sector. In this part of the study, information will be given about the studies made with DEA for the insurance sector in the sample of Turkey. Salimi Altan evaluated the efficiency of the insurance companies operating in the sector concerning each other using data envelopment analysis, based on 2005, 2006, and 2007 data of 25 insurance companies operating in the non-life branch of the Turkish insurance sector. He also explained how much of a percentage change in the number of inputs or outputs inactive units need to be effective.[22] Köse determined the efficiency values of life and life/pension companies operating in the Turkish insurance sector in the 2004–2008 period using an input-oriented DEA. In 2008, it was determined that eight of the 18 life and life/pension companies were relatively efficient in total, and the others were relatively ineffective.[23]

Akhisar and Tezergil using the equities, total assets, premiums received, period net profit (loss), and technical profit variables of 23 insurance companies operating in non-life branches in the Turkish Insurance Sector in the 2006–2010 period, their productivity is calculated by the Malmquist total factor productivity index.

---

[15] Masud et al. (2019), p. 241.
[16] Almulhim (2019), p. 1.
[17] Naushad et al. (2020), p. 297.
[18] Kaffash et al. (2020), p. 801.
[19] Naushad et al. (2020), p. 303.
[20] Masud et al. (2019), p. 246.
[21] Battal and Fahad p. 28.
[22] Salimi Altan (2010), p. 202.
[23] Köse (2010), p. 186.

According to the study results, the top five companies with the highest efficiency are listed according to Malmquist Index values from 2006 to 2010. It has been revealed that there is a decrease in the technical efficiency of all enterprises in the sector.[24] Külekçi and Saldanlı analyzed the efficiency of non-life insurance companies for each year, whose data could be obtained between 2011 and 2015, using the data envelopment method. According to the analysis, the ratio of companies active in the non-life insurance sector to those included in the study varied between 10% and 30%. It was determined that the year with the highest number of active companies was 2012 with nine companies, and the year with the lowest was 2014 with three companies.[25]

Karaca and Kılıçarslan analyzed 39 non-life insurance companies operating in 2018 with the output-oriented DEA method. As a result of the study, it was determined that eight insurance companies were effective, and thirty-one insurance companies could not reach the efficiency limit.[26] Naldöken and Kaya analyzed the insurance companies operating in the health branch in the top 20 according to the annual premium production order in 2018, using the input-oriented DEA method. They concluded that nine insurance companies were active in 2016, six in 2017, and eight in 2018.[27] Arslan, in the period 2006–2016, examined the technical activities of seven insurance companies selected from non-life insurance companies active in Turkey by the DEA method. The analysis used the number of agencies, employees, cash, and similar assets as inputs, while the written premiums, number of policies, and technical profit were used as output. The analysis calculated the total factor productivity index and technical efficiency, technological efficiency, scale efficiency, and pure efficiency values for the same firms. It has been concluded that Turkish insurance companies have structural problems and problems in terms of benefits/costs.[28]

Ekinci using the data of the insurance companies operating in the non-life branch of the Turkish insurance sector for the period 2010–2019, Data Envelopment Analysis was applied. According to the estimation results, under the assumption of constant returns to scale, the average efficiency level is 71.45%; it was found that it was 80.15% under the premise of varying returns to scale. It has been determined that the environmental factors affecting efficiency such as firm size, liquidity level, return on equity, loss premium ratio, concentration ratio, and economic growth affect efficiency positively. In contrast, the effect of the equity ratio and inflation variables is negative.[29]

Kavak and Cihangir tried to determine the efficiency levels of 7 insurance companies traded in the Istanbul Stock Exchange between 2013 and 2017 with a

---

[24] Akhisar and Tezergil (2014), p. 13.

[25] Külekci and Saldanlı (2018), p. 244.

[26] Karaca and Kılıçarslan (2019), p. 1379.

[27] Naldöken and Kaya (2020), p. 31.

[28] Arslan (2021), p. 56.

[29] Ekinci (2021), p. 402.

Table 2 Companies in the Insurance Sector

Company Code	Company Name
AGESA	AGESA LIFE AND PENSION INC.
AKGRT	AKSİGORTA INC.
ANSGR	ANADOLU ANONİM TURKISH INSURANCE COMPANY
ANHYT	ANADOLU LIFE AND PENSION INC.
RAYSG	RAY INSURANCE INC.
TURSG	TURKISH INSURANCE INC.

DEA analysis. The number of personnel, the number of agencies, and equity were selected as input variables, and the output variables were chosen as premium production amount and technical profit. As a result of the analysis, five companies in 2013, four in 2014, three in 2015, five in 2016, and four in 2017 were effective.[30]

A healthy and well-functioning insurance sector in developing countries has significant implications for the financial system's stability. Since Turkey is a developing country, the need for studies on the development of the insurance sector and the evaluation of its performance is increasing.

4 Purpose of the Research and Data

This study aims to measure the relative efficiency of companies in the insurance sector traded in Stock Exchange Market Istanbul and examine the change in efficiency values over periods. In the study, six companies in the insurance sector were examined. These companies are shown in Table 2.

The financial ratios of insurance companies calculated using the financial statements between the years 2016–2020 were used in the analysis. The Data Envelopment Analysis method for the input was used to calculate the efficiency values. In the study, first of all, which companies are effectively using Data Envelopment Analysis. Then, the change in the efficiency values of the companies during the period was measured using the Total Factor Productivity index method. The DEAP package program developed by Coelli was used to analyze the data.[31]

The essential part of measuring the efficiency of the companies is to determine the number of decision units and the input and output variables. The number of decision units (the number of companies) is determined by considering the number of inputs and outputs.[32] Two constraints are taken into account when determining the number of decision units. The first constraint; If the number of selected inputs is h, and the number of outputs is k, the number of decision units must be at least h + k + 1. The

[30] Kavak and Cihangir (2019), p. 126.

[31] Coelli (1996) pp. 1–49 <http://www.une.edu.au/econometrics/cepa. htm> accessed 11 November 2021.

[32] Kula et al. (2009), p. 195.

Table 3 Input and Output Variables

Inputs	Outputs
I1: Equity/Total Assets	O1: Return on Equity
I2: Liquidity Ratio	O2: Technical Profitability
I3: Gross Damage Premium Rate	

other constraint is that the number of decision units must be at least twice the number of variables.[33] Considering the first of these constraints, three input and two output variables were determined since the number of companies included in the study was 6. The input and output variables to be used in the study are given in Table 3.

5 Method of Research

In the study, the DEA method was used to determine the technical efficiency value of the companies, and the Malmquist Total Factor Productivity Index Method was used to analyze the change in technical efficiency, technological change, and total factor productivity change.

5.1 Data Envelopment Analysis (DEA)

Data envelopment analysis was first developed by Charnes et al.[34] DEA, one of the frequently used methods among non-parametric methods, is a linear programming-based analysis method used to measure the relative efficiency of decision units in cases where there are multiple inputs and outputs.[35] DEA is a form of static analysis that makes cross-sectional analysis using one-period data of decision units.

There are two basic models of DEA, input-oriented and output-oriented.[36]

1. Model CCR (Charnes, Cooper, and Rhodes); It is the input-oriented DEA model developed by Charnes, Cooper, and Rhodes in 1978. The CCR model examines how the most appropriate input combination should be used to produce a particular output combination.
2. Model BCC (Banker, Charnes, and Cooper); It is the output-oriented DEA model developed by Banker, Charnes, and Cooper in 1984. The BCC model examines how much output combination can be achieved with a given input combination.

[33] Boussofiane et al. (1991), p. 2.

[34] Charnes et al. (1978).

[35] Boussofiane et al. (1991), p. 3.

[36] Charnes et al. (1994), pp. 36–50.

The CCR model is based on the assumption of constant returns to scale. The mathematical expression of the input-oriented CCR model for m decision units with h inputs and k outputs is as follows:[37]

Purpose Function:

$$max.q_0 = \sum_{r=1}^{k} \mu_r \gamma_{ro} \tag{1}$$

Restrictive Terms:

$$\sum_{r=1}^{k} \mu_r \gamma_{rj} - \sum_{i=1}^{h} \omega_i x_{ij} \leq 0 \quad j = 1, 2, \ldots, m \tag{2}$$

$$\omega_i \geq 0 \qquad \text{i} = 1, 2, \ldots\ldots \text{h}$$

$$\mu_r \geq 0 \qquad \text{r} = 1, 2, \ldots\ldots \text{k}$$

Here, k is the number of outputs, h is the number of inputs and m is the number of decision units.

x_{ij}; The amount of input i used by the decision unit j

y_{rj}; The amount of output r produced by the decision unit j

x_i; The amount of input i used by the decision unit whose effectiveness is being investigated.

y_r; The amount of output r produced by the decision unit whose effectiveness is being investigated.

ω_i; The weight that the decision unit gives to the input i.

μ_r; The weight that the decision unit gives to the output r.

In the CCR model, the weighted average of the outputs of the decision units is aimed to be maximum. The weighted average of the inputs of the decision unit is equal to 1. Another condition of the model is that the weighted output averages for each decision unit are smaller than the weighted input averages. According to this condition, the weighted average of the outputs of the decision units for which the efficiency value is to be calculated is equal to a maximum of 1. Therefore, if the efficiency value is 1, the decision unit is effective, and if the efficiency value is less than 1, the decision unit is inactive.

With DEA, the technical efficiency values of each decision unit for each period are calculated. Technical efficiency consists of pure technical efficiency and scale efficiency. Pure technical efficiency refers to managerial efficiency, while scale efficiency refers to the company's production level at an appropriate scale. [38]

---

[37] Charnes et al. (1978), pp. 431–432.

[38] Türker Kaya and Doğan 2005), pp. 10–11.

5.2 Malmquist Total Factor Productivity Index

Malmquist Total Factor Productivity Index, which is based on distance functions, was developed by Malmquist in 1953 to calculate the change in total factor productivity of two observations as the ratio of the distances to standard technology.[39]

The distance function can determine the production technology where there is more than one output and input without requiring any assumptions such as cost minimization or profit maximization. Distance functions can be considered both as input axis and output axis. The input axis distance function refers to the generation technology that considers the minimum proportional contraction of the input vector, given the output vector. The output axis distance function considers the maximum proportional increase of the output vector when the input vector is given.[40]

If the output axis distance function is the set P with the y's produced with x, it is shown as follows.

$$D_0^s(x, y) = min\{\delta : (y/\delta) \in P\} \tag{3}$$

The distance function $D_0^s(x, y)$, takes the value one if the y-vector is on the P boundary (production limit), >1 if the y-vector describes a technically inactive point inside P, and <1 if the y-vector describes an impossible point outside P.[41] Fare et al. calculated the Malmquist total factor productivity change index according to the output between the t period and the following t+1 period, as in Eq. (4).[42]

$$M_0\left(x^t, y^t, x^{t+1}, y^{t+1}\right) = \sqrt{\left[\frac{D_0^t(x^{t+1}, y^{t+1})}{D_0^t(x^t, y^t)} \times \frac{D_0^{t+1}(x^{t+1}, y^{t+1})}{D_0^{t+1}(x^t, y^t)}\right]} \tag{4}$$

In Eq. (4), $D_0^s(x, y)$, shows the distance of the t+1 period observation from the t period technology. If the value of the M_0 a function is greater than 1, it indicates an increase in total factor productivity. If it is less than one, it indicates a decrease in total factor productivity.

The total factor productivity index measures the change in productivity with the help of two components: change in technical efficiency and technology change. The product of these two components gives the change in total factor productivity. The equation containing the components of the Malmquist total factor productivity index can be expressed as follows.

---

39 Malmquist (1953), p. 209.

40 Tarım (2021), pp. 152–153.

41 Caves et al. (1982), pp. 73–86.

42 Fare et al. (1994), pp. 70–71.

Table 4 Efficiency values of companies

	2016	2017	2018	2019	2020
AGESA	**1.000**	**1.000**	**1.000**	**1.000**	**1.000**
AKGRT	**1.000**	**1.000**	**1.000**	**1.000**	**1.000**
ANSGR	0.430	0.932	0,961	0.865	0.682
ANHYT	**1.000**	**1.000**	**1.000**	**1.000**	**1.000**
RAYSG	0.948	0.465	0.279	0.440	0.340
TURSG	0.809	**1.000**	0.360	0.633	**1.000**
Average	0.865	0.900	0.961	0.823	0.837

$$M_0\left(x^t, y^t, x^{t+1}, y^{t+1}\right) = \frac{D_0^{t+1}\left(x^{t+1}, y^{t+1}\right)}{D_0^t\left(x^t, y^t\right)} \times \sqrt{\left[\frac{D_0^t\left(x^{t+1}, y^{t+1}\right)}{D_0^{t+1}\left(x^{t+1}, y^{t+1}\right)} \times \frac{D_0^t\left(x^t, y^t\right)}{D_0^{t+1}\left(x^t, y^t\right)}\right]} \quad (5)$$

The ratio outside the square root in Eq. (5) measures the change in output-oriented technical efficiency between period t and period t+1. The expression in the square root explains the technology change. Decomposing the Malmquist total factor productivity index to technical efficiency change and technological change helps us determine both factors' contribution to total factor productivity. Thus, dividing the above equation into two parts can measure the change in technical efficiency and technology change separately.

6 Research Findings

In the study, firstly, the efficiency values of the companies every year were calculated using the input-oriented DEA method. The analysis gives only the technical efficiency value for each period. It does not allow comparisons between enterprises over time. For this reason, a comparison was made between enterprises and periods with the Malmquist Total Factor Productivity Index Method. The change in the factors that affected the efficiency value was investigated.

6.1 Results of Data Envelopment Analysis Method

The Efficiency values of six insurance companies handled for each year between the 2016-2020 periods were calculated using the input-oriented DEA method. According to the results of the DEA method, companies with an efficiency coefficient equal to 1 were determined as efficient companies. Efficiency companies are shown in bold. Technical efficiency values are given in Table 4.

According to Table 4, AGESA Life and Pension, Aksigorta, and Anadolu Life and Pension companies, whose efficiency values are equal to one, operated effectively in 2020 and in previous years. It has been determined that the Turkish

Table 5 Potential Improvement Rates of Ineffective Companies

Companies	Variables		Actual	Target	Potential Improvement
ANSGR	Inputs	I1	0.205	0.095	−0.537
		I2	0.368	0.252	−0.316
		I3	0.658	0.450	−0.316
	Outputs	O1	0.213	0.210	−0.014
		O2	0.063	0.060	−0.047
RAYSG	Inputs	I1	0.189	0.065	−0.656
		I2	0.656	0.224	−0.658
		I3	1.544	0.317	−0.999
	Outputs	O1	0.174	0.170	−0.022
		O2	0.045	0.040	−0.111

Table 6 Reference Sets and Density Values of Companies (λ)

	Reference Sets					
Company	Company	Λ	Company	λ	Company	λ
ANSGR	AGESA	0.010	ANHYT	0.101	AKGRT	0.453
RAYSG	ANHYT	0.113	AKGRT	0.295	AGESA	0.047

Insurance Company has been operating effectively in 2017 and 2020. The Turkish insurance company was restructured in 2020 by merging it with the public insurance companies under the Turkey Wealth Fund. This situation has put the company in a powerful financially. When we examined the average efficiency values of the periods, 2018 was more effective for the insurance sector than other years, while 2020 was less efficient.

DEA identifies the amount and sources of the inefficiency of each ineffective company and guides managers on the measures to be taken. In other words, potential improvement rates are calculated, which shows the amount of change that inefficient businesses need to make in their inputs and outputs to become effective. The potential improvement rate is calculated as follows.

If the amount of input X_2 needs to be used for company X, the amount of input used by X_1 is;

Potential improvement rate = $(X_2 - X_1) / X_1$.

Potential improvement rates have been calculated based on 2020 data and are given in Table 5. According to the data, it is seen that Anadolu Insurance and Ray Insurance companies need to reduce their inputs and outputs to be effective. The companies to be taken as reference by ineffective companies and their density values are given in Table 6.

For Anadolu Insurance and Ray Insurance companies to be effective, they must first refer to Aksigorta, then Anadolu Life and Pension, and finally AGESA Life and Pension.

6.2 Malmquist Total Factor Productivity Index Method

Suppose the Malmquist Total Factor Productivity Index and its components are less than one. In that case, it indicates a decline in productivity, and if it is greater than 1, it indicates a productivity improvement. The change in the Malmquist Total Factor Productivity Index and the values of its components according to the periods of the companies operating in the insurance sector are shown in Table 7.

As seen in Table 7, the change value in total factor productivity in AGESA Life and Pension companies is more significant than one from 2017 to 2018. This value shows that the company achieved an 84% productivity increase in 2018 compared to the previous year. In other periods, since this value remained below 1, there were decreases in productivity compared to the previous period. The fact that the change values in the total factor productivity of Aksigorta and Anadolu Life and Pension companies in the other periods, except for the 2016–2017 period, are more significant than one, indicates that there was an increase in productivity in those periods.

Table 7 Malmquist Total Factor Productivity Index Results of Companies by Periods

Company Code	Period	Technical Efficiency Change	Technological Change	Total Factor Productivity Change
AGESA	2016–2017	1.000	0.275	0.275
	2017–2018	1.000	1.840	1.840
	2018–2019	1.000	0.998	0.988
	2019–2020	1.000	0.833	0.833
AKGRT	2016–2017	1.000	0.879	0.879
	2017–2018	1.000	1.428	1.428
	2018–2019	1.000	1.318	1.318
	2019–2020	1.000	1.052	1.052
ANSGR	2016–2017	2.166	0.719	1.556
	2017–2018	1.030	1.444	1.488
	2018–2019	0.900	1.272	1.145
	2019–2020	0.789	1.093	0.862
ANHYT	2016–2017	1.000	0.956	0.956
	2017–2018	1.000	1.037	1.037
	2018–2019	1.000	1.203	1.203
	2019–2020	1.000	1.600	1.600
RAYSG	2016–2017	0.491	0.786	0.386
	2017–2018	0.600	1.419	0.851
	2018–2019	1.575	1.258	1.981
	2019–2020	0.773	0.999	0.772
TURSG	2016–2017	1.237	1.152	1.425
	2017–2018	0.360	1.031	0.371
	2018–2019	1.759	1.402	2.467
	2019–2020	1.581	1.117	1.766

To determine the source of the increases in total factor productivity, technical efficiency change and technological change values are examined. Technological change is the source of the increases in total factor productivity. In other words, it can be said that companies have increased their activities by making technological developments in the relevant periods, and they have reached the same output amount with less input amount.

Anadolu Insurance Company shows an increase in total factor productivity compared to the previous period, except for 2019–2020. The increase in total factor productivity is the change in technical efficiency in the 2016–2017 period, the change in technical efficiency and technology in the 2017–2018 period, and the technological change in the 2018–2019 period. Only in the 2018–2019 period, the change value in the total factor productivity of Ray Insurance Company is greater than 1. The company achieved an increase in productivity in 2019 compared to the previous year. This increase is the increase in both technical efficiency and change in technology. Except for the 2017–2018 period, the Turkish Insurance Company has increased its total factor productivity compared to the previous period. The source of the increases in total factor productivity is the increase in both technical efficiency and change in technology. The changes in the Total Factor Productivity Index of the companies in the insurance sector for the period 2016–2020 and the values of their components are given in Table 8.

According to the total factor productivity index, an average annual productivity increase of 5.6% was observed in the insurance sector during the 2016–2020 period. In this period, while the technology change increased by 7.2%, technical efficiency decreased by 1.5%. When we evaluate on a company basis, businesses with an increase in productivity in the 2016–2020 period; Turkey Insurance (23.2%), Anadolu Insurance (23%), Anadolu Life and Pension (17.5%), and AkSigorta (14.8%) businesses. In the 2016–2020 period, productivity losses of 19.4% and 15.8% were measured in AGESA and Ray Insurance companies. According to the periods, The change in the total factor productivity indices of the insurance sector is shown in Table 9.

As seen in the table, the highest increase in Total Factor Productivity was realized in 2018-2019. This period is given in bold in the table. The insurance industry

Table 8 Malmquist Total Factor Productivity Index (2016–2020)

Companies	Technical Efficiency Change (TEC)	Technological Change (TC)	Total Factor Productivity Change (TFPC)
AGESA	1.000	0.806	0.806
AKGRT	1.000	1.148	1.148
ANSGR	1.122	1.096	1.230
ANHYT	1.000	1.175	1.175
RAYSG	0.774	1.088	0.842
TURSG	1.055	1.168	1.232
Average	0.985	1.072	1.056

Table 9 Malmquist Total Factor Productivity Index Results of the Insurance Industry

Period	Technical Efficiency Change	Technological Change	Total Factor Productivity Change
2016–2017	1.047	0.729	0.763
2017–2018	0.778	1.339	1.042
2018–2019	**1.165**	**1.235**	**1.438**
2019–2020	0.994	1.094	1.087

achieved a 43.8% increase in productivity in 2019 compared to the previous year. The source of this increase is a 16.5% improvement in technical efficiency and 23.5% improvement in technology. The highest decrease in Total Factor Productivity was realized by 23.7% from 2016 to 2017. This decrease is due to technological regression. When the values are analyzed in terms of the components of Total Factor Efficiency, the highest progress in technical efficiency is in the 2018–2019 period, with a rate of 16.5%. The most significant decrease in technical efficiency was observed in the 2017–2018 period, with a rate of 22.2%. In the technology change, the highest progress was observed with a rate of 33.9% in the 2017–2018 period, while the highest decrease was observed in the 2016–2017 period with a rate of 27.1%.

7 Conclusion

Financial management of unexpected risks poses a significant challenge for governments and institutions worldwide. The insurance sector makes significant contributions to reducing financial fragility in the economy. Insurance companies are one of the financial institutes with a significant share in the economy in developed countries. The insurance sector's resource potential to transfer to financial markets is also significant for developing countries. The efficiency of insurance companies in developing countries positively impacts their financial markets.

While the ratio of premium products in the Turkish insurance sector to Gross Domestic Product was 2.05% in 2015, this ratio reached 2.78% in 2020. The profit amounts of the Turkish insurance sector have also increased continuously over the past five years. It is essential for Turkey that the sector develops daily and companies increase their performance. In this direction, the DEA method is used as an essential method in determining the financial performance of companies, in other words, the degree of efficiency.

This study measured the efficiency levels of 6 insurance companies traded in the Stock Exchange Market Istanbul in 2016–2020 using the non-parametric DEA method. According to the result of the analysis of the input-oriented CCR model, AGESA Life and Pension, Aksigorta, and Anadolu Life and Pension companies were found to be effective in all of the years 2016–2020. On the other hand, the

Turkish insurance companies were determined to be effective in 2017 and 2020. Ineffective Anadolu Insurance and Ray Insurance companies need to improve their inputs and outputs to be effective.

The changes in the efficiency values of the insurance sector during the period were measured using the Total Factor Productivity index method. The biggest change in the productivity index occurred in the 2018–2019 period. The insurance industry increased 43.8% in productivity in 2019 compared to the previous year. The source of this increase is a 16.5% improvement in technical efficiency and 23.5% improvement in technology. The most significant decline in Total Factor Productivity was 23.7% from 2016 to 2017. This decline is due to technological regression.

The results obtained in the study are similar to Masud et al. (2019)'s study on the Malaysian insurance industry. As in the case of Malaysia, the most crucial factor that increases the effectiveness of companies in the Turkish insurance sector is technological progress. It is thought that the reason for the decrease in activity in the sector in 2020 is the Covid-19 pandemic, which affects the whole world.

References

Akhisar İ, Tezergil S (2014) Malmquist Toplam Faktör Verimlilik Endeksi: Türk Sigorta Sektörü Uygulaması. Finansal Araştırmalar ve Çalışmalar Dergisi 5(10):1–14

Akhtar MH (2018) Performance analysis of takaful and conventional insurance companies in Saudi Arabia. Benchmark Int J 25(2):677–695

Al-Amri K, Gattoufi S, Al-Muharrami S (2012) Analyzing the technical efficiency of insurance companies in GCC. J Risk Financ 13(4):362–380

Almulhim T (2019) Analysis of takaful vs. conventional insurance firms' efficiency: two-stage DEA of Saudi Arabia's insurance market. Cogent Bus Manage 6:1–18

Arslan P (2021) Efficiency in non-life insurance companies (2006-2016). Human Sci 16:45–58

Barros CP, Barroso N, Borges MR (2005) Evaluating the efficiency and productivity of insurance companies with a Malmquist index: a case study for Portugal. Geneva Pap Risk Insur Iss Pract 30:244–267

Battal A, Jarwaan S, Fahad AY (2018) Estimating the total productivity growth of insurance companies listed in the Iraqi stock exchange. Proc Pap ICABEP 2018:20–29

Boussofiane A, Dyson RG, Thanassoulis E (1991) Applied data envelopment analysis. Eur J Oper Res 2(6):1–15

Caves DW, Christensen LR, Diewert WE (1982) The economic theory of index numbers and the measurement of input, output and productivity. Econometrica 50(6):1393–1414

Charnes A, Cooper WW, Rhodes E (1978) Measuring the efficiency of decision-making units. Eur J Oper Res 2:429–444

Charnes A, Cooper WW, Lewin AY, Seighford LM (1994) Basic DEA models. In: Charnes A, Cooper WW, Lewin AY, Seighford LM (eds) Data envelopment analysis. - theory, methodology, and applications. Kluwer Academic Publishers, Boston/Dordrecht/London, pp 23–47

Coelli T (1996) A Guide to Deap Version 2.1: A DEA Computer Program. CEPA Working Paper 96/08. University of New England

Ekinci R (2021) Türk Sigortacılık Sektöründe Etkinlik Ve Belirleyenleri: Veri Zarflama Analizi Ve Parçalı Regresyon Modeli Bulguları. J Financ Res Stud 13(25):374–406

Eling M, Luhnen M (2010) Efficiency in the international insurance industry: a cross-country comparison. J Bank Financ 34:1497–1509

Fare R, Grosskopf S, Norris M, Zhong Z (1994) Productivity growth technical progress and efficiency change in industry. Am Econ Rev Combine J Econ Liter J Econ Persp 84:66–80

Hwang S-N, Kao T-L (2006) Measuring managerial efficiency in non-life insurance companies: an application of two-stage data envelopment analysis. Int J Manag 23(3):699–720

Kaffash S, Azizi R, Huang Y, Zhu J (2020) A survey of data envelopment analysis applications in the insurance industry 1993–2018. Eur J Oper Res 284(3):801–813

Karaca FB, Kılıçarslan Ş (2019) Türkiye'de Faaliyet Gösteren Hayat Dışı Sigorta Şirketlerinde Veri Zarflama Analizi İle Etkinlik Tahmini. Turkish Stud Econ Finance Polit 14(4):1359–1381

Kavak B, Cihangir M (2019) Sigorta Şirketlerinin Etkinlik Düzeylerinin Saptanması: Borsa İstanbul'da Yer Alan Sigorta Şirketleri Üzerine VZA Modeliyle Bir Uygulama. J Eurasian Soc Econ Stud 6:115–128

Köse A (2010) Türk Sigorta Sektörü Hayat ve Emeklilik Şirketleri Etkinlik Analizi. Akademik Araştırmalar Dergisi 44:85–100

Kula V, Kandemir T, Özdemir L (2009) VZA Malmquist Toplam Faktör Verimlilik Ölçüsü: İMKB'ye Koteli Çimento Şirketleri Üzerine Bir Araştırma. SÜ İİBF Sosyal ve Ekonomik Araştırmalar Dergisi 9(17):187–202

Külekci I, Saldanlı A (2018) Türk Sigortacılık Sektöründe Hayat Dışı Sigorta Şirketlerinin Etkinlik Analizi. Ekoist: J Econometr Statis 14(29):225–246

Malmquist S (1953) Index Numbers and Indifference Curves. Trabajos De Estatistica 4:209–242

Mandal S (2014) A DEA-investigation of efficiency of the Indian general insurance during recession. J Adv Manage Res 11(1):115–136

Masud MM, Rana MS, Mia MA, Saifullah MK (2019) How productive are life insurance institutions in Malaysia? A Malmquist approach. J Asian Finance Econ Bus 6:241–248

Naldöken Ü, Kaya MV (2020) Türkiye' De Sağlık Sigorta Şirketlerinin Etkinliklerinin Veri Zarflama Analiziyle Ölçülmesi. Dumlupınar Univ J Soc Sci 65:21–33

Naushad M, Farıdı MR, Faısal S (2020) Measuring the managerial efficiency of insurance companies in Saudi Arabia: a data envelopment analysis approach. J Asian Finance Econ Bus 28(7-8): 297

Nourani M, Devadason ES, Kweh QL, Lu W-M (2016) Business excellence: the managerial and value-creation efficiencies of the insurance companies. Total Qual Manag Bus Excell 28:879–896

"OECD Insurance Statistics 2020" <https://www.oecd-ilibrary.org/finance-and-investment/oecd-insurance-statistics-2020_adfe5566-en> Accessed 11 March 2021

Özen E, Grima S (2020) The Turkish life insurance market: an evaluation of the current situation and future challenges. In: Borda M, Grima S, Kwiecien I (eds) In life insurance in Europe. Springer, pp 45–58

Report on Insurance and Private Pension Activities in Turkey in 2019 (Insurance and Private Pension Regulation and Supervision Agency (SEDDK), 2020) <https://seddk.gov.tr/tr/raporlar/sigortacilik-ve-bes-faaliyetleri> Accessed 11 March 2021 Yazılışı doğru mu

Salimi Altan M (2010) 'Türk Sigortacılık Sektöründe Etkinlik: Veri Zarflama Analizi Yöntemi İle Bir Uygulama. J Gazi Univ Faculty Econ Adm Sci 12(1):185–204

Swiss Re World insurance: The recovery gains pace. Sigma, 3 (Swiss re Institute 2021) <https://www.swissre.com/institute/research/sigma-research/sigma-2021-03.html> Accessed 11 March 2021

Tarım A (2021) Data Veri Zarflama Analizi: Matematiksel Programlama Tabanlı Göreli Etkinlik Ölçüm Yaklaşımı. Sayıştay Yayınları

Türker Kaya Y, Doğan E (2005) Dezenflasyon Sürecinde Türk Bankacılık Sektöründe Etkinliğin Gelişimi. Bankacılık Düzenleme ve Denetleme Kurumu ARD Çalışma Raporları

Turkish Insurance Association Sector Report (Turkish Insurance Association 2020) <https://tsb.org.tr/media/attachments/2020_YILI_SEKT%C3%96R_RAPORU.pdf> Accessed 5 October 2021

Serap Vurur has 18 years of experience in teaching. At present author is working as an associate professor in finance at the Faculty of Bolvadin Applied Sciences University of Afyon Kocatepe, Turkey. The author presented more than 29 papers at various national and international conferences and published more than 22 research papers in various reputed journals. Six books Chapters with the titles financial system, economics and cost stickiness have been published. The author has been involved in four scientific projects and has been awarded third prize in the 21st Finance Symposium. The author is a member of the Finance Science Platform and TEMA (Turkey Combating Soil Erosion, for Reforestation and the Protection of Natural Resources Foundation).

Letife Özdemir received her BSc in Business (2002), MSc in Business (2005), Ph.D. in Business Finance (2011) from the University of Afyon Kocatepe. At present the author is working as an associate professor in finance at the Faculty of Economics and Administrative Sciences, University of Afyon Kocatepe, Turkey. The author presented more than 17 papers at various national and international conferences and published more than 24 research papers in various reputed journals. Four book chapters on different Financial markets have been published. The author has been involved in two scientific projects and has been awarded third prize in the 21st Finance Symposium. The author is a member of the Finance Science Platform and TEMA (Turkey Combating Soil Erosion, for Reforestation and the Protection of Natural Resources Foundation).

The Impact of Capital Structure on the Financial Performance of Insurance Companies: An Econometric Analysis of the Insurance Industry in Kosovo

Fisnik Morina, Vlora Berisha, and Kastriot Idrizaj

Abstract The primary purpose of this chapter is to analyze the impact of capital structure on the financial performance of insurance companies in Kosovo. During the literature review process, the empirical findings of many studies by other authors that have addressed the issue of the impact of capital structure on the financial performance of insurance companies in different parts of the world have been analyzed.

Quantitative methods have been applied in this scientific research based on the secondary data of the annual statistical reports of the time series of the Central Bank of Kosovo as well as the audited annual financial statements of insurance companies in Kosovo. In order to analyze the impact of capital structure on the financial performance of insurance companies in Kosovo, it is necessary to consider many other factors that explain the correlation between these variables. The period included in this study is 17 years (2004–2021), the number of insurance companies included in the analysis is 12, and the number of observations reaches 110.

The insurance industry in Kosovo plays an important role for all businesses in that without insurance companies, businesses could end up facing bankruptcy due to their instability and dynamic business environment. The capital structure is an essential aspect for insurance companies in Kosovo because these firms need funds to finance their operation, settle their claims or pay damages at the time of

F. Morina
Faculty of Business, Department of Banking and Finance, University "Haxhi Zeka", Peja, Kosovo

Financial Institutions and Risk Management at University of Malta, Msida, Malta
e-mail: fisnik.morina@unhz.eu

V. Berisha (✉)
Faculty of Business, Department of Accounting and Audit, University "Haxhi Zeka", Peja, Kosovo
e-mail: vlora.berisha@unhz.eu

K. Idrizaj
Faculty of Business, Department of Accounting and Finance, University "Haxhi Zeka", Peja, Kosovo

M. Lima Rego, S. Grima (eds.), *Cross-Disciplinary Impacts on Insurance Law*, AIDA Europe Research Series on Insurance Law and Regulation 8,
https://doi.org/10.1007/978-3-031-38526-1_7

loss. The study concluded that the capital structure has a significant impact on the financial performance of insurance companies in Kosovo. Based on the econometric results of this study, we can conclude that all independent variables (funds contributed by the owners, retained earnings, general and specific reserves, asset and liability management) have a significant positive impact on the financial performance of insurance companies in Kosovo.

Keywords Financial performance · Capital structure · Insurance companies · Profitability

JEL Codes G22 · G28 · G32 · G52 · G24

1 Introduction

The enormous contribution of the insurance industry to the economic growth and development of developing and developed countries has been documented in the literature and recognized by global researchers. No country can experience meaningful development without the presence of the insurance industry. Authors (Yinusa and Taiwo 2013; Vincent Kiptum 2014; Maina and Ishmail 2014; Tornyeva 2013; Narang 2018; Batool and Sahi 2020; Ayuba et al. 2019; Almajali and Shamsuddin 2019; Adeyemi et al. 2017) as well as many others have analyzed the impact of capital structure on the financial performance of insurance companies in financial services systems of different countries around the world.

According to the authors (Yinusa and Taiwo 2013), the insurance industry's role in mitigating unexpected and destructive phenomena by stimulating economic growth can not be overemphasized in developed and developing countries, as the insurance sector contributes to economic growth, both sectoral and geographical.[1] According to their study in Nigeria, the insurance industry has grown steadily, and the total premium has gone up from 75 billion in 2005 to over 300 billion in 2017. A study conducted by (Vincent Kiptum 2014) on the effect of capital structure and value of insurance companies showed that firms' capital structure and value have a positive correlation.[2] (Maina and Ishmail 2014) investigated the effect of capital structure on the performance of insurance companies listed on the Nigerian Stock Exchange. Their results conclude that the correlation between performance indicators and capital structure is negative. It turns out that the capital structure is vital in determining the insurance company's performance.[3]

In his study, the author (Tornyeva 2013) analyzed the determinants of the capital structure of insurance companies in Ghana. This study shows a statistically significant correlation between firm size and financial leverage. This indicates that larger

[1] Yinusa and Taiwo (2013), pp. 218–224.

[2] Vincent Kiptum (2014), pp. 1–71.

[3] Maina and Ishmail (2014), pp. 209–223.

insurance companies have a lower probability of default and thus greater ability to use more debt funds. This supports the compromise theory, which suggests that the larger the firm, the lower the credit risk. Debt capital providers are safer in lending to large insurance companies than smaller ones because larger ones have the ability to diversify their operations and thus reduce their risk profile. Smaller insurance companies have used less debt in their capital structure due to the problem of information asymmetries.[4]

Narang (2018) study proves that the capital structure plays an essential role in the performance of an insurance company. The main objective of companies is to maximize their profits and, at the same time, minimize their costs. Most companies use a mix of capital and debt, which form the capital structure, so the choice of internal or external financing is one of a firm's serious concerns. The econometric results of this study show that the capital structure positively impacts the company's performance. Furthermore, the study's findings confirmed a positive correlation between the determinants of capital structure and firm performance. Insurance companies are very important to corporations, businesses and individuals because they protect these actors from financial loss. Therefore, the insurance sector is crucial financially in almost all developed and developing countries.[5]

In their study, the authors (Batool and Sahi 2020) have analyzed the determinants of the financial performance of insurance companies in the financial systems of two countries, the United Kingdom and the United States of America. According to the results of their study, the internal factors that affect the profitability of insurance companies in the US and the UK are firm size, liquidity, financial leverage and asset turnover. At the same time, external macroeconomic factors that affect the financial performance of insurance companies are gross domestic product (GDP), inflation and interest rate. In the US insurance industry, the study results show a high positive correlation of $R = 86\%$ of internal and external factors with profitability indicators: return on assets and return on capital. Whereas, in the insurance industry in the UK, the econometric results of their study show a high positive correlation ($R = 70\%$) between internal and external factors with indicators of the financial performance of insurance companies.[6]

In their study, the authors (Ayuba et al. 2019) analyzed the effect of capital structure on the financial performance of listed insurance companies on the Nigerian stock exchange for the period between 2012 and 2017. According to the results, capital structure has a significant impact on the financial performance of insurance companies. The firm's debt-equity ratio is an essential factor in the financial performance of listed insurance companies on the Nigerian Stock Exchange. The result shows that the debt-equity ratio had a positive effect on return on equity but a negative one on return on equity. The author of this study recommended that the senior management of any insurance company make prudent decisions to remain

[4]Tornyeva (2013), pp. 52–60, ISSN 2222-1697 (Paper) ISSN 2222-2847 (Online).
[5]Narang (2018), pp. 251–254.
[6]Batool and Sahi (2020), pp. 1–9.

profitable and competitive.[7] In their study, the authors (Almajali and Shamsuddin 2019) analyzed the correlation between capital structure and profitability of insurance companies in Jordan. Empirical results of this study show that short-term debt and long-term debt are positively related to (ROE) while negatively related to Tobin's Q. The study findings also show that financial leverage has a significant impact on the profitability of insurance companies in Jordan. These results confirmed that an increase in the loan position is associated with an increase in profitability.[8] Another study by the authors (Adeyemi et al. 2017) analyzed the effect of capital structure on the profitability of insurance companies in Nigeria. According to this study's econometric results, we can conclude that the capital structure measured by the debt ratio and the debt-equity ratio negatively correlates with the financial performance measured by ROA and ROE.[9]

When firms get insurance, they transfer their risk to insurance companies. Insurance companies have several advantages in taking on risk: first, they have considerable experience in ensuring similar risks to assess the probability of loss and determine the risk accurately. Second, they provide advice on measures that firms should take to reduce risk and may offer lower premiums for firms that accept this advice. Third, the insurance company can spread the risk by maintaining a diversified portfolio of policies. The requirements for individual policies can be very uncertain, but the requirements for the policy portfolio can also be very stable. Of course, insurance companies can not diversify macroeconomic risks. Instead, firms use insurance policies to reduce specific risks, and they find other ways to avoid risks at the macro level.

This chapter focuses on identifying how capital structure decisions affect insurance companies in the financial sector in Kosovo. According to the Central Bank of Kosovo data for 2021, the insurance sector in 2020 was characterized by an increase in assets, maintaining the level of premiums collected from the previous year and reducing the level of claims paid. The spread of the Covid-19 pandemic had a more pronounced effect on the decline in the level of claims paid (due to restrictions on movement), thus influencing the insurance sector to make a profit in 2020. The insurance sector assets reached in 2021 have reached the value of euro 220.5 million and marked an annual increase of 12.2%. Therefore, taking into account the fact that the financial stability of the financial system in Kosovo largely depends on the financial performance of insurance companies, this study emphasizes the importance of capital structure decisions in the profitability of insurance companies. Insurance companies that perform well can concentrate their investments on securities domestically and abroad. The research questions of this study are:

1. *How have the funds contributed by the owners affected the financial performance of insurance companies in Kosovo?*

[7] Ayuba et al. (2019), pp. 57–74.

[8] Almajali and Shamsuddin (2019), pp. 64–73.

[9] Adeyemi et al. (2017), pp. 8–15.

2. *What effect do retained earnings have on the financial performance of insurance companies in Kosovo?*
3. *What is the impact of general and specific reserves on the profit/loss of insurance companies in Kosovo?*
4. *What effect does asset and liability management have on the financial performance of insurance companies in Kosovo?*

This chapter will provide empirical and scientific evidence for future studies, which can be conducted by other researchers in the field of the insurance industry in Kosovo. The results of this study will serve as a reference basis for drafting financial policies in the field of insurance in Kosovo, and based on the results of this study, insurance companies in Kosovo will be able to design more effective strategies for managing capital structure, and also increase the financial performance of insurance industries, avoiding potential risks in the future. According to various studies in this field, there is a correlation and a positive effect between the capital structure and the financial performance of insurance companies in different financial systems. Based on the theories of capital structure and studies by other authors, the results of this study should find a correlation and a positive effect of the components of the capital structure on the financial performance of insurance companies in Kosovo.

2 Literature Review

Many studies have analyzed the impact of capital structure on the performance of insurance companies in different countries around the world. Referring to the econometric findings of studies by various authors, we have compiled a review of the existing literature on the capital structure and its impact on the financial performance of insurance companies.

The capital structure of a firm is the mix of its financial resources available to conduct the business and is a crucial determinant of how the business operates. While financial capital is uncertain and a critical resource for all firms, finance suppliers can exercise control over firms. The two main classes of financing for a business are debt and equity. In static trade-off theory, firms balance the tax benefits of debt versus costs and bankruptcy. Given that firms are allowed to deduct the interest paid on the debt from their tax liability, they favour debt over their capital. As a result, the present value of the profits resulting from the choice of debt over equity (the so-called tax shield) increases the firm's value. Without any additional debt compensation costs, this tax advantage would mean total debt financing.[10]

Agency problems exist between shareholders and managers. In this relationship, the shareholders are the chairpersons, and they do not have direct control over the actions of the managers (agents). One must remember that firms undertake projects

[10] Kraus and Litzenberger (1973), pp. 911–922.

with a positive net present value in a perfect market. Also, contracts are easily enforceable in a perfect market, and shareholder decisions are easy to contract. So creditors and shareholders sign a contract under which creditors will get their investments back. Shareholders will choose projects with positive net present value, or when projects are mutually excluded, shareholders will choose the project with maximum net present value. Therefore, when a firm takes on a risky project, it can create wealth for shareholders but deprive creditors of wealth. Jensen and Meckling (1976) first introduced the effects of asset substitution and risk transfer. This is considered one of the essential concepts in corporate finance.[11]

The pecking order theory says that companies prioritize their sources of financing (from internal financing to equity) and choose value equity financing as a last resort. So, according to this theory, domestic funds are initially applied, and when they are exhausted, debt is issued. If the company is not careful to issue more debt, then equity is issued. This theory states that businesses adhere to a hierarchy of funding sources and prefer domestic financing when available, and debt is preferred over equity if external financing is required (Table 1).[12]

From the review of the existing literature, we can conclude that in most studies by different authors, capital structure decisions positively impact the profitability of insurance companies in the financial systems of different countries of the world. Through these studies analyzed in the meta-analysis part, it has been emphasized that the management of insurance companies should make efforts to have an optimal capital structure by increasing their capital level and reducing debt dependence so that an illiquid state is avoided. Various investors in financial markets are often willing to provide ongoing financing for insurance companies when these companies have an optimal capital structure. Such decisions positively affect their financial performance and the development of insurance companies in future. Capital structure decisions that positively affect the financial performance of insurance companies will also have an impact on reducing the exposure of these companies to various financial risks.

Compared to the studies of other authors, this study will provide scientific and empirical evidence on the impact of capital structure components on the financial performance of insurance companies. In most of the works included in the meta-analysis part by different authors, the determinants of capital structure are included as independent variables. In this study, the independent variables are the components of the capital structure (contributed funds by owners, retained earnings, general and specific reserves, asset and liability management).

[11] Jensen and Meckling (1976), pp. 305–360.

[12] Caselli and Negri (2021).

Table 1 Summary of extant literature

Author	Year	Variables	Methods	Findings
(Salim and Yadav 2012)	1995–2011	ROA, ROE, EPS, Tobin Q, short term debt to total assets, long term debt to total assets, total debt to total asset, the logarithm of total assets, changes in total asset	Regression Analysis	According to the results of this study, the growth and size of the firm have a positive relationship with the performance of companies which ROA measures, while STD and LTD have negatively affected the company's performance. Furthermore, the empirical results of this study also show a significant positive correlation between firm growth and ROE. Total debt in relation to total assets has a significant negative correlation at the significance level of 1% in the firm's performance for three sectors: consumption, construction, and industrial production, which suggest that the increase in total debt will decrease firm performance.[a]
(Eladly 2021)	1999–2019	Debt Ratio, Return on Equity, Liquidity, Return on Investment	Pearson Correlation Matrix, Hausman Test for Correlated Random Effects, Fixed Effect Model	The econometric results of this study show a significant negative linear correlation between the independent variable in terms of return on equity, return on investment and the dependent variable on capital structure at the level of statistical significance (0.001). This study identifies an important correlation between capital structure and liquidity, but there is also an important relationship between capital structure, return on equity and return on investment.[b]
(Getahun 2016)	2004–2013	Return on Asset, Firm Leverage, Growth Opportunities. Firm Size, Tangibility of Fixed Asset, Liquidity of the Firm, Business Risk	Regression Analysis	The econometric results of this study show that financial leverage, size, the vulnerability of fixed assets, and business risk significantly impact the performance of insurance companies in Ethiopia. The results provide strong empirical evidence of capital structure theory, which states that financial leverage is essential for firm performance. Furthermore, a significant negative correlation exists between financial leverage and performance.[c]

(continued)

Table 1 (continued)

Author	Year	Variables	Methods	Findings
(Shamsuddin et al. 2020)	2007–2017	Short-term Debt, Long-term Debt, Equity Financing, Return on Asset (ROA), Return on Equity (ROE) and Tobin's Q	Regression Analysis	According to the empirical findings of this study, we find that the capital structure affects the profitability of insurance companies listed in Jordan. The results also reveal a significant positive relationship between long-term debt to total assets with profitability ratios: return on assets (ROA), return on equity (ROE), and Tobin's Q.[d]
(Jaishi 2020)	2013–2019	Return on Assets, Earnings per share, Total debt ratio, Equity to total assets, Leverage, Firm size, Liquidity, Assets tangibility	Regression Analysis	The main conclusion of this study is that the total debt ratio, the ratio of capital to total assets, leverage, firm size, liquidity and vulnerability to fixed assets are significant factors in determining the financial performance of insurance companies in Nepal. Insurance companies in Nepal suggest increasing their total debt ratio and tangible assets and reducing capital, firm size, and liquidity ratio to increase their financial performance.[e]
(Ajao and Ogieriakhi 2018)	2009–2017	Size, Performance, Leverage, Tangibility, Growth Rate, Premium Growth, Age	The Panel Regression Analysis	Based on the empirical results of this study, it can be concluded that there is a statistically significant correlation between the performance of insurance companies and the firm's age. Moreover, firm size and growth rate are firm-specific factors that significantly correlate with the insurance company's performance.[f]
(Morara and Sibindi 2021)	2009–2018	ROA, ROE, Solvency Ratio, Combined Ratio, Debt Ratio, Size, Reinsurance Ratio, Investment Ratio, Age	The Panel Regression Analysis	The empirical results of this study show that the financial performance and size of the insurer were positively correlated. Through this study, it was found that the financial performance of the insurer was negatively correlated with the age variable. The study also found that insurance companies with higher financial leverage performed better than those with lower financial leverage.[g]

(Kiptoo et al. 2021)	2013–2020	ROA, Credit Risk, Market Risk, Operation Risk, Liquidity Risk, Age, Size	Regression Analysis	The econometric results of this study show that insurance companies with a higher percentage of troubled accounts receivable than total receivables perform poorly. Consequently, these insurance companies need to design credit management strategies to ensure that receivables are collected within the stipulated time to avoid cases of non-performing receivables and to improve performance.[h]
(Olawale et al. 2019)	2013–2017	ROE, Short-term Debt Ratio, Premium Growth,	Regression Analysis	According to the econometric results of this study, it can be concluded that short-term debt has a negative and significant effect on the profitability of insurance companies listed in Nigeria. In contrast, long-term debt and an increase in premiums have a positive effect and a significant effect on the profitability of insurance companies listed in Nigeria.[i]
(Wanyama and Olweny 2013)	2007–2011	ROE, ROA, Board Size, Board Composition, CEO Duality, Leverage	Regression Analysis	According to the results of this study, there is a strong relationship between corporate governance practices and the financial performance of insurance companies. The size of the board was found to negatively affect the financial performance of insurance companies.[j]

Source: Meta-analysis processed by the authors (2021)
[a]Salim and Yadav (2012), pp. 156–166
[b]Eladly (2021), pp. 103–114
[c]Getahun (2016), pp. 45–53
[d]Shamsuddin et al. (2020), pp. 1310–1320
[e]Jaishi (2020), pp. 89–106
[f]Ajao and Ogieriakhi (2018), pp. 14–28
[g]Kamanda and Athenia Bongani (2021), pp. 566, 1–13
[h]Kiptoo et al. (2021), pp. 1997246, 1–17
[i]Olawale et al. (2019), pp. 13–22
[j]David and Tobias (2013), pp. 96–120

3 Scientific Research Methodology and Specification of Econometric Models

The primary purpose of this study is to analyze the impact of capital structure on the financial performance of insurance companies in Kosovo. During the literature review process, the empirical findings of many studies by other authors that have addressed the issue of the impact of the capital structure on the financial performance of insurance companies in different parts of the world have been analyzed.

Authors such as (Ajao and Ogieriakhi 2018), (Eladly 2021), (Getahun 2016), (Jaishi 2020), (Morara and Sibindi 2021), (Olawale et al. 2019), (Salim and Yadav 2012), (Wanyama and Olweny 2013) as well as many other studies by other authors have analyzed the impact of capital structure on the financial performance of insurance companies in different countries of the world.

The main goal of conducting this study is that the insurance industry is one of the critical sectors of a country's financial system. Therefore, it is crucial to analyze how the capital structure has affected the financial performance of insurance companies in Kosovo over the years.

Kosovo's insurance sector over the years has not had a satisfactory performance influenced by several factors, such as a turnover tax of 5% for insurers and damages caused by uninsured vehicles circulating in the territory of the Republic of Kosovo. Given this, the financial results of insurance companies over the past years have been negative. However, over the last two years, we have seen a significant improvement in the insurance sector's performance due to the supervisory and legislative measures taken by the CBK.

During these years, the insurance sector in Kosovo has performed exceptionally well, providing insurance products that the economy needs. Therefore, one can say that this sector is making a significant contribution to increasing security and, consequently, improving the environment to operate in Kosovo's economy. However, the 3% share of the insurance market in the total financial system of the country continues to remain low, with high room for growth and expansion in this sector. The Central Bank of the Republic of Kosovo is and continues to be committed to supporting the sustainable development of this sector. However, increased activity is needed to increase the financial education of the public in terms of products offered by the insurance industry.

The main hypotheses of this study are:

H1: Funds contributed by the owners have positively impacted the financial performance of insurance companies in Kosovo.

H2: Retained earnings have positively impacted insurance financial performance in Kosovo.

H3: General and specific reserves have positively impacted the profit/loss of insurance companies in Kosovo.

H4: Asset and liability management have had a positive impact on the financial performance of insurance companies in Kosovo.

Table 2 Description of variables included in econometric models

Variables	Description of the variable	Data source
Dependent variable (Y)	Financial performance—Profit/loss of the year (FP)	CBK Annual Reports—Time Series (2004–2021)
Independent variable (X_1)	Funds contributed by owners (FCO)	CBK Annual Reports—Time Series (2004–2021)
Independent variable (X_2)	Retained Earnings (RE)	CBK Annual Reports—Time Series (2004–2021)
Independent variable (X_3)	General and special reserves (GSR)	CBK Annual Reports—Time Series (2004–2021)
Independent variable (X_4)	Asset and Liability Management (ALM) – Asset Coverage Ratio	CBK Annual Reports—Time Series (2004–2021)

Source: Calculation of data by the authors (2021)

Quantitative methods have been applied to test these hypotheses based on the secondary data of the annual reports of the Central Bank of Kosovo, the Kosovo Security Bureau, the Tax Administration of Kosovo, the Ministry of Finance and the Kosovo Agency of Statistics. However, to analyze the impact of capital structure on the financial performance of insurance companies in Kosovo, it is necessary to consider many other factors that explain the correlation between these variables. To specify the econometric model, the authors based themselves on several studies by various authors that have analyzed the effects of capital structure on the financial performance of insurance companies in different countries of the world.

The period included in this study is 17 years (2004–2021), the number of insurance companies included in the analysis is 12, and the number of observations reaches 110. The data are processed in STATA and Microsoft Excel. For the authentication of the validity of the hypotheses of this study, we have applied the following statistical tests: linear regression, random effect, fixed effect, Hausman—Taylor Regression, GMM Model—Arellano Bond Estimation, as well as, linear trend analysis through historical and comparative method (Table 2).

The primary purpose of using these econometric models is that we deal with panel data and dynamic models. Through these statistical tests, most authors have identified the correlation between capital structure and financial performance of insurance companies.

To verify the validity of the hypothesis of this study, we have constructed this econometric model as follows:

$$FP_{it} = \beta_0 + \beta_1\ FCO_{it} + \beta_2\ RE_{it} + \beta_3\ GSR_{it} + \beta_4\ ALM_{it} + \gamma_{it}$$

Where: FP – Financial performance; FCO – Funds contributed by owners; RE – Retained earnings; GSR – General and special reserves; ALM – Asset and Liability Management; γ – stochastic variables (other factors not taken into account in the model); i – code and t – time period.

Financial performance is a subjective measure of how well a firm can use its core business model assets and generate revenue. There are many stakeholders in a company, including commercial creditors, bondholders, investors, employees and management. Each group has its own interest in tracking a company's financial performance. Financial performance identifies how well a company generates revenue and manages its shareholders' assets, liabilities, and financial interests. Financial analysis refers to studying and evaluating a company's financial statements—a collection of data and figures organized according to recognized accounting principles. The goal is to understand the company's business model, the profit (or loss) of its operations, and how it is spending, investing, and generally using its money.

Contributed capital, also known as paid-up capital, is the cash and other assets that shareholders have given to a company in exchange for shares. For example, investors make capital contributions when a company issues equity shares based on a price that shareholders are willing to pay for them. The total amount of capital contributed or paid in equity represents their shares or ownership in the company. Contributed capital may also refer to the balance sheet item of a company listed under shareholder equity, often presented with the balance sheet entry for additional paid-in capital. Contributed capital is reported on the equity portion of the balance sheet and is usually divided into ordinary shares and additional paid-in capital accounts. In other words, the contributed capital includes the par value—or par value—of the shares found in the ordinary share account and the amount of money above and above the par value that the shareholders were willing to pay for their shares—the premium of the stock is found in the additional paid-in capital account.

Retained earnings are the part of the company's net profit that remains after taxes and the distribution of dividends among shareholders, used for reinvestment purposes for development needs. Unallocated assets can be invested in the bulk, held in the form of cash balances or suitable for market circulation securities, used to finance the purchases of other firms, lend to customers, repay loans, or increase liquid assets. Compared to raising new capital by borrowing or issuing shares, retaining some of the profits are an alternative and more straightforward method of financing. For a company to grow and develop, it must invest its retained earnings in itself. If successful, in the long run, this will increase the company's profitability and increase its share price, i.e., investors will earn more money than if they initially demanded large dividends. Every company starts its activities to generate income. Therefore, the company members expect to have extra money, regardless of whether they will work in this enterprise or not. Profits held on the balance sheet are the company's remaining income after all debts owed to suppliers and employees of the company have been paid.

Total reserves: total reserves are not set aside for any specific purpose but the overall financial strengthening of the company.

Specific reserves: specific reserves are set aside for a specific purpose and can not be used for any other reason. Specific reserves are sometimes known as special reserves.

Capital reserves are created from capital gains—profits from sources other than ordinary trading activities. Capital reserves are usually set aside for capital losses. The General Reserve is the amount set aside from the profit earned by the company during its ordinary course of operations to meet future needs, such as unforeseen cases, strengthening the company's financial position, increasing working capital, paying dividends to shareholders, and compensating for specific future losses. The General Reserve is considered part of the profit and loss sharing account. It is generally used to cope with future uncertainties such as future business losses and future litigation, and there is no set percentage for creating reserves. It is at the company's discretion how much reserve it wants to accumulate. In case of losses, reserves are not created by the company. Instead, they are shown under the heading 'Reserves and surpluses' on the balance sheet liabilities side.

Asset/liability management is the process of managing the use of assets and cash flows to reduce the firm's risk of losing a liability on time. Well-managed assets and liabilities increase business profits. The asset/liability management process is typically applied to bank loan portfolios and pension plans. It also includes the economic value of capital. The concept of asset/liability management focuses on cash flow time because company managers have to plan the payment of liabilities. The process should ensure that assets are available to pay off debts on time and that assets or profits can be converted into cash. The asset/liability management process applies to different categories of assets on the balance sheet. The practice of asset and liability management can involve many factors, including strategic asset allocation, risk mitigation, and regulatory and capital frameworks adjustment. By successfully matching assets to liabilities, financial institutions are left with a surplus that can be actively managed to maximize the return on their investment and increase profitability. Asset and liability management is managing financial risks arising from discrepancies between assets and liabilities as part of an investment strategy in financial accounting.

4 Analysis of Linear Trends Between Financial Performance and Funds Contributed by Owners in the Insurance Industry in Kosovo (2004–2021)

This part of the chapter will present a linear trend analysis or comparative analysis between the leading indicators of the capital structure in the insurance industry in Kosovo and the financial performance that represents the profit or loss of the year for all licensed companies, according to the Central Bank of Kosovo for the period (2004–2021). This part of the analysis will initially present the linear trend between financial performance profit and loss expressed in millions of euros and funds contributed by owners for the period 2004–2021. The following tables show the linear trend between financial performance and funds contributed by owners, which represent one of the main items within the capital structure of insurance companies in Kosovo.

Based on the linear trend analysis in Table 3 and Fig. 1, we find an average cumulative upward trend between financial performance and funds contributed by owners. In 2004 it was €8.39M while in the year 2010 it increased by €19.39M.

Table 3 Linear trend between FP and FCO (2004–2010)

Year	Financial Performance (Profit & Loss of the year)—mil. €	Funds Contributed by the Owners—Mil. €	Trend
2004	1.7	20.6	8.39
2005	4	20.1	10.23
2006	1.6	23	12.06
2007	3.5	27	13.89
2008	3.4	30.5	15.72
2009	−3.1	33.8	17.56
2010	0.9	33.9	19.39

Source: Calculation of data by the authors (2021)

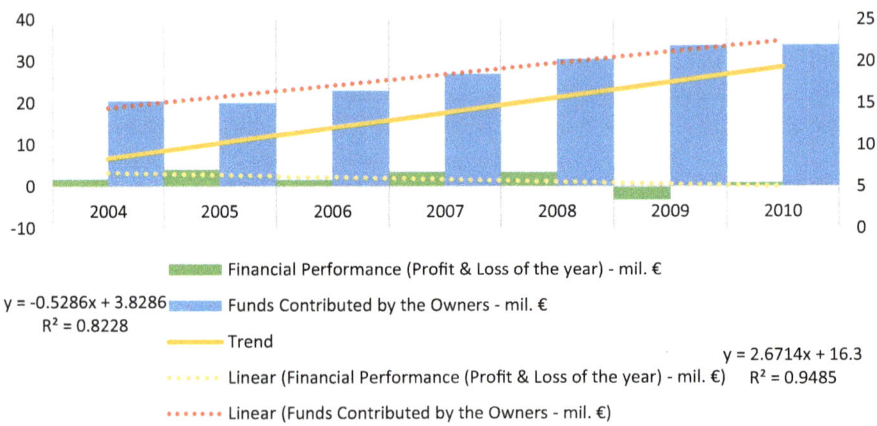

Fig. 1 Linear trend between FP and FCO (2004–2010). *Source:* Calculation of data by the authors (2021)

Financial performance between 2004 and 2007 was constantly increasing, while after 2007 until 2009 it decreased to −€3.1M. This was also a result of the consequences caused by the financial crisis in Kosovo's insurance sector and globally. Meanwhile, the funds contributed by the owners from 2004 to 2010 continuously marked an increase from €20.6M to €33.9M. As a result, the coefficient of determination of the linear trend between these two variables is 94.85%, which means we have a high level of explainability between these two variables for the analyzed period (2004–2010). As a general finding for this period analyzed, it is noted that the cumulative upward trend between these variables means that insurance companies, the more they have contributed through funds in the capital of insurance companies it has a positive impact on the profit of insurance companies for the relevant period (Table 4).

Based on Table 3 and Fig. 2, the linear trend between financial performance and funds contributed by owners for the period (2011–2021) is presented. Referring to the data in the table and the corresponding figure, we can conclude that there is a

Table 4 Linear trend between FP and FCO (2011–2021)

Year	Financial Performance (Profit & Loss of the year)—mil. €	Funds Contributed by the Owners—mil. €	Trend
2011	0.9	39.9	10.28
2012	−1.9	39.8	14.34
2013	−0.8	43.4	18.39
2014	−0.3	43.4	22.44
2015	−7.8	54.4	26.49
2016	−24.7	74.5	30.55
2017	6.4	81.6	34.60
2018	1.6	77.1	38.65
2019	−5.4	84.1	42.70
2020	4.2	91.3	46.76
2021	1.3	91.3	50.81

Source: Calculation of data by the authors (2021)

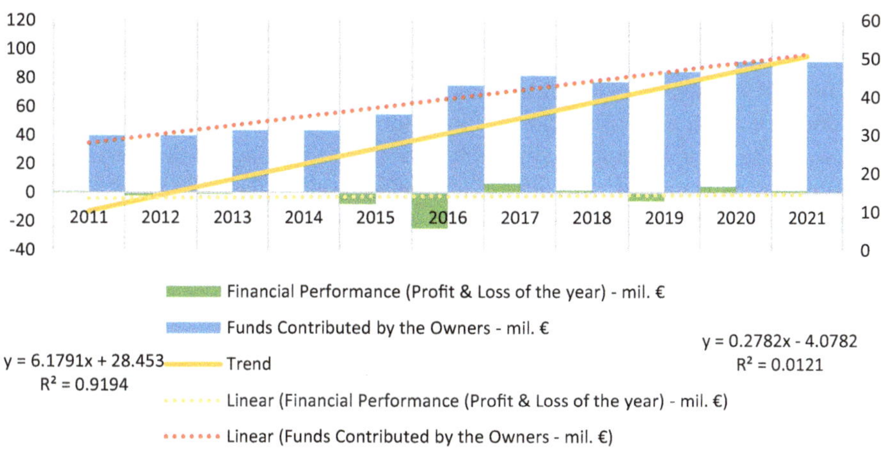

Fig. 2 Linear trend between FP and FCO (2011–2021). *Source:* Calculation of data by the authors (2021)

cumulative upward trend between these two variables; in 2011, the value of the average cumulative trend was 10.28, while in 2021, it is € 50.81 million, which means that we have an increase in the linear trend and that there is a positive correlation between these two variables.

The performance of insurance companies in Kosovo marked a continuous decline between 2011 and 2016; then, between 2017 and 2018, they operated profitably, while in 2019, they again suffered a negative performance with a value of - €5.4M. Meanwhile, the funds contributed by the owners from 2011 to 2021 have continuously increased from €39.9 million to €91.3 million. Based on the linear trend analysis results, as a general conclusion, we can estimate that the funds contributed by the owners have had a positive impact on financial performance, implying that the value of the trend is increasing. The coefficient of determination of the linear trend, in this case, is 91.94%, a relatively high level of explainability between these two variables. Based on this analysis of the linear trend between financial performance and funds contributed by owners for the period 2004–2021, it can be concluded that there is a cumulative linear upward trend between the two variables and that funds contributed by owners have positively affected the financial performance of insurance companies for the period under review.

5 Analysis of Linear Trends Between Financial Performance and Retained Earnings in the Insurance Industry in Kosovo (2004–2021)

This part of the chapter will present a linear trend analysis or comparative analysis between the leading indicators of the capital structure in the insurance industry in Kosovo and the financial performance that represents the profit or loss of the year for all companies which Central Bank of Kosovo licenses for the period (2004–2021).

This part of the analysis will initially present the linear trend between financial performance profit and loss expressed in millions of euros and profits held for the period (2004–2021). The following tables show the linear trends between financial performance and retained earnings, which represent one of the main items within the capital structure of insurance companies in Kosovo.

Based on the analysis of the linear trends in Table 5 and Fig. 3, we find an average cumulative downward trend between financial performance and retained earnings, wherein in 2004, the trend was €3.28 million, it declined to €0.14 million in 2010, which means that we have a negative correlation between financial performance and retained earnings for the period (2004–2010). Financial performance from 2004 to 2007 was constantly increasing, and after this year until 2009 decreased to −€3.1 million. Meanwhile, the profits from 2004 to 2006 continuously marked an increase from €0.7M to €4.4M, then a decrease until 2010 to −€2.4M.

Table 5 Linear trend between FP and RE (2004–2010)

Year	Financial Performance (Profit & Loss of the year)—mil. €	Retained Earnings mil. €	Trend
2004	1.7	0.7	3.28
2005	4	2.7	2.76
2006	1.6	4.4	2.23
2007	3.5	2.4	1.71
2008	3.4	0	1.19
2009	−3.1	2.3	0.66
2010	0.9	−2.4	0.14

Source: Calculation of data by the authors (2021)

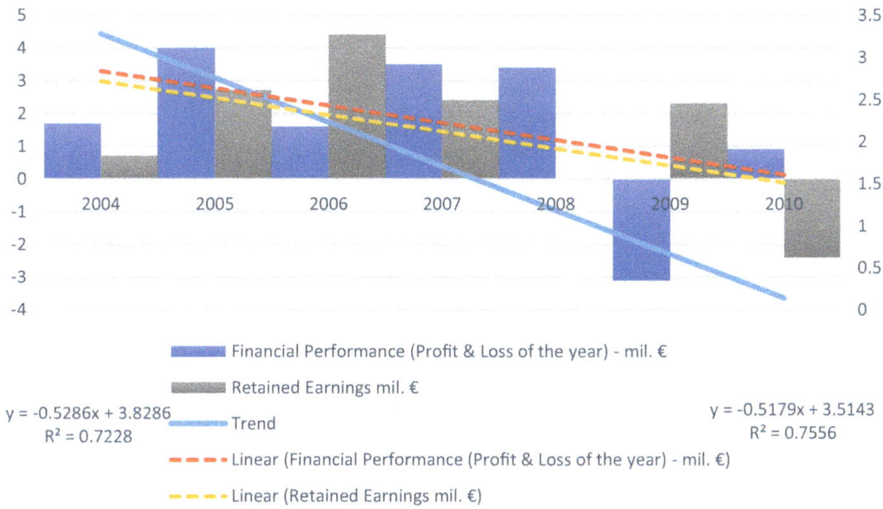

Fig. 3 Linear trend between FP and RE (2004–2010). *Source:* Calculation of data by the authors (2021)

Table 6 Linear trend between FP and RE (2011–2021)

Year	Financial Performance (Profit & Loss of the year)—mil. €	Retained Earnings mil. €	Trend
2011	0.9	−2.9	0.6
2012	−1.9	1.6	−2.0
2013	−0.8	−7.9	−4.6
2014	−0.3	−9.7	−7.2
2015	−7.8	−12.6	−9.8
2016	−24.7	−23.5	−12.4
2017	6.4	−44.8	−15.0
2018	1.6	−39.5	−17.6
2019	−5.4	−38.8	−20.2
2020	4.2	−43.6	−22.8
2021	1.3	−39.4	−25.4

Source: Calculation of data by the authors (2021)

In Table 6 and Fig. 4, the linear trend between financial performance and retained earnings for the period (2011–2021) is presented. Referring to the data in the table and the corresponding figure, we can conclude that there is a cumulative downward trend between these two variables; in 2011, the value of the average cumulative trend is 0.6, while in 2021, it is −€25.4 million, which means that we have an increase in the linear trend and that there is a negative correlation between these two variables. In terms of financial performance, they have marked a continuous decrease to −€24.7 million in 2016.Meanwhile, retained earnings have also marked a continuous

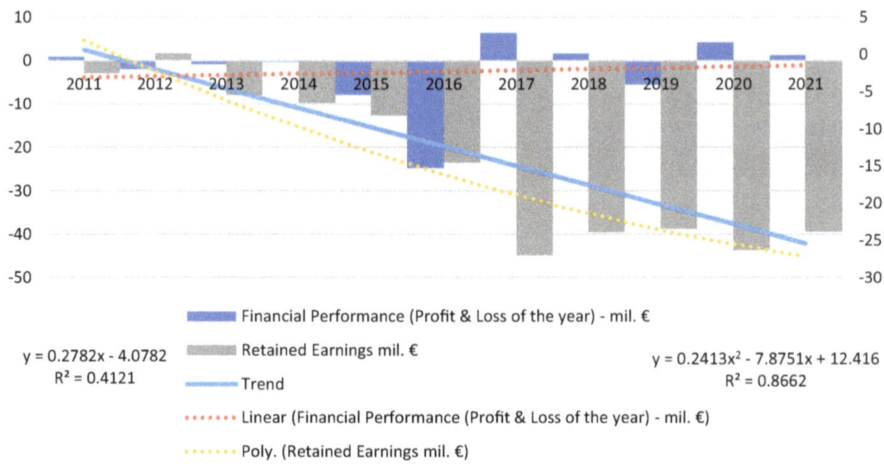

Fig. 4 Linear trend between FP and RE (2011–2021). *Source:* Calculation of data by the authors (2021)

decrease wherein, during 2021, the value reaches −€39.4 million. Based on the linear trend analysis results, as an overall finding, we can estimate that retained earnings have negatively impacted financial performance, implying that the value of the trend is downward. The coefficient of determination, in this case, is 86.62%, a fairly high level of explainability between these two variables.

As a general remark, it can be concluded that retained earnings have negatively affected the financial performance of insurance companies. Therefore, insurance companies in the future should allocate more funds to increase retained earnings because this is considered a fundamental determinant of capital structure. Furthermore, if insurance companies in Kosovo are exposed to various financial risks, then if they reinvest more retained earnings, it will positively affect the financial performance of insurance companies.

6 Econometric Results and Study Findings

This part of the chapter presents the results of descriptive statistics, and the hypotheses of this study are realized and tested to answer research questions. The data for testing the hypotheses of this study are processed in the STATA program; these data are secondary. Finally, they are presented in accordance with panel data based on statistical reports of the Central Bank of Kosovo, Kosovo Security Bureau, Tax Administration of Kosovo, the Ministry of Finance and the Kosovo Agency of Statistics.

The period analyzed in this study is between 2004 and 2021. This part of the study will present descriptive statistics. Correlation analysis and hypothesis testing

Table 7 Descriptive statistics for the variables included in this study

Variables	Obs.	Minimum	Maximum	Mean	Std. Deviation
FP	110	0.7245454	3.537484	−24.7	7.2
FCO	110	59.88091	25.10421	12.4	91.3
RE	110	−22.28182	19.97265	−48.7	6.8
GSR	110	5.21	3.591043	0	17.2
ALM	110	146.1755	52.1018	44.4	223.9

Source: Authors' calculations in the STATA program (2021)

are done through standard multiple regression analysis using different models such as the fixed effect model, the random effect model, the Hausman Taylor Estimation and the GMM Model using the Arellano Bond Estimation. Table 7 presents descriptive statistics for the variables included in the econometric models.

Referring to the data presented in Table 7, we can conclude that the number of observations included in this study is 110 for all variables.

- *Financial performance (FP) (dependent variable): it is noticed that there is an average of €0.724M with a standard deviation of 3.53; the minimum values are −€24.7M, and the maximum ones are €7.2M.*
- *Descriptive statistics for the main independent variable and the endogenous variable, which is the funds contributed by the owners (FCO), have an average value of €59.88M, with a standard deviation of 25.10, the minimum values are €12.4M, while the maximum is €91.3M.*
- *The other independent variable is retained earnings (RE); the average value is -€ 22.28M, with a standard deviation of 19.97, the minimum values are -€48.7M and the maximum ones are €6.8M.*
- *General and special reserves have an average of €5.21M, with a standard deviation of 3.59, the minimum values are €0, and the maximum value is €17.2M.*
- *As for the last asset and liability management variable, there is an average of €146.17M, with a standard deviation of 52.10, the minimum values are €44.4M, and the maximum is €223.9M.*

Table 8 shows the general correlations between the dependent and independent variables of this study. Firstly, the correlation between the financial performance and the funds contributed by the owners is given and based on this value, the correlation is R = 48%. This value shows that we have an average level correlation

Table 8 Pearson correlation analysis

Variables	FP	FCO	RE	GSR	ALM
FP	1.0000	0.48	0.784	0.85	0.712
FCO	0.48	1.0000	0.9625	0.1856	0.9694
RE	0.784	0.9625	1.0000	0.898	0.8942
GSR	0.85	0.1856	0.898	1.0000	0.3779
ALM	0.712	0.9694	0.8942	0.3779	1.0000

Source: Authors' calculations in the STATA program (2021)

and that between these variables, there is a positive linear correlation. Therefore, the increase in funds contributed by the owners will positively impact increasing the financial performance of insurance companies in Kosovo.

The correlation between the financial performance of insurance companies and retained earnings has a correlation value of R = 78.4%, so there is a fairly high correlation between these two variables which means that as retained earnings increase, this will have a positive effect on the growth of financial performance of insurance companies. Furthermore, the correlation between financial performance and general and special reserves is R = 85%, so we have a high positive correlation, which means that the increase in general and special reserves will positively impact the profit/loss of insurance companies. Finally, the correlation between financial performance and asset and liability management is R = 71.2%, i.e. a value of positive linear correlation and a high level of correlation between these two variables. This means that we will have a higher financial performance with more efficient management of assets and liabilities.

This part of the analysis presents the results of multifactorial regression analysis, using the small squares method (OLS) and statistical tests such as random effect, fixed effect, Hausman—Taylor Regression and GMM Model—Arellano Bond Estimation. The statistical data presented in the table below will analyze the impact of independent variables that are FCO, RE, GSR and ALM in the FP of insurance companies in Kosovo for the period analyzed (2004–2021) (Table 9).

Table 9 Empirical results for the first econometric model

Variables	Linear Regression	Random Effects – GLS Regression	Fixed–Effects Regression	Hausman Taylor Regression	GMM Model
FP	–	–	–	–	0.0246821 (0.839)
FCO	0.489299*** (0.001)	0.489299*** (0.001)	0.4448091*** (0.005)	0.44842*** (0.002)	0.8927333*** (0.000)
RE	0.3227106*** (0.000)	0.3227106*** (0.000)	0.3056475*** (0.000)	0.303425*** (0.000)	0.5587215*** (0.000)
GSR	0.4332853** (0.008)	0.4332853*** (0.007)	0.3702069** (0.038)	0.3998989** (0.015)	0.5469292*** (0.008)
ALM	0.1243618** (0.017)	0.1243618** (0.016)	0.1053726* (0.063)	0.1105416*** (0.002)	0.2094115*** (0.000)
Const.	6.9212409*** (0.000)	6.912409*** (0.000)	7.075626*** (0.000)	7.087153** (0.039)	2.089475*** (0.000)
R^2	0.7254	0.7145	0.6415	0.7680	0.7548
Adjusted R^2	0.7014	0.6923	0.6239	0.7256	0.7147

Source: Authors' calculations in the STATA program (2021)
Explanation: *p-values shown in parentheses: *** shows statistical significance at level 1%; ** shows the statistical significance at the level of 5% and * shows the statistical significance at 10%.*

According to the Hausman-Taylor regression model, we can conclude that all the independent variables of this study are at a significant level and are statistically significant. Furthermore, all these variables impact the dependent variable, which is the financial performance of insurance companies in Kosovo.

$$FP_{it} = \beta_0 + \beta_1\, FCO_{it} + \beta_2\, RE_{it} + \beta_3\, GSR_{it} + \beta_4\, ALM_{it} + \gamma_{it}$$

$$FP_{it=}\ 7.087 + 0.448\, FCO_{it} + 0.399\, RE_{it} + 0.110\, GSR_{it} + 0.448\, ALM_{it} + 0.232$$

β_0—if all other factors are constant, then the financial performance of insurance companies will be 7,087 units. This statement is correct because the significance level is $0.000 < 0.05$.

$\beta_1\ FCO_{it}$ —If the owners' funds increase per unit, keeping the other factors constant, then the financial performance of insurance companies in Kosovo will increase by 0.448 units. This statement is correct because the significance level is in the statistical confidence interval, i.e. it is $0.002 < 0.05$.

$\beta_2\ RE_{it}$ —if retained earnings increase by one unit while keeping other factors constant, then financial performance will increase by 0.303 units. This statement is correct because the significance level is $0.000 < 0.05$.

$\beta_3\ GSR_{it}$ —if total and specific reserves increase by one unit while keeping other factors constant, then financial performance will increase by 0.399 units. This statement is correct because the significance level is $0.015 < 0.05$.

$\beta_4\ ALM_{it}$ —if asset and liability management increases by one unit while keeping other factors constant, then financial performance will increase by 0.110 units. This statement is correct because the significance level is $0.039 < 0.10$.

As a general conclusion of the results of multifactorial regression analysis using the Hausman-Taylor Estimation model, we can conclude that all variables are significant, have statistical significance and positively affect the financial performance of insurance companies in Kosovo. These results are realistic and are comparable to the studies of other authors, who have analyzed the impact of capital structure on the profitability or financial performance of insurance companies in different countries of the world (Table 10).

According to the results presented in Table 8, we can confirm that multicollinearity and heteroskedasticity are not present in the econometric models. Since all the independent variables of this study have a variance inflation factor of less than 5, this implies a non-serious problem for the statistical stability of the

Table 10 Results of multicollinearity and heteroskedasticity in panel econometric models

Variables	FCO	RE	GSR	ALM
Variance Inflation Factor (VIF)	0.007634	0.013301	0.044118	0.285776
Breusch – Pagan Test (P-Value)	0.382	0.489	0.091	0.448

Source: Authors' calculations in the STATA program (2021)

econometric model. Furthermore, according to the Breusch–Pagan test results, all independent variables of the econometric model have a higher significance value than the standard value of 0.05. Therefore, we can conclude that there is no presence of heteroskedasticity and error term dispersion is constant for each observation.

7 Discussions

In this part of this study, we will discuss the hypothesis testing and the answer to the research questions we posed at the beginning of this chapter. These results will be compared with the findings of other authors who have analyzed the impact of capital structure on insurance companies in different countries worldwide.

7.1 How Have the Funds Contributed by the Owners Affected the Financial Performance of Insurance Companies in Kosovo?

H0: Funds contributed by the owners have negatively affected the financial performance of insurance companies in Kosovo.

H1: Funds contributed by the owners have had a positive impact on the financial performance of insurance companies in Kosovo.

Based on all the statistical tests that we have presented in the econometric results section, we can conclude that the funds contributed by the owners have had a positive impact on the financial performance of insurance companies since the primary independent variable is also endogenous. FCO is significant and statistically significant. In this case, hypothesis zero is rejected, and the alternative hypothesis is accepted.

7.2 What Effect Do Retained Earnings Have on the Financial Performance of Insurance Companies in Kosovo?

H0: Retained earnings have negatively affected the financial performance of insurance companies in Kosovo.

H2: Retained earnings have had a positive impact on the financial performance of insurance companies in Kosovo.

According to the results of statistical tests, we can conclude that the null hypothesis is rejected, and the second alternative hypothesis is accepted. Retained earnings have had a positive impact on the financial performance of insurance companies in

Kosovo, given that retained earnings are a crucial determinant of the capital structure which can be continuously reinvested and can contribute positively to the financial performance of the insurance industry for the analyzed period (2004–2021).

7.3 What Is the Impact of General and Specific Reserves on the Profit/Loss of Insurance Companies in Kosovo?

H0: General and specific reserves have negatively affected the profit/loss of insurance companies in Kosovo.

H3: General and specific reserves have had a positive impact on the profit/loss of insurance companies in Kosovo.

According to the results of statistical tests presented in this study, it can be concluded that the null hypothesis is rejected, and the third alternative hypothesis is accepted since the general and specific reserves variable is significant and statistically significant. Therefore, based on this, it can be concluded that if the value of GSR continues to increase, it could bring positive effects on the profitability or profitability of insurance companies in Kosovo.

7.4 What Effect Does Asset and Liability Management Have on the Financial Performance of Insurance Companies in Kosovo?

H0: Asset and liability management have negatively affected the financial performance of insurance companies in Kosovo.

H4: Asset and liability management have had a positive impact on the financial performance of insurance companies in Kosovo.

The results of statistical tests through various econometric models show that the null hypothesis is rejected, and the fourth or alternative hypothesis is accepted. Asset and liability management has had a positive impact on the financial performance of insurance companies in Kosovo, and based on these results, it can be concluded that effective management of assets and liabilities and proper investment of these accounting items will contribute positively to the financial performance of the insurance industry in Kosovo. These results and findings of this study are realistic, consistent and comparable to the results and findings consistent with the studies of various authors such as: (Ajao and Ogieriakhi 2018), (Eladly 2021), (Getahun 2016), (Jaishi 2020), (Morara and Sibindi 2021), (Olawale et al. 2019), (Salim and Yadav 2012), (Wanyama and Olweny 2013).

7.5 Conclusions and Recommendations

The insurance industry in Kosovo plays an important role for all businesses in that without insurance companies, businesses could end up facing bankruptcy due to their instability and dynamic business environment. In addition, the capital structure is an essential aspect for insurance companies in Kosovo because these firms need funds to finance their operation, settle their claims or pay damages at the time of loss.

This study has empirically analyzed the effect of capital structure on the financial performance of insurance companies in the insurance industry in Kosovo. The econometric results of this study used various statistical tests applied to examine the effect of capital structure on insurance companies in Kosovo. The analysis was based on the data of the time series of the Central Bank of Kosovo for the insurance industry in Kosovo, which includes 12 insurance companies that the CBK licenses and covers the period between 2004 and 2021, i.e. 17 years.

The study concluded that the capital structure has a significant impact on the financial performance of insurance companies in Kosovo. Furthermore, based on the econometric results of this study, we can conclude that all independent variables have a significant positive impact on the financial performance of insurance companies in Kosovo.

According to the findings of this study, it can be concluded that the funds contributed by the owners have a significant and positive impact on the financial performance of insurance companies in Kosovo. Based on this, it can also be concluded that FCOs are one of the most critical elements of the capital structure, which positively affects the financial performance of insurance companies. Therefore, this study recommends that shareholders of insurance companies in Kosovo should continuously increase their capital in insurance companies so that this amount of funds contributes to its growth and development and has positive effects on the profitability of insurance companies in Kosovo. Therefore, the increase of funds contributed by the owners has an impact on increasing the performance of insurance companies.

Based on the econometric results of this study, we can conclude that retained earnings have a positive and significant impact on the financial performance of insurance companies in Kosovo. According to this result, it can be concluded that the continuous increase of retained earnings and their reinvestment in the form of various assets of insurance companies will affect the higher performance of these insurance companies. Therefore, based on this study, it is recommended that insurance companies continuously increase retained earnings and reinvest, as this impacts the higher liquidity and profitability of these insurance companies so that they can withstand any financial difficulties, whether long-term or short-term, related to its performance.

According to the empirical findings of this study, another conclusion is that general and specific reserves have positive effects on the profitability of insurance companies in Kosovo. So, this variable is significant and positively impacts the financial performance of insurance companies analyzed in this study. Based on this correlation, we can recommend that all insurance companies in Kosovo increase the amount of general and specific reserves, as a larger volume of these reserves will positively affect the profitability of insurance companies. This makes it easier for them to manage the potential consequences that may come from the various risks that these companies face in the exercise of their activities. At the same time, these companies will be even more solvent, as they will also use various external financing that will have the ability to repay all liabilities and claims to third parties.

Based on the results or findings of this study, it can be concluded that the fourth independent variable of this study which is the management of assets and liabilities, has a significant and positive impact on the financial performance of insurance companies in Kosovo. Therefore, based on this correlation, it can be recommended that insurance companies should be cautious in managing assets and liabilities as effectively as possible in order to have positive effects on increasing the profitability of insurance companies, and these companies will be more successful in exercising their activity.

References

Adeyemi AZ, Unachukwu JC, Oyeniyi KO (2017) Capital structure and its effect on the financial performance of Nigerian insurance industry. Int J Bus Law Res 5(3):8–15

Ajao MG, Ogieriakhi E (2018) Firm specific factors and performance of insurance firms in Nigeria. Amity J Finance 3(1):14–28

Almajali M, Shamsuddin Z (2019) The effect of capital structure on performance of insurance companies: evidence from Jordan. Int J Account Finance Bus 4(20):64–73

Ayuba H, Ja'afaru Bambale A, Aminu Ibrahim M, Abdulwahab Sulaiman S (2019) Effects of financial performance, capital structure and firm size on firms' value of insurance companies in Nigeria. J Finance Account Management 10(1):57–74

Batool A, Sahi A (2020) Determinants of financial performance of insurance companies of USA and UK during global financial crisis (2007–2016). Int J Account Res 7(1):1–9

Caselli S, Negri G (2021) Private equity and venture capital in Europe Markets, Techniques, and Deals, 3rd edn

Eladly SM (2021) The impact of the financial performance on capital structure of insurance industry in Egypt. Int Bus Res 14(7):103–114. https://doi.org/10.5539/ibr.v14n7p103

Getahun M (2016) Capital structure and financial performance of insurance industries in Ethiopia. Glob J Manage Bus Res 16(7):45–53

Jaishi B (2020) Capital structure and its impact on financial performance in insurance companies of Nepal. J Nepalese Bus Stud 13(1):89–106. https://doi.org/10.3126/jnbs.v13i1.34708

Jensen MC, Meckling WH (1976) Theory of the firm: managerial behavior, agency costs and ownership structure. J Financ Econ 3(4):305–360. https://doi.org/10.1016/0304-405X(76)90026-X

Kiptoo IK, Samuel Nduati K, Kennedy Nyabuto O (2021) Risk management and financial performance of insurance firms in Kenya. Cogent Bus Manage 8(1997246):1–17. https://doi.org/10.1080/23311975.2021.1997246

Kraus Z, Litzenberger RH (1973) A state-preference model of optimal financial leverage. J Am Finance Assoc 28(4):911–922. https://doi.org/10.1111/j.1540-6261.1973.tb01415.x

Maina L, Ishmail M (2014) Capital structure and financial performance in Kenya: evidence from firms listed at the Nairobi securities exchange. Int J Soc Sci Entrep 1(11):209–223

Morara K, Sibindi AB (2021) Determinants of financial performance of insurance companies: empirical evidence using Kenyan data. J Risk Financ Manage, 14 (12), 566, 1-13. doi:https://doi.org/10.3390/jrfm14120566
Narang M (2018) Impact of capital structure on firm performance: a study of listed firms on national stock exchange. Int J Adv Educ Res 3(1):251–254
Olawale S, Muhammad M, Fawad A, Chibuzor O (2019) Effect of capital structure on the profitability of listed insurance firms in Nigeria. Int J Technical Res Sci 4(3):13–22. https://doi.org/10.30780/IJTRS.V04.I03.002
Salim M, Yadav R (2012) Capital structure and firm performance: evidence from Malaysian listed companies. Int Congr Interdiscip Bus Soc Sci Proc Soc Behav Sci 65:156–166. https://doi.org/10.1016/j.sbspro.2012.11.105
Shamsuddin Z, Al Majali MAK, Daud WMNW, Wan Sallha Y (2020) Analysis of capital structure and financial performance in the Jordian insurance sector. Human Soc Sci Rev 8(3):1310–1320. https://doi.org/10.18510/hssr.2020.83133
Tornyeva K (2013) Determinants of capital structure of insurance companies in Ghana. Res J Finance Account 4(13):52–60. ISSN 2222-1697 (Paper) ISSN 2222-2847 (Online)
Vincent Kiptum K (2014) Effect of capital structure on value of firms listed in Nairobi Securities Exchange. Research Project, School of Business, University of Nairobi, pp 1–71
Wanyama DW, Olweny T (2013) Effects of corporate governance on financial performance of listed insurance firms in Kenya. Public Policy Adm Res 3(4):96–120
Yinusa O, Taiwo A (2013) Insurance development and economic growth in Nigeria. J Econ Int Finance 5(5):218–224. https://doi.org/10.5897/JEIF2013.0498

Fisnik Morina is an Assistant Professor in the field of Banking, Finance, Economics and Econometrics at the Faculty of Business at University "Haxhi Zeka" in Pejë, Kosovo. Currently, Professor Fisnik Morina is Vice-Dean for Teaching, Student Affairs and Scientific Research at the Faculty of Business. In 2023, Fisnik Morina is continuing his post-doctoral research in the field of Banking and Finance at the Institute of Economics at the University of Graz in Austria. In 2022, Professor Fisnik Morina successfully completed his post-doctoral studies in the field of Financial Institutions and Risk Management at the University of Malta. He completed his doctoral studies in 2019 at the South East European University, Faculty of Business and Economics in the Republic of North Macedonia and gained the qualification of Doctor of Economic Sciences—Economics. Professor Fisnik Morina has an international experience in the field of scientific research, has several scientific papers published in international scientific journals and has participated in many international scientific conferences in many countries of the European Union. Professor Fisnik Morina is internationally certified by the Center for Economic Research and Graduate Education – Economics Institute (CERGE-EI) in the Czech Republic for contemporary teaching methods in Higher Education and is a senior trainer at the Center of Excellence at University "Haxhi Zeka" in Peja.

Vlora Berisha Dranqolli is an accomplished Assistant Professor of Accounting and Finance at Business College—UHZ, with a PhD degree in Bank, Accounting and Finance from University Hasan Prishtina, and a Fulbright Visiting Scholar postgraduate degree from Northern Arizona University. She also has a postdoctoral candidacy at Malta University. Vlora has contributed to several TEMPUS and ERASMUS + Projects, including CONSUS and T2P and CTPE Projects. Beyond academia, she has worked as a financial manager at Woman Wellness Center and served as a liaison officer for the Kosovo NGO network for gender equality and against domestic violence under IOM project. Her work has been published in numerous journals and presented at many conferences, and she is a member of the prestigious European Cooperation in Science and Technology (COST).

Kastriot Idrizaj has completed his master's degree studies in 2021 at the University "Haxhi Zeka" in Peja, Faculty of Business, Department of Accounting and Finance. Kastriot has experience in the field of scientific research and has participated in scientific conferences. Currently, Kastriot is a financial officer at the Family Medicine Center in Istog and is certified as an Accounting Technician by the Institute for Accounting, Auditing and Finance in Kosovo. In recent years, Kastriot has attended a significant number of trainings in the field of public finance management and in 2022 he was certified by the Swiss Tropical and Public Health Institute (Swiss TPH) in the field of financial management in the health sector.

Part III
The Impact of New Technologies and Other Recent Developments in Insurance Law and Regulation

Automatic Vehicles and Legal/Insurance Risks. A New British "Quasi-Legislative" Point of Observation and Glimpses of Liability in Tort in Italy

Camilla Della Giustina and Pierre de Gioia Carabellese

Abstract The chapter discusses the legal concept of automated motor vehicles pursuant to the UK statute, as well as the linkage with the pertinent insurance coverage, this analysis being carried out also in the light of the potential reverberations on the Italian legal system. Of the latter, on the other hand, the UK legislation may be regarded as the forerunner. The automated vehicles, including the most extreme forms of driverless vehicles, will seemingly be used in the UK in the imminent future. Meanwhile, in 2018, a piece of legislation has been passed whose purposes is to legislate on both the insurance contract (and the way the liability shall be apportioned among insurer, owner and, particularly, the manufacturer) and the administrative law (therefore, the regulation) of the automated vehicles, focused on a register kept by the Secretary of State.

Keywords Unmanned vehicles · UK · Insurance risk · Producer's liability · *Automated and Electric Vehicle Act 2018* · *Statute*

1 Introduction

Perfidious Albion or wonderful Albion: that is the question. A country such as the United Kingdom which, in leaving the European Union, seemed to be in decline, has now found a new impetus in the field of technology, as well as in both transport and automation.

C. Della Giustina
Università degli Studi Vanvitelli, Caserta, Italy
e-mail: camilla.dellagiustina@unicampania.it

P. de Gioia Carabellese (✉)
Advance HE, York, UK

Edith Cowan University, Perth, WA, Australia

Beijing Institute of Technology (Zhuhai Campus), Hong Kong Area, China

M. Lima Rego, S. Grima (eds.), *Cross-Disciplinary Impacts on Insurance Law*,
AIDA Europe Research Series on Insurance Law and Regulation 8,
https://doi.org/10.1007/978-3-031-38526-1_8

The theme of unmanned machines, or unmanned vehicles, i.e. devices that move without a driver/pilot, is one of the most fascinating ones, and at the same time the most difficult legal challenge that Italy too is currently facing.[1] However, as far as the UK is concerned, that legislation has been equipped since 2018 with a legal framework. The main goal of this legislation is to regulate a section of whole matter, specifically the one pertaining to the insurance policy of these "machines". Nevertheless, further legal frameworks will be probably passed in the future in order to govern, from an administrative point of view, the topic of automated machines, and in particular the actual vehicles (the "cars") that circulate on the road. From the same perspective, it is worth mentioning that in the UK, after this contribution had already been submitted, a joint report of both the Law Commission of England and Wales and of the Scottish Law Commission[2] was passed and this piece of work recommends that a broader and more comprehensive statute be passed in this area.[3] Remarkably, at the moment, driverless cars, which, moreover, are not permitted yet to circulate in the United Kingdom, making the same new insurance scheme still inapplicable, as far as that part is concerned.[4]

In 2018, the United Kingdom passed an insurance liability statute, applicable to vehicles that move, either wholly or partially, in an automatic way, therefore without a driver, provided that they are entered in an *ad hoc* list. The aforementioned piece of legislation is formally encompassed with the Automated and Electric Vehicle Act 2018 (hereinafter also "AEVA 2018"), in force since the month of July of the same year.[5]

The list is potentially open to "road" vehicles (actual "cars", in the common jargon), although the current implementation does not include cars yet, given the fact that the UK Government need still give their approval to the most extreme forms of driverless vehicles.

---

[1] Among the not many writings in the Italian language, in a perspective of law and economics: Calabresi and Al Mureden (2020), pp. 7–21; Ruffolo (2017); Pardolesi and Davola (2017), pp. 616–629.

[2] See Law Commission and Scottish Law Commission, Automated Vehicles. Joint report, Law Com No 404, Scot Law Com No 258, 25th January 2022.

[3] Such a prospective piece of legislation, as well as a detailed commentary on the Joint Report of the British Commissions on automated vehicles will be the subject matter of a separate work.

[4] See Noussia (2020), pp. 253–270; Manes (2020), pp. 129–168; Cheng and Deng (2018).

[5] *Royal Assent* was given on 19 July 2018, after the Westminster Parliament approval with no. 18. According to section 21 of the Act, the provisions of the Act will enter into force when the Secretary of State starts enacting the relevant regulations, through its Statutory Instruments. However, some provisions have already entered into force in coincidence with the promulgation of the law, namely: (a) section 20(2) to (7); (c) sections 22 and 23. With regard to the present law, see: Marson et al. (2020), pp. 395–416; Channon 2019 The latter Author underlines that, in general, the law is quite wide, given the lack of precise definitions or the same scope. Such a broad scope is clearly intended to ensure that legislation remains connected with technology. It can therefore be summarised by saying that there is a dynamic "proactive" approach of the legislator, which however leaves many uncertainties, in particular about the very nature of the regulatory provisions.

The fundamental pillar of the AEVA is - it is worth mentioning this since the beginning of this work—section 2(2). The 2018 AEVA states that CAVs (Connected and Autonomous Vehicles,[6] therefore vehicles that move alone, either wholly or partially) must be covered by an insurance policy under a single insurance contract, covering both the insured and the vehicle.[7]

In view of this, where an accident is caused by the CAV, to the extent to which at the time of the accident the self-propelled (or colloquially, the "driving itself") mode is in operation, the insurer is under an obligation to indemnify the third party, without prejudice to its recourse action against the producer of the CAV or, more directly, the person responsible for the accident.[8]

This overall painting is drawn in this contribution, in order to discuss and analyse the developments, in recent years, of this area of the United Kingdom legislation. For this purpose, a comparison with the Italian legal system, and with its controversial and debated legal concepts, will be made too. Third, the risk entailed to the circulation of unmanned vehicles is ascertained juxtaposed against the insurance legal framework applicable to this area in question.

In this chapter, also, a reference is made to a new concept, within the broader area of the Automated Vehicles System, the "use in charge". This has been introduced by the last "Automated Vehicles: Joint Report" of Law Commissions.[9]

2 Traditional Legal Risks in Transport in the UK: The Insurance Contract

"Machines", including vehicles, which move without a driver, are equipped with a support technology, provided by the manufacturer, which makes them operational, adapting them to the use of the user who is not necessarily the owner. The manufacturer "works", more often than not, in the best interests of the same owner. In other words, the manufacturer is to the owners, as employees are to their employers.

With this in mind, the operation of these machines may have negative consequences for the victims who are accidentally hit by them: the real dilemma for the victim is to establish whom the legal proceeding for the remedies (i.e. damages) shall be directed.

---

[6]Henceforth also CAV.

[7]In the United Kingdom, in relation to conventional vehicles, the Road Traffic Act 1988 requires the user of a vehicle (the user) to take out an insurance contract to cover his liability to third parties for damage caused by his negligence; by virtue of that contract, the insurer is obliged to compensate the third party as a victim. If there is no insurance contract at all, an organ, the Motor Insurers' Bureau, will compensate the victim.

[8]The phenomenon is reconstructed very precisely by Channon, *cit.*

[9]Law Commission of England and Wales, Law Commission No, 404, Scottish Law Commission, Scottish Law Commission No 258, *Automated Vechicles: Joint Report*, 25 January 2022, online.

The first possible answer would be that the manufacturer of the automatic vehicle shall be deemed responsible. Being the automatic vehicle, in its most extreme form, devoid of any proper driver, as already hinted above, from a theoretical perspective it is ultimately the manufacturer responsible for the damage.

It is worth noting, though, that under English law such an action is likely to be difficult to use by the injured party: the Consumer Protection Act 1987[10] was clearly issued in a context where no one would have thought about vehicles without drivers.[11]

Moreover, for the general principles applicable to traditional vehicles, the defendant, or defender in Scottish law, should be the owner of the vehicle according to the general rules which also apply in the United Kingdom and specifically in English law. However, the objection that the owner cannot be called into question—in the present case, given the lack of *mens rea*—may be overcome by the observation that the most "right defendant" must be the manufacturer. On the other hand, it is this manufacturer who has arranged for the machine and, above all, the software that makes it run. It should be added that in the operation in question it is usually the insurer who is sued, in place of the owner. To elaborate, in the case of unmanned machine, the real dilemma is to determine who, between either the insurer of the owner of the machine and the supplier, which has produced the vehicle, is responsible.

For traditional vehicles/machinery, whether road or not, driven by a driver or pilot, each issue across the Channel is defined in a straight-forward way. In the event of an accident, the owner activates an insurance policy and calls in the insurer's warranty. The responsibility of the owner towards those who have suffered the damage (such as, for example, a car accident) stems from the general principles, and in particular from the ancient case *Donoghue v Stevenson.*[12]

The Scottish case, "exported" also to English law, is paradigmatic, in common law, of the principle on which the entire area of tort law is based, that is the extra-contractual liability.[13] Given the dearth of a contract, or at least a contractual link between the owner/driver and the victim, no legal action, at least in contract, would be conceivable. Nevertheless, the victim can still be sued in tort. It was held, to the

[10]The strict liability regime has been recognised from the outset. See Newdick (1988), pp. 455–476; Stoppa (1992), pp. 210–217.

[11]One of these defences is that of section 4(1), and, which allows the manufacturer to avoid compensation by proving that the state of scientific and technological knowledge at the time of production was such that he could not detect the defect of the product. In this regard, the same jurisprudence of the Court of Justice of the European Union clarifies that the defence of the producer can be overcome by the consumer only by demonstrating that, at the time when the product was put into circulation, the relevant technical and scientific knowledge was already available to the producer. Cfr *Commission v United Kingdom* /Re the Product Liability Directive) (Case C-300/95) [1997].

[12]Smith and Burns (1983), pp. 147–163.

[13]See in the English legal system, Horsey and Rackley (2011). In Scottish law, the tort, whose principles are substantially similar, is defined delict, with concept of "delictual" liability. Thomson (2014).

benefit of the few jurists who may have forgotten the case, that, in the light of the breach of a duty of care, it is incumbent on any person who carries out a given activity which causes damage to others, whether or not a contract is in place.

On the other hand, in English common law, the call of the third insurer is an exception to the principle, or better pillar, which characterises the law of contracts "on this side of the Channel": more precisely the privity of contract. This is the principle according to which the contract does not have effects *vis-à-vis* third parties or beneficiaries covered by the same contract, since these are non-contracting parties which did not exist at the time of conclusion.[14] In fact, historically, the insurance contract represents one of the few exceptions to the principle of privity.[15]

There is no specific definition in the British legislation of insurance contract. Despite this, some correctly refer to the definition of Channell J. in *Prudential v Commissioner of Inland Revenue*:[16] "A contract of insurance, then, must be a contract for the payment of a sum of money, or for some corresponding benefit such as the rebuilding of a house or the repairing of a ship, to become due on the happening of an event, which event must have some amount of uncertainty about it, and must be of a character more or less adverse to the interest of the person effecting the insurance".[17]

"Legislative" definitions, and not jurisprudential definitions, of the insurance contract are found in the *ad hoc* discipline, relating to specific sectors. Reference is made to the Consumer Insurance (Disclosure and Representations) Act 2002, section 1, that is to say, to the regulation of consumer insurance contracts, in which the contract in question, precisely "consumer insurance contract means a contract of insurance between: (a) an individual who enters into the contract wholly or mainly for purposes unrelated to the individual's trade, business or profession, and (b) a person who carries on the business of insurance and who becomes a party to the contract by way of that business (whether or not in accordance with permission for the purposes of the Financial Services and Markets Act 2000); 'consumer' means the individual who enters into a consumer insurance contract, or proposes to do so; 'insurer' means the person who is, or would become, the other party to a consumer insurance contract".

The counterparty, on the other hand, is the institution which carries out the insurance business in a professional manner, and therefore the insurance company.

[14] On the concept of *privity*, See, among others, Taylor and Taylor (2017). This principle can be summarised with the expression: "No party can act upon a contract unless they are a party to it". Among the previous ones, see *Tweddle v Atkinson* [1861]; *Dunlop Pneumatic Tyre Co Ltd v Selfridge Ltd* [1915]; *Beswick v Beswick* [1968].

[15] Among the various exceptions, there is the one that of a legislative nature, *Road Traffic Act 1988*, about the "Third party insurance". More precisely: "the injured third party can sue the insurer and is not a party to the contract".

[16] (1904) 2KB 658.

[17] The dearth of a definition of the insurance contract in the United Kingdom is also reflected in the regulation, since the supervisory authority enjoys a wide discretion, which can in fact be limited only by the Judge. See Birds (2010), p. 7.

Further pieces of legislation consist of the Marine Insurance Act 1906, [18] which defines the contract of insurance of maritime nature: "A contract of marine insurance is a contract whereby the insurer undertakes to indemnify the assured, in manner and to the extent thereby agreed, against marine losses, that is to say, the losses incident to marine adventure".[19]

3 The Next UK Legislative Model of Responsibility for Automated Vehicles (*Automated Machines*)

In view of the general principles of insurance contracts for conventional vehicles in the United Kingdom, and obviously taking into account the relevant insurance legal framework,[20] the nitty-gritty of the matter relating to unmanned vehicles is to assess who, eventually, should bear the insurance costs.[21]

One possible solution is that, since the vehicle is intended to operate without proper driving, apart from the activity of the owner who operates it on a case-by-case basis, the manufacturer should also bear the costs of insurance for damage caused to third parties, and this throughout the lifespan of the vehicle. Such solution, however, appears expensive and with uncertain consequences, being unable the manufacturer to predict until the vehicle will operate.[22]

The insurance contract, concluded directly between the manufacturer and the insurer, means that, in the event of an accident caused by a vehicle without human driving, the paperwork of the insurance policy falls within the remit of the insurers and the manufacturers of unmanned vehicles. In the light of this, the owner would be relieved from the seeming legal issues and disputes, since these would be settled "upstream" between the major players (again, manufacturer and insurer).

Despite this, the main research question is whether the traditional regime of insurance is fit for CAVs or, alternatively, it is better for automated vehicles to be subject to an *ad hoc* insurance policy. In the latter case, though, the price of policy could be potentially higher. Additionally, such an *ad hoc* insurance contract would

[18] The *Marine Insurance Act* is a piece of legislation that has "codified", in its section 17, the judicial principle of utmost good faith, which must be referred to *Lord Mansfield in Carter v Boehm* (1766) 3 Burr. 1905. See Birds (2010).

[19] Please refer to Bennett (2006), pp. 669–692. Among Scholars, see Barlow (2008).

[20] For a general examination see *insurance contract* in English Law, see Merkin (2021); Clarke (2011).

[21] The Italian insurance discipline that is the background to this analysis is the traditional manual and general Italian literature. Donati and Volpe Putzolu (2019); Farenga (2016). It does not seem that, to date, the Italian university textbooks address the issue of insurance of automated vehicles. As far as treatises are concerned, see 2013. On the issue of the niche of the insurance contract and the protection of the person, see Schirone (2004).

[22] However, proceedings against the producer are subject to a three-year limitation period.

be governed by a correspondent statute, applicable specifically to automated vehicles, governing the conditions of the autonomous vehicle.

In UK, at the moment, it is not allowed to use vehicles that are without a driver (the driverless vehicles). However, regulation will be in force and it will allow the circulation of these vehicles in 2022. Accordingly, the new insurance principles enshrined in the AEVA 2018 will be applicable.

This piece of legislation does not cover every legal obligation on the manufacturer, in the event of a defect in the production of automated machines, such as the one related to the way in which the software was created. The practical objective of the AEVA is to dissuade from liability actions against the manufacturer, while promoting the way of the insurer's warranty call.

In reviewing the main precepts of the legal framework in question, section 1, "Listing of automated vehicles by the Secretary of State" should be recalled.

More specifically, "the Secretary of State must prepare and keep up to date a list of all vehicles that: (a) are in the Secretary of State's opinion designed or adapted to be capable, in at least some circumstances or situations, of safely driving themselves, and (b) may lawfully be used when driving themselves, in at least some circumstances or situations, on roads or other public places in Great Britain".

It is worth observing that, on the one hand, the list is exhaustive, while on the other hand its update is left to the discretion of the authority. The latter, however, enjoys wide discretion. In essence, by reading the parameters of the British legislature, not only does the list concern vehicles that move in a totally independent way (the driverless vehicles), but also it includes, more generally, those that are partially self-propelled. In this respect, Scholars hint at the proactive approach of the British legislator who, despite being inexperienced and perhaps misleading, opts for the technology driving the legislation, rather than vice versa. And this is a surreptitious choice on the part of a Parliament that could have been more clear, rather than been vague.

In accordance with section 2), the list "may identify vehicles—(a) by type, (b) by reference to information recorded in a registration document issued under regulations made under section 22 of the Vehicle Excise and Registration Act 1994, or (c) in some other way". However, the list kept by the Secretary of State is essential, as the "automated vehicle" is only the one that falls under the relevant section, for the purpose of the application of the discipline, and not others if not included.

Currently, the Secretary of State has issued a list of "automated machines", which does not currently include automated vehicles par excellence, namely driverless vehicles, although, as just mentions, it is likely that by 2022 the United Kingdom will allow such vehicles to run on its own roads. Furthermore, Scholars are of the opinion that this objective is not without an ethical justification: the automated vehicle, although it cannot avoid an accident, must be, at least, safer than the best of human pilots.[23]

[23] This is remembered, more recently, in the literature in English by Channon (2019).

The central point of the matter is to determine when the insurer can be held liable, and then be sued by the injured party.

To this end, section 2 stipulates that, in circumstance where (i) an automated vehicle has caused an accident when driving itself on a road or other public place;[24] (ii) such a vehicle is insured,[25] and finally (iii) if there is a damage suffered by an insured person or any other person as a result of the accident, "the insurer is liable for that damage". Despite these *caveats*, section 2(2) nonetheless defines the different circumstances where an accident is caused by a vehicle without a driver in a public road or other public place and is not insured at the time of the accident. In such cases, to the extent that section 143 of the Road Traffic Act 1988 (users of insured vehicles or guaranteed against third-party risks) does not apply to the vehicle, the vehicle owner (and not the insurer) must be held liable for the damage.

Furthermore, in section 3, a concept of damage is provided, which is particularly useful for Courts also in order to define the demarcation line of responsibilities. Damages shall be taken to be "death or personal injury, and any damage to property other that - (a) the automated vehicle, (b) goods carried for hire or reward in or on that vehicle or in or on any trailer (whether or not coupled) drawn by it, or (c) property in the custody, or under the control, of— (i) the insured person (where subsection (1) applies), or (ii) the person in charge of the automated vehicle at the time of the accident (where subsection (2) applies)."[26]

In accordance to subsection 5, section 2 will apply, subject to the legal provisions of the previous section 3.

Worthy of mention is also the legal provision encompassed with section 2(6), which stipulates the following: "Except as provided by section 4, liability under this section may not be limited or excluded by a term of an insurance policy or in any other way". In brief, the liability regime introduced by the legislation in question is imperative. This body of law is tainted with a public law nature: its ultimate binding scope is to prevent litigation.

According to subsection 7, it is established as follows: "The imposition by this section of liability on the insurer or vehicle owner does not affect any other person's liability in respect of the accident".

Section 3 then states that, if an insurer or vehicle is liable under section 2 to the person (the offended party) in relation to an accident and the accident or damage is

---

[24] In this respect, the arguable aspect is the constraint of the public road. Thus, the level of protection of the damaged party is reduced, since the victim would not be entitled to rely on the new rules, should the accident occur in a private road.

[25] As far as the second circumstance is concerned (ii), the new legislative framework is imperative, so long as an insurance policy is in place. However, somehow bizarrely, there no such thing as an obligation, on the part of the owner of a CAV, to have an insurance policy duly signed.

[26] The subsection 4 states that, in respect of damage to property caused by, or arising out of, any one accident involving an automated vehicle, "the amount of the liability under this section of the insurer or owner of the vehicle is limited to the amount for the time being specified in section 145(4)(b) of the Road Traffic Act 1988 (limit on compulsory insurance for property damage)".

partly due to the offended party, then the relevant liability will be subject to the limitation under the Law Reform (Contributory Negligence) Act 1945.[27]

This is a general rule which is linked to the principle, formalised in the 1945 law, which was previously discussed in the same law, according to which the injured party cannot raise claim for compensation caused by the same victim.

Partially connected is the norm referred to in section 3(2), according to which: "The insurer or owner of an automated vehicle is not liable under section 2 to the person in charge of the vehicle where the accident that it caused was wholly due to the person's negligence in allowing the vehicle to begin driving itself when it was not appropriate to do so". The regulation aims to protect the owner and insurer, in particular, in the event that a different person, however in control of the vehicle (for example an employee) decides, in violation of protocols or internal orders, to start the automatic driving of the machine.

Further legislative provision is that of section 4, under which "An insurance policy in respect of an automated vehicle may exclude or limit the insurer's liability under section 2(1) for damage suffered by an insured person arising from an accident occurring as a direct result of - (a)software alterations made by the insured person, or with the insured person's knowledge, that are prohibited under the policy, or (b)a failure to install safety-critical software updates that the insured person knows, or ought reasonably to know, are safety-critical".

It is clear that, without prejudice to the general responsibility of the manufacturer for damages caused by the automatic machine,[28] the owner will still be liable in cases of failure to adapt the software (first and foremost, the installation of updates) or for alteration of the same operating system. The initial software portrays places, contains maps and, more generally, situations that may soon become obsolete. Therefore, since they are misleading, they can also cause harm.

Moreover, the legal provision stipulates that, given the owner's obligation to update the software, a better system of protection for the manufacturer could be to have a register of automated machines, where registration takes place of the different owners who follow each other in the legal title of each automated vehicle. This would also prevent the producer from having to deal with speculative claims in cases of general uncertainty about the ownership of the assets, against which the producer could incur costs, which in fact are not justified.

[27] For comments on this law, please refer to the initial one of Williams (1946), pp. 105–186.

[28] It is undeniable that they have arranged for the vehicle to operate independently.

4 The 2022 Joint Report of the British Law Commissions: The Concept of "User-in-Charge"

Within the broader area of automated vehicles, the UK has made a further significant step forward, thanks to the publications of a Joint report of the Law Commissions (England/Wales and Scotland), just occurred last year.

While the report does not encompass, needless to say, binding rules, nevertheless it hints at future pillars of a prospective legislation in this area. Among these principles, there is, first and foremost, a new system of legal accountability which should be designed for automated vehicles, particularly for fully automated vehicles. In this respect, the recommendations of the Law Commissions suggests that the person in the driving seat, since she/he is no longer a driver, may be regarded as a "user-in-charge".

The definition of the "users-in-charge" is given by the same report. They can be thought of as a human in the driving seat while a vehicle is driving itself.

The underpinning philosophy of the Joint Commissions is that every vehicle driving itself should have a user-in charge: as a result, the user-in-charge would be regarded : "(1) an individual, that is, a human or "natural person", rather than an organisation; (2) who is in the vehicle: not standing nearby or in a remote operations centre; (3) in position to operate the driving controls: for current vehicle design, in the driving seat; (4) while an ADS feature requiring a user-in-charge is engaged. [..]".

As a result of this definition of "user-in-charge", she/he will no longer be prosecuted for offences which arise directly from the driving task. It is obvious that in this case the liability will lie on the producer of the automated vehicle. Thus, the user-in-charge would have immunity from a most offences, such as dangerous driving, violation of speed limits or to run a red light.

However, the user-in-charge will still retain some duties, such as "carrying insurance, checking loads or ensuring that children wear seat belts".

The user-in-charge, like any current driver of a traditional vehicle, shall have a driving licence (although the Join report refer to an unclear "qualification"), a well as fit to drive, "as they may be called on to take over driving if the ADS issues a transition demand". As a traditional driver, the user-in-charge "must not be under the influence of drink or drugs".

To ensure that this system cannot be circumvented, the Joint report makes a a criminal offence "to act as a user-in-charge while unfit or unqualified, or to cause or permit another person to do so". More in general, in connection with the new concept of user-in-charge, the Joint report draws a demarcation line between dynamic driving and not-dynamic one and, therefore, between dynamic and non-dynamic offences.

More in general, when the ADS feature is engaged, the user-in-charge will not be responsible "for the dynamic driving task", since they do not control the vehicle "through steering, accelerating or braking, and do not need to monitor the driving environment".

Similarly, while the user-in-charge is immune for all offences which arise from dynamic driving, she/he will face a criminal liability "where the user-in-charge took steps to override or alter the 18 system so as to engage the ADS when it was not designed to function, or deliberately interfered with the functioning of the ADS". Finally, a user-in-charge will retain other "non-dynamic" driver.

For the remaining responsibilities, which appear to be also the most serious ones, it will be the producer that will retain most responsibilities, including the criminal ones.

Finally, in the Joint Report of the Law Commissions, some useful guidelines are figured out, particularly with the reference to the "duty of candour",[29] a very new concept in the common law system At first glance, this is a quasi-moral or philosophical suggestion, addressed to the UK legislator, which in the imminent future is expected to engage in drafting of the actual regulation in this area.

More practically, should one envisage the future norms in this micro-area, there will be distinction of accountability, since the Report highlights two separate liability: the one of senior managers on the one hand;[30] the one of the nominated person on the other. In the first case, senior managers have the duty of an implementation a "safety-first culture" and to operating on the basis of openness and transparency. In the second case, concerned with the nominated person, he/she has the duty to submit correct and complete information. At first glance, the way this system of liability is shaped of, again the liability for nominated person, is reminiscent of the Corporate Manslaughter Act 2007, and, upon reflection, of the correspondent "Italian 231".[31]

[29] See Paragraph no. 5.

[30] In force of the text, senior manager is "a person who plays a significant role in: the making decision about how the ASDE/NUIC operator is managed or organised, or the management of the safety assurance process" (Paragraph. No. 5.8).

[31] In force of Paragraph no. 5.11. and, 5.12 with reference of the burden of proof, the Report said that "the burden of proof should lie in establishing the nominated person's failure to take precautions. One possibility is to require the prosecution to show beyond reasonable doubt that the offence was attributable to their neglect. The other possibility is to require the nominated person to establish a due diligence defence: that is, to show on the balance of probabilities that they took reasonable precautions and exercised all due diligence to prevent the wrongdoing. On balance, we have reached the conclusion that the nominated person should be required to establish a due diligence defence. This acknowledges the information asymmetry between the prosecution and nominated person. The safety of AVs is dependent on the openness and honesty of the ASDE or NUIC operator in sharing information with the regulator. This offence is intended to ensure personal responsibility for creating a culture of transparency.".

5 Futures Scenarios; The Driverless Cars

On the basis of what has been observed so far, the United Kingdom, with a recent regulation, has introduced a niche body of law on driverless vehicles, even if, at the moment, its law does not allow the circulation of pure driverless cars, therefore cars that drive themselves alone. However, it is the British Government itself which is seeking to pursue a traffic regime: the latter will in future provide that only such vehicles are used on the roads of the Kingdom.

Once, from an administrative point of view, autonomous motor vehicles will be able to circulate. This type of vehicles too will be included in the updated list of the Secretary of State and the relevant insurance scheme will be that of the law, commented here, of 2018, unless, in the meantime, new rules are introduced.

Prior to the current provisions, vehicle insurance policy covered drivers who were human (and owners), but there was a possibility, indeed not remote, that the owner/driver or insurer would avoid liability, if the vehicle had not been under the immediate control of the driver at the time of the accident. Those who, therefore, had suffered personal damage or injury as a result of the accident would have been at the mercy of the most complex provisions of the Consumer Protection Act, always in order to exercise a claim for compensation, which was itself made more difficult. On the other hand, the new legislation offers those who buy vehicles of an automatic nature an alternative way of compensation, based on insurance, instead of the manufacturer's liability for defective vehicles.

Such action, it should be recalled, is provided not only to third parties who have suffered damage from the automatic vehicle, but also to the driver of the automatic vehicle, whether he has suffered an injury and provided that he is under the control of the automatic vehicle at the time of the accident and, therefore, has not actually become a passenger.

It is clear that changes will be needed to the Road Traffic Act 1988 in order to extend the mandatory liability insurance to automated vehicles, in particular those that appear on the list. Furthermore, the Secretary of State will provide an updated list of automated vehicles, which will be covered by the new legislation. More generally in continental Europe and in the EU, where the compulsory insurance scheme is based on Directive 2009/103, far-reaching changes will also be necessary to substantive law, expected that such discipline was not in any way designed for automated vehicles, always having in mind the pilot, the human being.[32]

For automated vehicles not covered, nor included in the new law, there will only be a legal duty on the manufacturer, in order to ensure that the software installed is implemented correctly. It is therefore primarily for such vehicles not included in the list that the new traditional regime of producer liability will apply, rather than the insurance-based regime under the new law.

---

[32] "Car insurance is based on human driver capability and thus well-established logic is becoming problematic in respect of autonomous cars as the risk is transferred to the machine". Noussia, *Autonomous* cit. p. 264.

Broadly speaking, autonomous vehicles, with their growing use, could also lead to the end of traditional liability insurance policy for damages to third parties, since this matter could be better reserved to the relationship between producers and their insurance companies.

6 New Liability Profiles: Between Trolley Problem and Privacy

If in the near future there will be only unmanned vehicles, particularly driverless cars, along the roads, the burning question is not whether the insurance policy is going to disappear. Rather, the new conundrum is the actual way the prospective policies will be shaped. As to the latter, reference shall be made to both trolley problems[33] and data protection.

The first aspect (trolley problems) requires a costs/benefits analysis, that is to say, whether it is preferable to sacrifice one's life for the interests of society. Should the algorithm be designed in order to better prop up the society (and the concept of protection of the community), the life of the individual will turn out to be sacrificed. This approach will be defined "utilitarian". In adopting this utilitarian approach, both the programmer and the manufacturer of autonomous vehicles will carry out an *ex ante* and abstract an appraisal, strictly pegged with the principle of maximum usefulness. Nevertheless, this appraisal, insofar it is detached from the actual circumstances and events, would be merely theoretical. This solution, from a strictly economic point of view, would be optimal, in the way that the final solution is to benefit the community and the society to a potential detriment of the individual.

To elaborate, the Artificial Intelligence, like the ordinary driver of vehicles (the individual), shall comply with the road traffic legislation, therefore the give-way rules, as well as both prohibitions and mandatory conducts. The real difference, though, is that the AI system, unlike the human counterpart, does not have that unique survival instinct. The latter, usually, allows the human being, rather than the mere machine, to make the best decision, by also weighing the survival chances of its

[33] "The Trolley Problem describes a philosophical thought experiment often used in introductory philosophy classes to demonstrate two major modem philosophies: Utilitarianism and Deontology or Duty-based morality. The problem has many iterations, but is typically described as follows: a trolley is hurtling down a track towards five people. You are on a bridge under which it will pass, and you can stop it by putting something very heavy in front of it. As it happens, there is a very fat man next to you - your only way to stop the trolley is to push him over the bridge and onto the track, killing him to save five. Should you proceed? The two options demonstrate one of the philosophical positions; should one choose to sacrifice the fat man, they have taken the Utilitarian position by saving the five people on the track, netting four lives by their actions, while allowing the trolley to continue on its course without interference is the Deontological position, in which one respects the duty they owe to the fat man as a fellow human being and do not sacrifice his life in order to save the lives of the other people on the track". See Belay (2015), p. 121; Bradley Wendel (2018), pp. 129–164; Santoni (2017), pp. 411–429; Appiah (2008); Wu (2020), pp. 1–13.

passengers in the event of an accident. Similarly, the Artificial Intelligent is not in a position to assess the costs, in terms of physical safety of other people, while carrying out operations, usually programmed in advance by the algorithm, to ensure the survival of their passengers.[34] As a result, the utilitarian approach may not be considered the best one from a strictly philosophical point of view.

Given the above, the underlying question relate to how the AI may assess the value of the human life or also the one of the community, or more in general of objects which are not likely to be financially valued, such as monuments, pieces of art or the environment. While these assessments are unrelated to mere philosophical digressions, nevertheless they have significant practical implications. These ethical assessments are taken into account by the programmers and, therefore, they "unleash" their consequences on the real world.

Moreover, these assessments could be influenced by customers, particularly the ones of the manufacturer. Potential customers may want the vehicle to work in such a way as to protect pedestrians or private property and artistic heritage assets. By contrast, other customers, may wish the vehicle and its software could safeguard other values, should a decisions be made in the inextricable case of "tragic choice".[35]

If the reasoning described above is followed, a further problem arises. If one assumes that driverless car has total control over the lives of its passengers, it could potentially also have a duty to its manufacturers. This duty could take the form of protecting its passengers, and therefore the persons it transports, from any damage to their physical safety.[36]

This is not without its drawbacks. First, allowing AI systems to take potentially irrational decisions prevents the full economic benefit to society from being satisfied and thus does not eliminate the occurrence of accidents. Secondly, there may be a reluctance of programmers[37] and insurers to, respectively, produce and insure vehicles that are manufactured exclusively to protect the lives of passengers.

Thirdly, on the basis of the current state of affairs, the sole liability lies with the producers of the CAVs and, as a result, they are compensating for damage which would have been suffered by the insurers.[38]

---

[34] If the AI of a vehicle considers that taking extreme measures to protect its passengers in the event of an accident would result in greater damage to the property or life of another person or persons, would make the least extreme decision but would endanger the lives of their passengers.

[35] This is not a new issue for the legal literature which, indeed, is full of contributions in this area. The concept of "tragic choices", already mentioned, refers to both risk assessment and risk management. Both these features allow to achieve a balance between individual fundamental rights, on the one hand, and the right of "multiple individuals". In this assessment, the first ones result in being overwhelmed by the latter ones (multiple individuals' rights). See Calabresi (2016).

[36] The AI currently existing within the CAV is conceived and implemented in a way that decisions are made in order to protect the lives of its passengers, even if this decision may cause more damages to others, and even if this decision is more expensive from an economic point of view.

[37] It has been observed that manufacturers and programmers will prepare the software so that it can take decisions that minimize the risk of legal exposure to the manufacturer and programmer, precisely. Casey (2017), pp. 1347–1366.

[38] Kumar (2018), pp. 1–32.

Closely connected to this profile, it is the one concerned with the privacy.[39] In this area, the concept of data protection[40] may come under attack from numerous corners. For example, CAVs can influence and ultimately compress the autonomy of individuals by taking over their lives (e.g. the way they travel, the relevant itinerary and the places where they go). At the same time CAVs produce personal pieces of information about users to the point that this software can monitor, almost completely, the route taken by the user. The privacy aspect is complicated by two circumstances: it is not clear yet the way autonomous vehicles interact with people; secondly, the privacy[41] is a complex and multiform concept, therefore the relevant paradigm cannot be crystallised.

The size of the privacy issue will depend on the design and operation of the CAV. If the common aspect is that they will replace the driver, physical person, with artificial intelligence, the aspects of programming can follow different paths leading, potentially, to different results.

Should the AI replace the driver of a car, the vehicle systems would adopt and develop a set of data in order to assess the surrounding environment, including the possible presence of other vehicles. In order to assess the impact on privacy it is necessary to reflect on at least three aspects: (1) who controls artificial intelligence; (2) that amount of external data (caressed, presence of other vehicles and people) are collected and transmitted to the vehicle; (3) the transmission of data to other vehicles.

Autonomous vehicles shall be based on both external and internal sensors with the objective of collecting data on the presence of external obstacles, to detect the temperature and its operation, but also to report any malfunctions or activate safety mechanisms in the event of an accident or impact. Privacy becomes of central importance when a particular vehicle is associated with an individual, identified or identifiable: in this way the data become the role of personal information.

Further reflection concerns the distinction between CAVs that can be defined as "autonomous" from those that are interconnected. With regard to the former, they use only information that is generated internally without it being communicated to the outside or to other vehicles. Moreover, , the interconnected vehicles communicate, via Wifi, with a wider communication network with the aim, precisely, is to put more CAV in communication with each other. As a result, we are witnessing a continuous exchange of information concerning the surrounding road environment, the route it is taking and which will be taken, but also the messages that are exchanged by other passengers.

---

[39] "If people were not involved with autonomous vehicles, privacy would not be an issue". Gancy (2012), p. 1171.

[40] In force of last Report of Law Commissions, it is write that the "regulator should only authorise a system as self-driving if these systems comply with data protection law", Paragraph no. 3.18.

[41] It is recalled that it concerns not only "the right to be alone" but also the right to the protection of personal data, the expectation of confidentiality that a person can boast at the time when he is in a public place, "the right to be forgotten".

These two driverless car models have different privacy implications. The first model will not pose any problem given that the personal data that are collected remain within the vehicle itself. The second, precisely because it is designed to interact with an external network, may, alternatively, provide only the information deemed strictly necessary to determine the *modus operandi* of the other vehicles present, or, communicate also what happens inside.

It is clear, therefore, that the first model, namely that of autonomous CAVs can be considered more secure in terms of privacy as the others become susceptible to external control at least through two different ways.

First, a vehicle can be controlled by handling information that has been sent to another autonomous vehicle.[42] Secondly, it could be the network itself that imposes a command on the vehicle, causing a change in the destination initially chosen by the user. In the latter case, the passenger's decision-making autonomy is *de facto* erased.

In both hypotheses, despite the differences already highlighted, there is the existence of a track that is concerned with the information of passengers regarding their identity, the route they have taken and everything they have encountered during the journey.

Hence, it is quintessential, as far as "autonomous" CAVs are concerned, that the relevant manufacturer adopts special systems in order to protect personal data. This goal will be achieved either through encryption or via a regular disposal of data. However, the solution now envisaged would be less straight-forward to achieve for interconnected vehicles: the latter, in fact, require the adoption of a complex mechanism for the protection of personal data, because they are part of an integrated system. Nevertheless, also in this case, some solutions could be the use of cryptography or anonymisation,[43] which would ultimately protect passengers' privacy in the most meaningful way.[44]

[42] For example, the vehicle may change route due to information sent by another interconnected vehicle relating to the temporary closure of a given road.

[43] It should be borne in mind that when anonymous information is used, it does not generate personal information and, consequently, the risks appear to be very limited.

[44] The FIA (International Automobile Federation) has launched the project "My Car Data" with the aim of increasing the awareness of users regarding the personal data processed as well as to highlight the need to introduce specific legislation on the subject. It is inferable from the above project that the source of data from the connection between several vehicles can be both the customer provided data and the vehicle generated data. In the first case, the personal data are related to the owner of the vehicle's passengers and relate to the location of both the vehicle and the passengers, the routes taken and the information resulting from the synchronisation of the users' mobile phone. In the second case, the data are produced directly by the vehicle and concern personal data or technical data. Fédération internationale de l'automobile (FIA), *What EU legislation says about car data. Legal Memorandum on connected vehicle and data*, in *www.osborneclarke.com*, 2017, pp. 1 ff.

7 The Italian Approach

In turning the attention to the Italian legal system, Scholars, given the fundamental dearth of a regulation on driverless vehicles, are still asking themselves which legal provision, of those within its Italian Civil Code (henceforth also "ICC"), is to be applied in the event of damage arising out of the circulation of autonomous vehicles. Thus, the nitty-gritty of the issue is whether art. 2054, ICC, can be applied, since this legal provision, unlike art. 46 of the Italian Road Act (the *Codice della Strada*, as it is known in the Italian legal system), does not refer, in an express manner, to a human being driving, since it mentions, in a very generic way, the driver.[45] The definition of the last one, is potentially consistent with an "driver-algorithm" too. Nevertheless, this solution is very difficult to share, because, in our view, the last limb of art. 2054(1) may, indeed, warrant the opposite solution. [46] Somehow to support this, most Scholars seem to be inclined to subscribe to this sceptical interpretation.[47]

A further legal provision within the Italian Civil Code to potentially recall is art. 2051, ICC, concerned with the damages caused by things in custody, where the role of a caretaker is implied and/or required. Likewise, the ensuing question is whether such a caretaker will be held responsible for the operations of a fully autonomous vehicle, should the thing in custody be a CAV.

This provision could be applied, *mutatis mutandis*, to the CAVs too, if it was reasoned that the vehicle is the thing that directly causes the damage. In other words, the damage, for the same to be relevant under art. 2051, ICC, shall be caused by the thing, but not by using the thing. To further elaborate, the hypothesis contemplated under art. 2051 ICC implies that the damage derives from the "thing" (or the occurrence, within it, of a harmful event). However, such a liability must therefore be excluded, in the event that the thing has been the means used to carry out an independent action.[48] Should the latter be the interpretation of art. 2051, ICC (and there is no reason from departing from this entrenched approach), the automated vehicles would hardly fit into this legal provision.[49]

---

[45] According to article. 46 of the Italian Road Act by vehicle shall mean "all machines of any kind, circulating on roads guided by man" (our literal translation from Italian).

[46] The drive shall be held responsible "if he does not prove that he did everything possible to avoid the damage" (our literal translation from Italian).

[47] For an individual to be qualified as a driver, she/he must have the possibility to determine the trajectory of the vehicle. See De Bruyne and Tanghe (2017), p. 339.

[48] Italian Supreme Court, n. 12300/1995.

[49] In details, the scope of art. 2051, ICC, requires that it is not the injured person who has to provide the Court with the proof of the defect or the danger of the thing. The burden of proof is shifted to the custodian, who in turn will be entitled to exercise a recourse action against the producer (Belfiore 2018, p. 1580; Fernández Cruz and León Hilario 2005, pp. 9–76). At the last (lastly), assumption of the activation of the responsibility of art. 2051 ICC concerns the occurrence of damage during the operation of the res and that these can be traced to a malfunction suitable to assume causal relevance. Despite the above, it is difficult to argue that passengers can be considered as custodians of the CAV, given that the custody cannot result in the mere use and enjoyment of the property

Despite these misgivings, the liability under art. 2051, ICC, is a "strict" one and its source must be located in the relation existing between a "player", the custodian, and the object of custody, the *res*. Consequently, the grounds of this liability shall be found in the risk, duly assessed in advance, by the custodian in using the thing or in allowing the use of it by other parties.[50] Admittedly, though, while this norm is more favourable to the damaged party, it greatly increases the responsibility of the owner, if compared with what happens for "traditional" vehicles, should the owner be the keeper of the thing too.

In conclusion, it is possible to highlight that, given the dearth of *ad hoc* legal provisions in this area, a possible precept of the ICC to apply would be art. 2051, ICC., at least in following an Italian school of thought, although it is still very difficult to imagine who the custodian is, in dealing with CAVs.[51] However, it is more realistic to accept that there is a huge loophole in this area within the Italian legal system. Again, the Italian legislature could batten down the hatches with an *ad hoc* regulation, given the unsatisfactory solutions that are otherwise available in the current literature.

To think that there is now an osmosis between legal systems, it can be considered that, where and when the Italian law deems it appropriate to regulate the movement of driverless vehicles[52] and, as a result, introducing its own system of liability insurance for the conduct of such vehicles would inevitably be a model of a certain charm; however, it should be noted that there are several doubts as to whether the same legislation can be reproduced in Italy, if not in some marginal aspects, given the flexible (purposive) nature of the regulations under discussion, which also reflects the system of belonging, of common law.

---

without any possibility of interference in its destination, maintenance and conservation. Italian Supreme Court, no. 15429/2004, no. 26086/2005.

[50] Albanese (2021), pp. 955–1044.

[51] The hypothesis of art. 2051 seems to refer to a relationship (the custodian-owner) very distant from the one between the manufacturer, the owner, the programmer of CAVs.

[52] There is no doubt that the process is inevitable. And on the other hand, the logic of prohibitions in one order, when in others it is allowed, does not seem to be the winning one. In this regard, they can only recall the words of Calabresi and AL Mureden, p. 9: "From this point of view, it appears that, first of all, an approach based on a policy of prohibition aimed at authoritatively inhibiting the spread of driverless cars should be excluded. Such a measure would be ineffective: in fact, would not prevent other systems more favourable to the spread of driverless cars to opt for a policy of openness and incentive to take over in the long run and to overwhelm the choices of safeguard made by countries perched on positions of prohibition". (Our not literal translation from Italian).

8 Conclusions

The AEVA 2018 represents an "open-ended proactive" legislation that allows its subject matter to rule itself, on the basis of an almost "blank check" delegation. Automated machines, in their strict form, totally without a driver, have not yet been introduced into British law, yet a law of 2018 well in advance regulates an aspect of liability for damages to third parties of the CAV.

The objective is, therefore, to compensate with sufficient clarity the damaged party, on the basis of an insurance policy, and, as highlighted in this paper, tend to avoid that the damaged third party can activate a—otherwise deemed dangerous—legal action against the manufacturer, currently based, Overseas, on a law not designed for the type of machinery in question.[53]

It must also be said that the law in question also aims to ensure the insurance industry, against what would otherwise be the uncontrolled trend to see its range of responsibilities expanded.[54]

Some aspects, as explained by this contribution, remain open: the definitions, broad and perhaps too broad; the ways in which the insurer can obtain reimbursement from the producer.

Soft law should provide flexibility, which is particularly required in an area such as the one under consideration, where the definition of automatic vehicle itself can change rapidly, also in order to take account of technological developments, more than traditional law does.

A flexible "purposive" approach to interpreting the law in the sense that it applies could also be adopted to the subtle causal issues related to damages caused by CAVs. In this respect, it is likely that there may be "causation gaps", therefore gaps in the causal link between the CAV's unlawful conduct and damages. In other words, by rigidly applying the causal theories of English law, some harmful phenomena might not find a real justification. These gaps, in the British legislation, will be filled in by Courts through the use of a reasonableness that, moreover, constitutes the quintessence of common law.

The view advocated in this contribution is that, should the British legislation be adopted, this would be the preferable solution, because of its extremely practical flavour. However, the Italian legal system, because of its EU membership, is the recipient of solutions, adopted in the community, which are not totally convincing. In this respect, the EU law, establishing a legal liability for robots,[55] may be one of the stark examples. More specifically, within the Resolution "Civil Law Rules on Robotics",[56] the European Parliament asked the Commission for a number of

[53] On the theory of Market Enterprise Responsibility (MER) as a suitable tool to achieve a balanced allocation of accident costs in the new automated traffic system. Abraham and Rabin (2019), pp. 127–171; Geistfeld (2017), p. 1635; Al Mureden (2019), p. 895.

[54] This is mentioned by Chagas Lessa and Bulunt (2020), pp. 331 ff., more specifically p. 338.

[55] In the specific case of CAV and European Union law, see Santoni (2017), pp. 411–429.

[56] European Parliament, Resolution of the European Parliament of 16 February 2017.

interventions extended to algorithms and, more generally, to damages produced by algorithms.[57] Although this EU statute in the area of robotics may appear a fascinating theme, some legal issues remain unresolved. The most serious danger lies, particularly, in the fundamental vagueness of the current EU legal provisions, which means that, for specific cases and/or event, it would be pretty impossible to identify the legal provision to apply.[58] Thus, the British Regulation could serve as a model for the development of a European legislation in this area of law, not only the Italian limb. It is true that what has been drawn up so far in "Albion" in this area could work as a mere reference framework, given the fundamental diversity of the different legal

[57] In particular, the Commission was invited to: (1) adopt "common Union definitions of cyber physical systems, autonomous systems, smart autonomous robots and their subcategories by taking into consideration the following characteristics of a smart robot: — the acquisition of autonomy through sensors and/or by exchanging data with its environment (inter-connectivity) and the trading and analysing of those data; — self-learning from experience and by interaction (optional criterion); — at least a minor physical support; — the adaptation of its behaviour and actions to the environment; — absence of life in the biological sense"; (2) "Considers that a comprehensive Union system of registration of advanced robots should be introduced within the Union's internal market where relevant and necessary for specific categories of robots, and calls on the Commission to establish criteria for the classification of robots that would need to be registered; in this context, calls on the Commission to investigate whether it would be desirable for the registration system and the register to be managed by a designated EU Agency for Robotics and Artificial Intelligence"; (3) "Considers that the future legislative instrument should be based on an in-depth evaluation by the Commission determining whether the strict liability or the risk management approach should be applied"; (4) "Calls on the Commission, when carrying out an impact assessment of its future legislative instrument, to explore, analyse and consider the implications of all possible legal solutions, such as: (a) establishing a compulsory insurance scheme where relevant and necessary for specific categories of robots whereby, similarly to what already happens with cars, producers, or owners of robots would be required to take out insurance cover for the damage potentially caused by their robots; (b) ensuring that a compensation fund would not only serve the purpose of guaranteeing compensation if the damage caused by a robot was not covered by insurance; (c) allowing the manufacturer, the programmer, the owner or the user to benefit from limited liability if they contribute to a compensation fund, as well as if they jointly take out insurance to guarantee compensation where damage is caused by a robot; (d) deciding whether to create a general fund for all smart autonomous robots or to create an individual fund for each and every robot category, and whether a contribution should be paid as a one-off fee when placing the robot on the market or whether periodic contributions should be paid during the lifetime of the robot; (e) ensuring that the link between a robot and its fund would be made visible by an individual registration number appearing in a specific Union register, which would allow anyone interacting with the robot to be informed about the nature of the fund, the limits of its liability in case of damage to property, the names and the functions of the contributors and all other relevant details; (f) creating a specific legal status for robots in the long run, so that at least the most sophisticated autonomous robots could be established as having the status of electronic persons responsible for making good any damage they may cause, and possibly applying electronic personality to cases where robots make autonomous decisions or otherwise interact with third parties independently". See no. 1, no. 2, no. 53, no. 59 (a) of Resolution.

[58] Infantino (2019), pp. 1762–1794.

systems. Nonetheless, this new statute does have the advantage of being a coherent system of practical precepts, which could be "imported" almost immediately.[59]

We have put forward the theory that, while the current legislation—whether of a British or of a "Community" origin—holds the manufacturer responsible for the damages caused by vehicles, a new form of liability of the insurer can be conceived. To such an end, it has been pointed out that CAVs too engender privacy problems that, either "by design" or "by default", are potentially instrumental in a manufacturer's responsibility.

However, this does not rules out the possibility that the owners of the driverless cars can enter into policies to be insured against the possible data breach that could potentially lead to the dissemination of personal data of the passengers of their vehicle. Therefore, we could see the surge of new models of insurance contracts, whose purpose is to cover the damage caused by any cyber-attacks against autonomous vehicles, in both their version "autonomous" and in the one interconnected via Wifi network.

According to the same line of reasoning, provided that robots[60] are held as entities responsible for damages caused to third parties,[61] new models of insurance contracts may arise, with the aim of compensating third parties for damages they may suffer as a result of the interaction with synthetic entities.[62] The interesting aspect to study and to deepen concerns the different degrees of the psychological elements attributable to the robot, that is if it is still possible to distinguish between wilful misconduct and negligence.

Finally, it is possible to affirm that the "match" is over, since also the most innovative and forward-looking guideline encompass a warning for the legislature. To elaborate, the scope of recommendations is to set up, in the matter of safety insurance, a new *ad hoc* regulation with particular attention to powers and responsibilities. In order to do this, it is inferable that three main warnings shall be addressed to the British Parliament: (1) to make an assessment on the safety of AV, compared with conventional driving; (2) to investigate the potentially road traffic infractions; (3) to ensure that Authorised Self-Driving Entities (ASDEs) give clearly and effectively information.[63]

[59] We are aware that in Italy, according to the Decree of 28 February 2018 (Smart Road Decree) has authorized the testing of autonomous vehicles.

[60] Please note that robots have already been granted rights, See Caughill (2017); Bertolini (2013), pp. 214–247.

[61] For a deepening see La Torre (2019), pp. 323–336.

[62] An embryo of the above is referred to points no. 57 and no. 58 of "European Parliament resolution of 16 February 2017 with recommendations to the Commission on Civil Law Rules on Robotics (2015/2103(INL))".

See Amato Mangiameli (2019), pp. 107–124; Lobianco (2020), pp. 1080–1097.

[63] See Paragraph no 3.19 and 3.20 of the last Joint Report.

References

Abraham KS, Rabin RL (2019) Automated vehicles and manufacturer responsibility for accidents: a new legal regime for a new era. Virginia Law Rev 1:127–171
Al Mureden E (2019) Autonomous cars e responsabilità civile tra disciplina vigente e prospettive de iure condendo. Contratto e impresa 3:895–924
Albanese A (2021) La responsabilità civile per i danni da circolazione di veicoli a elevata automazione. Europa e Diritto Privato 4:955–1044
Amato Mangiameli AC (2019) Algoritmi e big data. Dalla carta sulla robotica. Rivista di Filosofia del Diritto 1:107–124
Appiah A (2008) Experiments in ethics. Cambridge University Press, Cambridge
Barlow LG (2008) Insurance law handbook. Bloomsbury, Haywards Heath
Belay N (2015) Robot ethics and self-driving cars: how ethical determinations in software will require a new legal framework. J Legal Profess 40:119–130
Belfiore A (2018) Responsabilità (Struttura del giudizio e prestazione risarcitoria), Le parole del diritto. In Scritti in onore di Carlo Castronovo. Jovene, Napoli
Bennett H (2006) The marine insurance act 1906. reflections on a centenary. Singapore Acad Law J 3:669–692
Bertolini A (2013) Robots as products: the case for a realistic analysis of robotic applications and liability rules. Law Innov Technol 5:214–247
Birds J (2010) Birds' modern insurance law. Sweet & Maxwell, London
Bradley Wendel W (2018) Economic rationality and ethical values in design-defect analysis: the trolley problem and autonomous vehicles. Calif West Law Rev 1:129–164
Calabresi G (2016) The future of law and economics. Yale University Press, New Haven and London
Calabresi G, Al Mureden E (2020) Driverless car e responsabilità civile. Rivista diritto bancario:7–21
Casey B (2017) Amoral machines, or: how roboticists can learn to stop worrying and love the law. Standf Law J 5:1347–1366
Caughill R (2017) An artificial intelligence has officially been granted residence. Futurism
Chagas Lessa JC, Bulunt B (2020) A New Era, a New Risk! A study on the impact of the developments of new technologies in the shipping industry and marine insurance market, in InsurTech: a legal and regulatory view. In: Marano P, Noussia K (eds) InsurTech: a legal and regulatory view. Springer, London
Channon M (2019) Automated and electric, vehicles Act 2018: an evaluation in light of proactive law and regulatory disconnect. Eur J Law Technol
Cheng DLK, Deng R (2018) Cryptocurrency, fintech, Insuretch, and regulation. Elsevier, London
Clarke M (2011) An introduction to insurance contract law. In: Burling J, Lazarus K (eds) Research handbook on international insurance law and regulation. Edward Elgar Publishing, Cheltenham and Northampton
De Bruyne J, Tanghe J (2017) Liability for damage caused by autonomous vehicles: a Belgian perspective. J Eur Tort Law 8: 324–371
Donati A, Volpe Putzolu G (2019) Manuale del diritto delle assicurazioni. Giuffré, Milano, p 2019
Farenga L (2016) Manuale di diritto delle assicurazioni private. Giappichelli, Torino
Fernández Cruz G, León Hilario L (2005) La reedificación conceptual de la responsabilidad extracontractual objetiva. Derecho PUCP 58:9–76
Gancy DJ (2012) Privacy in autonomous vehicles. Santa Clara Law Rev 4:1171–1240
Geistfeld M (2017) A roadmap for autonomous vehicles: state tort liability, automobile insurance, and federal safety regulation. Calif Law Rev 105:1611–1694
Horsey K, Rackley E (2011) Tort law. Oxford University Press, Oxford
Infantino G (2019) La responsabilità per danni algoritmici: prospettive europeo-continentali. Responsabilità Civile e Previdenza 5:1762–1794

Kumar AM (2018) The modern trolley problem: ethical and economically-sound liability schemes for autonomous vehicles. Case West Res J Law Technol the Internet 9:1–32
La Torre A (2019) I robot fra responsabilità e assicurazione. Assicurazioni 3:323–336
Lobianco R (2020) Veicoli a guida autonoma e responsabilità civile: regime attuale e prospettive di riforma. Responsabilità Civile e Previdenza 4:1080–1097
Manes P (2020) Legal challenges in the realm of insur-tech. Eur Bus Law Rev 1:129–168
Marson J et al (2020) The automated and electric vehicles act – Part I and beyond: a critical review. Statute Law Rev 3:395–416
Merkin R (2021) Marine insurance. A legal history. Edward Elgar
Newdick C (1988) The development risk defence of the consumer protection act 1987. Cambridge Law J 47:455–476
Noussia K (2020) Autonomous vehicles: legal considerations and dilemmas. In: Marano P, Noussia K (eds) InsurTech: a legal and regulatory view. Springer, London
Pardolesi R, Davola A (2017) In viaggio col robot: verso nuovi orizzonti della rc auto ("driverless")? Danno e Responsabilità:616–629
Ruffolo U (2017) Self-driving car, auto driverless e responsabilità, in Intelligenza artificiale e responsabilità. Giuffrè, Milano
Santoni F (2017) Killing by autonomous vehicles and the legal doctrine of necessity. Ethical Theory Moral Pract 2:411–429
Schirone A (2004) Il contratti di assicurazione. La protezione della persona. Giappichelli, Torino
Smith JC, Burns P (1983) Donoghue v. Stevenson: the not so golden anniversary. Mod Law Rev 46:147–163
Stoppa A (1992) The concept of defectiveness in the consumer protection act 1987: a critical analysis. Legal Stud 12:210–217
Taylor R, Taylor D (2017) Contract law. Oxford University Press, Oxford
Thomson J (2014) Delictual liability. Bloomsbury Professional, Edinburgh
Williams GL (1946) The law reform (contributory negligence) Act, 1945. Mod Law Rev 9:105–186
Wu SS (2020) Autonomous vehicles, trolley problems, and the law. Ethics Inf Technol 22:1–13

Camilla Della Giustina (Juris Doctor summa cum laude) is a Ph.D. candidate in Law at Campania University, Luigi Vanvitelli, Italy.

Her research interests mainly relate to human rights (autonomous vehicles, privacy, cryonics) and business law (i.e., employment law, banking law and corporate law).

She is the author of more than fifty peer-reviewed research papers, chapters in edited books and books, in both English and Italian. She is also the author of two monographs.

She is a full qualified lawyer in Italy.

Pierre de Gioia Carabellese (Ph.D. - LL.M. - PGCAP - MA – CMI – Juris Doctor summa cum laude) is Fellow of Advance HE (York, UK), professor (full) of business law and regulation (ECU, Perth, Australia) and professor (full) of banking and financial law (Beijing Institute of Technology, Hong Kong Area). He has been a full professor of Law in England since 2017 (Huddersfield). Prior to this, he was associate professor of business law at Heriot Watt University (Edinburgh, UK). Professor de Gioia Carabellese is also Notary Public in Edinburgh, Solicitor in the UK and Avvocato in Italy.

Exploring the Suitability of the Protected Cell Company Structure for Shipping Business: A Call for Further Discussion and Research

Luke Bonello Ghio

Abstract This chapter examines the use of protected cell company (PCC) structure in the maritime industry. The study provides an overview of the origins and general characteristics of PCCs, which are a type of corporate structure that allows a business to create separate cells or "protected cells" within the company, each of which is treated as a separate legal entity for the purposes of liability. The research then explores the potential applications of the PCC in the maritime sector, specifically how it can be used to substitute the traditional single-ship company corporate structure, the current corporate landscape of ship-owning, and its implications for ship-owners and crew management companies. Additionally, an in-depth analysis of the Shipping and Aviation Business Cell Company Regulations, which were introduced under Maltese Law in 2020, is provided. The analysis covers the definition of shipping business, the formalities required for the creation of a cell company, the obligation to inform third parties, the separation of assets and liabilities, the creation of cells, and the liquidation process. The study also highlights the limitations of PCCs in the maritime industry, including the potential challenges of cross-jurisdictional recognition and the risk of sister-ship arrest, as well as the incompatibility of the structure with the tonnage tax flag link requirements. The chapter concludes by providing recommendations for the implementation of PCCs in the maritime industry and suggesting areas for further research.

Keywords Protected cell company structure · Maltese law · Shipping business · Malta · Aviation business · Regulations · Maritime industry

---

L. Bonello Ghio (✉)
Commercial Law, Faculty of Laws, University of Malta, Msida, Malta
e-mail: lukebonello.16@um.edu.mt

M. Lima Rego, S. Grima (eds.), *Cross-Disciplinary Impacts on Insurance Law*, AIDA Europe Research Series on Insurance Law and Regulation 8,
https://doi.org/10.1007/978-3-031-38526-1_9

1 Introduction

The maritime industry is one of the oldest and most traditional business sectors globally and is of vital importance to Malta's economy. As a seafaring nation, the maritime sector accounts for 14% of the country's gross domestic product, contributing to the employment of more than 20,000 people. Besides this, Malta boasts the largest ship registry in Europe, and the sixth largest in the world, with 86.1 million tonnes at the end of 2021, representing an 82% increase since 2012. Malta has placed itself at the forefront of shipping activities, bringing significant benefits to the Maltese economy.[1]

In recognising its unique position within the maritime industry, Malta has continuously invested heavily in the various marine and maritime fields of activities, thus establishing itself as a hub for shipping requirements. Besides providing necessary facilities such as ship repair, cruise and passenger terminals, berthing facilities and so forth, Malta has also undertaken innovative approaches to attract ships to the Malta flag and businesses to establish themselves and operate in Malta. Indeed, Malta has successfully attracted companies involved directly or indirectly with the maritime sector because it has achieved a balance between regulation on the one hand and creating an industry-friendly environment on the other. For instance, the exemption of income tax on shipping activities, reasonable incorporation and registration costs for companies and vessels, and the introduction of a new and revised Commercial Yacht Code are a few examples of how Malta has managed to attract business while being able to offer an alternative to other jurisdictions.

Another example of such innovation is the recent extension of the cell company concept to aviation and "shipping business". The maritime industry is a vast and complex sector that encompasses a wide range of activities, including ship management, shipbuilding, port operations, cruise liners, the carriage of passengers and offshore oil and gas exploration. These activities are often subject to significant risks, and as such, it is important for businesses operating in the maritime industry to have effective risk management strategies in place. It has been suggested that one such potential tool for managing risk in the maritime industry is the use of the protected cell company structure.

On the 16th of June 2020, the legislator introduced new regulations which allow companies within the shipping and aviation sector to benefit from the cell company structure, more commonly attributed to insurance, investment funds, the securitisation vehicle industry and repackaging. Legal Notice 248 of 2020, the Companies Act (Shipping and Aviation Cell Companies) Regulations (the Regulations) had been welcomed by practitioners, with some remarking that the impact of the COVID-19 global pandemic has brought about the need for corporate restructuring and that this novel concept allows companies within the shipping and aviation sector to do just that in a seemingly cost-effective and efficient manner.

[1] Arena (2022).

Since June 2020, Malta has registered 19 protected cell companies in terms of the Regulations with a total of 126 cells, all of which are aviation cell companies.[2] With so many aviation cell companies registered in such a short time since the introduction of these Regulations and none related to the shipping industry, calls into question the suitability of the framework for companies involved in shipping business.

While it is noted that these Regulations were created with the aviation sector in mind, as seen by the number of aviation PCC registrations, this chapter will attempt to understand why Malta has decided to expand the use of the cell company beyond insurance law. Therefore, this chapter will focus on the application of the Regulations to shipping business. It will explore the potential use of the PCC structure in the maritime industry in more detail, examining the benefits and limitations of using this structure by considering the concepts and implementation of the PCC in the insurance industry and how they can be applied to the maritime industry.

Thus, although the concept of the cell company is not new, it is nonetheless an innovative product within the shipping industry. As it is unlikely that stakeholders within the shipping sphere are aware of the concept of the cell company, this Chapter will delve into the origins of the cell company legislation and examine how the concept of statutory segregation of assets and liabilities came to be, before delving into the practical use of the cell structure for shipping business. It will also provide a commentary on the Regulations.

Owing to the vital importance that the maritime sector plays, this Chapter aims to determine how a shipping company might be able to benefit from abandoning its traditional corporate structure in favour of this novel framework. This will be achieved by examining these questions; if a shipping company decides to adopt the cell company format, how might it be structured? What are the benefits of using this corporate vehicle? Would jurisdictions that do not provide for the segregation of assets and liabilities recognise and respect such a corporate structure regarding a claim that arises in their jurisdiction? And finally, what are the risks and limitations of using this corporate vehicle?

2 Methodology

As this is the first-ever study on the application of the cell company to shipping business, this chapter, will therefore provide a detailed analysis of S.L 386.22 Companies Act (Shipping and Aviation Cell Companies) Regulations employing the 'Black Letter' method. To assist in the interpretation of the Regulations, where suitable, reference will also be made to other Cell Company regulations, namely the Companies Act (Cell Companies Carrying on Business of Insurance) Regulations. Furthermore, references will also be made to local and foreign cases to substantiate

[2] Appendix 1.

specific claims. Reference will mainly be made to the facts of the case. These cases shed light on the issues under review; (1) the concept of segregating assets and liabilities and restricting the rights of creditors to a separate fund, (2) examining the purpose for placing a ship in a cell of a cell company, in this instance reference will be made to a US case whereby the company in question was structured in the US equivalent of a cell company, and (3) to show how legislation is subject to the interpretation of the court.

Complementing the black letter method of research, the study will also use the 'Desk Research' method. Reference will be made to authoritative texts dealing with (1) protected cell companies and (2) shipping companies. Furthermore, publications dealing with the management, incorporation and uses of the protected cell company will also be examined. Such an exercise will provide a comprehensive understanding of (1) how the cell company is used in already established industries, (2) how shipping companies are managed and operated, and (3) how shipping companies could make use of the cell company structure.

3 Literature Review

While the literature on protected cell companies is scarce, there is a plethora of literature relating to ship management and applicable relevant maritime and merchant shipping laws. Since the cell company concept has only been recently expanded to include shipping business, there is no literature examining such an entity. However, several texts deal with individual components which cumulatively form the focus of this study. In this regard, the author has consulted with texts that deal with protected cell companies generally and within specific industries, namely captive insurance and investment funds.

The leading authoritative text covering the protected cell company is *Protected Cell Companies: A guide to their implementation and use* by Nigel Feetham and Grant Jones.[3] This is the only reference book on the subject of cell companies which provides comprehensive legal analysis and guidance on the use of cell companies. This authoritative text was cited by the Federal Court of Montana, USA, in May 2015. This Chapter will make continuous references to this text.

While there appear to be no texts that deal entirely with the application of the cell company to shipping business, the author has come across many texts and notes that seemingly allude to the possibility that a cell company can set up cells to hold a vessel. One such example is *The Curacao Protected (Trust) Cell Company*, published in the *Trusts & Trustees* journal by Maike Bergervoet and Jeroen Starreveld.[4] While stating that a cell company can be established for the purposes of managing ships, these texts do not provide any detailed information how such a

[3] Feetham and Jones (2010).

[4] Bergervoet and Starreveld (2014), pp. 568–572.

structure will function. Given the limited literature available, this chapter will focus on the application of the Regulations within the context of ship owning companies.

Relevant literature regarding the traditional corporate structure of shipping companies has also been consulted. This includes two theses, the first, *Shipping Group of Companies: The Phenomenon of One-Ship Companies and Protection of Creditors* by Nicolaos Mitsakis,[5] which provides a detailed examination of the historical developments in the shipping industry that led firstly to the creation of the limited liability company and then how such companies utilise the corporate group structure to minimise exposure to risk and more importantly sister-ship arrest. The second is *Sister Ship Arrest and the Problem of the One Ship Company* by Nargys Hasan-Cakir,[6] which also examines the single-ship company structure. Finally, the author has also consulted with *Modern Maritime Law Volume 1: Jurisdiction and Risks* by Aleka Mandaraka-Sheppard,[7] which assisted with the understanding of how the single-ship company is used in the context of ship arrest.

3.1 Origins of the Cell Company

The PCC, which is also known as the 'segregated portfolio company', the 'segregated accounts company' or the 'series LLC' depending on the jurisdiction, has been around for almost 30 years since its inception in Guernsey in 1997 and further development in the Cayman Islands and Gibraltar. Since then, the PCC has enjoyed relative success, particularly within the insurance and investment funds industry, with the concept being adopted by a number of jurisdictions, including Malta and the US.

The principal objective of the PCC is to segregate the assets and liabilities between separate operations within a single business organisation. This is achieved by placing certain identifiable assets and liabilities into divisions of cells held separately from the assets and liabilities of another cell. The ultimate aim is that the activities and assets of one cell are ring-fenced and protected from the liabilities of another. Therefore, the creditors of a specific cell cannot use the assets of another cell to make good for any liabilities, the end result being that different and separate patrimonies are held by a single corporate body and ring-fenced from each other.

Typically, the PCC corporate structure is used for captive insurance, investment funds, securitization, and repackaging.[8] Indeed, PCC legislation was introduced in Guernsey to address the emerging needs of the captive insurance market amid heavy lobbying from industry players that wished to take advantage of the captive approach

[5] Mitsakis (1986).

[6] Hassan-Cakir (2019).

[7] Mandaraka-Sheppard (2013).

[8] Feetham and Jones (2010), pp. 3

to risk management but did not want to establish their own captive.[9] Prior to the introduction of PCC legislation, the segregation of assets and liabilities of a captive insurance company was realised through contractual arrangements between the various participants. This was achieved by incorporating a limited liability company for which the promoters would hold ordinary voting shares, the subscription monies of which would constitute the company's general assets. Third parties would then be able to enjoy equity participation through non-voting redeemable preference shares, with each different type of preference share constituting a separate fund. This would enable the preference shareholder to have risks underwritten through the company with respect to the insurance business undertaken and to receive dividends from the segregated funds of their respective underwriting activities. Thus, the preference shareholder would enjoy a dual relationship with the company, firstly as a shareholder and secondly as a policyholder. The Articles of Association would regulate their relationship as shareholders and the rights of a member qua member. Therefore, it would be possible to limit claims to specific assets on the condition that such limitation is enforceable only against the members of the company. Therefore, in order for the company to limit their claims to a particular fund through their relationship as policyholders, the preference shareholder would enter into a shareholders' agreement for the purpose of limiting claims to a prescribed and defined fund. The objective of cell segregation is consequently achieved through contractual arrangements.[10]

Even within the traditional limited liability company structure, it has always been possible to provide for some form of contractual segregation. This can be achieved by creating separate groups of assets, with each class of shareholders being contractually entitled to only receive the benefit of a particular group of assets. For example, a company owning two properties could create a contractual arrangement whereby only particular property and the profits or losses attributable to it would be enjoyed or suffered by only one class of shares, while the profits and losses of the other property would be attributed to a second class of shares.[11]

While it is possible to achieve the objective of asset segregation through contractual principles, whereby creditors contractually limit their claims to particular assets through non-recourse agreements, it is nonetheless easy to identify the limitations of such an agreement. If a company fails to establish a legally binding non-recourse agreement with all its creditor or is challenged by an involuntary creditor (who is not a party to any such contract and who therefore cannot have their claims limited), then this could result in cross-contamination of liabilities whereby all the assets of the company are made available. This point is highlighted by Feetham and Jones, who explain that a potential weakness of a contractual cell captive structure is that all of the company's liabilities, regardless of whether they are linked to specific assets or restricted by contract, could potentially be pursued or enforced against the company

[9] Moss (2001), pp. 14–15.

[10] Feetham and Jones (2010), pp. 6–9.

[11] Curmi (2009), p. 63.

and its assets. This could be especially problematic in the event of insolvency, as the mandatory rule of pari passu would take precedence over any contractual provisions. This may be particularly relevant in cases where policyholders' rights under individual insurance contracts are not limited in value but, rather, are only tied to specific assets. During insolvency proceedings, it is the total value of the available assets that is considered to satisfy the company's liabilities.[12] PCC legislation was introduced to address the limitations of contractual segregation of assets and liabilities by creating a legal framework for statutory 'ring-fencing' protection by having assets and liabilities held in distinct, segregated and separate patrimonies.

3.2 General Characteristics of the Protected Cell Company

Unlike other general trading companies, the PCC enjoys legislative protection for the segregation of its assets and liabilities which are kept physically separate and identifiable. It is a single legal entity and like any other company, a PCC has a single separate legal personality distinct from its members. Unlike traditional companies, the PCC is able to create an unlimited number of cells. The creation of a cell does not create, in respect of that cell, a legal person separate from the PCC, even though there are certain instances where for the purposes of company law, the cell is treated as though it were a separate company. Accordingly, where a cell wishes to contract with another party, it does so through the PCC acting for and on its behalf.[13]

A PCC is created in the same way as any other limited liability company and accordingly exhibits all the usual characteristics of a traditional company.[14] In order to be incorporated, it must have a Memorandum and Articles of Association, a registered office, a share capital, shareholders and a board of directors.[15] The revenue streams, assets and liabilities of each cell are kept independent from all other cells and from the core and it is possible for each cell to have its own shareholders.[16]

A cell company operates in two parts— the company core and cells. The core part comprises all non-cellular assets, including the company's core share capital, investments, liabilities, etc. Non-cellular assets are also known as core assets. The core must be solvent at all times. A cell company can create one or more cells within its company structure. The cells are independent of each other and are protected from each other from a legislative point of view. This is done by the issue of cell shares with respect to each individual cell, the proceeds of which form part of the so-called cellular assets attributable to that cell. Each shareholder of a cell receives its own

[12] Ibid, p. 13.

[13] Feetham and Jones (2010), p. 29.

[14] *Ibid*, p. 30.

[15] Finance Malta (2016).

[16] Appleby Global (2019).

Fig. 1 PCC structure

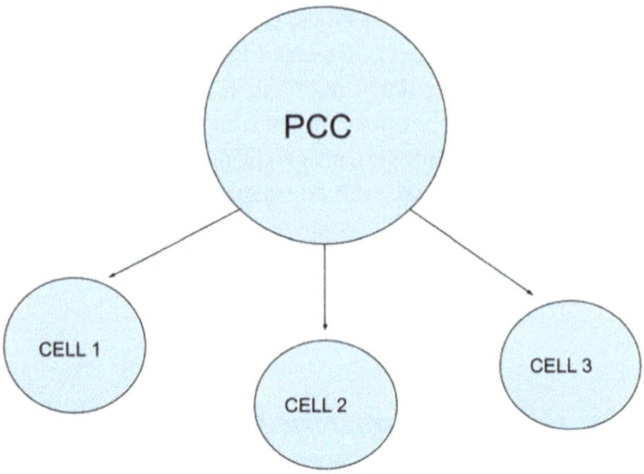

dividend stream. For tax purposes, each cell is treated as a separate entity and even has its own individual tax number.[17]

The PCC has a single board of directors that takes responsibility for the transactions within the core and each of the cells and the company's statutory and regulatory compliance and corporate governance requirements. The assets of any particular cell are only available to the shareholders and creditors of that cell—creditors of another cell have no recourse against them.[18]

This unique legal nature enables the PCC to establish multiple portfolios under one corporate entity, with liability for each specific portfolio limited to specific pools of assets, rather than exposing all assets of the company as a whole (Fig. 1).[19]

4 Overview of the Shipping and Aviation Cell Companies Regulations

Before a discussion on the practical usefulness, if any, of the PCC regulations as they relate to shipping business can ensue, it is firstly important to consider the provisions of the Legal Notice 248 of 2020, which introduced the new regulations in the Companies Act pertaining to the establishment of shipping cell companies.

As noted earlier, the concept of a cell company is not novel and has existed for almost three decades since its introduction in Guernsey. Likewise, Cell Companies have been regulated under Maltese law for some time. The concept was introduced in 1998 through amendments to other laws contemplated by the new Insurance Business Act promulgated at the time. It was not until 2011, through the enactment

[17] Finance Malta (2016).

[18] *Ibid.*

[19] Appleby Global (2019).

of the Companies Act (Incorporated Cell Companies Carrying on Business of Insurance) Regulations, that it became possible to use cells in practice. Since then, Malta has established itself as an attractive jurisdiction for entities utilising this corporate vehicle. Cell company regulations within the Maltese legal system which preceded the Regulations are the following:

- S.L 386.10 Companies Act (Cell Companies Carrying on Business Insurance) Regulations
- S.L 386.14 Companies Act (SICAV Incorporated Cell Companies) Regulations
- S.L 386.16 Securitisation Cell Companies Regulations

Whereas the mechanism for the use of PCC is already well established in Malta and other jurisdictions, the novelty of these regulations is that industries for which the PCC may be utilised have been extended to both the shipping and aviation sectors in an attempt by Malta to create a new and innovate product within both industries in order to appeal to industry players. Generally, jurisdictions implementing PCC legislation restrict this type of corporate medium to defined business activities (such as Malta's case, which creates separate regulations for the different business activities that may use the PCC framework as listed above). Historically, the use of this type of company has been reserved for insurance companies and captives, securitisation and investment schemes. Through the promulgation of Act V of 2020, the introduction of the new article, section 84E, to the Companies Act established the power to make regulations regarding Cell Companies carrying on or engaged in shipping or aviation business, thereby creating more specialised rules for both industries.

Article 84E of the Companies Act provides the following:

84E (1) (a) The Minister may make regulations in order to:

(i) provide for the formation, constitution, authorisation and regulation of cell companies carrying on or engaged in shipping or aviation business;
(ii) make it possible for a company carrying on or engaged in shipping or aviation business to convert into a cell company;
(iii) provide for all other matters that may arise in connection therewith; and
(iv) provide for the better carrying out of the provisions of this sub-article, and, without prejudice to the generality of the foregoing, may, by such regulations, in particular regulate the matters referred in Article 84A(1)(a) to (f), which shall also apply to this article.

4.1 Definition of Shipping Business

It is essential to note the difference in the definition of 'shipping business' in terms of Article 84E of the Companies Act and the definition of 'shipping activity' as caught by Article 84Z of the Merchant Shipping Act. Noticeably, Act V of 2020 adopts a much broader definition of the term 'shipping business' than 'shipping activity' as provided in the Merchant Shipping Act.

With regards to the Companies Act, shipping business has the following meaning:

> 84E. (1)(b)(i) the ownership, operation (under charter, lease or otherwise), administration and management (including personal engagement, employment or management whether on board or otherwise) of any ship [. . .] and the carrying on of all ancillary financial, security, commercial and other activities in connection therewith; or
>
> (ii) the holding of shares or other equity interests in any undertaking, whether Maltese or otherwise, established solely or mainly for the carrying on or carrying out of any one or more of the activities referred to in this definition and the carrying on of all ancillary financial, security, commercial and other activities in connection therewith; or
>
> (iii) the activities of a parent company which holds share or other equity interests in undertakings, whether Maltese or otherwise, where any one or some of these undertakings is established solely or mainly for the carrying on or carrying out of any one or more of the activities referred to in this definition and the carrying on of all ancillary financial, security, commercial and other activities in connection therewith; or
>
> (iv) the raising of capital through loans, the issue of guarantees or the issue of securities by an undertaking when the purpose of such activity is to achieve the objects or activities stated in the preceding sub-paragraphs for the undertaking itself or for any other undertaking within the same group; or
>
> (v) the carrying on of such other objects or activities within the maritime [...] sector and related or connected matters which the Ministry may, on the advice of the Authority, from time to time prescribe by regulations.

Such a wide definition of the term 'shipping business' includes not only the ownership or operation of a vessel, but also the administration and management of ships, including crew management (crewing companies), and all ancillary activities connected therewith. Therefore, the regulations attempt to encompass all and any shipping and vessel-related operations. Additionally, the definition also refers to creditors and other financial activities. Therefore, the term shipping business does not refer only to ship owners or operators but also to any entity granting financial assistance, such as financiers and providers of security, to companies carrying out the activities as mentioned above. Likewise, parent or holding companies with subsidiaries also fall within this definition. This provision can be contrasted with the Companies Act (Cell Companies Carrying on Business of Insurance) Regulations 2004, which provides a more restrictive definition to the term 'business of insurance' and specifies that 'business of insurance' refers to insurance and reinsurance companies, affiliated insurance and reinsurance companies, insurance managers and insurance brokers. Furthermore, Article 84A of the Companies Act states that only those companies that are authorised under the Insurance Business Act may establish themselves as a PCC.

4.2 *Formalities for the Creation of a Cell Company*

The regulations allow a PCC to be constituted in either of two ways:

(a) A company may be formed or constituted as a PCC,[20] or
(b) An existing company may be converted into a PCC[21]

It must have at least one Cell for the purposes of segregating and protecting the cellular assets of the company in relation to the conduct of shipping business, it must state that it is a PCC incorporating the terms 'Mobile Asset Protected Cell Company' or MAPCC in its company name,[22] it's Memorandum and Articles of Association must also provide that the company is a PCC,[23] and each cell must have its own distinctive name or designation.[24] Failure to do so would not enable the company to benefit from the PCC regulations.[25]

Additionally, while the Insurance Business PCC regulations expressly require the approval of the Regulator in order to be formed[26] such authorisation is not provided for in the Shipping PCC Regulations. However, as a consequence of the wide definition of the term shipping business, the Regulations provide a general statement that the company must still obtain the required licences or authorisation, as the case may be, in accordance with the law governing the relevant activity.[27] Therefore, if the purpose of the PCC is to own and manage ships, then it must be licenced to do so in terms of the Merchant Shipping (Licensing of Shipping Organisations) Regulations. The requirement set out by Article 84Z(1) of the Merchant Shipping Act must nonetheless be complied with. This example shows how there is an interplay between the different legislations and that the Regulations, while afforded *lex specialis* status, do not operate in isolation from other laws.

4.3 *Obligation to Inform Third Parties*

The Cell Company has a duty to inform third parties interacting with it that they are contracting with a PCC and that the transaction is attributable to a particular cell.[28] If the creditor is not adequately informed, there remains the possibility for that person to attack the company as a whole. For this reason it is important that the official letterhead of the company mentions that it is a PCC and where applicable the name of the cell being transacted with.[29]

[20] Shipping Cell Companies Regulations - Reg 4(1)(a).
[21] Ibid Reg 4(1)(b).
[22] Ibid Reg 5(1).
[23] Ibid Reg 5(2).
[24] Ibid Reg 5(4).
[25] Ibid Reg 5(3).
[26] Companies Act (Cell Companies Carrying on Business of Insurance) Regulations - Reg 5(1).
[27] Shipping Cell Companies Regulations - Reg 4(1)(c).
[28] Ibid Reg 10.
[29] Ibid Reg 5(5).

4.4 Separation of Assets and Liabilities

This notion is the cornerstone of PCC legislation worldwide and is dealt with extensively in these Regulations. The directors of the PCC have the responsibility to ensure proper segregation of all assets and liabilities within the company at all times. It is their duty to keep cellular assets separately identifiable from the assets of other cells[30] and the non-cellular assets.[31] However, the directors may permit the cellular and non-cellular assets to be held by a company whose shares and capital interests may be a combination of cellular assets and non-cellular assets.[32]

The assets may be collectively managed by an investment manager provided that the assets remain identifiable. Provided the requirements of the Regulations are complied with, the rights of creditors are limited to the assets of the cell for which they are creditors.[33]

It is a consequence of their cellular nature that a PCC must keep its assets separately identifiable at all times. Thus, the directors are obligated to keep separate records, accounts, statements and other documents which must be appropriately designated to evidence the assets and liabilities of each cell as distinct from those of other cells and the core.[34]

It is fundamental, therefore, that liabilities be attributable to an identifiable cell or the core. Such attribution enables the liability to be accounted for properly in the books of the PCC, such that the liability is limited to the relevant assets to which it is attributable.[35] Any liability that cannot be attributed to a cell must fall on the core.[36] This ensures that each cell is legally protected and operates as a separate business from other cells within the same entity.[37]

Older PCC regulations, such as in the case of insurance business, provide cellular creditors with a right of secondary recourse to the non-cellular assets. Thus, the cellular assets will primarily be used to satisfy any liability and non-cellular assets will only be used once the cellular assets have been exhausted.[38] Interestingly, the Shipping Business PCC Regulations do not provide for such secondary recourse thus providing an absolute water-tight ring-fencing mechanism whereby only the cellular assets must be made available to the creditor in respect of the cell with which the creditor has transacted with.

---

[30] Ibid Reg 8(2)(b).

[31] Ibid Reg 8(2)(a).

[32] Ibid Reg 7.

[33] Ibid Reg 8.

[34] Ibid Reg 8(1)(c).

[35] Ibid Reg 13(1)(a).

[36] Ibid Reg 13(2).

[37] Feetham and Jones (2010), p. 42.

[38] Companies Act (Cell Companies Carrying on Business of Insurance) Regulations - Reg 14(1).

Table 1 Comparison between creditor recourse provisions of the Insurance Business PCC Regulations and the Shipping Business PCC Regulations

Regulation 14 of the Insurance Business PCC Regulations:	*Regulation 13 of the Shipping Business PCC Regulations:*
14 (1) Subject to the provisions of regulation 15, where any liability arises which is attributable to a particular cell of a cell company— (a) the cellular assets attributable to that cell shall be primarily used to satisfy the liability; (b) the company's non-cellular assets shall be secondarily used to satisfy the liability, provided that the cellular assets attributable to the relevant cell have been exhausted; and (c) any cellular assets not attributable to the relevant cell shall not be used to satisfy the liability.	13 (1) Where any liability arises which is attributable to a particular cell of a cell company: (a) only the cellular assets attributable to that cell shall be used to satisfy the liability; and (b) any cellular assets not attributable to the relevant cell shall not be used to satisfy the liability.

Guernsey's PCC legislation used to allow for secondary recourse to the core assets, however this has since been removed[39] and the default position is the one replicated in the Shipping Business PCC regulations (Table 1).

Regulation 11 further clarifies this point. All rights are protected within its own cell, Regulation 11 clarifies that in every transaction, no party shall seek, whether in proceedings or by any other means whatsoever, to make or attempt to use cellular assets attributable to a cell to satisfy a liability not attributable to it.[40] If, however, a creditor succeeds in doing so, they shall be liable to pay a sum to the PCC equal to the value of the benefit obtained.[41]

If an executive warrant is issued and enforced on the assets of a cell in respect of a liability that is attributable to another cell and it is impossible to restore or compensate the assets lost by the cell, then the PCC must instruct its auditors to establish the true value of the assets lost by the cell,[42] and transfer such amount to the cell from the assets to which the liability was originally attributable.[43] If a cell has insufficient funds, then the PCC must make up for the deficiency from its noncellular assets.[44]

4.5 Creation Of Cells

The formation of a cell is a fairly simple process and begins when the PCC passes a resolution to this effect clearly stating the name of the cell and the assets to be

[39] Curmi (2009), p. 77.

[40] Companies Act (Cell Companies Carrying on Business of Insurance) Regulations. Reg 12(2)(a).

[41] Ibid Reg 12(2)(b).

[42] Ibid Reg 11(4)(a).

[43] Ibid Reg 11(4)(b).

[44] Ibid Reg 11(5).

attributed to this. The resolution is filled with the Malta Business Registry, which, being satisfied that all requirements have been complied with, shall register the cell. The cell is not created until the Registrar publishes such notice.[45]

The creation of a cell does not, in respect of that cell, create a legal person distinct from the PCC.[46] Thus, the assets of a PCC are owned by that PCC and not by the individual cells. Cells are unable to contract with each other nor can they contract with the core, as this would be analogous to a person contracting with themself.[47]

4.6 Liquidation

In the event of insolvency of a cell, that insolvency will have no effect on the solvency of the other cells or the core of the PCC itself. The Regulations in recognising that each cell has its own creditors, provides that on liquidation each cell must be treated as if it were its own company. The reason for this is that although each cell has its own separate patrimony, it does not enjoy a distinct personality. Therefore, in treating each cell as it is its own legal person ensures that the liquidation proceedings are able to take effect without disrupting the cellular nature of the cell company. In other words, proceedings in relation to one cell shall not have any effect on the assets of any other cell of the PCC and the core. The Potential Uses of the Cell Company for Shipping Business: An Evolution of the Single-Ship Company.

4.7 Current Ship-Owning Corporate Landscape

As observed in the previous chapters, PCC legislation aims to create one corporate entity capable of representing a number of diverse economic interests. While the concept of statutory intervention for such companies to operate is new, the underlying objective of asset segregation and limitation of liability through the corporate medium is not.[48] This is well exemplified in the shipping industry through the notion of the group of companies and the establishment of the one-ship company.

Historically, shipping has been considered a high-risk, high-investment and expensive venture. For this reason, industry players have sought innovative means of spreading risk and limiting liability. As we understand it today, the concept of the limited liability company owes its origins to the maritime sector when in the seventeenth-century, merchant organisations were founded for colonial

[45] Ibid Reg 7.

[46] Ibid Reg 4(2).

[47] Feetham and Jones (2010), p. 45.

[48] Feetham and Jones (2010), pp. 4–5.

undertakings. With this in mind, it is said that the Dutch East India Company is the earliest example of a limited liability company, formed in 1602 through an association of shipping companies. Therefore, the shipping industry pioneered concept of the limited liability company, which presently remains the corporate vehicle of choice for shipping business undertakings.

In the past, a single shipping company would have owned and operated several vessels. However, deficiencies in this corporate structure exposed the shipping company to a number of dangers, namely that a creditor enforcing a claim against the company could do so against all the assets of the company. This, coupled with the introduction of the notion of sister-ship arrest, led to another pioneering innovation in the shipping industry: the development of the shipping corporate group and one-ship companies.[49]

The group company is the typical form of business organisation and is composed of a holding-subsidiary company relationship whereby one company is owned and operated by a parent company. The primary advantage of incorporating a subsidiary is the notion of limited liability. Thus, the parent company is insulated from the debts of its subsidiaries, much like in the case of the PCC structure, where the liabilities of the core and each cell are ring-fenced from each other.[50] Incorporating and conducting business through a subsidiary reduces the risks of insolvency of the entire group, making such a corporate structure attractive for high-risk ventures such as shipping.[51]

In fact, it is common practice for a ship owning company to place the ownership of ships in its fleet in a number of one-ship companies. Instead of operating the entire fleet under one company, the shipping company would establish sister companies or subsidiaries for every ship in their fleet.[52] This is done for the purposes of limiting liability up to the assets of the company (where the vessel would be the sole asset) with the effect that each ship is isolated from potential liability from the other vessels in the fleet. Therefore, shipping companies have utilised the general principles of company law in order to segregate their assets and liabilities and limit the risk of exposure to their liabilities. This is made possible because each one-ship company of the parent company represents a distinct legal entity. A ship owned by one company cannot be held liable for a claim against another company. In other words, the advantage of such corporate structuring is to make efficient use of the shield provided by the notion of legal personality: that the creditor of a transaction linked to the operation of a ship will only be able to act against the company that owns the ship. The creditor will not be able to act against the shipping company operating another ship in the same fleet with which they have not contracted with, even though these two companies are owned and financed by the same parent company (Fig. 2).[53]

[49] Mitsakis (1986), p. 18.

[50] Muscat (2019), p. 1500.

[51] Curmi (2009), p. 35.

[52] Mandaraka-Sheppard (2013), p. 13.

[53] Delebecque (1996), p. 1.

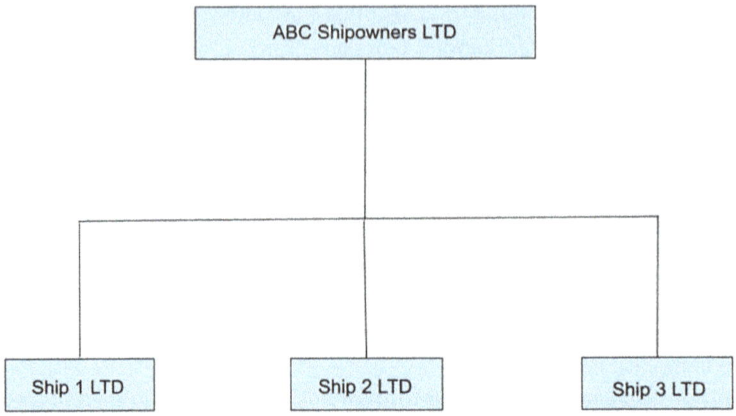

Fig. 2 Traditional shipping corporate group structure

Another critical development essential for the spreading of risks involved in shipping activities is the principle of limitation of shipowners' liability. Generally, the entire assets of a company should be made available to meet its liabilities. However, this principle, which was applied before limited liability under company law was introduced, holds that the liability of shipowners was limited to the value of the ship and its freight. Thus, much like in the field of segregated business forms today, the shipping industry has long attempted to limit the liability of creditors to identifiable available assets. This is exemplified in the historic judgement of Judge Ware in 1831 in The Rebecca, Case No 11,619, District Court, D. Maine. where the claimant tried to argue that to limit liability to a particular fund was contrary to public policy:

> The maritime law... has, on principles of general policy, restricted him [a creditor] to a particular fund, it not only permits him to proceed directly against it in specie, but gives him a privilege against it over the general creditors of his debtor [shipowner]. This privilege, so far from being dangerous and embarrassing to commerce, as it was represented at the argument, appears to me to be perfectly natural and just, and entirely in harmony with the general spirit of maritime law...This form of contract was probably suggested by the extreme perils attending on all commercial operations, in those ages of barbarism and disorder, and more particularly on those of maritime commerce.
>
> The profits of trade in those times were great and tempting, in proportion to the greatness of the risk, and by this contract men of capital were enabled to participate in these profits, without putting at hazard their whole property. It therefore had a direct and powerful influence in drawing out dormant capital, and putting it into a state of activity, and by thus giving a new impulse and greater extension to commerce, to render capital at once more productive to the owner and more beneficial to the community. It was, in fact, in the primitive ages of trade, one of the most powerful springs by which maritime commerce was carried on.

This principle is now embodied in international conventions. In Malta, the limitation of liability for maritime claims is governed by the Liability Claims for Maritime Claims Regulations (S.L 234.16), which gives effect to the Convention on

Limitation of Liability for Maritime Claims (1976). Once a claim is limited to liability, the claimant can only attack the assets attributed to the limitation of the liability fund. A limitation of liability is a privilege enjoyed and known by shipowners, and the claimants cannot challenge the right to limit liability. By exercising this right, shipowners can limit their liability up to a maximum amount, regardless of the actual amount of damages. This is done not only to protect shipowners from financial ruin and bankruptcy but also ensures that claimants are granted payment.[54]

4.8 PCCs and Ship Owners

The above examination of the current corporate landscape of ship owning companies shows that the shipping industry has preceded the objectives that PCC legislation aims to achieve through innovative practices and legislative inroads. In other words, the rationale for creating segregated cells is to separate pools of assets and liabilities and limit what funds and assets are available to creditors has already been achieved by shipping companies through the establishment of subsidiaries and the limitation of liabilities regime.

Accordingly, the PCC structure seems to provide the same protections that a group company structure afford. The question now is, what are the additional benefits offered by the PCC structure to shipping business using the corporate group structure?

As the extension of the PCC concept by Malta to shipping business is new, there are currently no examples of any shipping company registered as a MAPCC. However, there is an example in the US of a company established in the US equivalent of a PCC, known as a Series LLC, and which created a cell, the sole asset of which was a vessel. The company purchased a custom-built vessel and formed a cell known as a "series" of "limited liability company interest" for the purpose of holding title to and operating the vessel in question. The contract to construct the vessel was entered into by GxG Management LLC and the title of the vessel was held by the 'cell' in the name of "GxG Management LLC (Series B). This Series B was formed for the purpose of holding the assets/liabilities associated with the vessel, including the vessel itself.[55]

This example gives us some indication of how a shipping business PCC incorporated in Malta might be able to manage and structure itself. The idea would be for the shipping company (if already established) to convert the parent company that owns the single-ship companies into a PCC in terms of regulation 4(1)(b) of the Regulations and then pass a resolution creating a separate cell for each ship in its fleet. The core will maintain the ships' management, control, and operation, and each vessel will retain its ring-fencing against each other vessels and the core. It is also

[54] Williams et al. (2005).

[55] 2007 WL 551761 (D. Me. 2007) at page 2.

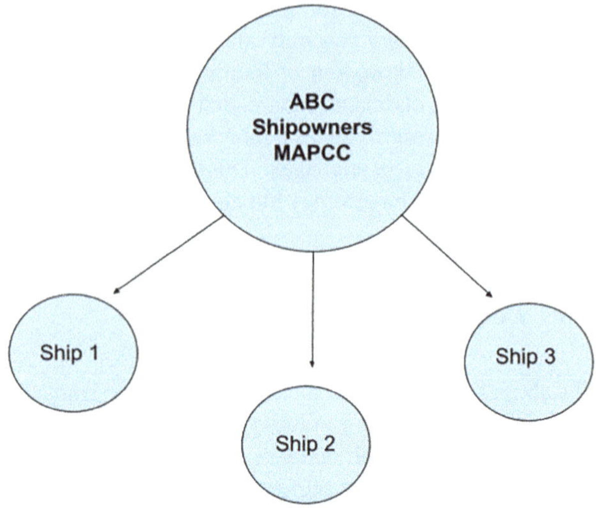

Fig. 3 Shipowning PCC structure

submitted that a shipping company is generally composed of a holding/parent non-ship owning company that is responsible for the shipping operation such as crewing, provisioning, bunkering, engineering, maintenance, freight collection, sales, and funds management. Because of the wide definition of the term 'shipping business' as discussed earlier, it would be possible for the shipping company to create other cells in respect of its activities that would be caught by the definition of 'shipping business', such as its crew management. Therefore, by being able to place each vessel in a separate cell, as well as any other shipping business activity, the PCC framework allows the shipping company to do away with the complex web of parent, sister, subsidiary companies usually associated with shipping companies, thus making huge corporate structures unnecessary (Fig. 3).

Another benefit usually associated with PCCs, especially within the insurance industry, is cost savings and reduced administrative burden. However, a closer look casts doubt upon this advantage.

The formation of a PCC and also of a traditional Limited Liability Company imposes filing and registration fees. These fees are listed in the Schedule to the Companies Act (Fees) Regulations. The fees for the registration of either corporate format are identical and vary according to the authorised share capital and are established by the Companies Act (Fees) Regulations, 2008. Interestingly, Regulation 7(1) of the Regulations provides that the fees set out in item (a) also apply for the registration of a cell, as it provides the following:

> 7. (1) [...] A cell company shall pay the fee prescribed in item (a) of the Schedule to the Companies Act (Fees) Regulations for each cell created.

This is something that the directors should consider when deciding whether they wish to establish a new subsidiary or a cell within a PCC. While the minimum share capital requirement to establish a company in Malta is €1164.69, there is no such minimum requirement for the consideration of cell share capital as such it is common practice for the authorised cell share capital to be set at €1. Regardless of whether the directors decide to establish a new subsidiary or a new cell, the registration fee owed to the Malta Business Registrar (MBR) would be the same in terms section 7 of the Regulations. That is to say, a company whose authorised share capital is €1200 and a PCC that establishes a cell with authorised cell share capital of €1 must both pay an equal amount of €100 (or €245 if in paper format) to the MBR by way of registration fees.

Furthermore, while the PCC regulations make no reference to the reporting of annual returns, the assumption is that because each cell must keep separate records, then the PCC must have each cell and the core individually audited and register separate annual returns to the MBR. Therefore, the shipping cell company would still need to produce as many annual reports and audits as it would generally have done under the single-ship corporate structure.

There are, however, some benefits with regards to the administration of the PCC when compared to the limited liability company. Firstly, for each company that is formed a Memorandum and Articles of Association must be drafted. This is not the case with respect to a cell of the PCC. There is no requirement under the Regulations that any form of constituting documents be prepared in respect of the creation of a cell, as the only required document for the creation of a cell is a resolution to that effect. However, in practice most shipping companies have a draft Memorandum and Articles of Association prepared so that they can quickly open a new company with the acquisition of a new ship.

Since the PCC represents only a single entity, there will only be one set of directors managing the affairs of the PCC structure as a whole and only one annual general meeting in respect of the entire PCC. Therefore, the directors would only owe their duties to one corporate group as opposed to all the single-ship companies that they would be directors of. However, it must be pointed out that due to the unique nature of the PCC, it imposes on the directors' increased obligations which do not exist in the case of general trading companies, namely the duty to inform and keep cellular assets separate and separately identifiable from both non-cellular assets and other assets of other cells. Failure by the director to conform with these duties might impose personal liability. With regards to the annual general meetings, although it is true that each company must have its own annual general meeting, usually in the case of single-ship companies, these are held at group level during the AGM of the parent or holding company.

On this same point, the fact that the PCC is a single entity may contribute to the reduction of certain operating expenses. For instance, each cell is able to benefit from the use of any licences and certificates held by the PCC, without the need for each cell to apply individually for such licence or certificate. For example, Article 84Z of the Merchant Shipping Act provides that a shipping organisation must obtain a licence from the Registrar-General for the ownership, operation, administration and management of a ship.[56] Within the single-ship company structure, each individual ship owning company would therefore each have to apply for the licence. Since the licence is issued for each company and not per cell, then the PCC managing a fleet of vessels in individual cells would only have to apply for one licence issued in the name of the PCC.

Thus, while this Chapter has discussed the benefits and advantages that the PCC corporate vehicle provides, it appears that these benefits have already been achieved by setting up a shipping holding company with one or more subsidiary single ship owning companies.

4.9 PCCs and Crew Management

As noted earlier, the Regulations provide a broad definition of ship owning companies, it must be pointed out that other areas of shipping business could benefit from the PCC regime. The PCC framework could be advantageous to companies engaged in any shipping business activity that do not utilise the corporate group structure but would nonetheless like to benefit from the possibility of segregation of assets and liabilities.

Such an area of shipping business that could use the cell structure is crew managing companies. In defining shipping business, the law expressly states that the term 'shipping business' includes personnel engagement and employment.

Typically, the crew of ships and yachts are not always employed directly by the company or owner managing and operating the vessel. Instead, they are recruited and employed by a separate company that then assigns them to a ship under their management. Such a crew management company could have multiple agreements for different vessels. The risk in such a facility is that if one client fails to pay the crew manager the amount required to employ the crew working on the vessel, there would be a shortfall between the amount of cash in hand and what is owed to the crew. This could have an adverse effect on the crew manager and the other ships under its management, especially if the crew manager uses funds, paid in advance by other clients, to pay the crew of a client who has failed to pay the crew manager.

In such a scenario, the crew manager could use the PCC structure to ensure funds are not inadvertently misused risk of becoming insolvent due to the inability of one client to make payments. In this situation, it might be advantageous to segregate each client's payments received from and liabilities attributable to them by placing them into separate cells. Likewise, the crew would also be placed into the cell representing the ship they work on. However, it must be pointed out that since the PCC is traditionally used for insurance and investment funds, the typical assets within a cell are corporate entities. As such, cells of a PCC do not tend to have employees.[57]

[56] Merchant Shipping Act Ar 84Z (1)(a).

[57] Feetham (2017).

Nevertheless, there are examples of crew managing companies registered as a PCC and where each cell acts as a dedicated crew employer. Therefore, if the purpose of the introduction of the PCC Regulations is to encourage more companies to choose Malta, it would be interesting to see if there would be any future change of domicile of such crew managing PCCs from Guernsey to Malta.

5 Limitations

5.1 *Cross-Jurisdictional Recognition and Risk of Sister-Ship Arrest*

Due to the uniqueness of the shipping world, it is often the case that the shipping company is registered in one country, and the ship itself is registered under the flag of another country. Therefore, international disputes often arise concerning maritime claims. There may be a conflict of laws when determining which laws are applicable and which court or tribunal has jurisdiction over the case. This results in forum shopping, whereby parties to an international dispute attempt to commence proceedings in a jurisdiction of their choice to their advantage.[58]

The use of the PCC structure is faced with the challenge of uncertain extra-territorial recognition. This refers to the recognition of the PCC's legal validity by foreign jurisdictions that do not have laws in place for this type of structure. In such cases, the assets protected by the PCC's segregation of liabilities, such as ships, may be located or be subject to claims in a foreign jurisdiction that may recognise the PCC's cellular segregation. This could invalidate the protective mechanism provided by a PCC and make all assets available to a creditor to the detriment of the PCC as a whole.[59]

This would not be the case where the proceedings were to be instituted in the courts of the jurisdiction of incorporation of the PCC. The courts would apply national laws, even if the asset is located overseas. Likewise, this would be the case if the proceedings are instituted in a foreign jurisdiction that recognises some concept of the PCC framework. In that case, the foreign court should respect the segregation of assets and liabilities accordingly.

The issue is that the PCC framework's protection might be lost when a claim is instituted in a jurisdiction that does not provide for a similar segregated cell legislation. This would depend on how the foreign court interprets the PCC Regulations under the rules of private international law.[60] In other words, legislative protection may not be sufficient and much depends on the interpretation and enforcement of the framework by the courts.

[58] Baatz (2018).

[59] Moss (2001), p. 19.

[60] Feetham and Jones (2010), p. 32.

Despite the lack of case law on cross-jurisdictional recognition of PCCs, there are examples in the maritime sphere where a legislative right or security was challenged. One such example is the *Bright Star* saga.[61]

This was a legal dispute that arose when a court in Jamaica ordered the sale of the vessel *Bright Star*. The defendant company, Jebmed, had registered a mortgage over the vessel in its favour. On 28 June 2017, the Jamaican Courts arrested and put the ship up for sale at the request of Jebmed and other creditors. Jebmed then filed a legal claim in Jamaica to try and gain possession of the ship as a mortgagee, but this claim was rejected by the Jamaican Court as it would have prejudiced the position of the ship's owner, who had protested the lawfulness of the arrest. The ship was sold to its current owners on 9 January 2018.

On 19 June 2018, the ship, now under new ownership, was re-arrested by an Executive Warrant of Arrest in Malta,[62] as Jebmed claimed to still hold the mortgage on the ship. The ship then sought to revoke the executive warrant of arrest,[63] but this request was rejected by the First Hall Civil Court on procedural grounds. The Court of Appeal upheld the validity of the Executive Warrant in respect of the ship on the grounds that, according to the court, Jebmed still held a valid and executable executive title.[64] At the time of the arrest the vessel was under a time charter party and was transporting maize to Venezuela. Due to the arrest, the time charter was suspended and the new ship owner had to deposit €779,346.61 in order to release the vessel and complete the voyage.

These decisions did not amount to a sentence, but rather a decree, as the procedure used was a summary procedure. The creditor only needed to show on a prima facie basis that they held an executive title. Due to the summary nature of the procedure, the Court was under no obligation to investigate the validity or merit of the title itself, but only to assess the executive act.

Following this, on 14 August 2018, the ship's owners instituted an ad hoc action on the merits, asking the court to declare the arrest illegal and to hold the arresting parties liable for damages. It wasn't until 12 January 2023 that the Superior Court of Appeal confirmed that the arrest of the vessel was illegal and that the ship was sold free and unencumbered.

The mere fact that this particular case arose, notwithstanding national legislation and customary international law that ships sold under court order are sold free and unencumbered, raises serious alarm bells within the context of ships held in a cell of a PCC. Using the *Bight Star* saga as a point of departure, the rationale here is that a creditor might use the lack of formal PCC legislation to their benefit in a foreign court to facilitate sister-ship arrest.

Article 742D(b) of the COCP provides that an action *in rem* may be brought before the civil courts of Malta against "*any other vessel of which, at the time when*

[61] Dr. Ann Fenech *noe* -vs- Jebmed SRL Civil Court of Appeal (Superior) 12/01/2023.

[62] Executive Warrant of Arrest no 998/18.

[63] Code of Organisation and Civil Procedure, CAP 12 Laws of Malta, Ar 280(1).

[64] Jebmed SRL -vs- M/V Bright Star Civil Court of Appeal (Superior) 12/07/2019.

the action is brought, the relevant person is the owner or beneficial owner as respects all shares in it." The 1952 Convention on Arrest of Ships similarly provides that "*a claimant may arrest the ship in respect of which the claim arose*" or "*any other ship which is owned by the person who was, at the time when the maritime claim arose, the owner of the particular ship*...".

The concept of sister-ship arrest affords maritime creditors the right to an arrest *in rem* of a vessel that has no immediate connection with the cause of action but which is under the same ownership.[65] It has been established that a PCC is a single corporate entity and that the creation of a cell, does not in respect of that cell, create a legal person separate from the company and that the assets of a PCC are owned by the PCC itself as the corporate entity and not by the individual cells.[66] Thus, should a jurisdiction fail to recognise the true nature of the PCC, it may simply decide that sister-ship arrest is available as all the ships in the PCC structure are registered to the same owner.

This issue is further compounded with regard to the registration of the ship. Although the PCC might be incorporated in Malta, this does not necessarily mean that its vessels would likewise be registered in Malta. If the ship registry in question does not have procedures in place to register ships in a cell of a PCC and only registers ships in a company, then the creditor may use this to their advantage. In other words, the inability of a ship registrar to distinguish between company and cell could further facilitate sister-ship arrest as the creditor could easily point out that the ships have the same owner according to the certificate of registration. Therefore, it is crucial that the words "*in respect of [name of cell]*" follow the company name on the certificate of registration so that the ship registration certificate should read as follows:

> M/V [NAME OF SHIP] [NAME OF PCC] MAPCC in respect of [NAME OF CELL] IMO Company No: [...] - Sole Owner

Accordingly, the creditor need only to convince the court at prima facie basis that the ships are all owned by one and the same company in order to validate sister-ship arrest. Following from the *Bright Star* case as discussed above, the PCC, would be able to argue on the merits that a creditor who has transacted with one cell has done so with the knowledge that the company is a PCC (insofar as the company has fulfilled its duties to inform third parties), and that therefore the creditor has chosen to contract freely at their own risk in the knowledge that their claims are limited to the assets of that cell. Any attempt by such a creditor to proceed against the assets of another cell should be seen by the foreign courts as an attempt by the creditor to evade the application of the contract they have entered into.[67] Just like the creditor in *Bright Star* was found to have acted in bad faith when they sought the arrest of the vessel, so to would a creditor who uses the uniqueness of the PCC structure to force

[65] Hassan-Cakir (2019), p. 22.

[66] Feetham and Jones (2010), p. 45.

[67] Feetham and Jones (2010), p. 34.

an arrest of a sister-ship. While any court would be able to come to such reasonable conclusion, this is however a lengthy and costly process as observed through the *Bright Star* case and an issue which may have a negative impact on world trade and global supply chains and may quite paradoxically expose the ship-owner to unnecessary risk and losses.

It is recommended, therefore, that any PCC entering into a contract with a creditor should ensure that they are well informed that they are contracting with a PCC and that the creditor is made to accept that there is no right of action against the assets of the other cells and the core. Such a clause in the contract could read as follows:

> Notwithstanding any other provision of this Agreement, all persons claiming under or with respect to or seeking to effect this Agreement agree and acknowledge that the extent of the liability of the PCC is limited to the assets attributable to [NAME OF THE CELL] and that in the event of the exhaustion of the assets attributable to [NAME OF THE CELL], there shall be no liability on the part of any other Cell established by the PCC or the non-cellular assets of the PCC and that the PCC has no obligation whatsoever to use any of its property or assets, other than the assets attributable to [NAME OF THE CELL], to satisfy any claim or liability in the event of the exhaustion of the assets attributable to [NAME OF THE CELL].

5.2 Incompatibility with Tonnage Tax Flag Link Requirement

The Merchant Shipping (Taxation and Other Matters relating to Shipping Organisation) Regulations, exempt from income tax any income derived from shipping activities.[68] A shipping organisation is able to benefit from the tax tonnage system upon the satisfaction of certain compliance obligations, including that at least 60% of the ships registered under one Malta company need to be registered under the flag of an EU/EEA state. This requirement is applicable for each company, and not per cell. Therefore, a shipping company with a large fleet of different flagged vessels and making use of the single-ship company will be able to benefit from this tax tonnage regime provided that the company owning the vessel is registered in Malta and that the flag is of an EU/EEA state. Thus, if in a particular fleet of 10 ships (each owned by a single-ship company in a group structure), two ships are Malta flagged and the other eight are registered in say Panama, those two single-ship companies owning the Malta flagged vessels will be able to benefit from the tax tonnage system, as long as the company in which they are registered is also a Malta registered company.

If this corporate group wishes to convert into a PCC and place all the ships in its fleet into different cells within the PCC, then that company would no longer benefit from the tonnage tax regime as the flag link requirement has not been satisfied. Therefore, it is recommended that either all ships in the PCC be registered in Malta or within the EU/EEA, or that the PCC creates individual cells only in respect of the

[68] Merchant Shipping (Taxation and Other Matters relating to Shipping Organisations) Regulations Reg 5.

vessels that comply with the tax tonnage regime. In the example above, on conversion the PCC should create only two cells, one for each of its Malta flagged vessels and retain the single-ship company structure for the Panama flagged vessels.

6 Conclusions and Recommendations

Although the PCC is credit great success in the investment and insurance funds industries in Malta and overseas jurisdictions, this discussion contends that using this type of entity for shipping business may be risky. Firstly, because of the possibility that the cell structure would not be recognised in a foreign jurisdiction. Secondly, the outcome of any litigation involving a PCC would be uncertain because of the limited case law both in Malta and worldwide involving a PCC. For this reason, it is suggested that the PCC should not hold any assets abroad and rather should keep the assets in the PCC jurisdiction.[69] However, this would not be possible in the shipping industry since, due to the globalisation of trade and commerce, vessels hardly ever find themselves in the waters of their flag state or the state of their registered owners. Other ways that the directors could reduce such risk include adopting choice of law clauses in contractual agreements and including provisions in such contracts that reinforce the statutory provisions of the PCC legislation, thereby having the contracting party agree to and acknowledge the PCC structure and segregation of assets and liabilities.

Furthermore, as already mentioned the PCC statutory framework was devised in response to the emerging needs of the insurance and investment funds industries. However, the same could not be said for the shipping industry. It does not appear that there has been any form of lobbying from the shipping industry to make use of such PCC legislation, as opposed to the aviation sector, this is evidenced by the number of aviation PCCs registered in Malta. Thus, while the PCC concept appears to offer a flexible corporate vehicle that aids corporate structures and business, the limitations of its practical use by shipping companies, the level of uncertainty as regards foreign recognition, the risk of sister ship arrest and the possibility to lose everything places the system in an unfavourable position as far as shipping companies are concerned.

On the other hand, the benefits and advantages provided by its use have already been achieved by shipping companies, i.e. the segregation of assets and liabilities, ring-fencing, asset protection, creditor protection and the limitation of liability. Other aspects of corporate governance and administration between the two structures appear unchanged and mirror each other such as keeping separate records and filing separate annual returns. Thereby seemingly replicating the current situation instead of improving corporate efficiency. In any case, the directors would need to weigh up these benefits against the risks of using the PCC medium in favour of the traditional corporate structure, which is well understood and accepted globally.

---

[69] Feetham and Jones (2010), p. 37.

In conclusion, it is not recommended that a shipping company structured on the traditional corporate model utilise the PCC corporate vehicle, and practitioners should not recommend it to their clients until such time that the limitations discussed in the above are addressed. The risks of using this untested corporate vehicle outside the insurance and investment funds industries are too high, and the benefits are seemingly few.

Furthermore, it is submitted that this Chapter considered the application of the PCC to Shipping Business in two limited cases only; ship owning companies and crew management. However, as discussed, the definition of 'shipping business' is vast as it attempts to capture any and all maritime-related activities. As such, there may be other instances where the application of the PCC concept might appear more beneficial. To this end, it is recommended that further study be conducted to identify other shipping business activities and examine the PCC structure applied to such activity, for instance, in the field of yachting in the case of a yacht chartering and a crew management company.

As pointed out in the introduction, it seems that the Regulations were adopted with the aviation sector in mind. Additionally, whereas the PCC originated by addressing the emerging market and business needs of the insurance and investments funds industry, it does not appear that the same is true in the case of shipping business Thus, it is further recommended that there should be more consultation with the shipping industry to truly identify gaps in the market and then see how and in which ways the PCC model could lend itself to the industry's needs. Doing so would place Malta in a better position to identify which shipping business activity could benefit from the PCC regime and thus present this innovative product to such sectors accordingly.

Finally, the most significant risk to the use of the PCC framework by a shipowner is the matter surrounding the vessel's registration certificate. While the non-recognition of the PCC structure could be argued on its merits, the fact that a ship registration certificate does not mention that the ship is held by a cell of a cell company could be used by creditors to circumvent the ring-fencing mechanism in favour of sister-ship arrest. Therefore, it is recommended that ship registries world-wide adopt procedures for the recognition and registration of ships in a cell of a PCC making reference to the name of both the PCC and the cell.

While praising Malta's initiative to enact legislation to extend the use of PCC beyond traditional areas of insurance and investment the Regulations appear unfavourable to some activities that it tries to cater for. As opposed to applying a wide meaning to the term aviation and shipping business in an apparent attempt to cater for the industries as a whole, the Regulations could have done more by identifying only those specialised areas of shipping business that can truly benefit practically from its use. It is now in the hands of practitioners to continue this discussion on the usefulness of the cell company to shipping business and identify ways and means for its proper implementation.

Acknowledgements This chapter is based on the thesis *Is the Introduction of the Cell Company Useful to Shipping Business Based on the Traditional Corporate Structure?* by Luke Bonello Ghio, written in partial fulfilment for the degree of Bachelor of Laws (*Hons*), Faculty of Laws, University of Malta, April 2022.

Appendix 1: List Of Malta Registered Mobile Assets Protected Cell Companies

Malta Registered Mobile Assets Protected Cell Companies (MAPCC) as at April 2022

Registration no.	Company name	Registration date	Company status	Number of cells
C 101510	FractionJet Malta MAPCC Ltd.	Feb 09, 2022	Active	0
C 100524	VistaJet 2021-1 9H EETC MAPCC Limited	Oct 20, 2021	Active	20
C 101312	VISTAJET 2021-1 N EETC MAPCC LIMITED	Jan 13, 2022	Active	9
C 95155	VISTAJET EETC1 MAPCC LIMITED	Mar 09, 2020	Active	13
C 86864	VISTAJET MALTA AIRCRAFT EIGHTEEN MAPCC LIMITED	Jun 19, 2018	Active	5
C 76915	VISTAJET MALTA AIRCRAFT ELEVEN MAPCC LIMITED	Aug 18, 2016	Active	6
C 73736	VISTAJET MALTA AIRCRAFT FOUR MAPCC LIMITED	Dec 23, 2015	Active	7
C 76916	VISTAJET MALTA AIRCRAFT FOURTEEN MAPCC LIMITED	Aug 18, 2016	Active	6
C 75166	VISTAJET MALTA AIRCRAFT NINE MAPCC LIMITED	Apr 08, 2016	Active	4
C 90934	VISTAJET MALTA AIRCRAFT NINETEEN MAPCC LIMITED	Mar 05, 2019	Active	3
C 71351	VISTAJET MALTA AIRCRAFT ONE MAPCC LIMITED	Jul 08, 2015	Active	3
C 74488	VISTAJET MALTA AIRCRAFT SIX MAPCC LIMITED	Feb 23, 2016	Active	4
C 76913	VISTAJET MALTA AIRCRAFT THIRTEEN MAPCC LIMITED	Aug 18, 2016	Active	31
C 76914	VISTAJET MALTA AIRCRAFT TWELVE MAPCC LIMITED	Aug 18, 2016	Active	5
C 100138	VISTAJET MALTA AIRCRAFT TWENTY-FOUR MAPCC LIMITED	Sep 07, 2021	Active	7
C 96456	VistaJet Malta Aircraft Twenty-One MAPCC Limited	Sep 02, 2020	Active	2
C 99816	VistaJet Malta Aircraft Twenty-Three MAPCC Limited	Jul 29, 2021	Active	1
C 99740	VISTAJET MALTA AIRCRAFT TWENTY-TWO MAPCC LIMITED	Jul 21, 2021	Active	2
C 98949	XO MALTA AIRCRAFT ONE MAPCC LIMITED	Apr 26, 2021	Active	1

Table of Statutes

Chapter 12 of the Laws of Malta - Code of Organisation and Civil Procedure
Chapter 234 of the Laws of Malta - The Merchant Shipping Act
Subsidiary Legislation 234.41 - Merchant Shipping Act (Licensing of Shipping Organisations) Regulations
Subsidiary Legislation 234.43 - Merchant Shipping Act (Taxation and Other Matters Relating to Shipping Organisations) Regulations
Chapter 386 of the Laws of Malta - Companies Act
Subsidiary Legislation 386.03 - Companies Act (Fees) Regulations
Subsidiary Legislation 386.10 - Companies Act (Cell Companies Carrying on Business of Insurance) Regulations
Subsidiary Legislation 386.10 - Companies Act (Shipping and Aviation Cell Companies) Regulations

Table of Judgements

Malta

Jebmed SRL -vs- M/V Bright Star Civil Court of Appeal (Superior) 12/07/2019
Dr. Ann Fenech *noe* -vs- Jebmed SRL Civil Court of Appeal (Superior) 12/01/2023

United States

The Rebecca, 20 F. Cas. 370 (1833)
GxG Management, LLC v. Young Bros. & Co. (2006)

Bibliography

Books

Baatz Y (2018) Maritime law, 4th edn. Informa Law
Feetham N, Jones G (2010) Protected cell companies: a guide to their implementation and use, 2nd edn. Spiramus Press
Mandaraka-Sheppard A (2013) Modern maritime law: risks and jurisdiction, Jurisdiction and risks, vol 1, 3rd edn. Routledge. (2 vols)
Muscat A (2019) Principles of Maltese company law, vol 3, 2nd edn. Malta University Press. (3 vols)
Williams R et al (2005) Limitation of liability for maritime claims, 4th edn. LLP

Online Journals

Bergervoet M, Starreveld J (2014) The curacao protected (trust) cell company. Trusts Trustees 20(6):568–572. https://doi.org/10.1093/tandt/ttu071

Moss G (2001) Protected cell companies - legal issues. J Pension Manag 7(1):14–22. https://link.springer.com/article/10.1057/palgrave.pm.5940178

Dissertations

Curmi N (2009) Segregated cells within legal organisations: their introduction & implementation in Maltese law. Faculty of Laws, University of Malta

Hassan-Cakir N (2019) Sister ship arrest and the problem of the one ship company. LLM Dissertation, University of Essex Repository, University of Essex, UK. http://repository.essex.ac.uk/26944/1/1804620_Dissertation.pdf. Accessed 28 Mar 2022

Mitsakis N (1986) Shipping groups of companies: the phenomenon of one-ship companies and protection of creditors. LL.M Thesis, McGill University, Canada

Websites

Appleby Global (2019) Guide to cell companies in Guernsey. https://www.applebyglobal.com/insights/cell-companies-in-guernsey-a-guide-2019.pdf. Accessed 4 Feb 2022

Delebecque P (1996) Les single ship companies. Arbitrage Maritime. https://www.arbitrage-maritime.org/CAMP-V3/fr/Misc/Singleshipcompany.pdf. Accessed 3 Apr 2022

Feetham N (2017) Protected cell company structure cited in employment case. Hassans International Law Firm. https://www.gibraltarlaw.com/insights/protected-cell-company-structure-cited-employment-case/. Accessed 7 Apr 2022

Finance Malta (2016) Protected cell companies. Fact sheet. Atlas PCC News, Finance Malta. http://www.atlaspcc.eu/wp-content/uploads/2016/03/FM-Fact-Sheet-Protected-Cell-Companies-and-Protected-Cells-Insurance-and-Reinsurance-2015.pdf. Accessed 22 Mar 2022

Newspaper Articles

Arena J (2022) Maritime sector now accounts for 14% of Malta's GDP. Times of Malta, 14 February 2022. https://timesofmalta.com/articles/view/maritime-sector-now-accounts-for-14-of-maltas-gdp.934546. Accessed 20 Apr 2022

Further Readings

Dingli K (2020) Legal implications arising from the decision of the Maltese Court of appeal regarding the bright star (ex trading fabrizia) case. Id-Dritt XXX 2:141–156

Mertens S (2009) Series limited liability companies: a possible solution to multiple LLCs. Chi-Kent Law Rev 84(1):271

Goods and Services Tax Implications on the Insurance Sector: Assessment of Awareness and Knowledge

M. P. Akhil and Gabriel Simon Thattil

Abstract The GST, or Goods and Services Tax, is an indirect tax reform for the Indian economy. The long-delayed GST Bill was approved by Lok Sabha on August 8, 2016. After a very lengthy trip filled with obstacles, conflicts, and other unpleasant experiences, it is getting betterment day by day. The tax system between the federal government and the states changed as a result of GST. This chapter aims to give readers a broad picture of peoples' awareness on how the GST affects the insurance sector. Utilizing primary data, this study was created utilising an exploratory research process. The study provides evidence that the insurance business will not be immune to its effects. The service tax has increased by 3%. The 15% service tax on banking and insurance services has been replaced with an 18% GST. It will undoubtedly influence both policyholders and the insurance sector.

Keywords GST · Insurance sector · Insurance policy · Service tax · Awareness · Indirect tax · Tax planning

1 Introduction

There are numerous economic factors that affect an economy's growth and cause ups and downs. The GST is now seen as a crucial tool in the process of economic expansion. A tax on products and services that is imposed at each point of sale or provision of services, as well as when they are moved from one site to another, is known as GST.[1] In India, the GST is an indirect tax that will replace all other taxes imposed by the federal and state governments.[2] The 2006–2007 Union Budget

[1] Bedi and Sharma (n.d.).

[2] Priya and Harshitha (2018).

M. P. Akhil (✉)
Alliance University, Bengaluru, India

G. S. Thattil
University of Kerala, Thiruvananthapuram, India

M. Lima Rego, S. Grima (eds.), *Cross-Disciplinary Impacts on Insurance Law*, AIDA Europe Research Series on Insurance Law and Regulation 8,
https://doi.org/10.1007/978-3-031-38526-1_10

Speech in India was the first to mention the GST concept. GST is another name for a unified sales tax. For a layperson GST is a single comprehensive tax applied on products and services used in an economy.[3]

An effective way to guard against financial loss is insurance. It is a technique for managing risks that is largely employed to protect against the danger of a potential uncertain loss. The insurance sector in India has advanced significantly, notably in the past 10 years.[4] Historically, consumers have primarily considered insurance as a tax planning and investing tool because they believe it offers better returns while reducing onerous taxes.[5] In a nation like ours, where social security is non-existent and retirement plans are unviable, looking for protection for the future becomes a pressing concern and that is where getting insurance into action.[6] As opposed to the old service tax of 15%, insurance is included in the 18% slab of the four GST slabs i.e. 5%, 12%, 18%, and 28%. The rise in indirect taxes runs counter to the successful steps taken over the past few years to advance this industry.[7] Governments all throughout the world are renowned for creating favourable conditions for insurance protection, even in more developed markets. Life insurance frequently falls outside of the GST's purview. For general insurance, a few nations, including Australia, Singapore, and South Africa, use a cash flow system.[8] Tax is levied for the latter and credit is given for paid claims. Tax is payable on the premiums received. Taxability on the gross premium for pure risk plans is against the value addition taxing principle under India's GST system. GST is a tax on value addition, and the net value addition is the net premium after claim deduction. It is exceedingly challenging to separate the savings component and identify a value that may be used as the right tax basis, especially for each premium transaction over the course of an insurance policy's life. Although this sector has so far had significant growth, the growth momentum needs to be maintained. More people should be covered by insurance if financial literacy is spread, Indian households are encouraged to convert their savings from tangible to intangible assets, and the distribution network is expanded to rural areas. The direction of this industry's growth and stability will be determined by the political and regulatory landscape, as well as customer behaviour, in the ensuing years. If insurance businesses use the proper kind of solution-based selling strategies, insurance purchases would continue. In this regard, a favourable indirect taxation structure would have been beneficial. The penetration of insurance in India has been increased thanks in part to the efforts of the country's insurance companies. We hope that the industry receives the attention and support that it justly deserves as the nation moves into a new economic era.

[3]Ramkumar (2018).

[4]Chatzara (2020).

[5]Ayers et al. (2009).

[6]Tackie et al. (2022).

[7]Rao (2009).

[8]Pennanen et al. (2010).

There are primarily three types of life insurance products: term insurance plans, ULIPs, and endowments with money-back options. The three of them do not apply the same service tax in the current format to their premium. The premium for life insurance covers two things: risk protection and savings. Only the risk component of the premium is subject to the service tax; the savings component is not. In accordance with the GST regulations, the value of services on which GST is to be levied in connection with the life insurance company shall be: The gross premium less the sum designated for investment or savings on behalf of the policyholder; 10% of the single premium paid by the policyholder for single premium annuity policies; In all other circumstances, 25% of the premium in the first year and 12.5% in the following years. The GST of 18% will be applied to the total premium if the policyholder only pays for the risk coverage in life insurance, such as in term insurance plans. Due to the increase in the rate of tax on insurance following the implementation of the GST, the immediate impact of the GST would therefore be the higher outlay premium increased by GST portion in case of term and endowment insurance policies. Theoretically, this might result in a 3% premium increase across life, health, and general insurance, however some of this could be offset if tax on services used by the sector is allowed to be considered to reduce insurers' tax paid. Only if the insurance companies are permitted to take advantage of the input tax credit could the policyholders expect to gain. Given the intricacy of the state and central structure of the GST, this is somewhat disputed; it could result in misunderstanding as well as additional administrative and compliance expenses for insurers. Prices may increase or decrease if these costs are not passed on to consumers, but it will have an impact on the market's ability to function and financial stability.

So, in this study, it is determined to what extent consumer households are aware of how the GST may affect the insurance industry.

2 Review of Literature

One of the most significant fiscal reforms in India's independent history will be the GST. Both at the federal and state levels, there were several indirect taxes levied. Most indirect taxes, including VAT/Sales tax, excise duty, service tax, etc., are included in the GST. Through the adoption of the GST in India, a growth of one to two percent in the GDP is anticipated. The Economic Survey 2015–16 predicts that the introduction of the GST will result in an increase in tax revenue of Rs. 3.3 lakh crores.[9] The study found that hoteliers had difficulty adapting to the new system, their compliance costs increased, and there was a general increase in the price of the goods and services. The hotel industry in India is one of the economy's

[9] Arora et al. (2016).

fastest-growing industries. However, with the implementation of the increased prices, the majority of hotels have voiced confidence in the system.[10]

Every individual is required to pay tax on output under the Goods and Service Tax mechanism, and they are also eligible for credit for any paid input taxes. Only the value-added is subject to tax. Additionally, the full adoption of GST will set a record in history. Hopefully, this greatest historical reform will make conducting business in India easier.[11] From the factory to the customer, various levies were to be replaced with the GST. This article helped readers comprehend the fundamental idea, advantages, and effects of the GST on various economic sectors as well as the numerous kinds of GST returns. This essay came to the conclusion that by removing tax barriers and implementing a uniform GST, the nation would become a single market, resulting in increased production efficiencies and supply chain effectiveness.[12]

The GST has a considerable effect on the textile industry. It makes note of the effects of GST on the expansion, employment, and export potential of the textile sector as well as calculates the revenue-neutral GST rates for the pertinent textile segments. It also highlights the adjustments that must be made to the government's support and subsidy policies after the GST regime replaces the current system of indirect taxes.[13] India's tax structure is complicated to calculate and comprehend. The government proposed replacing all indirect taxes with GST and all direct taxes with DTC in order to address these issues. It is crucial that the government works to implement the GST nationwide under clear legislation that is also business-friendly so that the economy, industry, and consumers may all benefit.[14]

Jasmine[15] explains how the GST was developed and its features, as well as the historical history of the Indian tax system. People are confused and filled with a variety of doubts as a result of the GST's adoption. It has been hailed as a paradigm-shifting reform that will catalyse the expansion of the Indian economy and move it in a more positive direction. Additionally, the GST would establish a common national market by releasing interstate trade from tangles of paperwork and antiquated processes, as well as, more crucially, from the cascade of levies that have been driving up corporate costs without producing any advantages. According to some, India has the potential to become the world's most powerful economy, and the implementation of the GST can be very important in this regard.[16]

With the implementation of the GST, numerous modifications have been made to the administrative and revenue structure. The establishment of the GST Council and other institutional structures can be used to examine the tax policy and another

[10] Abraham and Mathew (2019).

[11] Kaur (2018).

[12] Nunoo-Mensah et al. (2020).

[13] Gupta (2016a).

[14] Ajay Kumar (2017).

[15] Jasmine (2017).

[16] Gupta (2016b).

coordinating mechanism. The effectiveness of the GST changes depends on the creation of suitable institutional and organisational frameworks.[17] GST would be advantageous for all parties involved. An important step towards its implementation is the fact that all states have agreed in principle on a uniform indirect taxes system. However, it appears that there are still significant differences across States in terms of the details of the GST.[18]

The researcher concludes that GST has strengthened India's tax structure and had a favourable effect on a number of industries. Analytical study is more necessary to meet the competing interests of all the stakeholders and to achieve the true goal of implementing GST.[19] The fourth-largest sector of the Indian economy is the fast-moving consumer goods (FMCG) industry. This study examines both the potential advantages and disadvantages of GST implementation on the FMCG industry. A "transition of tax" is not all that the GST changeover is. It has an effect on every facet of how the firm operates, so a "whole of business" strategy is needed to ensure a smooth transition. As a result, the researcher came to an equivocal conclusion, and the authors raised some future concerns.[20]

Nayyar and Singh[21] studied the history of the tax system and carefully examined the GST in India. GST undoubtedly gives India a transparent and unambiguous tax system, but as this article will demonstrate, it also comes with a number of difficulties. Although the introduction of GST has various effects on the fisheries industry, one way to communicate all of those effects is through an increase in the annual cost of fishing. The majority of respondents, the researchers discover, are unclear of how the introduction of the fuels GST will affect fishing, and the majority of respondents are unaware of how the GST will affect the fisheries sector. Besides, it is expected that the technology-driven fishing investment may take a back stage due to increasing taxes on navigational equipment brought by the introduction of GST.[22]

The major goal of GST is to establish a single tax system for the production and sale of commodities across the nation, at both the Central and State levels. The economy is said to benefit from the GST. The Central government and the State governments do not work together to implement the GST. Even though, if implemented, the States would still be responsible for collecting the taxes.[23] It is crucial to realise that the GST is not a tax relief programme where the government lowers tax rates, causing all products and services to become more affordable. Along with this, the government should impose GST in order to protect the underprivileged population from potential inflation.[24] By strengthening the transparency of the tax

[17] Kishore (2012).

[18] Khan et al. (2012).

[19] Mussaiyib (2016).

[20] Naik (2017).

[21] Nayyar and Singh (2018).

[22] Salim et al. (2019).

[23] Sankar (2017).

[24] Shanta and Nandargi (2018).

collecting system and making tax evasion more difficult, the GST is supposed to foster a business-friendly climate and enhance the government's financial health. GST may result in a shared benefit for all of its participants, including consumers and the federal and state governments.[25]

Shukla[26] explains how regular people in Uttar Pradesh feel about the GST. The author explains that our country has undergone a number of changes, such as demonetisation and the eradication of corruption, which eventually cleared the way for the introduction of the GST single tax system. According to the study's conclusions, the general public opposes the GST. The study focuses on merchants because they are the essential component of marketing. The competitiveness of industries, exporters, and businesses has increased since the state and federal taxes were combined.[27] Sridevi[28] highlighted how the Coimbatore district's shops were affected by the GST. The retail industry has a significant impact because it creates a lot of jobs in both the rural and urban areas and allows for a lot of transactions. GST has a favourable impact on the retail industry because it lowers indirect taxes, makes input tax credits more smooth, and boosts supply chain effectiveness.

The current tax system is not satisfactory to the Indian government because it has some flaws. Every political party should stick to one term in order to implement GST. The GST is a taxation strategy that is acceptable by the government for new changes in our nation and is applicable to approximately 160 countries. It is also the preferred indirect tax structure for all countries.[29] It underlined its intention to pass a "flawless" GST in order to protect India's economy from growing international competition brought on by globalisation and liberalisation. Even though there are a number of obstacles to the proposed transition, it would be beneficial to look at the GST's positive benefits on India's many economic areas before it is put into place.[30]

The report from Ernst & Young has asserted that GST will bring about a far-reaching reform in the Indian economy. This would be possible by creating a common and unified Indian market. From the above literature, it seems GST will simplify a lot of taxation anomalies leading to a better business environment. It is expected to reduce transaction cost, remove cascading tax effect, simplify taxation procedure, seamless flow of ITC chain, reduce logistics cost, unify the market etc.

---

[25] Shaik and Firoz (2015).

[26] Shukla (2018).

[27] Sreekumar and Suvarnalakshmi (2018).

[28] Sridevi (2018).

[29] Dixit (2018).

[30] Akhil and Thattil (2018).

3 Objective of the Study

The study aims at analysing the awareness of household consumers in Kerala on GST implications on Insurance sector. For achieving this objective, we have studies awareness on GST basics, awareness on Insurance aspects and ultimately awareness of GST impact on insurance.

4 Research Methodology

The study is analytical in nature. Study uses both secondary as well as primary data to reach at conclusion based on the stated objectives. Primary data were collected from household consumers having any kind of insurance policy. Data were collected from 384 respondents using questionnaire. Collected data were tabulated and analysed with the help of SPSS software and the results generated were presented as follows.

5 Results and Discussion

5.1 Level of Awareness of Household Consumers on GST Implications on Insurance Sector

The level of awareness of household consumers on GST implications on insurance sector is analysed under three heads:

Part 1: GST Basics
Part 2: Insurance aspects
Part 3: GST impact on Insurance

5.2 Level of Awareness of Household Consumers on GST Basics

The level of awareness on GST Basics is ascertained based on response to the following statements.

- GST is a consumption tax
- Tax rates of GST
- Goods & Services exempted from GST
- Goods & Services do not come under GST
- Goods & Services come under GST

Table 1 Level of awareness of Household Consumers on GST Basics

Statement	Mean	SD
GST is a consumption tax	2.72	1.499
Tax rates of GST	2.83	1.150
Goods exempted from GST	2.59	1.487
Goods not come under GST	3.07	1.180
Goods come under GST	3.02	1.176
GST registered dealers should disclose GSTIN in front of the shop	2.76	1.431
GST should be shown in the bill separately	3.27	1.146
Combined Mean & SD	2.89	.928

Source: Primary Data

- GST registered dealers should disclose GSTIN in front of the shop
- GST should be shown in the bill separately

Mean value was used to ascertain awareness level on a five-point scale, where 4–5 indicated a very high level of awareness, 3–4 high level of awareness, 2–3 moderate level of awareness, 1–2 low level of awareness, and very low when it was below 1.

It was observed that the overall level of awareness on GST Basics was moderate (Mean = 2.89). It was, however high on 'displaying GST amount in the bill separately' (Mean = 3.27), on 'Goods not coming under GST' (Mean = 3.07) and 'Goods coming under GST' (Mean = 3.02). It was moderate on the factors 'GST is a consumption Tax, 'Tax rates of GST, 'Goods exempted from GST' and 'Disclosure of GSTIN by GST dealers. Details are given in Table 1.

5.3 Level of Awareness of Household Consumers on Insurance Aspects

The level of awareness on Insurance Aspects is ascertained based on response to the following statements.

- Term insurance
- Motor insurance
- Health insurance
- ULIPs
- Endowment plans

Mean value was used to ascertain awareness level on a five-point scale, where 4–5 indicated a very high level of awareness, 3–4 high level of awareness, 2–3 moderate level of awareness, 1–2 low level of awareness, and very low when it was below 1.

It was observed that the overall level of awareness on Insurance Aspects was moderate (Mean = 2.81). It was, however, high on 'Term insurance' (Mean = 3.25) and 'motor insurance' (Mean = 3.19). It was moderate on the factors 'Health insurance', 'ULIPs' and 'Endowment plans'. Details are given in Table 2.

Table 2 Level of awareness of Household Consumers on Insurance Aspects

Statement	Mean	SD
Term insurance	3.25	1.275
Motor insurance	3.19	1.167
Health insurance	2.82	1.347
ULIPs	2.35	1.268
Endowment plans	2.43	1.279
Combined Mean & SD	2.81	1.067

Source: Primary Data

Table 3 Level of awareness of Household Consumers on GST impact on Insurance

Statement	Mean	SD
Tax on Pure risk insurance/term insurance increased from 15% to 18%	2.96	1.246
Tax on Motor insurance increased from 15% to 18%	2.82	1.329
Tax on Health insurance increased from 15% to 18%	2.91	1.259
Tax on ULIPs increased from 15% to 18%	2.87	1.238
Tax on endowment plans increased from 3.75% to 4.5% (First year) and 1.88% to 2.25% (Second year)	2.64	1.233
Combined Mean & SD	2.84	1.007

Source: Primary Data

5.4 *Level of Awareness of Household Consumers on GST Impact on Insurance*

The level of awareness on GST impact on insurance is ascertained based on response to the following statements.

- Tax on Pure risk insurance/term insurance increased from 15% to 18%
- Tax on Motor insurance increased from 15% to 18%
- Tax on Health insurance increased from 15% to 18%
- Tax on ULIPs increased from 15% to 18%
- Tax on endowment plans increased from 3.75% to 4.5% (First year) and 1.88% to 2.25% (Second year)

Mean value was used to ascertain awareness level on a five-point scale, where 4–5 indicated a very high level of awareness, 3–4 high level of awareness, 2–3 moderate level of awareness, 1–2 low level of awareness, and very low when it was below 1.

It was observed that the overall level of awareness of GST impact on insurance was moderate (Mean = 2.84). It was moderate on all the factors such as 'Tax on Pure risk insurance/term insurance increased from 15% to 18%', 'Tax on Motor insurance increased from 15% to 18%', 'Tax on Health insurance increased from 15% to 18%', 'Tax on ULIPs increased from 15% to 18%', 'Tax on endowment plans increased from 3.75% to 4.5% (First year) and 1.88% to 2.25% (Second year)'. Details are given in Table 3.

5.5 *One-Sample T-Test*

Test of Hypothesis
Research Question:

How aware are the household consumers about GST?

To test the significant difference between the mean values of the variables measured against the average test response of 3 (mean score), the following hypotheses were framed and tested:

Household consumers are evidenced of having awareness on GST Basics.
Household consumers are evidenced of having an awareness of Insurance aspects.
Household consumers are evidenced of having an awareness of GST impact on insurance.

Table 4 shows the one-sample t-test result regarding the level of awareness on GST implications in insurance sector among household consumers in Kerala. Awareness was tested on three broad categories, namely: awareness on GST basics, awareness on Insurance aspects and awareness of GST impact on insurance. The overall

Table 4 Level of Awareness of household consumers on GST & Insurance

Statement	t-value	p-value
GST is a consumption tax	−3.712	<.001
Tax rates of GST	−2.928	0.004
Goods exempted from GST	−5.456	<.001
Goods not come under GST	1.168	0.244
Goods come under GST	.347	0.729
GST registered dealers should disclose GSTIN in front of the shop	−3.316	0.001
GST should be shown in the bill separately	4.585	<.001
Overall awareness	−2.270	0.024
Term insurance	3.883	<.001
Motor insurance	3.235	0.001
Health insurance	−2.615	0.009
ULIPs	−10.023	<.001
Endowment plans	−8.741	<.001
Overall awareness	−3.499	0.001
Tax on Pure risk insurance/term insurance increased from 15% to 18%	−.614	0.539
Tax on Motor insurance increased from 15% to 18%	−2.649	0.008
Tax on Health insurance increased from 15% to 18%	−1.378	0.169
Tax on ULIPs increased from 15% to 18%	−2.020	0.044
Tax on endowment plans increased from 3.75% to 4.5% (First year) and 1.88% to 2.25% (Second year)	−5.751	<.001
Overall awareness	−3.103	0.002

Source: Primary data
Test value = 3

t-values of the three broad categories are significant at the 5% level. This was true for all the individual statements. This shows that there is a significant difference in the level of awareness on GST implications in insurance sector among household consumers. Hence, the research hypotheses are supported.

5.6 *Awareness Level of Household Consumers on GST Implications on Insurance Sector Based on Demographic Profile*

To understand the impact of demographic variables on the level of awareness, the major demographic variables which were found to be relevant as per the previous studies were checked with statements measuring the level of awareness under three broad categories, namely: awareness on GST basics, awareness on Insurance aspects and awareness of GST impact on insurance. For this purpose, Multivariate Analysis of Variance (MANOVA) with a two-way variant was used. The primary purpose of the two-way MANOVA is to understand if there is an interaction between the two independent variables on the two or more dependent variables.

Research Question:

Is there any influence of demographic variables on the level of awareness of household consumers?

The following hypotheses were framed and tested:

There is a significant interaction effect between paired demographic variables on the combined dependent variable (Awareness on GST basics)

There is a significant interaction effect between paired demographic variables on the combined dependent variable (Awareness on Insurance aspects)

There is a significant interaction effect between paired demographic variables on the combined dependent variable (Awareness on GST impact on insurance)

Identified paired demographic variables are:

- Age and Area
- Income and Education

Box's Test of Equality of Covariance Matrices checked the assumption of homogeneity of covariance across the groups using $p < 0.001$ as a criterion. Box's M value was significant, p (0.000) < (0.001)—indicating that there are significant differences between the covariance matrices. In this situation, Pillai's trace test will be the most suitable.[31] (Details are given in Table 5).

The two-way MANOVA result revealed that the interaction effect between combined variables area and age is not significant. But when we look into the

[31] Hintze and Kaysville (2007).

Table 5 Box's Test of Equality

Equality of Covariance Matrices	
Box's M	574.888
F	2.724
df1	196
df2	73699.194
Sig.	<.001

Source: Primary data

individual effect of the independent variable on the level of awareness on GST basics, Insurance aspects and GST impact on insurance, the Age factor shows the significant result. For GST basics, the p-value was significant at 1% level with Pillai's Trace =0.264, F = 5.130. For Insurance aspects, the p-value was significant at 1% level with Pillai's Trace =0.204, F = 5.451. For GST impact on insurance, the p-value was significant at 1% level with Pillai's Trace =0.210, F = 5.618.

Likewise, in the case of the interaction effect between combined variables income and educational qualifications, it was found to be insignificant. But when we look into the individual effect of the independent variable on the level of awareness on GST basics, Insurance aspects and GST impact on insurance, the income factor shows a significant result. For GST basics, the p-value was significant at 1% level with Pillai's Trace =0.392, F = 7.910. For insurance aspects, the p-value was significant at 1% level with Pillai's Trace =0.152, F = 3.939. For GST impact on insurance, the p-value was significant at 1% level with Pillai's Trace =0.129, F = 3.333 (See Table 6).

Since MANOVA shows a significant difference, we have to carry out a follow-up posthoc analysis. Table 7 shows the multiple comparison results of the post-hoc Tukey Honest Significant Difference (HSD) test. As the MANOVA result shows a difference in the awareness level of household consumers with reference to age and income, it is necessary to find out which category differs in respect of awareness.

Regarding GST basics, in the case of age groups, the awareness level of 'below 30 years' age group respondents was significantly different from the awareness level of '31–40 years' age respondents with respect to statements such as GST is a consumption tax, GST registered dealers should disclose GSTIN in front of the shop, and GST should be shown in the bill separately. Coming to the '41–50 year' age category respondents, their awareness level was significantly different from the 'below 30 years' age group respondents in terms of GST is a consumption tax, Tax rates of GST and GST should be shown in the bill separately. The awareness level of 'below 30 years' age group respondents was significantly different from the awareness level of 'above 50 years' age respondents with respect to statements such as GST is a consumption tax, Tax rates of GST, GST registered dealers should disclose GSTIN in front of the shop, and GST should be shown in the bill separately.

Regarding GST basics, in the case of different income groups, the awareness level of respondents having income 'up to Rs. 20000' is significantly different from the awareness level of respondents with income range 'Rs. 20,001–30000' in terms of statements such as GST is a consumption tax and Tax rates of GST. The awareness

Table 6 Level of awareness of household consumers on GST implications on Insurance sector based on demographic factors

Factor	Demographics	Test-statistic value	F value	p-value
GST Basics	Area	0.023	1.268[b]	0.265
	Age	0.264	5.130	<0.001
	Area*Age	0.080	1.463	0.081
	Income	0.392	7.910	<0.001
	Education	0.036	.963	0.490
	Income*Edu.	0.115	1.032	0.415
Insurance aspects	Area	0.004	.284[b]	0.922
	Age	0.204	5.451	<0.001
	Area*Age	0.041	1.044	0.407
	Income	0.152	3.939	<0.001
	Education	0.026	.955	0.482
	Income*Edu.	0.075	.945	0.552
GST impact on insurance	Area	0.026	2.818[b]	0.358
	Age	0.210	5.618	<0.001
	Area*Age	0.047	1.202	0.263
	Income	0.129	3.333	<0.001
	Education	0.036	1.369	0.190
	Income*Edu.	0.054	0.683	0.902

Source: Primary data
Note. Test-statistic: Pillai's Trace

level of respondents with income range 'Rs. 30,001–40000' and income 'up to Rs. 20000' is different in the case of GST is a consumption tax statement. The awareness level of 'up to Rs. 20000' income group and 'above Rs. 40000' income group differ in statements Tax rates of GST and Goods not come under GST. The awareness level of 'above Rs. 40000' income groups also differ with income group 'Rs. 20,001–30000'in terms of GST is a consumption tax, Goods come under GST, and GST should be shown in the bill separately; whereas with 'Rs. 30,001–40,000′ income group in terms of GST is a consumption tax, Goods not come under GST, Goods come under GST, GST registered dealers should disclose GSTIN in front of the shop, and GST should be shown in the bill separately.

Regarding Insurance aspects, in the case of different age groups, the awareness level of 'below 30 years' age group respondents was significantly different from the awareness level of '31–40 years' age respondents with respect to statements such as Motor insurance, Health insurance, ULIPs and Endowment plans. Coming to the '41–50 year' and 'above 50 years' age category respondents, their awareness level was significantly different from the 'below 30 years' age group respondents in terms of Term insurance, Motor insurance, Health insurance, ULIPs and Endowment plans. The awareness level of 'above 50 years' age group respondents was significantly different from the awareness level of '31–40 years' age respondents with respect to statements such as Term insurance, Motor insurance, Health insurance; and with '41–50 year' age groups in terms of Health insurance, ULIPs.

Table 7 Multiple comparisons—Level of Awareness of Household Consumers on GST based on Demographic profile

Factors	Demographic				
GST Basics	Age		31–40	41–50	>50 years (+)
		<30 years (−)	GB1, GB6, GB7	GB1, GB2, GB7	GB1, GB2, GB6, GB7
	Income		20,001–30,000	30,001–40,000 (+)	>40,000 (−)
		<20,000	GB1, GB2	GB1	GB2, GB4
		20,001–30,000			GB1
		30,001–40,000			GB1, GB4
		>40,000	GB5, GB7	GB5, GB6, GB7	
Insurance aspects	Age		31–40	41–50	>50 years (+)
		< 30 years (−)	IA2, IA3, IA 4, IA 5	IA1, IA2, IA3, IA4, IA5	IA1, IA2, IA3, IA4, IA5
		31–40			IA1, IA2, IA3
		41–50			IA3, IA4
	Income		20,001–30,000	30,001–40,000 (+)	>40,000 (−)
		<20,000		IA3, IA5	IA1, IA2, IA3
		20,001–30,000			
		30,001–40,000			IA4, IA5
		>40,000		IA1, IA2, IA3	
GST Impact on Insurance	Age		31–40	41–50	>50 years (+)
		<30 years (−)	GI 1, GI 3, GI 4, GI 5	GI 2, GI 3, GI 4, GI 5	GI 1, GI 2, GI 3, GI 4, GI 5
		31–40			GI 2, GI 3
		41–50			GI 1, GI 2, GI 3
	Income		20,001–30,000	30,001–40,000 (+)	>40,000 (−)
		<20,000	GI 3, GI 4	GI 2, GI 3, GI 4, GI 5	
		20,001–30,000		GI 2, GI 5	GI 1, GI 3, GI 4, GI 5
		30,001–40,000			GI 2, GI 3, GI 4, GI 5

Source: Primary data

Regarding Insurance aspects, in the case of different income groups, the awareness level of respondents having income 'up to Rs. 20000' is significantly different from the awareness level of respondents with income range 'Rs. 30,001–40000' in terms of statements such as Health insurance, and Endowment plans. The awareness level of respondents with income 'above Rs. 40000' and income 'up to Rs. 20000' is different in the case of Term insurance, Motor insurance and Health insurance. The awareness level of 'Rs. 30,001–40000' income group and 'above Rs. 40000' income group differences in statements Term insurance, Motor insurance, Health insurance, ULIPs and Endowment plans.

Regarding GST impact on insurance, in the case of different age groups, the awareness level of 'below 30 years' age group respondents was significantly different from the awareness level of '31–40 years' age respondents with respect to statements such as Tax on Pure risk insurance/term insurance increased from 15% to 18%, Tax on Health insurance increased from 15% to 18%, Tax on ULIPs increased from 15% to 18%, Tax on endowment plans increased from 3.75% to 4.5% (First year) and 1.88% to 2.25% (Second year). Coming to '41–50 year' age category respondents, their awareness level was significantly different from the 'below 30 years' age group respondents in terms of Tax on Motor insurance increased from 15% to 18%, Tax on Health insurance increased from 15% to 18%, Tax on ULIPs increased from 15% to 18%, Tax on endowment plans increased from 3.75% to 4.5% (First year) and 1.88% to 2.25% (Second year). The awareness level of 'above 50 years' age group respondents was significantly different from the awareness level of 'below 30 years' age respondents with respect to statements such as Tax on Pure risk insurance/term insurance increased from 15% to 18%, Tax on Motor insurance increased from 15% to 18%, Tax on Health insurance increased from 15% to 18%, Tax on ULIPs increased from 15% to 18%, Tax on endowment plans increased from 3.75% to 4.5% (First year) and 1.88% to 2.25% (Second year). The awareness level of 'above 50 years' age groups is also different with '31–40 years' age groups in terms of Tax on Motor insurance increased from 15% to 18%, Tax on Health insurance increased from 15% to 18%; whereas with '41–50 year' age group in terms of Tax on Pure risk insurance/term insurance increased from 15% to 18%, Tax on Motor insurance increased from 15% to 18%, Tax on Health insurance increased from 15% to 18%.

Regarding GST impact on insurance, in the case of different income groups, the awareness level of respondents having income 'up to Rs. 20000' is significantly different from the awareness level of respondents with income range 'Rs. 20,001–30000' in terms of statements such as Tax on Health insurance increased from 15% to 18%, Tax on ULIPs increased from 15% to 18%. The awareness level of respondents with income range 'Rs. 30,001–40000' and income 'up to Rs. 20000' is different in the case of Tax on Motor insurance increased from 15% to 18%, Tax on Health insurance increased from 15% to 18%, Tax on ULIPs increased from 15% to 18%, Tax on endowment plans increased from 3.75% to 4.5% (First year) and 1.88% to 2.25% (Second year). The awareness level of 'Rs.20001–30000' income group and 'Rs. 30,001–40000' income group differences in statements Tax on Motor insurance increased from 15% to 18%, and Tax on endowment plans increased from 3.75% to 4.5% (First year) and 1.88% to 2.25% (Second year); whereas with 'above Rs. 40000' income group differences in statements Tax on Pure risk insurance/term insurance increased from 15% to 18%, Tax on Health insurance increased from 15% to 18%, Tax on ULIPs increased from 15% to 18%, Tax on endowment plans increased from 3.75% to 4.5% (First year) and 1.88% to 2.25% (Second year). The 'above Rs. 40000' group of respondents also different with 'Rs.

30,001–40000' respondents with regard to statements Tax on Motor insurance increased from 15% to 18%, Tax on Health insurance increased from 15% to 18%, Tax on ULIPs increased from 15% to 18%, Tax on endowment plans increased from 3.75% to 4.5% (First year) and 1.88% to 2.25% (Second year).

In a nutshell, the post-hoc multiple comparison analysis revealed where the difference lies. From the output, it was found that respondents with age group 'above 50 years' are more aware of GST Basics, Insurance Aspects and GST impact on insurance when compared to all other age groups. The awareness was least among respondents with 'below 30 years' age categories. In the case of income, the respondents with income range 'Rs. 30,001–40000' are more aware of GST Basics, Insurance Aspects and GST impact on insurance when compared to all other income categories; whereas awareness was low among respondents having income 'above Rs. 40000'.

5.7 *Awareness Level of Household Consumers on GST Implications on Insurance Sector Based on Gender*

On GST Basics, awareness was high on 'Displaying GST amount in the bill separately' for both Male (3.08) and Female (3.45) respondents, whereas it was moderate on all other basic factors for male respondents. For Female respondents, it was high on factors—'Goods that come under GST' (Mean = 3.17) and 'Goods that do not come under GST' (Mean = 3.20). For all other factors, it was moderate.

Test of Hypothesis
Research Question:

Is there any difference between male and female household consumers regarding awareness level on GST implications on Insurance sector?

To test the significant difference between Male and Female household consumers, the following hypothesis was framed and tested.

There is a significant difference between male and female household consumers regarding awareness level on GST implications on Insurance sector.

Since Levene's test for equality of variance significance shows values which is more than 0.05, equal variance can be assumed. Since the p-value is less than 0.01, the research hypothesis is supported at a 1% level with regards to the statement 'goods exempted from tax', 'Tax on Pure risk insurance/term insurance increased from 15% to 18%','Tax on Motor insurance increased from 15% to 18%'. Hence there is a significant difference between the opinion of male and female respondents towards this statement. Considering the opinion of respondents towards the statements such as 'GST is a consumption tax', 'Goods do not come under GST', 'Goods come under GST' and 'Tax on endowment plans increased from 3.75% to 4.5% (First year) and 1.88% to 2.25% (Second year)': the p-value is less than 0.05; thus

Table 8 Gender-wise difference in the awareness level of Household Consumers on GST

Statement	Male		Female		t value	p-value
	M	SD	M	SD		
GST is a consumption tax	2.54	1.541	2.89	1.438	−2.294	0.022
Tax rates of GST	2.77	1.175	2.89	1.124	−.976	0.330
Goods exempted from GST	2.50	1.486	2.67	1.487	−3.198	0.001
Goods not come under GST	2.94	1.174	3.20	1.174	−2.217	0.027
Goods come under GST	2.87	1.188	3.17	1.147	−2.534	0.012
GST registered dealers should disclose GSTIN in front of the shop	2.70	1.451	2.81	1.413	−.748	0.455
GST should be shown in the bill separately	3.08	1.195	3.45	1.067	−1.133	0.258
Term insurance	3.24	1.292	3.27	1.260	−1.411	0.159
Motor insurance	3.17	1.201	3.21	1.135	−1.318	0.188
Health insurance	2.73	1.406	2.91	1.283	−1.251	0.212
ULIPs	2.26	1.247	2.44	1.285	−.200	0.842
Endowment plans	2.34	1.264	2.52	1.290	−.349	0.727
Tax on Pure risk insurance/term insurance increased from 15% to 18%	2.69	1.277	3.23	1.154	−4.403	<0.001
Tax on Motor insurance increased from 15% to 18%	2.64	1.346	3.00	1.290	−2.670	0.008
Tax on Health insurance increased from 15% to 18%	2.81	1.294	3.02	1.217	−1.625	0.105
Tax on ULIPs increased from 15% to 18%	2.73	1.205	3.01	1.257	−2.196	0.029
Tax on endowment plans increased from 3.75% to 4.5% (First year) and 1.88% to 2.25% (Second year)	2.55	1.214	2.72	1.250	−1.367	0.172

Source: Primary data

the research hypothesis is supported at 5% level. With respect to all other statements, the research hypothesis is not supported at the 5% level. Details are given in Table 8.

5.8 GST Source of Information of Household Consumers

The major sources of information for household consumers were Friends/Family, Print Media, Visual Media, Internet and GST Authorities. Analysis was done based on multiple responses. The most important source of information for household consumers was the Internet (33%), followed by print media (29%) and visual media (18%). There was a significant difference in the most important source of information; it was print media for rural respondents, while it was the internet for urban respondents.

It can be concluded that the important sources of information were print media and the internet for rural household consumers, while the internet took the first place for urban household consumers. Details are given in Table 9.

Table 9 Source of information regarding GST among household consumers

	Rural		Urban		Total			
Source of Information	Res. Yes	%	Res. Yes	%	Res. Yes	%	Z test value	p-value
Friends/Family	53	15	57	15	110	15	−0.4515	.65272
Print Media	136	38	72	20	208	29	6.5548	.00001
Visual Media	67	19	61	17	128	18	0.6495	.5157
Internet	85	24	152	42	237	33	−7.0341	.00001
GST Authorities	13	4	22	6	35	5	−1.5957	.1096
Total	354	100	364	100	718	100		

Source: Primary data

Test of Hypothesis
Research Question:

Is there any difference in the source of information used by rural and urban respondents for getting information on GST?

The following hypothesis was framed and tested.

There is a significant difference between rural respondents 'opinion proportion and urban respondents' opinion proportion regarding the source they have been using for getting GST information

Table 9 shows a two-sample z-test percentage comparison regarding sources which were helped the respondents to get information regarding GST. The p-values of print media and the internet show a significant difference; hence research hypothesis is supported. The result indicates that most of the rural respondents depend on print media like newspapers for getting information about GST, whereas, in the case of urban respondents, the internet is the prime source of information on GST.

6 Conclusion

GST regime implemented in a hurried manner due to the fragile state of the Indian economy. The production and consumption of goods and services are surely rising, the application of GST can provide a more straightforward, user-friendly, and transparent tax system. The influence on the insurance business will also not be limited. Both policyholders and the insurance sector will undoubtedly be impacted. Policyholders often pay service tax on the risk portion of the premium component, but the investment portion of the policies is typically exempt from service tax. For insurers, the GST regime is likely to present both promising prospects and challenging obstacles. To improve their current company processes, spot possibilities, and gain a competitive edge, they must think of GST as a business transformation force.

Although the impact of the GST on insurance price increases is minimal, a large portion of policyholders find the higher insurance costs to be exorbitant. It is mainly due to lack of proper awareness and knowledge among the household consumers. Therefore, it is advised to organise well-focused awareness promotion campaigns for the identified stakeholders.

References

Abraham A, Mathew T (2019) A study on the impact of goods and services tax reform on hotels in Kerala. Int J Manag Stud VI:54

Ajay Kumar K (2017) A journey of goods and services tax (GST) and structural impact of gst on the growth of GDP in India. Adv Sci Humanit 3:50

Akhil MP, Thattil GS (2018) GST: a global facet. Int J Sci Res Comp Sci Appl Manag Stud 7:5. www.ijsrcsams.com

Arora AK et al (2016) Jim Quest:12

Ayers BC, Jiang J, Laplante SK (2009) Taxable income as a performance measure: the effects of tax planning and earnings quality. Contemp Account Res 26:15

Bedi B, Sharma K (n.d.) Moving to goods and service tax in India: impact on India. S Growth 36

Chatzara V (2020) FinTech, InsurTech, and the regulators, p 3

Dixit DR (2018) GST simplified tax system: challenges and remedies, vol 1. http://conference.nrjp.co.in/index.php/GST/article/view/89. Accessed 5 Mar 2021

Gupta CAU (2016a) Integrated goods and services tax (Igst). Natl Law Sch India Rev 28:134. http://www.jstor.org/stable/26201830

Gupta T (2016b) An impact of good & service tax on Indian textile industry. Int J Sci Eng Res 7: 1248. https://www.ijser.org/researchpaper/An-Impact-of-good-Service-Tax-on-Indian-textile-industry.pdf

Hintze JL, Kaysville U (2007) User's guide IV. NCSS

Jasmine VM (2017) GST & evolution of tax system in India. IRA Int J Manag Soc Sci 7:65

Kaur A (2018) A research paper on impact of GST on Indian economy, No. 07, p 534

Khan M, Azam K, Shadab N (2012) Goods and services tax (GST) in India: prospect for states. Budget Res Rev 4:38. www.econstor.euwww.buget-finante.rowww.buget-finante.ro. Accessed 5 Mar 2021

Kishore P (2012) Administering goods and services tax in India: reforming the institutional architecture and redesigning revenue agencies. Econ Polit Wkly 47:84

Mussaiyib AM (2016) IJRIAS I(VII). www.ijrias.org. Accessed 29 Mar 2020

Naik RH, Sudina TA (2017) A study on perspective impact of GST on FMCG sector in India. Int J Res Bus Stud 2:2455

Nayyar A, Singh I (2018) A comprehensive analysis of goods and services tax (GST) in India. Indian J Financ 12:57

Nunoo-Mensah JW et al (2020) COVID-19 and the global impact on colorectal practice and surgery. Clin Colorectal Cancer 19:178

Pennanen T, Hilli P, Koivu M (2010) Cash-flow based valuation of insurance liabilities. Optimization

Priya DCJ, Harshitha MC (2018) Impact of GST on the Indian economy. Int J Trend Sci Res Dev 2: 60

Ramkumar G (2018) Consumer perceptions towards goods and services tax implementation-an economic approach. ELK Asia Pac J Market Retail Manag 9:21–35

Rao MG (2009) Goods and services tax: some progress towards clarity. Econ Polit Wkly 44:8

Salim SS, James HE, Meharoof M (2019) Goods and services tax (GST) reforms and implementation: an economic analysis in the marine fisheries sector of Kerala, South India. Indian J Fish 66:135

Sankar R (2017) GST: impact and implications on various industries in Indian economy. J Internet Bank Commer 22:2. http://www.icommercecentral.com

Shaik S, Firoz S (2015) Does goods and services tax (GST) leads to indian economic development? IOSR J Bus Manag 17:2319. www.iosrjournals.org

Shanta A, Nandargi R (2018) Impact of GST on the Indian economy and consumer experience. Int J Res Sci Innov 5:101

Shukla VK (2018) Attitude of common people towards gst (goods and services tax) in India. Sch Res J Humanity Sci Engl Lang 6

Sreekumar PG, Suvarnalakshmi V (2018) Gst: A boon or a curse- a study with special reference to retailers in Thrissur District, Kerala. Int J Bus Manag Invent 7:58

Sridevi MR, Phil M (2018) A study on impact of GST system to retailers with special reference to Coimbatore District. Int J Res Eng Appl Manag 4:2

Tackie G et al (2022) Tax planning and financial performance of insurance companies in ghana: the moderating role of corporate governance. Cog Bus Manag 9:2144097. http://www.editorialmanager.com/cogentbusiness

Akhil MP is an Assistant Professor at the Alliance School of Business, Area of Finance & Accounting, Alliance University, Bangalore. He holds a Ph.D. from University of Kerala in the domain of Commerce. His thesis work is focused on understanding the challenges and potential of newly introduced Goods and Services Tax (GST) regime in the economy. He has cleared UGC Junior Research Fellowship (JRF) as well as National Eligibility Test (NET) and holds an M. Com degree (with a specialization in Finance). He also comes with industry experience in central school education sector. He has presented papers in various National and International events/forums/conferences. He has also published research papers/articles/book chapters in journals and books of repute in diverse areas of business studies and management. His current research interest includes working in areas related to Direct and Indirect Taxation, Sustainable Development Goals (SDG), Green Finance & Climate Finance, Circular Economy, Metaverse etc.

Gabriel Simon Thattil is a Professor in Commerce at University of Kerala. He has over 28 years of teaching and research experience—teaching at the under-graduate and Post graduate levels for M Com, MBA, MPhil and other P G Diplomas and guiding M. Phil and doctoral work. Has successfully guided 25 PhDs and 49 M. Phils. Is the author of 3 books and has published 48 research articles. Was the co-ordinator of a major research project of the Govt. of India undertaken by the Department, was the co-ordinator of UGC SAP project approved by the UGC for the Department. He is the former General Secretary of Indian Accounting Association and current Chief Editor, Indian Journal of Accounting, Life member of the Indian Commerce Association, Professional member of the National Institute of Personnel Management and member of All India Management Association (MIMA status). Governing Board Member of Centre for Development Studies. Currently the Director of Internal Quality Assurance Cell, University of Kerala.

The Effectiveness of Recent Policyholder-Friendly Laws at Addressing Complaints in India

Uma Shankar Yadav, Kiran Sood, and Simon Grima

Abstract In 1999, the government of India established the Insurance Regulatory and Development Authority of India (IRDAI), intending to establish effective insurance sector regulation. The creation of this regulatory body was motivated primarily by a desire to promote consumer safety and insurance market growth. Since then, this group has been doing everything in its power to safeguard policyholders' interests and foster a conducive regulatory environment for the development of the insurance industry. Life insurance businesses are improving their offerings, customer service, and grievance resolution mechanism in response to the institution's stringent regulations, which aim to ensure that policyholder complaints are resolved in a reasonable amount of time (TAT). After reviewing the secondary sources, it is easy to conclude that this organisation looks out for its customers and keeps its money safe. The examination of secondary data shows that insurance companies are paying more attention to their client's needs and resolving their complaints more quickly than in the past. This explains why, by the end of 2017–2018, only 0.13% of complaints had not been addressed.

Keywords Complaints · IRDAI · Rules · The regulatory agency · TAT

U. S. Yadav
Motilal Nehru National Institute of Technology Allahabad, Prayagaraj, India

K. Sood (✉)
Chitkara Business School, Chitkara University, Rajpura, Punjab, India

S. Grima
Department of Insurance and Risk Management, Faculty of Economics, Management and Accountancy, University of Malta, Msida, Malta

M. Lima Rego, S. Grima (eds.), *Cross-Disciplinary Impacts on Insurance Law*,
AIDA Europe Research Series on Insurance Law and Regulation 8,
https://doi.org/10.1007/978-3-031-38526-1_11

1 Introduction

Due to the lack of a regulatory body, the insurance sector oversaw 1938 when the first act (the Insurance Act of 1938) and effective action in 1956, called the life insurance act of 1956.[1] Later, there was the need for a robust regulatory act in 1999 when IRDA was made that regulated all insurance in India, either life insurance or motto insurance, since the beginning of liberalization, privatization, and globalization in the financial sector. The government has been analyzing to create a level playing field for private insurance businesses to engage with government undertaking insurers that had a monopoly before liberalization by establishing a regulatory institution to organize the insurance industry.

The government's motivation for creating the regulator was crystal clear: it saw that private life insurance companies were entering the market, and it knew that. As a result, the industry's fundamental business model was about to shift from socialism to capitalism. These companies would soon do whatever they could to secure a larger market share. This trend toward market share acquisition could give rise to a savage contest. Only a strong and autonomous overseer could properly handle this situation by safeguarding the interests of insurance policyholders while fostering the industry's expansion.

The government's high standards compelled the insurance industry's watchdog to establish stringent guidelines for the industry, to protect consumers' and policyholders' best interests and ensure that any complaints from policyholders would be resolved as quickly as possible by the regulator's established timeline. As a result of the rigorous rules, insurance providers had little choice but to priorities the needs of policyholders when responding to complaints.

1.1 Why People in India Need Life Insurance

In 1818, a British insurance company called oriental life insurance company was established in Kolkata under the European settlement. In 1870 Bombay mutual life company was the first Indian insurance company established by Indians. Then in 1938 Indian insurance company was established, and it was adequately regulated by the government of India in 1956 and nationalized on the first of September 1956. GOI merged it with 245 small insurance companies and medium insurance businesses as a single body called the life insurance corporation of India. This newly created company's starting capital was five crores (or 500 million) Indian rupees. Following the establishment of IRDA in 1999, private companies once again have access to the insurance market.

The primary goal of purchasing a life insurance policy is to protect one's family from financial ruin in the event of an unforeseen event. It's common knowledge that

[1] Venugopal (2015).

Table 1 Indian LIC history from private to public company and then again to the private company

Up to August 1956	About 245 private insurance firms were operating in India.
Nationalization	01.09.1956 When LIC was established, the insurance sector was nationalised.
Private Again	The IRDA Act of 1999 led to its re-privatisation.
Life Insurance Co.	24 (1 Public Sector +23 Private)
Largest Player	69.36% share of the premium and 75.7% share of Policies
FDI Limit	I (26% when privatized again, 49% currently)
Total Share Capital	27264.27 Crore as of 31.03.2018 (26956.94 Crore in 2016–17)
Listed through IPO	03-Insurance Act of 1938, Sections 3: ICICI-Pru, SBI, and HDFC
Relevant Act	1938-Insurance Act
Insurance Regulator	(IRDA-Act,1999)

Sources: Table compiled by authors

life is fleeting, that people die, and that no one can predict how long they'll live. Therefore, from a financial point of view, a policy related to life insurance provides the guarantee/assurance to the people as a whole family if they have a first-grade blood relationship in the family that a particular sum will be handed to the nominee/legal heir in the event of the death of the policyholder. It is also possible to create an estate in its earliest stages by paying the first payment to the insurance firm, provided that the policy should have been issued, the insurance proposal was accepted, or the first insurance premium receipt was produced. For private to the public company about insurance, please refer to Table 1.

Table 1 shows that players in the inside erec sector have different roles, and their share differs for holding organisations. Insurance falls under the contract act, making it legal. Contracts between insurers and proposers (Buyers) issue life insurance policies (seller). This contract guarantees the insurance company that the proposal form is accurate. However, if the premium has been paid regularly, the insurer promises to pay the agreed amount to the policyholder or nominee upon maturity or death/illness.

1.2 IRDA Formation

Parliament enacted the IRDA bill in December 1999, and the president signed it in January 2000. On the 19th of April, 2000, the regulatory body began. This authority was established to restrict expansion and protect life insurance consumers. IRDA effectively regulates the insurance industry with eternal succession. On the 26th of December, 2014, it became IRDAI.

The regulatory authority issues new recommendations regularly to protect policyholders' interests and create an equal market for all insurance businesses.

Because of insurance's shift from a social to a commercial activity, the regulatory body understood that competing insurers would employ any means to win over new customers and increase their market share, making it more difficult to exert regulatory oversight and protect the IRDAI.

1.3 Regulation

Life insurance businesses give the government the most investable funds. The main issue for any administration is investing public money so that the public gains the most and protects their investment. The Government of India established IRDAI as a regulator to manage insurance businesses by drafting regulations to preserve public money, maximise policyholder returns, and grow this sector.

Since its founding, the authority has enforced high standards of integrity to accelerate orderly expansion in the insurance market and defend policyholder interests (Investor). The regulatory authority started with 47 regulations and has 130 as of 31.03.2018. For insurance business growth and policyholder protection, new regulations are being created.

1.4 IRDA, 2017–18 and Annual Report

Few of these announced regulations safeguard life insurance policyholders. "IRDA (Protection of Policy Holders' Interest) Regulations, 2002" was the first. As needed, the authority announces new policyholder-benefitting criteria. IRDA's life insurance policyholder protection requirements are listed below in Table 2.

In Table 2, year-wise insurance regulation has been given. Other than the preceding regulations, notification of IRDAI's Ref: CA/Gen/CS/2011 orders insurers to deal with policyholders living in the TAT territory (Turnaround Time). The adage "justice delayed is justice denied" inspired these rules.[2] There are some categories related to different insurance organizations and turnaround times in Table 3.

1.5 Significance of the Study

This chapter has an essential role in understanding the role of Indian insurance companies and the role of IIRDA as the regulatory body since its founding in India. It also helps the client know their right and function when their money collapses or dips into debt. It is focused on the Ombudsman, and it's essential when clients complain are not cared for by the company.

---

[2]Gaba and Agarwal (2018); Nawal and Rajpurohit (2016).

Table 2 For the protection of the interest of policyholders and Specific Regulations

Regulation	Circular/notification no/year
IRDA (Protection of Policyholders' Interest) Regulations 2002	New Delhi, Notification, 16-4-2002
IRDA (Protection of Policyholders" Interest) 2002	IREDA regulation act 2002(amendment) registration number/10/2002 on 16-10-2002
Guidelines for Grievance Redressal by Insurance Companies	3/YPB/10/CA/GRV/2010-11, 27-07-2010
The interest of policyholder and their protection	CA/Gen/CS/2011
Insurance ombudsman and award for Non-Compliance	Ref: IRDAI/Cir/Misc/194/11/2015

Sources: Table compiled by authors about regulation of IRDA

Table 3 Notification of IRDA regulation and Turnaround Time (TAT)

Services	TAT
Maturity claim/Penal interest did not pay/Survival Benefits	15 day
Proceeding of communication and Proposal of decisions/cancellation/issue of policy/ including requirements	30 day
Proposal and obtained result	10 day
Error correction/proposal deposit refund requests made after a policy has been issued, as well as other post-policy-issue service requests that are not claims-	10 day
Life insurance	
Pension processing/Annuity/Surrender Value/	15 day
After claim Raising claim requirements	5 day
Death Claim settlement without investigation Requirements	10 day
The process of settling or disputing a death claim, including any Requirement/ investigation	15 day
Grievance acknowledgement	10 day
Grievance resolving	15 day

Sources: Ref: CA/Gen/Cs/2011 secondary data has been used from sourced of IRDA 2012 and Table compiled by the author

2 Research Objective

This study uses secondary data from government site IRDA reports, reputed Scopus, and SSCI journals. Mostly IRDA reports report has been; based on the regulation of insurance policies in India. The study's overarching goal is to ascertain whether or not IRDA's policyholder-friendly laws are effective at addressing complaints from insurance buyers and whether or not life insurance providers are held to adequate standards for the prompt resolution of customer complaints. This research zeroes in on the specific IRDA rules that aim to ensure policyholders' best interests and force life insurance providers to address their concerns as quickly as possible. A growing population means a growing number of insurance complaints. Still, a robust regulatory framework ensures that policyholders' needs are met, and disputes are resolved cordially, regardless of the annual growth in insurance consumers.

3 Literature Review

In his study paper "Insurance Business in India: Challenges and Opportunities," Venugopal notes that the Indian insurance market has overgrown since the founding of IRDA and the 2000 government opened for the private sector.[3] IRDAI explain in their study article "The influence of Regulatory and Development Institution (IRDA)" that IRDA is an autonomous statutory authority that controls and directs Indian insurance sector authorities.[4] Their study article "IRDA: Regulator of the insurance industry in India[5] explains IRDA's primary goals: regulating, monitoring, controlling and directing this industry's activities.

In their paper "The Role of Insurance Ombudsman and Grievance Management in the Life Insurance Services in the Indian Perspective," Nawal & Rajpurohit[6] and Prakash[7] define grievance as an unlawful or immoral act that warrants a complaint. The study found that insurance ombudspersons are crucial to grievance management and that policyholders trust them. As a statutory and autonomous body, IRDA develops and regulates the Indian insurance market; according to Rajshekhar and Hymavathi, the authority regulates insurance company investment money, the margin of safety, and policyholder interests.[8] As an Indian government insurance company IRDA has had a significant role in the insurance industry's growth since its founding. Mukandam & Deo[9] and Nawal and Rajpurohit[10] claim in "IRDA: Regulator of Insurance Sector in India" that the Indian insurance sector is rising by 15% to 20% annually. They advise traders/sellers to satisfy customers, business ethics, and society as much as possible. In their essay "Promoting Consumer Complaints in the Financial Sector," Jane Goodman and Delahunty encourage clients to complain. Internal communication must be reasonable.[11] In their paper "Indian insurance industry and Role of Development and regulation try authority," it is stated that the IRDA Act passed in 1999 changed various insurance sector policies.[12]

[3]Venugopal (2015).

[4]IRDAI (2017).

[5]Hira and Bhargdi (2016); Prakash (2015a).

[6]Nawal and Rajpurohit (2016).

[7]Prakash (2015b).

[8]Rajshekhar and Hymavathi (2014).

[9]Mukandam and Deo (2016).

[10]Nawal and Rajpurohit (2016).

[11]IRDAI Annual Reports (2001-2018); Gaba and Agarwal (2018).

[12]IRDAI Annual Reports (2001-2018); Mittal et al. (2020).

Venugopal[13] and Mittal and Jhamb[14] protects insurance policyholders and implements policies to support the Indian insurance sector's growth.

Rajshekhar and Hymavathi's study (About the Indian insurance industry and consumer protection laws) found that the insurance industry has increased.[15] However, insurance companies must also satisfy customers. The study explores insurance consumer protection laws in India. This study covers insurance consumer protection.[16]

The insurance sector is crucial to economic development, and customer grievance redressed is crucial to enhance customer relationship management. The study examined insurance grievances.[17] People-centric and Market-driven service sectors like insurance require better customer relationship management.

This brochure covers IRDA's history and economic reforms since 1991 in the insurance industry. The booklet covers the **Amphora committee**. Another Booklet Printed by IRDA, "Introduction to Insurance", covers insurance's ideas, principles, and the Indian insurance business.[18]

4 Research Methodology

Data mining is the practice of amassing relevant information to solve an issue. It is a method for systematically and deliberately locating a workable answer to an issue. To arrive at a workable conclusion, researchers must collect and analyse data using a dependable method. A systematic inquiry into describing, explaining, predicting, and controlling the observable phenomenon," writes American Sociologist Earl Robert Babbie. When conducting research, it is necessary to use both inductive and deductive approaches. The research employs both inductive and deductive strategies, both of which are founded on logical reasoning.[19]

Secondary data for this study came from IRDAI's and life insurance company's annual reports and IRDAI's journal and life insurance companies' grievance policies. In addition to these select online resources, we studied several previously published research articles. The paper's data set extends from 2000 to 2001 to the current year's figs.

A complaint is an unfavourable experience arising from interaction with a provider of products or services. Complaints about a company's goods or services

[13] Venugopal (2015).

[14] Mittal and Jhamb (2016).

[15] Rajshekhar and Hymavathi (2014).

[16] Mittal and Jhamb (2016); Muddumadappa et al. (2022).

[17] Nawal and Rajpurohit (2016).

[18] Venugopal (2015).

[19] Mittal and Jhamb (2016); Dutta (2020).

can make you less likely to buy from them again.[20] To put it another way, a complaint is defined as "customer discontent concerning any paid product or service." A grievance is a formal complaint lodged by an unhappy customer or consumer. A complaint occurs when a customer is unhappy with the service they received and wants something done about it.[21] Disputes arise when customers need clarification on what was promised and what was provided.

4.1 Grievances and Their Redressal

According to the study's findings, the involvement of IRDAI in resolving consumer complaints is crucial from the perspective of the expansion of this industry and vital from the consumer's reading. The (IRDA) is working to develop all necessary regulations to ensure that policyholders' interests are safeguarded concurrently with the expansion of the industry. The regulatory authority, called the "Insurance Regulatory and Development Authority", significantly emphasises and mandates that insurance companies immediately address consumer complaints. Insurers' complaints are being addressed, and policyholder trust is being built thanks to regulations by the "Insurance Regulatory and Development Authority of India if there has been a reduction in the number of pending complaints and a decrease in the trends of complaints filed compared to past years.[22]

Grievance redressal is a significant obstacle for every business, so every life insurance company runs its grievance redressal cell. This allows the companies to manage the complaints of their policyholders in a timely and efficient manner. It increases the likelihood that the policyholders will appreciate the company's efforts (Table 4)..

5 Data Analysis, Findings and Results of Grievance Data

1. An examination of secondary data reveals that the rate at which life insurance customers' complaints are resolved is relatively high, which can be attributed to the stringent regulatory framework at IRDAI.[23] The fact that IRDAI complaints are being resolved at a high rate demonstrates that the agency's regulations are working effectively. The outcome of the grievance redressal shows that the Regulatory Authority is in a positive (plus) position.

---

[20] Mittal et al. (2020).

[21] Yadav and Sudhakar (2017).

[22] Muddumadappa et al. (2022).

[23] Mukandam and Deo (2016).

Table 4 Grievances Status of the Life Insurance Industry as a Whole

Year	Received	Disposed	Disposal %	Outstanding grievances	Outstanding %
2003–2004	519	65	12.52	454	87.48
2004–2005	1433	308	21.49	1125	78.51
2005–2006	2516	737	29.29	1779	70.71
2006–2007	2640	299	11.33	2341	88.67
2007–2008	2057	1188	57.75	869	42.25
2008–2009	2811	2353	83.71	458	16.29
2009–2010	2907	2512	86.41	395	13.59
2010–2011	10,051	9797	97.47	254	2.53
2011–2012	309,867	308,331	99.50	1536	0.50
2012–2013	342,294	341,070	99.64	1224	0.36
2013–2014	375,844	374,664	99.69	1180	0.31
2014–2015	280,172	274,063	97.82	6109	2.18
2015–2016	210,810	209,875	99.56	935	0.44
2016–2017	121,782	121,535	99.80	247	0.20
2017–2018	154,367	154,413	99.87	201	0.13

Source: During 2003–2004 to 2017–2018, annual reports submitted by IRDA (Gaba and Agarwal 2018)

2. The downward trend in the number of grievances filed from 2014–2015 to 2016–2017 indicates that customers are now sufficiently satisfied with the operation of insurance firms compared to past years; this is why the rate of submitting grievances is low.[24] It could be the consequence of rapid grievance redressal willingness on the part of insurance companies or the result of the rigorous role played by IRDAI regulations; either way, it is a good indicator for the entire insurance market or industry. Once more, it demonstrates good portrayals of IRDAI (plus signs).
3. In the current year, 2017–2018, the number of complaints has increased by approximately 28% compared to the previous year. This may be viewed as a positive sign for the industry because it demonstrates that IRDA is successfully educating policyholders to fight for their rights; however, it may also be considered a negative sign for the industry. The consumer education campaign known as "Jago Grahak Jago" is well recognised and is generally accepted as the most effective educational programme by the Indian public. The Insurance Regulatory and Development Authority (IRDA) runs a consumer education website and a separate website to educate individuals about insurance products and their rights and obligations. It is also a positive (+) indicator for the industry and the regulator since it implies that consumers are now well-educated about the products offered by insurance companies, their rights, duties, and the importance of having life insurance. Additionally, it demonstrates the efficacy of regulations imposed by the IRDAI.

[24] IRDAI Annual Reports (2001-2018).

4. The number of complaints may rise due to the expanding market size by an amount equal to or greater than 12% yearly. However, there is no need for concern because the IRDA has rigorous regulatory rules that force insurance companies to address customer complaints as soon as possible. According to the available data, the rate of complaints being resolved is greater than 99%, which is highly encouraging.
5. The outstanding ratio of unresolved grievances has been less than 0.50% every year since 2011–2012, except 2014–2015; this implies that the IRDA regulatory power is forcing insurance companies to remedy customer complaints promptly. Additionally, it exemplifies the good (plus) side of the picture of this organization.[25]

6 Suggestions and Future Challenges

Every regulator faces a few hurdles, which become more complicated as the market grows. IRDA is also confronted with new issues daily due to the dynamic nature, intense competition, and rapid expansion of the insurance sector. Insurance providers are exerting every effort to win over new customers, and one of the ways they are working toward this goal is by doing all in their power to deliver the highest possible customer service to existing policyholders. On the other side, customers are becoming increasingly aware of their rights. They are exerting pressure on insurance providers to provide a prompt remedy or a settlement for the problems they have experienced. Both of these circumstances/stages are conflicting, which presents the regulator with several issues to manage. The insurance sector is growing, and the regulating body is trying to accommodate insurers' and policyholders' needs. For future market growth and a consumer-friendly environment, it has been proposed that insurers, consumers, and regulators need to cultivate a cooperative partnership.

6.1 Ombudsman

The government formed the Insurance Ombudsman post to solve the problems related to the public grievance in 1978. In the same year, it was notified in the official Gazette on the 11th of November, 1998. This establishment was given the authority in subsection (1) of section 114 of the Insurance Act of 1938.

The government established this institute to resolve policyholder complaints expeditiously, objectively and economically without resorting to the judicial system. The primary objective was to look out for the best interests of policyholders while also working to earn their trust in the insurance sector. In India, 17 different offices

[25] Hira and Bhargdi (2016).

are responsible for serving as ombudsmen. The primary duties of an insurance ombudsman are to mediate disputes and determine appropriate compensation for policyholders.[26]

The following categories of complaints are most frequently presented to an **Ombudsman**:

1. If a policyholder makes a complaint with the insurance company and is either denied or not responded to the policyholder's satisfaction level within thirty days of receiving the complaint, the policyholder is eligible for a refund.
2. The complaint is related to any insurance policy purchased in an individual's capacity, and the total value of the claim, including any expenses, must not exceed thirty lacs.
3. No other consumer forum, court, or arbitrator should hear the same complaint while one is pending with the ombudsperson to achieve justice.
4. If there is required documentation for the complaint being submitted, those documents should be attached to the complaint.
5. Any individual dissatisfied with the treatment they received from an insurance provider has the right to make a complaint with the Ombudsman, either directly or through their legal heirs, assignee, or nominee.

6.2 *Grievance Redressal Process*

The Ombudsman acts in a capacity similar to that of a mediator. In settling a complaint, written consent is obtained from both parties, and the Ombudsman delivers an appropriate recommendation to both parties within 1 month of the day the complaint was received. Suppose the complainant agrees to the advice and settles the complaint based on the recommendations. In that case, the insurance company is informed and given 15 days to resolve the issue or face further action from the Ombudsman.[27] If the complainant does not accept the advice and does not agree to settle the grievance based on such recommendations, the same is not notified to the insurance company (India Nair 2019).

If the claim cannot be resolved through conciliation, the complaint is disposed of by passing a speaking order within 3 months of the date on which the complaint was received. Both parties are informed of any ex-gratia payments that are permitted, if any are. Suppose the decision persuades the complaint. In that case, they must communicate acceptance of it in writing to the insurance company within a month for the award to be implemented.

Because of the limitations imposed by the Public Grievances Redressal Rules, 1998, an insurance company is not permitted to appeal against the order issued by the Ombudsman, except when an apparent error is discovered in the decision. This is

[26]Muddumadappa et al. (2022).

[27]Dutta (2020).

Table 5 Grievances Status of the Ombudsman in India

Year	Received grievances	Disposed grievances	Outstanding grievances
2001–2002	1967	1506	461
2002–2003	2940	1915	1025
2003–2004	4429	3289	1140
2004–2005	6033	5020	1013
2005–2006	5993	4926	1067
2006–2007	6500	5418	1082
2007–2008	6647	5778	869
2008–2009	6622	5586	1036
2009–2010	10,003	8636	1367
2010-2011	12,384	9551	2833
2011–2012	15,186	11,850	3336
2012–2013	19,047	14,673	4374
2013–2014	21,886	15,672	6214
2014–2015	20,553	16,156	4397
2015–2016	21,654	19,645	2009
2016–2017	18,753	17,377	1376
2017–2018	14,795	9475	5320

Data Collection IRDA Annual Reports 2001–2002 to 2017–2018
Sources: collected from IRDA annual reports 2016
Note: Previous unresolved complaints are added to the total of the current year figure

an essential point to understand in this context. In such a scenario, the insurance company has the legal right, as outlined in Article 226 of the Indian Constitution, to appeal with the Honorable High Court. Suppose the policyholder disagrees with the decision made by the Ombudsman. In that case, the policyholder has the right to file an appeal with any court that has jurisdiction over the matter for grievance status about the ombudsman-related data given in Table 5.

6.3 Performance Analysis of Ombudsman Grievance Data

According to the data, up until 2016–2017, the number of complaints has been steadily growing practically every year, and the number of complaints, that has been resolved is growing in proportion.[28] Compared to previous years, the number of policyholder complaints received in 2017–2018 was significantly lower. It suggests that policyholders are increasingly pleased with their experiences. These figures speak for themselves, showing that the IRDAI and Ombudsman, both of which are institutions, are successfully defending the interests of policyholders and developing

[28] Nawal and Rajpurohit (2016).

a thread of trust among policyholders and insurance companies. This is a positive indicator for the expansion of this industry.[29]

7 Conclusion

Consumers hold the utmost influence in every sector of the economy since the existence of any sector of the economy depends on consumers. Customers' trust in the insurance sector is the primary factor driving its growth. Once upon a time, the renowned author Norman Cousins penned the following: Death is not the most significant loss in life. The greatest tragedy occurs within us even as we continue to live. If customers in the insurance industry are not treated with respect, trust will wither away, slowing the industry's progression and detrimental to its overall health. IRDAI is making its utmost effort to preserve policyholders' faith in the industry as a whole to facilitate the growth of the industry as a whole based on policyholders' trustworthiness. Insurance firms have realised the importance of maintaining their policyholders' trust, so they are working diligently to address any problems that may arise. The brilliant author Tracy McMillan is credited with saying, "Caring about people, about things, and life is an act," Insurance companies are also hard at work with this thought in mind. According to the study's findings, IRDAI regulations successfully protect the interests of life insurance customers and compel insurance companies to pay serious attention to redressing policyholders' complaints on a priority basis within the turnaround time (TAT). IRDAI's policy for safeguarding consumers indirectly contributes to developing an environment favourable to expanding the insurance business and market.

7.1 The Implication of the Research

This article has focused on various regulations of IRDA and LIC. This has been given and provided safe data for researchers and policymakers to make it more robust per public demand in the digital era. It also gives an idea about the marginal level to take the right decision at the right time for the company's welfare, as well as public and dissatisfied. FII from another country to make LIC and such types of private companies strong and give easy insurance to the public in India. It has social implications in India because it will give the population to ensure ease and safety purposes of their family life even after the injury and unwanted accident.

[29] Muddumadappa et al. (2022); Chen and Su (2022).

References

Chen L, Su S (2022) Optimization of the trust propagation on supply chain network based on blockchain plus. J Intell Manag Decis 1(1):17–27

Dutta MM (2020) Health insurance sector in India: an analysis of its performance. Vilakshan XIMB J Manag 17(1/2):97–109. https://doi.org/10.1108/XJM-07-2020-0021

Gaba R, Agarwal A (2018) A critical analysis of IRDAI regulations on life insurance consumers' grievances in UP. Thesis, 1-223. UP

Hira H, Bhargdi H (2016) Role of insurance regulatory and development authority in Indian insurance sector. Indian J Finance 14(2):19–32

India Nair S (2019) A comparative study of the satisfaction level of health insurance claimants of public and private sector general insurance company. J Insur Instit India VI(I):33–42

IRDAI (2017) Introduction to insurance. IJAR 19(3):234–241

IRDAI Annual Reports (2001-2018) Annual reports of IRDA. Annual Reports of IRDAI

Mittal A, Jhamb D (2016) Determinants of shopping mall attractiveness: the Indian context. Procedia Econ Finance 37:386–390

Mittal A, Aggarwal A, Mittal R (2020) Predicting university students' adoption of mobile news applications: the role of perceived hedonic value and new motivation. Int J E-Serv Mob Appl 12(4):42–59

Muddumadappa PMB, Anjanappa SDK, Srikantaswamy M (2022) An efficient reconfigurable cryptographic model for dynamic and secure unstructured data sharing in the multi-cloud storage server. J Intell Syst Control 1(1):68–78

Mukandam AP, Deo P (2016) IRDA: regulator of insurance sector in India. Worldwide J 5(6)

Nawal R, Rajpurohit P (2016) Grievance redressal mechanism in Indian life insurance industry: an exploratory study on quantifying relationship. Pac Bus Rev Int 8(7):101–109

Prakash P (2015a) Role of insurance regulatory and development authority of India. IJAR 2(3):2

Prakash PJ (2015b) Role of insurance regulatory and development authority in Indian insurance sector. Ann Oper Res Study 12(3):128–134

Rajshekhar D, Hymavathi T (2014) Life insurance industry in India - an overview. GJCMP 3(2): 50–59

Venugopal R (2015) If dissatisfied, please tell us; if satisfied, tell others. IRDA, pp 12-16

Yadav SC, Sudhakar A (2017) Personal factors influencing purchase decision making: a study of health insurance sector in India. Bimaquest 17:48–59

Uma Shankar Yadav is a senior research fellow in the department of humanities and social science. He has worked as a research associate in the same Department on the ICSSR-sponsored project. He has published over 45 research papers in a reputed international journal in Scopus, ABDC and UGC care list journals. He has also written a book. He serves as an editorial board member in several journals and a peer reviewer in reputed journals and publications like Springer Nature, Taylor Francis, and SAGE Iinderscience.

Kiran Sood is a Professor at the Chitkara Business School, Chitkara University, Punjab, India. She is also an Affiliate Professor at the University of Malta, Msida MSD 20280, Malta. She earned her Undergraduate and Postgraduate degrees in commerce from Panjab University in 2002 and 2004, respectively. Panjabi University, Patiala, India, awarded her a Doctor of Philosophy in Commerce with a focus on Product Portfolio Performance of General Insurance Companies in India. Kiran has 19 years of teaching experience in four organisations. She has written numerous publications in peer-reviewed journals and presented papers at international conferences. She is an Editor for several refereed journals, including the IJBST International Journal of BioSciences and Technology, MDPI, PLOS, the International Journal of Research Culture Society, and the Journal of Corporate Governance, Insurance, and Risk Management (JCGIRM). Her research largely focuses on insurance regulations, marketing and finance, insurance management, economics, and insurance innovation management. She has edited over 15 books for international publishers including Emerald, CRC, Taylor & Francis, AAP, WILEY scrivener, IET, Rivers Publishers, Elsevier and IEEE.

Simon Grima is a professor and Dean in the Department of Finance and Accounting at malta university. He has 25 years of experience in the research and teaching field. He is a guest editor in Sustainability, IJRFM, and many others, which resulted in the journal. He has published many edited books in respected publications like Emerald, springer nature, and Taylor Francis. Sage, another journal. He has published more than 100 research papers in reputed journal.

GPSR Compliance
The European Union's (EU) General Product Safety Regulation (GPSR) is a set of rules that requires consumer products to be safe and our obligations to ensure this.

If you have any concerns about our products, you can contact us on

ProductSafety@springernature.com

In case Publisher is established outside the EU, the EU authorized representative is:

Springer Nature Customer Service Center GmbH
Europaplatz 3
69115 Heidelberg, Germany

www.ingramcontent.com/pod-product-compliance
Ingram Content Group UK Ltd.
Pitfield, Milton Keynes, MK11 3LW, UK
UKHW022212051026
15624UKWH00001B/126

* 9 7 8 3 0 3 1 3 8 5 2 5 4 *